Quantum AI and its Applications in Blockchain Technology

Christo Ananth
Samarkand State University, Uzbekistan

Nitin Mittal
Shri Vishwakarma Skill University, India

IGI Global
Scientific Publishing
Publishing Tomorrow's Research Today

Published in the United States of America by
IGI Global Scientific Publishing
701 East Chocolate Avenue
Hershey, PA, 17033, USA
Tel: 717-533-8845
Fax: 717-533-8661
E-mail: cust@igi-global.com
Website: https://www.igi-global.com

Library of Congress Cataloging-in-Publication Data

ISBN13: 9798369371657
EISBN13: 9798369371671

British Cataloguing in Publication Data
A Cataloguing in Publication record for this book is available from the British Library.

Table of Contents

Detailed Table of Contents

AI-Driven Autonomous Combat Vehicle with Quantum Network Integration is poised to transform military operations by significantly reducing casualties and minimizing the physical presence of soldiers on the battlefield. Advances in edge computing, 5G networks, machine learning, and quantum networking have driven the expansion of this technology, enabling real-time data analysis and decision-making at the device level with unprecedented speed and reliability. This innovative approach enables us to protect our nation without endangering our soldiers' lives, simultaneously advancing our technological capabilities and social media platforms. Beyond this, the Indian military plays a crucial role in ensuring national security, providing supplies, and training to promote safety and democracy within our borders. In times of conflict, soldiers defend the nation against enemy forces, with the military also capable of executing offensive operations as directed by national leadership.

IoT, which stands for "Internet of Things," is a term that describes the network of linked objects as well as the technology that is utilized for communication. Sensors are now included into commonplace equipment like toothbrushes and vacuum cleaners, allowing them to collect data and deliver intelligent replies to their users. The proliferation of low-cost computer chips and high-speed telecommunications has resulted in billions of digital devices being linked to the internet globally. Smart IoT applications are further secured using Quantum Blockchain technology and are advantageous to nearly all sectors, including logistics and transportation, retail, manufacturing and healthcare; and the Real estate is no exception. Tracking raw materials, analysing sales leads data, property tracking, and energy savings are some of the tedious tasks that could now be achieved with efficiency. The future of IoT in real estate is very bright and is already growing at an exponential rate.

Cloud computing has revolutionised service delivery over the internet, providing significant benefits in flexibility, scalability, and efficiency. Despite these advantages, security concerns remain a critical issue, particularly regarding data integrity and confidentiality. This paper proposes a novel approach to address these concerns through an advanced public auditing technique overseen by a third-party auditor (TPA), integrating the Blowfish algorithm for robust data protection. Quantum AI employs the principles of quantum computing to deliver more efficient encryption methods and improve the scalability of blockchain networks. By combining advanced cryptographic techniques with third-party oversight and leveraging quantum AI, our approach addresses critical security challenges, significantly contributing to the security posture of cloud computing environments and blockchain technology. This research paves the way for more secure cloud-based services and blockchain networks, fostering greater trust in outsourced data storage systems.

In the rapidly evolving healthcare sector, effective diagnosis and payment systems are crucial for improving patient care and operational efficiency. This paper presents a system that integrates disease prediction with Polygon Matic cryptocurrency payments, all supported by blockchain technology. The system allows users to enter symptoms for disease prediction, select specific healthcare providers, and pay consultation fees using cryptocurrency. By utilizing advanced machine learning algorithms, specifically the Multinomial Naïve Bayes algorithm, the system accurately

ensuring safe charging operations. Challenges such as efficiency enhancement, foreign object detection, and standardization are addressed, alongside potential solutions and ongoing research endeavors. This paper contributes valuable insights into the creation and application of static transmission of power wirelessly for charging the EV, laying the groundwork for further advancements in this vital technology.

The Quantum-AI Inspired Blockchain-Assisted Crowdsourced Energy Systems is to integrate cutting-edge technologies like blockchain, AI, and quantum computing to completely transform the production, distribution, and consumption of energy. The objective of this system is to improve energy efficiency, dependability, and sustainability by utilising blockchain's decentralised structure to establish a safe and transparent energy transaction platform. Crowdsourcing energy from different renewable sources would be made possible by the proposed system, enabling people and communities to contribute to and profit from a shared energy pool. The system aims to produce a more resilient and adaptable energy infrastructure that can satisfy the changing needs of modern society through this creative combination of technology. We provide a blockchain-driven spatial crowdsourcing platform where participants validate or invalidate task accuracy. In order to promote correct spatial information collection, all participants get rewards based on both spatial and non-spatial reward components.

The goal of this research is to leverage Quantum AI and blockchain technology applications to develop a Subaquatic Anomaly Detection and Hazard Alert System for divers and marine researchers. By using electromagnetic (EM) fields in an embedded system, we aim to simulate the frequency domain characteristics of seawater channels for efficient underwater communication. Quantum AI will be employed to analyze and predict anomalies in the subaquatic environment, providing real-time hazard

Preface

The convergence of quantum AI and blockchain technology presents a compelling opportunity to enhance decentralized systems. Quantum Artificial Intelligence merges the power of quantum computing and artificial intelligence, resulting in enhanced computational abilities. This integration plays a pivotal role in optimizing the efficiency of blockchain by expediting transaction validation and verification processes, particularly in critical sectors such as finance and supply chain management. utilization of quantum AI in blockchain networks enables streamlined data analysis. Its remarkable capability to swiftly handle extensive datasets enables the extraction of valuable insights, identification of patterns, and implementation of predictive analytics. This collaboration proves particularly beneficial in sectors like healthcare, where it aids in identifying trends and optimizing resource allocation, thereby driving advancements in patient care and medical research. Additionally, in the realm of finance, the integration of quantum artificial intelligence and blockchain can significantly bolster fraud detection mechanisms and enhance overall cybersecurity. Consequently, the integration of quantum artificial intelligence and blockchain has the potential to revolutionize not only transaction speed but also data-centric decision-making across diverse industries. Many Quantum-AI Inspired industries are going to benefit from quantum computing, learning how to better secure data from potential hackers in sectors such as finance, cybersecurity, and chemical and pharmaceutical companies like Testing chemical experiments which is an expensive process, and researchers could quickly test a lot more methods. These simulations can solve chemistry and physics challenges — improving R&D and manufacturing efficiencies leading to better products. Algorithms are currently being tested in this area for improving the cost, size, and charging speed of batteries for renewable energy. Across industries such as consumer goods and aerospace and transportation, creating and testing material designs can create new possibilities faster and simultaneously reduce costs.

The chapter entitled *AI-Driven Autonomous Combat Vehicle with Quantum Network Integration* emphasizes that the AI-Driven Autonomous Combat Vehicle with Quantum Network Integration is poised to transform military operations by significantly reducing casualties and minimizing the physical presence of soldiers on the battlefield. Advances in edge computing, 5G networks, machine learning, and quantum networking have driven the expansion of this technology, enabling real-time data analysis and decision-making at the device level with unprecedented speed and reliability. This innovative approach enables us to protect our nation without endangering our soldiers' lives, simultaneously advancing our technological capabilities and social media platforms. Beyond this, the Indian military plays a crucial role in ensuring national security, providing supplies, and training to promote safety and democracy within our borders. In times of conflict, soldiers defend the nation against enemy forces, with the military also capable of executing offensive operations as directed by national leadership..

The chapter entitled *Application of Quantum Blockchain technology in Real Estate Sector* discusses that IoT, which stands for "Internet of Things," is a term that describes the network of linked objects as well as the technology that is utilized for communication. Sensors are now included into commonplace equipment like toothbrushes and vacuum cleaners, allowing them to collect data and deliver intelligent replies to their users. The proliferation of low-cost computer chips and high-speed telecommunications has resulted in billions of digital devices being linked to the internet globally. Smart IoT applications are further secured using Quantum Blockchain technology and are advantageous to nearly all sectors, including logistics and transportation, retail, manufacturing and healthcare; and the Real estate is no exception. Tracking raw materials, analysing sales leads data, property tracking, and energy savings are some of the tedious tasks that could now be achieved with efficiency. The future of IoT in real estate is very bright and is already growing at an exponential rate.

The chapter entitled *Enhancing Data Privacy and Integrity in Cloud With Cutting Edge Through Data Auditing Techniques and Quantum AI Applications in Blockchain Technology* proposes that Cloud computing has revolutionised service delivery over the internet, providing significant benefits in flexibility, scalability, and efficiency. Despite these advantages, security concerns remain a critical issue, particularly regarding data integrity and confidentiality. This paper proposes a novel approach to address these concerns through an advanced public auditing technique overseen by a third-party auditor (TPA), integrating the Blowfish algorithm for robust data protection. Quantum AI employs the principles of quantum computing to deliver more efficient encryption methods and improve the scalability of blockchain networks. By combining advanced cryptographic techniques with third-party oversight and leveraging quantum AI, our approach addresses critical security challenges, significantly contributing to the security posture of cloud computing environments and blockchain technology. This research paves the way for more secure cloud-based services and blockchain networks, fostering greater trust in outsourced data storage systems.

The chapter entitled *Next Generation healthcare Online Disease Prediction Consultation and Quantum Blockchain Based Payment Framework* proposes that in the rapidly evolving healthcare sector, effective diagnosis and payment systems are crucial for improving patient care and operational efficiency, This paper presents a system that integrates disease prediction with Polygon Matic cryptocurrency payments, all supported by blockchain technology. The system allows users to enter symptoms for disease prediction, select specific healthcare providers, and pay consultation fees using cryptocurrency. By utilizing advanced machine learning algorithms, specifically the Multinomial Naïve Bayes algorithm, the system accurately predicts diseases based on user-submitted symptoms, facilitating timely medical intervention. Blockchain integration ensures that transactions are transparent, secure, and immutable, fostering trust among stakeholders and protecting sensitive healthcare data. This pioneering initiative at the intersection of healthcare, predictive analytics, and blockchain technology promises to revolutionize healthcare accessibility, efficiency, and security.

The chapter entitled *ProtectoLink Ease DeFi and Investing With Quantum AI and Its Applications in Blockchain Technology* investigates that in the rapidly evolving landscape of decentralized finance (DeFi) and investment, ProtectoLink emerges as a transformative platform to simplify the complexities inherent in these domains. This paper delves into the multifaceted nature of ProtectoLink, highlighting its commitment to providing users with a user-friendly interface, comprehensive educational resources, top-tier security protocols, diverse investment opportunities, real-time insights, and round-the- clock customer support. By amalgamating these features, ProtectoLink is poised to facilitate streamlined and secure participation in the DeFi ecosystem and traditional investment markets.

The chapter entitled *Quantum AI, Cybersecurity, and their Impact on Bitcoin, Cryptocurrency, and Blockchain-Based Financial Systems* explains that the the convergence of quantum artificial intelligence and online protection presents huge ramifications for Bitcoin, digital currencies, and blockchain-based monetary frameworks. Quantum figuring's capability to change information handling could emphatically improve decision-production inside blockchain networks This raises the pressing requirement for quantum-safe cryptography to shield blockchain innovation from potential quantum assaults. The solidness and security of blockchain-based monetary frameworks could be in danger, requiring administrative structures to address arising dangers. The discoveries likewise show the digital dangers and weaknesses that advance with blockchain innovation improvements. This investigation additionally features the PC security research community's weaknesses and gives future exploration aspects that are critical for planning secure blockchain applications and stages..

The chapter entitled *Quantum Computing and Generative Adversarial Networks (GANs): Ethics, Privacy and Security* explains that Advancement in technology has demonstrated a shift in application, interpretability, and technological acceptance. Quantum Computing and Generative Adversarial Networks (GANs) represent two transformative domains with immense potential for innovation and disruption. This study examines the rise of ethical, privacy, and security considerations accompanying these technologies, highlighting their importance and defining the core emphasis on overlapping ethical, data privacy, and security problems and their mitigation. Starting with an overview of quantum computing and GANs, the study outlines their principles and practical applications, elucidating quantum algorithms' revolutionary power and unique challenges. It explores how generative models reshape industries while examining ethical dilemmas introduced by synthetic content generation. Privacy concerns are evaluated, focusing on privacy-enhancing technologies. Security challenges are scrutinized, proposing strategies to fortify these technologies against adversarial threats.

The chapter entitled *Quantum Networks and AI Technologies for Electric Vehicle Charging* explores static WPT systems tailored for electric vehicle (EV) charging without relying on plug-in connections. Static transmission of power wirelessly permits the electrical energy to be transferred from stationary energy source for a vehicle parked over a charging pad, offering convenience and doing away with the requirement for physical cords. . Additionally, the paper examines critical components such as power electronics, coil design, and control strategies, highlighting their significance in optimizing system performance and ensuring safe charging operations. Challenges such as efficiency enhancement, foreign object detection, and standardization are addressed, alongside potential solutions and ongoing research endeavors. This paper contributes valuable insights into the creation and application of static transmission of power wirelessly for charging the EV, laying the groundwork for further advancements in this vital technology.

The chapter entitled *Quantum-AI Inspired Blockchain-Assisted Crowdsourced Energy Systems* discusses that The Quantum-AI Inspired Blockchain-Assisted Crowdsourced Energy Systems is to integrate cutting-edge technologies like blockchain, AI, and quantum computing to completely transform the production, distribution, and consumption of energy. The objective of this system is to improve energy efficiency, dependability, and sustainability by utilising blockchain's decentralised structure to establish a safe and transparent energy transaction platform. Crowdsourcing energy from different renewable sources would be made possible by the proposed system, enabling people and communities to contribute to and profit from a shared energy pool. The system aims to produce a more resilient and adaptable energy infrastructure that can satisfy the changing needs of modern society through this creative combination of technology. We provide a blockchain-driven spatial crowdsourcing platform where participants validate or invalidate task accuracy. In order to promote correct spatial information collection, all participants get rewards based on both spatial and non-spatial reward components.

The chapter entitled *Subaquatic Anomaly Detection and Hazard Alert System for Divers and Marine Researchers Based on Quantum AI and Blockchain Technology Applications* discusses that the goal of this research is to leverage Quantum AI and blockchain technology applications to develop a Subaquatic Anomaly Detection and Hazard Alert System for divers and marine researchers. By using electromagnetic (EM) fields in an embedded system, we aim to simulate the frequency domain characteristics of seawater channels for efficient underwater communication. Quantum AI will be employed to analyze and predict anomalies in the subaquatic environment, providing real-time hazard alerts to divers and marine researchers. The integration of blockchain technology ensures secure and immutable data transmission, safeguarding the integrity of the communication system. By combining these advanced technologies, we aim to revolutionize underwater communication and safety, addressing the inherent challenges posed by the underwater environment.

The chapter entitled *Unmasking the Shadows: Leveraging AI and Machine Learning for Dark Web and Cryptocurrency Forensics* explores the digital forensics of cryptocurrencies and the dark web, focusing on the role of blockchain in their formation and evidence gathering. It emphasizes the need for artificial intelligence and machine language in dark web forensics and the critical gap in research on host-based cryptocurrency forensics, especially mobile-based forensics. Most studies on host-based forensics focus on outdated operating systems or platforms, emphasizing the need for more up-to-date versions. Cryptocurrency forensics primarily analyzes publicly accessible blockchains using clustering heuristics and machine learning-based analysis to identify anonymous entities or provide investigation guidance. Security and vulnerability assessment studies are crucial for examining forensic methods for cryptocurrencies, providing insights into potential exploits or attacks useful for forensic investigations. While research in Blockchain-based forensics is advancing organically alongside technological advancements, there is a need for focused attention on host-based forensics for cryptocurrency..

Quantum AI and its applications in BlockChain Technology is highly promising, as it anticipates the development of advanced algorithms specifically designed for blockchain applications. By harnessing the unique properties of quantum computing, such as topological qubits, the evolution of quantum hardware will lead to the emergence of more reliable quantum computers. This, in turn, will facilitate the widespread adoption of blockchain technology across various industries. The integration of Quantum AI and blockchain has the potential to revolutionize these industries by creating secure, scalable, and efficient blockchain networks. Moreover, Quantum Artificial Intelligence's capabilities extend beyond just improving existing systems, as it also offers innovative opportunities for businesses and individuals through new consensus mechanisms, privacy techniques, and decentralized organizations. The threat to security has led to work on post-quantum cryptography, or quantum-resistant cryptographic algorithms, which are cryptographic systems that are secured even if they face quantum computer attacks. However, once quantum-resistant cryptography is developed and incorporated properly into the blockchain, it makes the blockchain immune to the security threats that quantum computers pose. The book will open doors for Quantum Computing Professionals to come up with real world applications of Quantum AI as an Effective tool to Crypto Upgrades and Hard Forks, Create a Powerful Synergy, adopt robots-as-a-service (RaaS), Quantum Dots and Photonic Quantum Computers. This Book will be a Key Reference for Students, Practitioners, Professionals, Scientists and Engineer – Researchers to combat the shortcomings of the Quantum AI – Blockchain Models.

The target audience will be Students, Practitioners, Professionals, Scientists, Industrialists and Engineer – Researchers of various sectors.

Christo Ananth
Samarkand State University, Uzbekistan

Nitin Mittal
Shri Vishwakarma Skill University, India

Chapter 1
AI-Driven Autonomous Combat Vehicle With Quantum Network Integration

S. Sarupriya
Velammal Engineering College, India

D. Archana
Velammal Engineering College, India

P. Hemalatha
Velammal Engineering College, India

A. Mohsina
Velammal Engineering College, India

ABSTRACT

AI-Driven Autonomous Combat Vehicle with Quantum Network Integration is poised to transform military operations by significantly reducing casualties and minimizing the physical presence of soldiers on the battlefield. Advances in edge computing, 5G networks, machine learning, and quantum networking have driven the expansion of this technology, enabling real-time data analysis and decision-making at the device level with unprecedented speed and reliability. This innovative approach enables us to protect our nation without endangering our soldiers' lives, simultaneously advancing our technological capabilities and social media platforms. Beyond this, the Indian military plays a crucial role in ensuring national security, providing supplies, and training to promote safety and democracy within our borders. In times of conflict,

DOI: 10.4018/979-8-3373-1657-4.ch001

soldiers defend the nation against enemy forces, with the military also capable of executing offensive operations as directed by national leadership.

I. INTRODUCTION

IoT and automation technologies have advanced significantly in recent years. A military tank is a large, tracked, heavily armored vehicle used in front-line battle. Tanks may fire powerful weaponry like cannons. They are an essential component of contemporary forces, offering mobility, protection, and firepower on the battlefield. They were vital in several battles of the 20th century. Some people need assistance from a computer interface or a remote control. The goal of our initiative is to advance technology. Through "Teleoperation," soldiers will be able to remotely operate the robotic panzer tank from any location on Earth with an unrestricted range over the internet. Soldiers may see and designate targets, manage the Panzer tank's firing mechanism, and operate the firing system remotely by using cameras with video displays. The development of a remote-controlled battle tank that can be commanded from anywhere in the world will enable soldiers to operate the vehicle safely and pleasantly in a remote location. With the help of a variety of tools and gadgets, including the firing systems and camera, users will be able to control the battle tank, or tank, from a distance. We can easily connect to the panzer thanks to our 4G/LTE or 5G towers. Our top goals are to increase military safety and prevent unnecessary deaths on the battlefield. During World War I, military tanks first arrived on the scene, demonstrating the need for a mobile, armored platform that could traverse difficult terrain. An essential component of World War II was the tanks. The development of tanks persisted during the Cold War, with a focus on enhancing mobility, armor, and firepower. Tanks built after the Cold War are equipped with the latest technological innovations, such as composite armor, sophisticated targeting systems, and more automation. The military tank has changed significantly to accommodate evolving tactics and technological breakthroughs. Tanks are still essential to ground operations today. Since its invention during World War I, the military tank, a powerful armored vehicle, has seen substantial evolution. While contemporary tanks were once created for trench warfare, they now incorporate cutting-edge technology for protection, mobility, and firepower. A military tank is an intricate piece of equipment with both offensive and defensive functions. The objective of this project is to investigate the evolution, essential elements, and state-of-the-art developments in the field of military tanks. The pervasiveness of security concerns in contemporary times has compelled the development of sophisticated monitoring systems to safeguard vital resources, public areas, and national security. The identification and development of weapons continue to be the most important of these issues. We are ushering in a new era of proactive, adaptable, and threat-aware intelligent surveillance systems by using rovers' capacity to detect weaponry.

II. LITERATURE SURVEY

The War Field Spy Robot is a device that can be used for military purposes to engage in armed conflict to achieve specific objects and invite the use of military force to attain strategic goals (B. S. Jebaraj,2023). To detect the weapons while moving according to the user's need. Intelligent Rover is controlled by using smart-phones and uses Raspberry Pi and Arduino(S. S. Chiwande, 2023). Controlling a Robot is done using a Raspberry Pi processor. These military applications are more comfortable. It is capable of walking on any surface and providing monitoring over an area(S. M. Sali, 2023). Robotic technology is increasingly being utilized in autonomous military systems. while battlefields are integral to warfare, efforts to prevent conflicts resolve disputes through diplomatic means, and maintain global peace and stability(M. Rane,2023).Allowing a soldier to the responsibility of surveillance comes with various challenges such as mental strain, human limitations, risk to personal safety, and resource intensive, there is an increasing reliance on technological solutions such as unmanned surveillance systems. (J. L. Prasanna, 2022). In military service, they have a new gadget to minimize their actions and beat their enemies in the war. A new high-tech machine and weapons with advanced technology because in the state of peace(H. Udaykumar,2022). We developed a robot for this project that will be useful in military operations on the front lines. It's mostly used for covert observation when in enemy territory. To save a soldier's life, this robot can also be used to ask for assistance and indicate the condition of a wounded soldier in a war zone. In addition to these features, robots are also used for security. The robot can swivel at any angle on its axis, drive forward in reverse, turn left or right, and reverse direction instantly because it is constructed like a tank circuit. A wireless camera mounted on the top of the robot transfers audio and video from the battleground to the observation platform (M. Sabarimuthu,2022). Once a landmine has been located using a GPS and GSM module, it will also give latitude and longitude information (P. S. Kumar,2022). The battlefield is now a crucial component of national security in every nation. Soldiers in the Army have a vital duty to play. Many of the protectors are lost from their unit after suffering injuries in battle or while on search and rescue missions. Soldier safety has been the focus of numerous initiatives. This paper's primary goal is to track the soldier's location and use sensors to warn them when they are in danger (K. Janani,2022). Currently, the army is essential to the security of the nation. In this regard, their correspondingly better tracking and health are more important for self-defense (P.

A. H. Vardhini,2022). Aside from military uses, unmanned armed vehicles are becoming more and more common in commercial settings. As technology advances unmanned armed vehicles are used more frequently (R. Kabilan,2022).

III. PROPOSED METHOD

In a bold leap towards modernizing military operations, our project unveils a groundbreaking approach: harnessing the power of a mobile phone as a sophisticated transmitter to commandeer a tank. With a simple tap on a specially designed app installed on the mobile device, users gain unprecedented control over the tank's steering system, dictating its movements with seamless precision. This revolutionary control mechanism is facilitated by an intricate Internet of Things (IoT) infrastructure, leveraging cutting-edge technologies like 5G networks, advanced machine learning algorithms, and quantum network integration. But our innovation doesn't stop there. Imagine tracking the tank's every move through sensors ingeniously embedded within the vehicle itself. These sensors feed real-time location data directly to the mobile app, allowing for strategic maneuvering and unparalleled situational awareness. Yet, our ingenuity extends beyond mere navigation. Integrating seamlessly with popular messenger apps like Telegram, our system provides a multifaceted communication hub. Users can not only monitor essential tank metrics, such as ammunition levels, but also coordinate operations with unprecedented efficiency. However, the most groundbreaking feature lies in our utilization of micro-camera technology. By outfitting the tank with a discreet micro-camera, accessible and controllable through the mobile app, we transcend traditional reconnaissance methods. This miniature marvel offers vital visual feedback and opens the door to covert surveillance and reconnaissance operations. Through this, our project transcends the conventional role of military equipment. Our endeavor isn't merely about innovation; it's about revolutionizing warfare itself. Our mobile-driven approach empowers soldiers to operate with unparalleled efficiency and safety. No longer mere instruments of battle, these tanks become strategic assets, capable of observing, analyzing, and adapting to the ever-shifting theater of war. From tracking enemy movements to recording vital intelligence, our project heralds a new era in military strategy.

IV. HARDWARE REQUIREMENTS

Breadboard: Used for prototyping and connecting various components.
Node MCU (ESP8266): Acts as the main microcontroller of the system.
Battery: Powers the entire system.

DC Motor: Used for the wheel mechanism.

L293D Driver: The motor driver used to control the DC motors.

Jumper Wires: Connect various components on the breadboard.

ESP32 Camera: Possibly for additional functionality not detailed in the provided information.

Software Requirements

Arduino IDE: Used to write and upload code

The code controls the behavior of the system, including motor movement and LED indication. It likely interfaces with the laptop for input control.

Tinker Card Software: Not specified but may be used for designing circuits or simulations.

Blink app: This application is used control during the steering control.

System Mechanism

The wheel mechanism is controlled by the Node MCU, which receives instructions from the Arduino IDE software. The Arduino code provides instructions for the ESP8266 module to control various components. Digital pins from D0 to D8 are used for connecting DC motors and the LED. Pins D0, D1, D2, and D3 are specifically used for motor control, while D8 is used for the LED. The LED serves as an indicator for the shooting action: ON indicates the shooting action started, and OFF indicates the shooting action stopped. The L293D is used for power segregation and supply to the DC motors and LED. Alkaline batteries are used to power the motors and LED.

Steps for controlling the army tank

Step 1: Forward Steering Control

Embark on the simulation journey with a single click igniting the start button to set the stage in motion. Use the remote control (mobile phone) to operate the tank in a forward direction by pressing the 'upper' button When the 'upper' button is pressed, two motors connected in the simulation move parallelly in the same right-side direction.

Step 2: Backward Steering Control

Operate the tank in a backward direction by pressing the 'downward' button on the remote. When the 'downward' button is pressed, two motors connected in the simulation move parallelly in the same left-side direction.

Step 3: Left-side Steering Control

Control the tank for the left side direction by pressing the 'leftward' button on the remote. When the 'leftward' button is pressed, two motors connected in the simulation move in opposite directions, simulating a left turn similar to a car's steering system.

Step 4: Right-side Steering Control

Maneuver the tank for the right side direction by pressing the 'rightward' button on the remote. When the 'rightward' button is pressed, two motors connected in the simulation move in opposite directions, mimicking a right turn akin to a car's steering system.

Step 5: Firing Operation

This mechanism is controlled by a separate mobile phone. Initiate the tank's firing mode by pressing the fire button on the remote. When the fire button is pressed, two LED bulbs switch on, indicating that the army tank is in shoot mode. These steps outline the seamless control mechanism for the army tank, facilitated through a mobile phone acting as a remote control in the original project.

Figure 1. Block Diagram

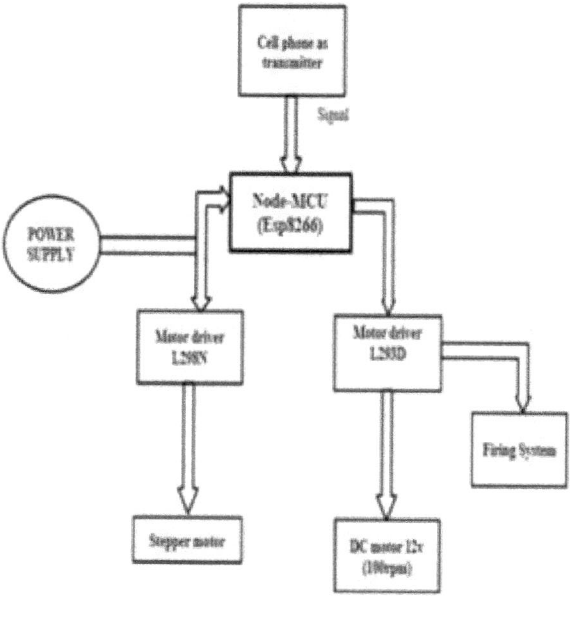

Figure 2. Flow Chart

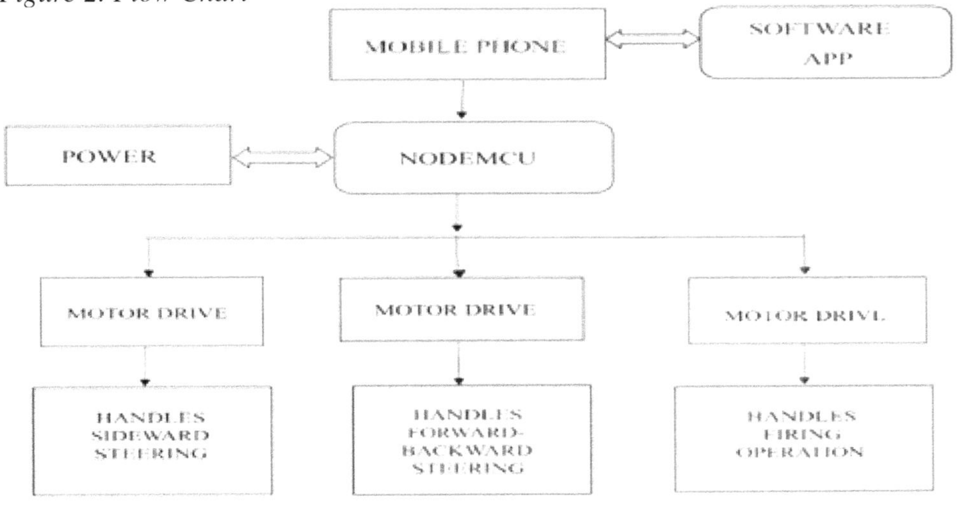

Figure 3. Mechanism

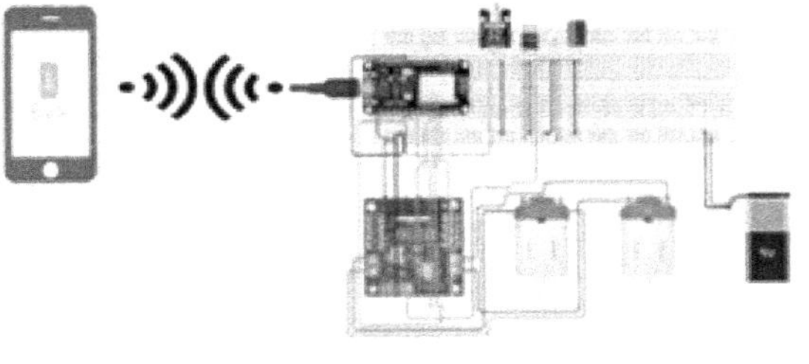

Figure 4. Final Project

V. CONCLUSION

The development and integration of automated unmanned armed vehicles represent a significant paradigm shift in military technology, offering several operational advantages. These vehicles provide a reduction in risk to human personnel, extended mission durations, and enhanced precision in target engagement. Equipped with advanced sensors, artificial intelligence, and connectivity, they bolster situational awareness and decision-making capabilities on the battlefield. The strategic flexibility they afford, spanning roles from reconnaissance to combat, is a notable asset for military forces. However, challenges such as cybersecurity vulnerabilities, ethical concerns, and the imperative of establishing clear rules of engagement must be addressed to ensure responsible use. Humans over unintended consequences and comply with international laws and norms.

Despite potential cost-efficiency through reduced operational expenses, a delicate balance between strategic advantages and ethical, legal, and operational challenges must be struck. Real-time monitoring through IoT sensors provides continuous data for better situational awareness, and predictive maintenance ensures optimal vehicle conditions. Communication and control facilitated by IoT enhance efficiency, emphasizing the overall positive impact of IoT-based technology on the battlefield. It is imperative to navigate these advancements with a commitment to responsible use, adherence to international laws, and ethical principles

VI. REFERENCES

Budiharto, W., Andreas, V., Suroso, J. S., Gunawan, A. A. S., & Irwansyah, E. "Development of Tank-Based Military Robot and Object Tracker," (2019) 4th AsiaPacific Conference on Intelligent Robot Systems (ACIRS), Nagoya, Japan, 2019, pp. 221-224, DOI: 10.1109/ACIRS.2019.8935962

Chiwande, S. S., Nimje, N., Barbaile, S., Singh, A., Dhote, A., & Pathade, A. (2023) "War Field Spy Robot with Metal Detection and Live Streaming," *7th International Conference on Intelligent Computing and Control Systems (ICICCS)*, Madurai, India, 2023, pp. 1688-1691, DOI: 10.1109/ICICCS56967.2023.10142415

Donghao, C., Bohua, Z., Chaomin, O., & Zhiyu, C. (2021) "Research on Military Internet of Things Technology Application in the Context of National Security," *2nd International Conference on Electronics, Communications and Information Technology (CECIT)*, Sanya, China, 2021, pp. 992-998, DOI: 10.1109/CECIT53797.2021.00177

Gotarane, V., & Raskar, S. (2019) "IoT Practices in Military Applications,"*3rd International Conference on Trends in Electronics and Informatics (ICOEI)*, Tirunelveli, India, 2019, pp. 891-894, DOI: 10.1109/ICOEI.2019.8862559

Janani, K., Gobhinath, S., Santhosh Kumar, K. V., Roshni, S., & Rajesh, A. (2022)"Vision Based Surveillance Robot for Military Applications,"*8th International Conference on Advanced Computing and Communication Systems (ICACCS)*, Coimbatore, India, 2022, pp. 462-466, DOI: 10.1109/ICACCS54159.2022.9785152

Jebaraj, B. S., Sekar, S., & Priyadharshini, S. (2023) "Automated Surveillance and Bomb Diffusing System for Military Applications," *International Conference on Computational Intelligence and Sustainable Engineering Solutions (CISES)*, Greater Noida, India, 2023, pp. 353-357, DOI: 10.1109/CISES58720.2023.10183517

Kabilan, R., R. MallikaPandeeswari, N. Lalitha, E. Kanmanikarthiga,C. Karthica and L. M. H. Sharon, (2022)"Soldier Friendly SmartAnd Intelligent Robot On War Field," Second International Conference on Artificial Intelligence and Smart Energy (ICAIS), Coimbatore, India, 2022, pp. 666-671, doi: DOI: 10.1109/ICAIS53314.2022.9742909.65

Kumar, P. S., Naveen, I. G., Parameshachari, B. D., & Ramachandra, A. C. (2022, November). Military Robot Design and Implementation For Wireless Communication. In *2022 IEEE North Karnataka Subsection Flagship International Conference (NKCon)* (pp. 1-6). IEEE.

Prasanna, J. L., Ravi Kumar, M., Santhosh, C., Aswin Kumar, S. V., & Kasulu, P. (2022) "IoT based Soldier Health and Position Tracking System," *6th International Conference on Computing Methodologies and Communication (ICCMC)*, Erode, India, 2022, pp. 417-420, DOI: 10.1109/ICCMC53470.2022.9754096

Rane, M., Jain, M., Kashyap, A., Jajoo, A., Kadam, H., & Kadam, D. (2023) "Mine Detecting Military Bot Using IoT," *International Conference on Emerging Smart Computing and Informatics (ESCI)*, Pune, India, 2023, pp. 1-6, DOI: 10.1109/ESCI56872.2023.10100211

Sabarimuthu, M., Krishna, M. P., Sundari, P. M., Aarthi, L., & Juhair, P. M. and G. GowthamRaj,(2022) "IoT Based Soldier Status Monitoring Using Sensors and SOS Switch, "Second International Conference on Computer Science, Engineering and Applications (ICCSEA), Gunupur, India, 2022, pp. 1-6,DOI: 10.1109/ICCSEA54677.2022.9936125

Sali, S. M., & Joy, K. R. (2023) "Intelligent Rover: An IoT Based Smart Surveillance Robotic Car for Military," *2nd International Conference on Computational Systems and Communication (ICCSC)*, Thiruvananthapuram, India, 2023, pp. 1-6, DOI: 10.1109/ICCSC56913.2023.10143011

Udaykumar, H., Rathod, S. J., Vinaykumar, R., Pradeep, S., & Savitha, P. B. (2022) "IoT-Based Quadcopter with Automatic Landing System and Object Detection," Fourth International Conference on Emerging Research in Electronics, Computer 64 Technology(ICERECT),Mandya,India,2022,pp.0104, RECT56837. 2022.10059649. DOI: 10.1109/ICERECT56837.2022.10059649

Vardhini, P. A. H., & Babu, K. M. C. (2022). *"IoT based Autonomous Robot Design Implementation for Military Applications," IEEEDelhi Section Conference.* DELCON., DOI: 10.1109/DELCON54057.2022.9753507

Chapter 2
Application of Quantum Blockchain Technology in Real Estate Sector

Utpal Saikhedkar
NICMAR University, India

Deepak Sundrani
https://orcid.org/0000-0002-7217-8911
NICMAR University, India

ABSTRACT

IoT, which stands for "Internet of Things," is a term that describes the network of linked objects as well as the technology that is utilized for communication. Sensors are now included into commonplace equipment like toothbrushes and vacuum cleaners, allowing them to collect data and deliver intelligent replies to their users. The proliferation of low-cost computer chips and high-speed telecommunications has resulted in billions of digital devices being linked to the internet globally. Smart IoT applications are further secured using Quantum Blockchain technology and are advantageous to nearly all sectors, including logistics and transportation, retail, manufacturing and healthcare; and the Real estate is no exception. Tracking raw materials, analysing sales leads data, property tracking, and energy savings are some of the tedious tasks that could now be achieved with efficiency. The future of IoT in real estate is very bright and is already growing at an exponential rate.

DOI: 10.4018/979-8-3373-1657-4.ch002

IOT IN DAILY LIFE

IoT has revolutionized numerous significant operations that would have otherwise consumed a significant amount of resources, including financial ones. IoT is a robust technology where many devices are connected with each other and perform smart functionalities. The Internet of Things is a concept that brings together commonplace objects and the internet. The IoT has rapidly expanded its market due to its scalable and autonomous services. The addition of sensors and processors to various things has been a daily practice for computer engineers ever since the 1990s. The massive and weighty chips caused the initial steps to move at a snail's pace. Initially, radio frequency identification (RFID) tags, which are computer chips with a low power consumption and may be used to identify expensive equipment, were deployed. The size of computing devices decreased, which resulted in these processors becoming both faster and more sophisticated.

Putting processing power into smaller items is now far more affordable than it was in the past. With the Alexa voice services feature, it is possible to connect with Alexa voice service capabilities for microcontroller units (MCUs) that have less than one megabyte of embedded Random-access memory (RAM). This allows for the addition of connectivity, such as light switches. The Internet of Things (IoT) devices that are used in our homes and companies have given rise to an entirely new sector. Smart objects have the capability of transmitting data to the internet in an automated fashion. Internet of Things is a term that refers to all of these computing devices that are not visible to the naked eye and the technology that they use.

We now interact with the things that we use on a daily basis in a different way as a result of the Internet of Things. They are able to transform commonplace equipment into intelligent devices that are able to communicate wirelessly with one another and give consumers the ability to modify and automate the functioning of the devices. In addition to being beneficial to businesses, they may also be utilized in a variety of ways to benefit individuals.

Businesses can get numerous benefits from the implementation of intelligent technology. Retail establishments have deployed Internet of Things applications in order to collect important customer data and analyse buying patterns. Complex algorithm been developed and applied for the quantitative treatment of quantum blockchain (Ablayev, 2018). They then make the necessary adjustments to the company, even if it means relocating a product that is already in stock, in order to enhance the quality of service they provide to customers and to boost sales.

Typically, the Internet of Things (IoT) system functions by collecting and distributing data in real time. An Internet of Things system is comprised of three components:

1) Electronic gadgets

For example, a television, a camera, or other security equipment can be monitored and controlled by this electronic gadget, which can also be used to monitor and control computing. First, this gadget gathers data from the surrounding environment as well as user inputs or patterns, and then it sends that information to its Internet of Things application through the internet.

2). Implementation of the Internet of Things

An Internet of Things application (IoT app) is a collection of software and services that aggregate data from various Internet of Things devices. Artificial intelligence (AI), machine learning, or AI technology is utilized by this program in order to assess the data and create choices that are based on accurate information. The Internet of Things gadget becomes aware of these decisions and reacts in a thoughtful manner.

3) A user interface that is designed with aesthetics in mind

The Internet of Things devices or fleets of IoT devices can be managed through the use of a graphical user interface (Chuntang, 2020). It is possible to control and register smart gadgets with the use of a mobile application or a website.

Integrating Internet of Things into the Real Estate Sector

The Internet of Things has the potential to supply a wealth of information regarding properties and how they are utilized. The analysis and monitoring of their portfolios can be accomplished with the use of this information by real estate professionals. This gives them the ability to conduct risk evaluations that are more in-depth. Additionally, this information can be utilized to ascertain the surplus capacity of the property and to enhance the efficiency with which it is utilized.

Internet of Things will soon become a significant player in fields such as big data. The Internet of Things (IoT) is a method that allows for the rapid collection of massive volumes of data and the identification of the most secure location for it.

It is conceivable for machine learning and the internet of things to be interrelated in the real estate industry. The human species stands to gain a great deal from the development of learning machines. They are also able to acquire further knowledge about the world that surrounds them and improve their comprehension of it.

In addition, the Internet of Things is further improvised by Quantum blockchain technology. The Internet of Things (IoT) is a popular method for rapidly moving money across various online businesses. With Internet of Things, quantum blockchain technology can simply monitor the measurement of sensor data. This eliminates the possibility of harmful data being replicated. As a result of the Internet of Things being incorporated into security measures, it is more difficult for cybercriminals to obtain critical financial information.

For a real estate company that is looking to establish itself in a competitive market, it is recommended that they develop their own platform. In order for the organization to begin considering Internet of Things solutions for project management, it is imperative that the app incorporate the Internet of Things capabilities that the clients will require the most first. Because it is fully driven by the Internet of Things, the entire procedure does not require a representative of the real estate company to be physically present at the location.

It is recommended that the corporation think about developing add-ons or gadgets that are specifically designed for its Internet of Things initiative. Following the consideration of the firm's most important software requirements for the future, the organization should subsequently turn its attention to the implementation of technology-based solutions.

The Internet of Things platforms that are considered trustworthy are those that offer the essential functionalities for the company's application and are regularly updated.

It would be beneficial for the organization to create a repository of information that the customers require. It is essential that they have rapid and easy access to it in order to fulfil their requirements. By creating data governance, the organization may assist its consumers in feeling more at ease when it comes to providing their personal information.

Data that is saved on devices, particularly those that are connected to smart homes, ought to be encrypted by the company. Two-factor authentication is one method that may be utilized to guarantee the safety of the Internet of Things applications and devices. It is advised that real estate data be stored in encrypted cloud storage and using protected server networks because malware assaults can always target real estate data.

Over the past few years, the application of Internet of Things (IoT) and Quantum blockchain technology has been rapidly adopted in a variety of different businesses, making it a potential new digital technology. Despite the fact that there are some dangers involved, the Internet of Things has the potential to be an excellent investment for the future of the real estate organization.

There are several reasons why a real estate company should have a mobile application for their business. Within the realm of real estate, digitalization is a significant factor. Homebuyers do not need to physically visit a large number of real estate agencies or brokers in order to select the property that best suits their needs. People are able to swiftly view several homes and properties from their smartphones, which is made possible by smartphones. There have been reports that before making a purchase, the majority of people living in urban areas conduct Internet searches for available real estate. On an annual basis, it is anticipated that this figure would rise.

The smartphone being used by a significant number of homebuyers. The majority of homebuyers believe that virtual tours are the most useful feature that can be found in a real estate website. Mobile phones are now being utilized by individuals, including homebuyers, real estate companies, and even brokers, in order to do searches within the real estate market.

Young people are very tech-savvy. When it comes to urban homebuyers in India, the average age is currently 31 years. All of these young people who are looking to buy a home do their research online. As a result of mobile phones, it has become very common (Josh, 2021).

The tendency of conducting property searches online is on the rise, which has resulted in high levels of competitiveness within the real estate industry. The vast majority of real estate companies operating in metropolitan India have websites that showcase their available homes.

Building a website, on the other hand, is a rather minor step when we are discussing the enormous amount of competition that exists. It is essential for a real estate company to have a mobile application if it wishes to achieve a position of leadership within the real estate sector. For consumers to be able to download and utilize the real estate app, it needs to stand out from the crowd of apps that are already available in app stores that are already overloaded.

Benefits of IoT in the Real Estate

Before we start with the benefits of IoT and Quantum blockchain technology in real estate, let us quickly discuss the two vital terms, i.e. IoT and commercial real estate. IoT is a robust technology where many devices are connected with each other and perform smart functionalities. That network of smart devices communicates with each other and automates various operations for providing ease and efficiency to their users. Things like smart home, autonomous vehicles, security systems, and even smart healthcare applications are some of the leading examples of IoT and Quantum blockchain technology applications. The main purpose of IoT in any field is to save time, money and extra efforts while reducing the human errors in business operations. Commercial real estate market is also benefiting from IoT in the same manner. Meaning, smart home automation devices are making it easier for real estate marketers to enhance their customer satisfaction and make more profits in each project (Bitton, 2023).

The major benefits are as following:

1. More Energy Efficient Spaces: The first and foremost benefit of IoT in real estate is better and smarter spaces. Whether we talk about energy efficiency, heating, ventilation, or air conditioning, IoT efficiently enhances the overall spacing of the property. The smart home automation devices allow the user to have complete control of their home environment whether it is the temperature or the lighting. For instance, with a smart HVAC system, the customers could seamlessly set their preferred temperature or can switch ON/OFF the lighting while sitting remotely. That will not only help to enhance the customer experience but also saves energy and house management cost.
2. Better Safety: Safety is another aspect that has benefited from the integration of IoT in real estate. Whether it is at the construction site, or even after the owner has moved to the site, security and safety play a crucial role. Even the slightest mistake could risk the life and property of the owner and the workers. That's why, today, many leading real estate and construction companies leverage IoT-enabled security systems in their sites. IoT solutions for real estate keeps a track of the workers at the site and sends immediate alerts in real-time if there is an emergency. Likewise, once the construction work is completed, the security systems monitor the indoor and outdoor of the house and inform the user if they sense something abnormal or threatening. A common example of this type of IoT systems is cameras, wearables, etc. which not only help to avoid any hazardous accidents but even keeps the work smooth and efficient.
3. Seamless Predictive Analysis: Few of the biggest advantages of the IoT is the power to anticipate the threat or problem before it arises. With IoT solutions for real estate, that thing has become possible today! All thanks to IoT for its predictive analysis, the house owners and managers can get to know about the problem and can even solve it before it creates any serious issue. Whether it is regarding the elevator or the parking access, home appliances or the wiring issues, or the water tank issues, the IoT in real estate alerts for all those issues and also gives solutions for it (Dilmegani, 2024). That means, the owners could seamlessly track their energy and utility consumption and can even get notifications over maintenance. All in all, the IoT in real estate, send you reminders or alarms in advance!
4. Better and Quicker Property Decisions: It is often seen that buying any property requires hundreds of site viewings and property visits. You have to continuously struggle over your mobile phones or with your realtors to get that perfect property for yourself. However, all those tedious tasks could now be easily solved with IoT solutions for real estate. IoT in real estate has brought many innovative solutions to the global market. One such technique is predictive analysis (https://www.matellio.com/hoa management-software) that enables the realtors to showcase every little detail of the property to the relevant customer.

So, instead of viewing hundreds of other sites, the customers could leverage this predictive analysis information to make better and quicker decisions. The best example of that is House Canary that uses IoT solutions for real estate. Under its predictive analysis feature, the lenders and investors could verify each and every little detail of the property and can even anticipate the problems much before they arise. That not only helps them to make better decisions but even showcase the true value of a property.

5. Enhanced House Hunting Experience: As mentioned, the house-hunting procedure requires a lot of work and resources. As such, the investors or buyers either get frustrated and settle for anything, or they cancel their plan to buy any property. Under both these conditions, customer satisfaction is not achieved and that hampers the value of your real estate business! However, that problem could also be solved with smart IoT solutions for real estate. Thanks to the digital world we live in, today we have smart IoT applications that could provide a complete picture of any property along with its nearby locations and utility conditions in no time. Meaning, the customers could check every detail ranging from water supply to lightning condition, roads, and nearby infrastructure seamlessly with the help of IoT applications. Beacons is one such smart application that is helping the realtors to communicate with the customers more easily. With beacons, one could easily send messages or the links of the site to the nearby people who are in their network range. And now, instead of the realtors, the site talks with the customers and provides complete detail with the best graphics. That not only saves the time of realtors but also cut the costs and enhances customer experience!
6. Workplace Optimization: Analysing data in real-time is the foremost need of any industry and real-estate in no exception. However, the traditional methods of collecting and processing data in the real estate industry were not very reliable. With smart IoT applications, real-estate marketeers can seamlessly analyse large volumes of data too in real-time. They can understand what employees are into, and where most of the marketing resources were being utilized. Plus, they have a perfect timesheet of the working hours of the employees that would be beneficial for the clients.
7. Cybersecurity: Real estate brokers and buyers alike could be anxious about data security. The cameras, monitors, or sensors inside the houses or on the premises could be infiltrated by hackers. This provides them with street images, data on the movement of people, and more. In addition, the home buyers' data on mobile applications and on websites are also prone to be exploited. Technology development in IoT now enables better protection of the clients' and customer's data from cyber-attacks.

IoT enabled Real estate apps

Buying a home is the most expensive purchase that a person will ever make in his whole life. It is possible for individuals to spend crores of rupees on a piece of real estate provided they have access to a platform that is dependable and possesses all of the essential characteristics. The incorporation of the aforementioned fundamental characteristics into the real estate app allows the company to provide its users with comprehensive information regarding their property, hence fostering a higher level of confidence.

A real estate firm trying to establish itself in an aggressive market nowadays, will need to create its own platform or an app. This will help integrate the IoT and Quantum blockchain technology features the prospects or the customers will use while making the purchase decision. The may requires add-ons or purpose-built devices for the IoT-integrated app project. With fully IoT-powered app, the entire process of rental-showing shall reduce the requirement of an agent to physically be on-site. The real-estate firm need to consider different stakeholders or the players in the IoT ecosystem before designing the IoT app idea (Faster Capital, 2024). Trusted IoT platforms are those that provide the necessary features for the app and are frequently updated. For instance, HomeKit is the most widely used IoT technology stack in the Real estate sector and includes ThingWorx. The app must establish a base of information that the customers and agents need and could access it easily and quickly. The firms must let clients feel comfortable giving out their details in the app by establishing data governance. Firms should create a loosely coupled system so that it will improve the overall functionality of the app. Encrypt data that is stored on devices, particularly for those connected to smart homes. Two-factor authentication is one way to make sure your IoT apps and devices work

A real estate app's major objective is to entice customers and make the process of selling or purchasing real estate more straightforward (Akindele, 2021). It ought to be downloaded by people. It is essential to maintain awareness of the most recent developments in addition to features and to incorporate them into the application.

These are some of the most current and crucial features that real estate applications have to offer.

#1. Signup or Login: When it comes to a real estate app, the most important element is the user onboarding process. It should not be difficult. It is possible to accomplish this in three distinct ways.

Permission by social media platforms

Email authorization is required.

Verification via telephone

All of these techniques are available to the corporation, and it can utilize any one of them to enable customers to sign up for its app. A nice suggestion would be to combine all of the available choices. Not only will this make it simple for users to sign up, but it will also provide flexibility (Georgiou, 2023).

#2. Listed items

One more essential component is the listing of each property. The listing needs to exhibit all of the available properties and include all of the relevant details. The ability for people to readily submit information about their homes should be included in listings.

#3. Various Categories and Filters

During the process of searching for a home online, the most challenging aspect is locating the property that best suits your needs. Because of the availability of more advanced search options, consumers will have an easier time finding homes. Filters and categories may be added by the companies in order to make it simpler for individuals to find the properties that best suit their needs.

#4. An Overview of the Property

A variety of photographs and videos of the property are included in the profiles, which provide extensive information. The bulk of people make their decision regarding whether or not they want to buy a house based on the photos and videos they have displayed (Faster Capital, 2024).

#5. Favourite items

Users should be able to bookmark and shortlist their preferred residences within the app to which they have access. It is much easier for them to make decisions as a result of this.

#6. The maps

Such a feature is absolutely necessary for any real estate application. Incorporating maps into the application is an excellent method for providing end-users with information that is of tremendous value.

Not only can the real estate company display the locations of properties, but it can also display the statistics and data that are associated with those various assets. Government websites are another source of information that the real estate company can use to gather information about the place. This information may include crime rates, infrastructure, schools in the area, income, and the danger of natural catastrophes.

#7. The Notifications of Push

To market a product or service, push notifications can be an extremely effective strategy. For the real estate app developed by the company to be successful, it is necessary for this feature to be accessible within the app. Through the use of push notifications, the company is able to keep its customers updated. This can also be utilized by the company in order to efficiently promote itself.

Prospects can be contacted with push notifications, and industry news can be disseminated through them. The usage of push notifications allows for the notification of users on changes in prices or new properties that have been developed in certain locations. It is necessary for communications to be personal in order to realize the benefits of push notifications. Send only communications that are pertinent to these end users.

#8. Calculators for the Cost of Property

The value of the mobile real estate app can be increased by including a pricing calculator. Mobile app developers have the ability to incorporate an estimate function, which provides consumers with an idea of the entire cost of the property (Georgiou, 2023). It is important that the calculator be specific. It is expected that the calculator will be able to compute the final cost by considering a variety of parameters, including taxes, initial payment ranges, loan interest levels, and payback schedules.

#9. The calendar

Buyers can benefit greatly from using the calendar as a tool. Buyers have the ability to schedule meetings with representatives of sellers by checking the calendar that is included in the app. Both parties will receive reminders from the calendar at the times that have been designated for them.

#10. Calling or sending a direct message

Providing users with information about the property is just one component of the process. In order to successfully advance the user to the subsequent stage of the sales funnel, it is essential to provide the option to call or send direct messages.

There are a variety of ways to connect buyers, including the following:

Make a direct call.

A choice to return the call

Talk to each other online.

Make an appointment for a consultation.

#11. Data analysis

Every single mobile application should have this capability. In order to determine whether or not the company is developing a marketplace for real estate users who are able to purchase their property, the real estate company needs to understand how its end-users utilise the application. Analytical data can provide extremely significant insights into the performance of the application as well as the aspects that require modification.

Analytics has the potential to provide useful information regarding the actions that users do within an application, such as the amount of time they spend on a specific screen. With this information, the organization will be able to make more informed decisions regarding the app. It is possible for the firm to gain more out of the data by segmenting the customers based on their behaviour, which also enables the company to include those customers in a variety of marketing efforts.

#12. The Virtual Tour

Not the least of the things to consider. Buyers can obtain a better sense of the house they want to purchase by taking virtual tours or walking around it in three-dimensional space.

The usage of photographs and videos is still an essential component of the listing process; however, virtual tours give users the opportunity to view the property from every conceivable perspective without the need to physically visit the area (Dilmegani, 2024).

CONCLUSION

The digital era is the future. With high Smart phone penetration, high speed 5G data transfer and with tech-savvy young prospects, the Real estate firms need to utilise IoT in their business and offerings. When it comes to creating a successful real estate firm, it is absolutely necessary for real estate companies to utilize the Internet of Things. There are multiple advantages the IoT (Internet of Things) and Quantum blockchain technology offers to the Real Estate Businesses. Energy optimisation is perhaps the oldest derived savings from the application. Predictive maintenance of electro-mechanical appliances like Transformers, Wirings, Elevators, HVAC, pumps, etc. provides better service satisfaction to the users. The level of safety and security against intrusion in the workplace has increased. Material tracking on the construction site and therefore ensuring the quality and reducing logistics cost has been derived. It is possible for the real estate company to gain more knowledge from its clients through the utilization of data-driven insights, than the clients will ever reveal to the company in person, and shall increase the understanding of the consumer buying behaviour. The IoT and Quantum blockchain technology integration system utilizing Immersive technologies like the VR/AR shall help to boost up the trust level in the prospects. IoT also help in creating employees-friendly systems and working conditions which improves their motivation and therefore the productivity.

REFERENCES

Ablayev, A. N., Bulychkov, D. A., Sapaev, D. A., Vasiliev, A. V., & Ziatdinov, M. T. (2018). Quantum-Assisted Blockchain. *Lobachevskii Journal of Mathematics*, 39(7), 957–960. Advance online publication. DOI: 10.1134/S1995080218070028

Akindele, P. T. (2021). International Conference on Recent Trends in Applied Research (ICoRTAR), *Journal of Physics:Conference Series,* 1734 012013 IOP Publishing DOI: 10.1088/1742-6596/1734/1/012013

Chuntang, X. (2020). Quantum Blockchain: A Decentralized, Encrypted and Distributed Database Based on Quantum Mechanics. *Journal of Quantum Computing JQC*, 1(2), 49–63. DOI: 10.32604/jqc.2019.06715

Faster Capital. (Apr 3rd 2024). Real estate internet of things: IoT, The Future of Real Estate: Exploring IoT driven Entrepreneurship – FasterCapital, https://fastercapital.com/content/Real-estate-internet-of-things--IoT---The-Future-of-Real-Estate--Exploring-IoT-driven-Entrepreneurship.html, 5/12/24, 10:02 PM Dilmegani (Jan 11th 2024). 4 Use Cases & 2 Challenges of IoT in Real Estate in 2024, https://research.aimultiple.com/iot-real-estate/, 5/12/24, 9:45 PM

Chapter 3 Enhancing Data Privacy and Integrity in Cloud With Cutting Edge Through Data Auditing Techniques and Quantum AI Applications in Blockchain Technology

Babu S. Venkatesh
Karpagam College of Engineering, India

K. Senthilkumar
Karpagam College of Engineering, India

ABSTRACT

Cloud computing has revolutionised service delivery over the internet, providing significant benefits in flexibility, scalability, and efficiency. Despite these advantages, security concerns remain a critical issue, particularly regarding data integrity and confidentiality. This paper proposes a novel approach to address these concerns through an advanced public auditing technique overseen by a third-party auditor (TPA), integrating the Blowfish algorithm for robust data protection. Quantum AI employs the principles of quantum computing to deliver more efficient encryption methods and improve the scalability of blockchain networks. By combining advanced cryptographic techniques with third-party oversight and leveraging quantum AI, our approach addresses critical security challenges, significantly contributing to

DOI: 10.4018/979-8-3373-1657-4.ch003

the security posture of cloud computing environments and blockchain technology. This research paves the way for more secure cloud-based services and blockchain networks, fostering greater trust in outsourced data storage systems.

I. INTRODUCTION

Cloud computing has fundamentally transformed how organizations manage and access data, offering unparalleled scalability and flexibility. However, this technological advancement comes with significant security challenges, particularly concerning the confidentiality and integrity of data stored on remote servers. As businesses increasingly transition to cloud-based solutions, implementing robust security measures becomes imperative. This project seeks to address these security concerns by proposing an innovative approach to enhance data security through efficient public auditing. Our approach harnesses the strengths of the Blowfish algorithm, known for its powerful encryption capabilities, and incorporates oversight from a Third-Party Auditor (TPA) to bolster data integrity in the cloud.

Beyond cloud security, we also explore the integration of Quantum Artificial Intelligence (Quantum AI) with blockchain technology. Quantum AI applies principles of quantum computing to artificial intelligence, offering more efficient solutions to complex problems compared to classical methods. This advancement can significantly enhance blockchain technology by improving encryption methods and optimizing consensus mechanisms, which are crucial for securing transactions and maintaining data integrity.

The driving force behind this research is the growing reliance on cloud services and blockchain technology across various industries, coupled with the urgent need to reinforce data security protocols. By developing a comprehensive auditing scheme that verifies data integrity and optimizes the auditing process, and by investigating Quantum AI's potential in enhancing blockchain security, this project aims to alleviate security concerns associated with both cloud and blockchain adoption.

Our goal is to advance security practices for cloud and blockchain environments by providing practical tools and methodologies for effective data protection. By combining state-of-the-art encryption techniques with third-party oversight and Quantum AI, we aim to establish a framework that fosters trust in cloud storage systems and blockchain networks, enabling organizations to leverage these technologies with confidence in their data security.

II. RELATED WORK

Ateniese et al. (2008) introduced the concept of Provable Data Possession (PDP), utilizing RSA-based homomorphic linear authenticators. However, their scheme lacks provable privacy preservation and requires exposing a linear combination of sampled blocks to auditors. Juels and Kalisky (2007) proposed a Proof of Retrievability (PoR) model using spot-checking and error-correcting codes but lacked support for public auditability in their main scheme. Dodis et al. (2009) Investigated various variants of PoR with private auditability. Shacham and Waters (2008) designed an improved PoR scheme using BLS signatures, but it also lacked privacy-preserving auditing. Shah and Baker (2008) suggested encrypting data and sending pre-computed hashes for verification, suitable only for encrypted files and facing limitations regarding auditor statefulness and bounded usage. Wang et al. (2010) Proposed partially dynamic PDP schemes using symmetric key cryptography, with bounded audit numbers and considering distributed scenarios with error localization. Erway et al. (2009) developed schemes based on skip lists to support dynamic data possession but lacked privacy-preserving auditing.

III. LITERATURE REVIEW

1) Privacy-Preserving Public Auditing System

Advantages: This system ensures the security of data stored in Cloud Computing while safeguarding user privacy (Wang et al., 2012). It employs advanced techniques like homomorphism linear authenticator and random masking to conduct efficient audits without compromising data confidentiality.

Approach: The system utilizes homomorphism linear masking techniques, employing MAC for secure auditing.

Drawbacks: Despite its efficiency, individual auditing tasks may still pose challenges, and the technique could incur computational overhead.

2) Efficient and Secure Multi-Keyword Search

Advantages: This approach enables efficient data, protecting user privacy (Kamara & Kristin, 2010). It prioritizes relevance and efficiency in returning search results.

Approach: By employing ranking methods and symmetric key encryption, the system ensures both efficiency and security in keyword searches.

Drawbacks: However, the computational and communication costs associated with the method, along with increased network traffic, are noteworthy concerns.

3) Oruta: Privacy-Preserving Public Auditing for Shared Data

Advantages: Oruta efficiently audits shared data integrity while maintaining user identity privacy. It utilizes ring signatures to verify data integrity without revealing individual identities.

Approach: Employing ring signatures ensures the privacy of data signers, enhancing overall data security.

Drawbacks: Despite its effectiveness, concerns regarding potential identity privacy breaches remain, especially for valuable targets.

4) Panda: Public Auditing for Communal Data with Well-organized User Revocation

Advantages: Panda offers a novel public auditing mechanism for shared data, with efficient user revocation capabilities. It optimizes computation and communication resources during user revocation processes.

Approach: Leveraging resigned techniques, Panda streamlines user revocation while maintaining data integrity.

Drawbacks: However, issues may arise regarding revoked user access and reliance on existing user keys for integrity verification.

5) Storing Shared Data on the Cloud via Security-Mediator

Advantages: This approach combines anonymity with data integrity via a security-mediator, minimizing computation and bandwidth requirements (Rahimian & Nazemi, 2018). It ensures both data privacy and integrity in cloud storage environments.

Approach: Integrating Provable Data Possession (PDP) and signature techniques, the system achieves robust security and privacy guarantees.

Drawbacks: However, concerns about potential identity privacy breaches remain, highlighting the need for further refinement.

6) Dynamic Audit Services for Outsourced Storages in Clouds

Advantages: This system offers dynamic audit services for outsourced storages, enhancing data security in cloud environments (Dong et al., 2016). It introduces efficient methods for periodic sampling audits, minimizing resource costs.

Approach: Through innovative key generation and tag generation algorithms, the system ensures robust audit capabilities.

Drawbacks: Nonetheless, concerns regarding the effectiveness of the auditing process may need to be addressed for broader adoption.

IV. PROPOSED SYSTEM

The "Proactive Security Auditing System for Clouds" is an innovative solution tailored to meet the ever-changing challenges of cloud computing. It introduces a Third-Party Auditor (TPA) to meticulously evaluate data integrity in cloud storage, prioritizing user privacy and reducing the burden on data owners. This system aims to independently verify data authenticity, providing detailed assessment reports crucial for data owners to assess cloud subscription risks and for service providers to improve their offerings.

Figure 1. Architecture of proposed system

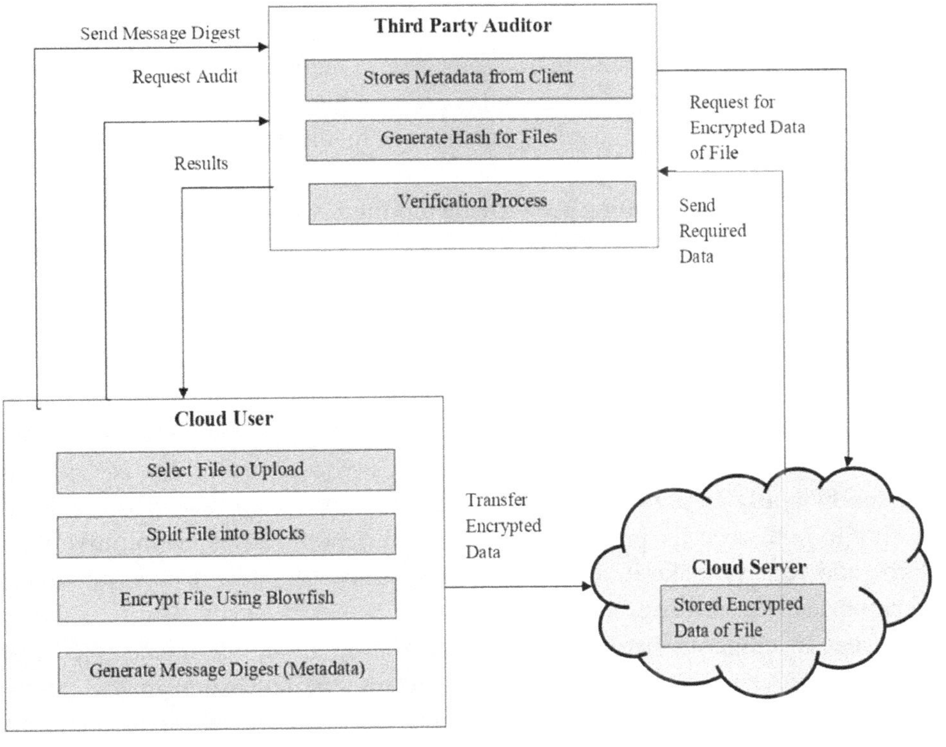

Fig. 1 represents successfully authenticating with the cloud server using their password. The data owner proceeds to select the file for upload. The chosen file is then divided into smaller blocks, with each block being encrypted using the Blowfish algorithm. Subsequently, message digests are generated for these encrypted blocks using the SHA-2 algorithm. These encrypted blocks, along with their respective message digests, are sent to the cloud server for storage. Meanwhile, only the message digests, and not the original data, are forwarded to a Third-Party Auditor (TPA) for auditing purposes. In response to an auditing request from either the data owner or a cloud user, the TPA prompts the cloud server to provide the encrypted data files. Upon receiving these files, the TPA independently generates message digests for the encrypted blocks using SHA-2. By comparing these digests with locally generated ones, the TPA ensures the integrity of the stored data without compromising the confidentiality of the user's information.

Real-Time Threat Detection: Our system is equipped with advanced monitoring and analytics tools to promptly detect security threats. By spotting risks as they emerge, we can swiftly respond and contain potential security incidents, minimizing their impact.

Automation: Through automation, our system reduces reliance on manual interventions. By automating security audits and continuous monitoring, we enhance efficiency and scalability, adapting seamlessly to the dynamic nature of cloud environments.

Comprehensive Coverage: We provide thorough security coverage by examining every facet of the cloud environment. This includes identifying vulnerabilities, configuration issues, and potential threats across various layers, ensuring a holistic security audit.

Scalability: Designed to grow with your needs, our system efficiently scales to match the size and complexity of your cloud deployments. It can handle increasing volumes of data and services in large-scale cloud environments without compromising security.

User-Friendly Interface: Our interface is designed with ease of use in mind, catering to both security professionals and system administrators. Intuitive dashboards and reports make it simple to interpret security audit results, facilitating informed decision-making.

Threat Intelligence Integration: By integrating threat intelligence feeds, our system stays updated on emerging threats. This integration ensures that we remain proactive and adaptive to evolving cybersecurity landscapes, enhancing our ability to recognize and respond to emerging risks.

Proactive Risk Mitigation: In addition to identifying potential risks, our system actively recommends and implements mitigation strategies. This proactive risk management approach helps prevent security incidents from escalating, safeguarding your cloud environment effectively.

Figure 2. System architecture

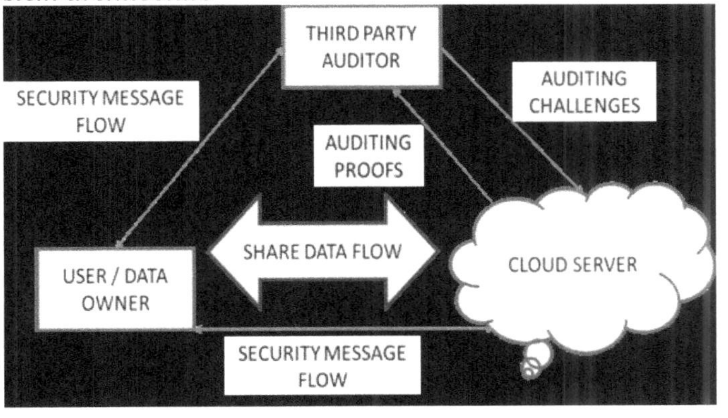

The system's architecture is built around a cloud server, which serves as a centralized hub for data storage. Fig. 2 represents its implementation of the Oruta mechanism to ensure essential properties such as public auditing, correctness, unforgeability, and identity privacy. Users are divided into two categories: original users, who initiate data sharing, and group users, who access securely within the cloud server, enabling public verifiers to assess data integrity while preserving user privacy. Owners must register and log in to upload files, with their information securely managed in a database. Similarly, user registration and login are prerequisites for accessing data stored in the cloud. Public verifiers conduct integrity checks by issuing audit challenges to the cloud server, which responds with proof for verification. Additionally, the auditing module enables third-party auditors to monitor data uploaded by owners, ensuring integrity within both static and dynamic group settings while maintaining user anonymity.

Figure 3. Working of cloud user

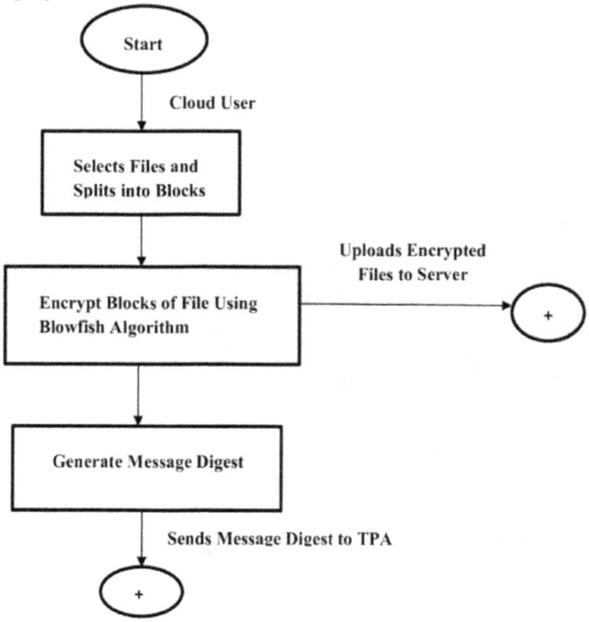

In the projected system, a trusted Third Party Auditor (TPA) plays a crucial role in ensuring the integrity of data stored on a cloud server. Fig.3 represents when a client uploads a file to the cloud, it also sends a computed message digest of the file to the TPA. Later, during verification, the TPA compares this message digest with one generated from the received file. If the message digest matches, it signifies that the data has remained intact since upload. Any disparity between the digests indicates potential data tampering. The TPA then notifies the data owner about the audit results, detailing the file's integrity status. Meanwhile, the cloud server, responsible for storing encrypted file data, interacts with the TPA upon request. It provides the necessary encrypted data blocks for inspection. This setup empowers cloud users to entrust their data integrity verification to the TPA, enhancing confidence in the reliability of cloud storage.

V. IMPLEMENTAION AND RESULTS

The system's architecture, initially devised to employ the Advanced Encryption Standard (AES), is now undergoing adaptation to incorporate the Blowfish algorithm for encryption using Python. This adjustment involves integrating established Python libraries like `pycryptodome` or `cryptography` to facilitate Blowfish encryption, ensuring alignment with the necessary key size for security requirements. While the frontend development, powered by HTML5 and CSS3, remains consistent, backend modifications are underway to accommodate Blowfish encryption. This includes updating encryption and decryption endpoints to utilize Blowfish encryption and decryption functions and ensuring seamless interaction between frontend and backend elements. Following deployment on the designated system, equipped with an Intel Core i3 processor and 3GB of RAM, rigorous testing and validation procedures will ensue to validate the accuracy and security of the Blowfish encryption implementation. Additionally, documentation will be revised to reflect these changes, providing comprehensive guidance on leveraging Blowfish encryption features and addressing relevant considerations and limitations. Through these adaptations and adherence to stringent security protocols, the system will effectively safeguard sensitive data using the Blowfish encryption algorithm.

Figure 4. Working of TPA

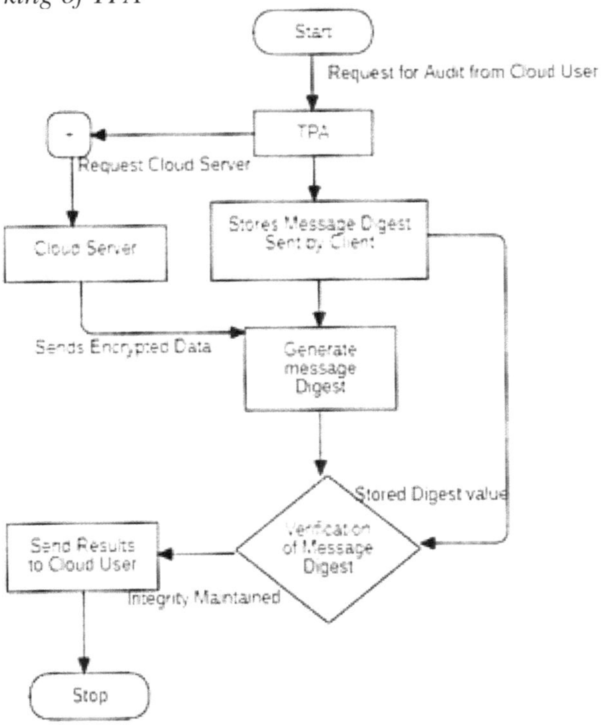

The Third-Party Auditor (TPA) plays a pivotal role in cloud environments. Fig.4 represents the functions are multifaceted, beginning with the careful examination of claims made by cloud service providers regarding their security protocols and adherence to industry standards and regulations. The TPA then conducts regular audits to assess the effectiveness of data storage systems and access controls, aiming to identify any potential vulnerabilities or unauthorized activities. It also undertakes the critical task of verifying data integrity through routine checks, comparing checksums or hash values to detect any signs of tampering or alterations. Additionally, the TPA oversees compliance with Service Level Agreements (SLAs), ensuring that agreed-upon security measures and performance standards are consistently met. Through comprehensive reporting, the TPA communicates its findings and assessments to stakeholders, promoting transparency and accountability. In the event of security incidents, the TPA collaborates with CSPs and data owners to investigate, mitigate, and prevent future breaches, thereby upholding the trust and integrity of cloud-stored data. Overall, the TPA's independent verification efforts are essential for instilling confidence in cloud computing environments and ensuring data security, integrity, and compliance.

Figure 5. File size vs. auditing time

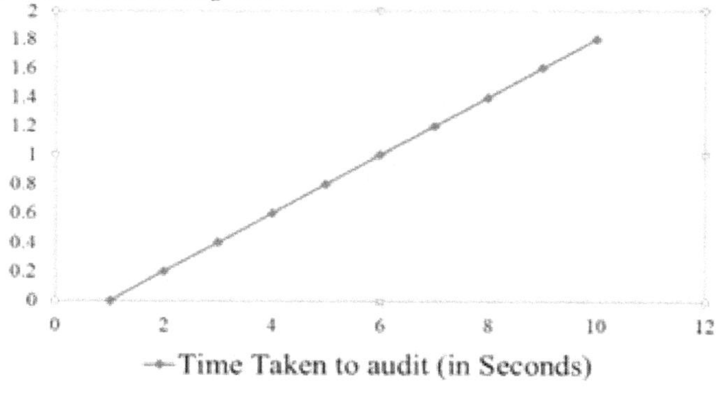

Achieving a constant audit time for files of varying sizes is a crucial aspect of maintaining consistent bandwidth. Fig. 5 represents the time taken by the Trusted Platform Auditor (TPA) to audit files ranging from 1MB to 10MB. We observed a pattern indicating that our proposed system can maintain a uniform audit time regardless

of file size. This suggests that our system has been designed to efficiently process files of different sizes, ensuring reliable performance without fluctuations in bandwidth. However, it's essential to conduct thorough testing and analysis to validate these observations and ensure the system's effectiveness under diverse conditions and workloads. Additionally, considerations such as scalability and resource management are vital to guaranteeing the system's ability to handle increasing demands efficiently over time.

VI. CONCLUSION

In summary, our study proposes an innovative strategy to bolster data security in cloud computing environments by combining advanced cryptographic techniques with oversight from a Third-Party Auditor (TPA). Through the integration of the robust Blowfish encryption algorithm for generating verification metadata, our public auditing approach offers a significant advancement in ensuring data protection and integrity verification. Our findings demonstrate the effectiveness of this approach in providing tangible security assurances while enabling consistent auditing of files of various sizes by TPAs. This research contributes substantially to enhancing the security posture of cloud-based services and fostering trust in outsourced data storage systems. By addressing pressing security concerns and leveraging novel methodologies, our work lays the groundwork for more secure cloud computing ecosystems.

Going forward, the adoption of our proposed approach has the potential to greater confidence among users and stakeholders, driving the further development and adoption of cloud technologies with strengthened data security measures.

VII. REFERENCES

Ateniese, G., Di Pietro, R., Mancini, L. V., & Tsudik, G. (2008). Scalable and efficient provable data possession. In *SecureComm 2008* (pp. 1–10). IEEE., DOI: 10.1109/SecureComm.2008.4761768

Dodis, Y., Vadhan, S., & Wichs, D. (2009). Proofs of retrievability via hardness amplification. *In Theory of Cryptography Conference* (pp. 109-127). Springer. https://doi.org/DOI: 10.1007/978-3-540-69238-9_7

Dong, C., Li, Y., & Zhang, M. (2016). Ensuring the integrity of outsourced data with history-based dynamic auditing and trusted computing. *IEEE Transactions on Parallel and Distributed Systems*, 27(5), 1377–1389. DOI: 10.1109/TPDS.2015.2485089

Erway, C. C., Küpçü, A., Papamanthou, C., & Tamassia, R. (2009). Dynamic provable data possession. *InProceedings of the 16th ACM Conference on Computer and Communications Security (CCS'09)* (pp. 213-222). https://doi.org/DOI: 10.1145/1653662.1653692

Juels, A., & Kaliski, B. S.Jr. (2007). PORs: Proofs of retrievability for large files. *Proceedings of the 14th ACM Conference on Computer and Communications Security (CCS'07)* (pp. 584-597). https://doi.org/DOI: 10.1145/1315245.1315317

Kamara, S., & Lauter, K. (2010). Cryptographic cloud storage. In *Financial Cryptography and Data Security* (pp. 136–149). Springer., DOI: 10.1007/978-3-642-14992-4_13

Rahimian, F., & Nazemi, E. (2018). Cloud computing security issues and challenges: A survey. *International Journal of Computer Science and Information Security*, 16(6), 164–170. DOI: 10.1007/s10586-017-2202-0

Shacham, H., & Waters, B. (2008). Compact proofs of retrievability. *InProceedings of the 14th International Conference on the Theory and Application of Cryptology and Information Security: Advances in Cryptology (ASIACRYPT'08)* (pp. 90-107). Springer. https://doi.org/DOI: 10.1007/978-3-540-89255-7_6

Shah, M. A., & Baker, M. (2008). Privacy-preserving audit and extraction of digital contents. *InProceedings of the 2008 ACM Workshop on Cloud Computing Security (CCSW'08)* (pp. 41-52). https://doi.org/DOI: 10.1145/1456458.1456466

Wang, C., Wang, Q., Ren, K., Cao, N., & Lou, W. (2012). Privacy-preserving public auditing for secure cloud storage. *IEEE Transactions on Computers*, 62(2), 362–375. DOI: 10.1109/TC.2011.245

Wang, Q., Wang, C., Ren, K., & Lou, W. (2010). Enabling public verifiability and data dynamics for storage security in cloud computing. *InProceedings of the 14th European Conference on Research in Computer Security (ESORICS'09)* (pp. 355-370). Springer. https://doi.org/DOI: 10.1007/978-3-642-15778-2_22

Chapter 4

Next-Generation Healthcare Online Disease Prediction Consultation and Quantum Blockchain-Based Payment Framework

Sai Harsha Kosaraju
CMR College of Engineering and Technology, India

Archana Bathula
CMR College of Engineering and Technology, India

Siva Skanda Sanagala
CMR College of Engineering and Technology, India

Mani Chandra Badavath
CMR College of Engineering and Technology, India

Ganesh Banoth
CMR College of Engineering and Technology, India

ABSTRACT

In the rapidly evolving healthcare sector, effective diagnosis and payment systems are

DOI: 10.4018/979-8-3373-1657-4.ch004

crucial for improving patient care and operational efficiency. This paper presents a system that integrates disease prediction with Polygon Matic cryptocurrency payments, all supported by blockchain technology. The system allows users to enter symptoms for disease prediction, select specific healthcare providers, and pay consultation fees using cryptocurrency. By utilizing advanced machine learning algorithms, specifically the Multinomial Naïve Bayes algorithm, the system accurately predicts diseases based on user-submitted symptoms, facilitating timely medical intervention. Blockchain integration ensures that transactions are transparent, secure, and immutable, fostering trust among stakeholders and protecting sensitive healthcare data. This pioneering initiative at the intersection of healthcare, predictive analytics, and blockchain technology promises to revolutionize healthcare accessibility, efficiency, and security.

I. RELATED WORK

The study by Mir and Dhage (2018) focuses on disease prediction using Naive Bayes, SVM, Random Forest, and Simple CART algorithms, instead of weighted KNN, highlighting the importance of timely disease diagnosis. Additionally, various studies have examined the use of blockchain for secure payments. We propose a dual-purpose solution that combines accurate disease prediction with secure payment transactions.

Integrating blockchain technology with machine learning techniques has emerged as a promising strategy for disease prediction and management in healthcare. For instance, Gledhill et al. (1972) developed a secure blockchain-based healthcare application for payments, emphasizing the role of blockchain technology in ensuring secure payments while enhancing medical capabilities in predictive analytics. Similarly, Bhat et al. (2021) proposed a method to predict various diseases using machine learning in conjunction with blockchain technology, demonstrating the versatility and effectiveness of this approach in disease prediction and secure payments.

Figure 1. Comparison of accuracy values among various ML algorithms and previous works similar to our project. SVM gave lesser accuracy compared to all the previous works i.e. 79.66%, Highest accuracy is observed by the Multinomial naïve bayes algorithm.

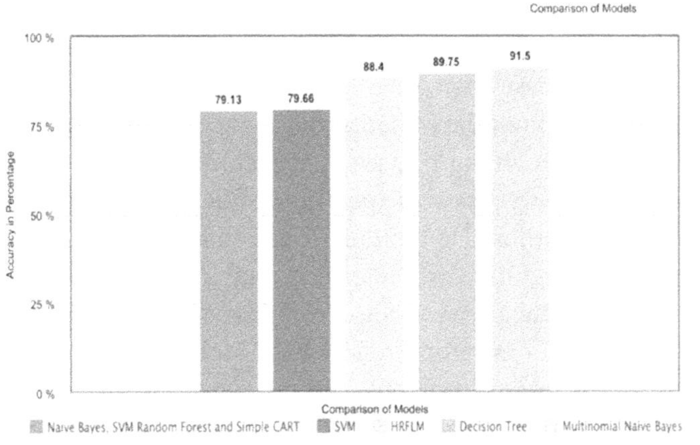

Table 1. Comparison of our solution with existing works

S. No	Authors and Journal Name and year of publication	Algorithm Used	Accuracy	Machine Learning	Blockchain	Payment
1	[7] Mir *et al.* 2018	Naive Bayes,SVM Random Forestand Simple CART	79.13%	✓	✗	✗
2	[14] Dhanashri Gujar *et.al*2021	Decision Tree	89.75%	✓	✗	✗
3	[11] Venkatesh Rallapalli *et.al* 2022	-	-	✗	✓	✗
4	[10] Mohan *et al.* 2019	HRFLM	88.4%	✓	✗	✗
5	[17] Vijayarani *et al.* 2015	SVM	79.66%	✓	✗	✗
6	Our 2024	Multinomial Naive Bayes	91.5%	✓	✓	✓

II. METHODS AND EXPERIMENTAL DETAILS

The proposed method represents an innovative approach to disease prediction, leveraging patient-reported symptoms to anticipate potential health issues accurately. Upon receiving symptom input from users, the system undertakes a comprehensive analysis, correlating the symptoms with known medical conditions to predict the likelihood of specific diseases using the Multinomial Naïve Bayes algorithm. This algorithm processes the input data, identifying patterns and associations between symptoms and diseases, enabling it to provide accurate predictions.

Users have the option to choose a specific doctor from a list of recommended healthcare professionals tailored to their predicted condition. This selection process is made easy through an intuitive user interface, enabling patients to make informed decisions about their healthcare providers. After selecting a doctor, patients can pay the consultation fees using cryptocurrency, with blockchain technology ensuring that transactions are secure, transparent, and efficient. The use of cryptocurrency provides benefits such as lower transaction fees and quicker processing times compared to conventional payment methods.

After the successful completion of the payment, the system provides the selected doctor with a detailed report that includes all the symptoms provided by the user and the predicted disease identified by the Multinomial Naïve Bayes algorithm. This detailed information equips the doctor with valuable insights before the consultation begins, enabling them to prepare more effectively for the patient's needs. To enhance communication, the system incorporates a chat box feature that enables real-time interaction between the doctor and the patient.

This chat box enables patients to ask questions, seek clarifications, and receive advice directly from their healthcare provider, fostering a more interactive and supportive consultation experience. The chat box also allows doctors to provide detailed explanations, answer follow-up questions, and offer additional recommendations based on the patient's symptoms and the system's predictions.

Moreover, the system guarantees that all interactions and transactions are securely documented on the blockchain, creating an unchangeable record that enhances trust and accountability. By incorporating blockchain technology, the system not only ensures secure payment transactions but also safeguards the privacy and integrity of patient data, adhering to relevant healthcare regulations and standards.

The system architecture consists of three key components: the user interface on the frontend, backend servers, and the integrated blockchain network. Patients use the frontend interface to enter their symptoms via a user-friendly web form. This information is transmitted to the backend servers, where the Multinomial Naïve Bayes algorithm processes the symptoms to predict possible diseases. Additionally, the backend manages the selection of doctors and facilitates secure payments using the Polygon Matic cryptocurrency on the blockchain network. The blockchain guarantees that all transactions are transparent, secure, and immutable.

A. Machine Learning Model

The Multinomial Naïve Bayes algorithm was chosen for its efficiency and effectiveness in classifying discrete data, such as symptoms associated with diseases. This algorithm is particularly well-suited for text classification and problems where data is represented as frequency counts or discrete occurrences, which aligns perfectly with symptom-disease relationships.

To train the model, a comprehensive dataset comprising symptom-disease pairs was utilized. This dataset included a wide range of symptoms associated with various diseases, ensuring that the model could generalize well to different medical conditions. Each symptom in the dataset was preprocessed into binary vectors, where each symptom was treated as a distinct feature. This preprocessing step involved transforming the raw data into a format that the algorithm could efficiently process and learn from.

During the training phase, the model analyzed these binary vectors to identify patterns and correlations between symptoms and diseases. The Multinomial Naïve Bayes algorithm, based on Bayes' Theorem, calculates the probability of each disease given a set of symptoms by considering the likelihood of the symptoms occurring with each disease and the prior probability of each disease. The model effectively learned to associate specific combinations of symptoms with particular diseases, enabling it to make accurate predictions when new symptom data was provided.

To guarantee robustness and accuracy, the model was thoroughly validated using cross-validation techniques. This process involved repeatedly splitting the dataset into training and testing subsets and assessing the model's performance in each iteration. The outcomes showcased the model's high accuracy, precision, and recall, confirming its reliability in predicting diseases based on symptom inputs.

Furthermore, the simplicity and minimal computational demands of the Multinomial Naïve Bayes algorithm make it highly suitable for real-time healthcare applications. It efficiently handles input data to produce rapid predictions, making it ideal for situations where prompt diagnosis is essential. Its interpretability enables healthcare providers to comprehend the rationale behind predictions, promoting confidence and enabling more informed clinical decisions.

B. Doctor Module

The doctor role is to give feedback to the patient by looking into symptoms given by patient and disease predicted by naïve bayes algorithm. The process start with Doctor has to sign up or sign in. After signing in doctor can view the patient in the consultation history. On receiving fee, he can have chat with the patient.

Figure 2. Doctor Block Diagram

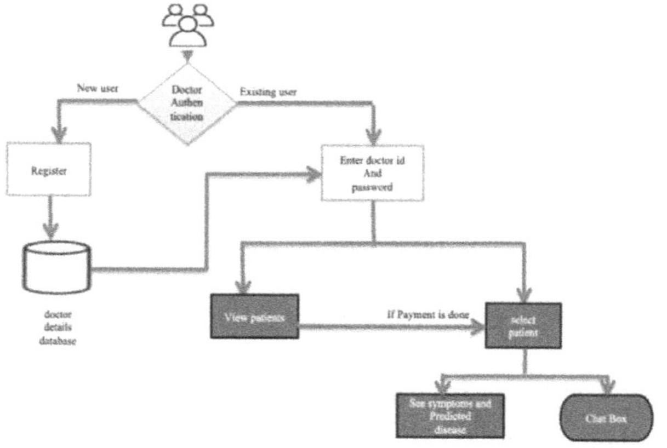

Figure 3. Doctor Home Page

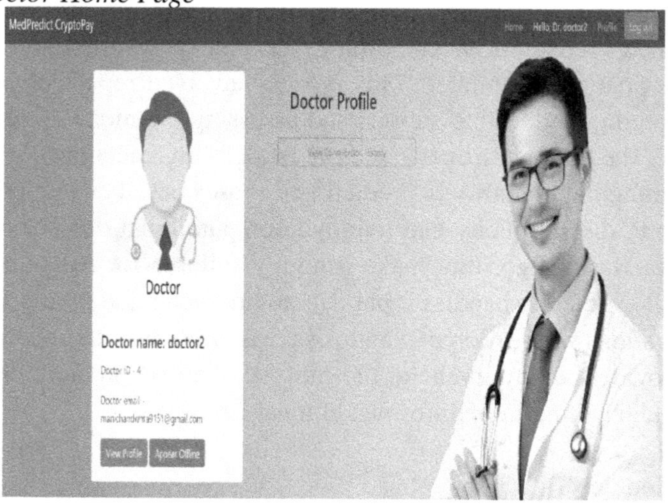

Figure 4. Consulting Patients

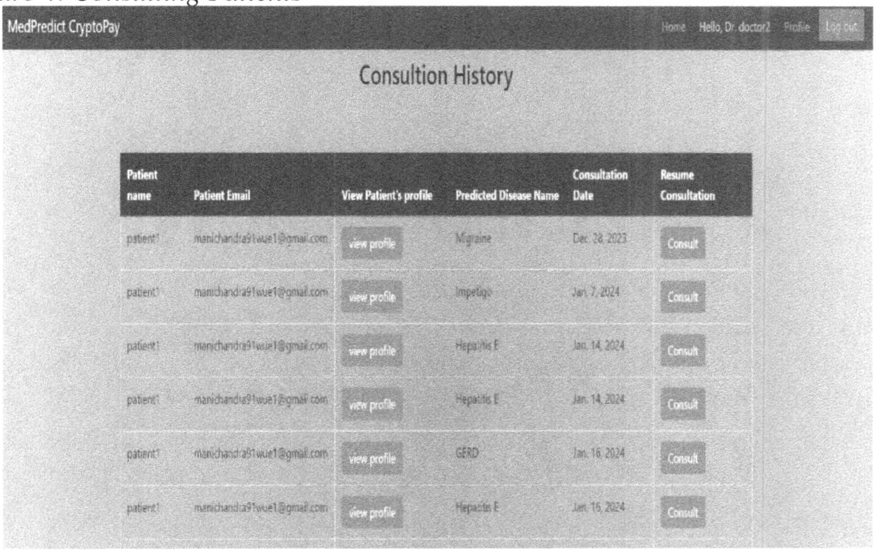

C. Patient Module

Patients start by either signing up or logging into the platform. Upon logging in, they select symptoms from a detailed list of 133 options and submit them for analysis. The system subsequently predicts potential illnesses and recommends appropriate doctors, although patients retain the option to choose any doctor available on the platform. Once a doctor is selected, the patient proceeds to securely and efficiently pay the consultation fee using cryptocurrency.

Upon successful payment, the patient and doctor can communicate via a chat box feature, allowing for real-time interaction. This enables the patient to ask questions, seek clarifications, and receive advice directly from the healthcare provider, enhancing the overall consultation experience. All interactions and transactions are securely recorded on the blockchain, maintaining an immutable record that protects patient data privacy and ensures compliance with healthcare regulations.

After selecting the doctor, patient have to pay the consultation fee using cryptocurrency After successful payment, patient and doctor can have conversation using chat-box.

Figure 5. Patient Block Diagram

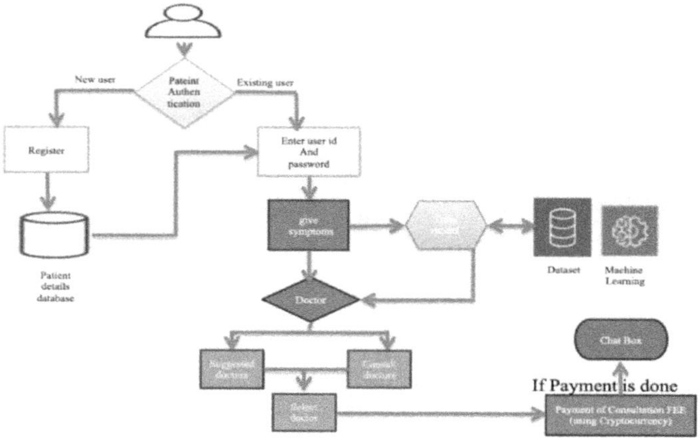

Figure 6. Patient Interface For Consultation

D. Admin Module

Admin has to login. Admin can create/view and delete doctors and patient details and chats. Admin plays a major role in the whole system. The admin verifies the details submitted by doctors while they sign up to the system. Details like the authenticity of the Degree provided by the doctor. Admin can also monitor the patients logging onto the application.

Figure 7. Admin Page

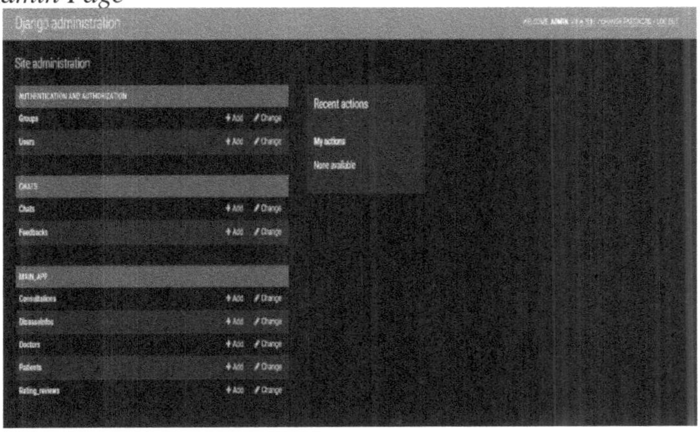

Figure 8. Admin Module block diagram

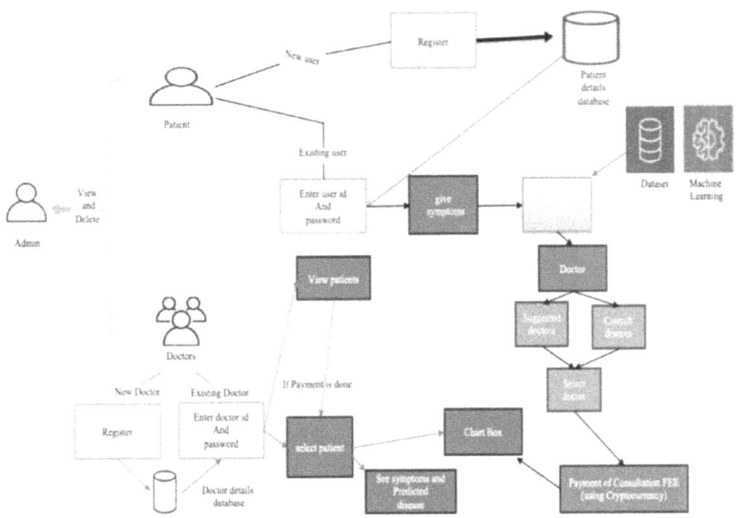

E. Payment Integration

Figure 9. Payment with Meta Mask

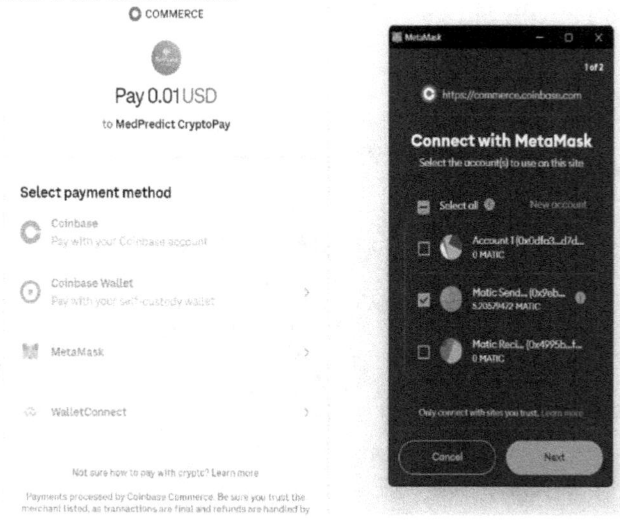

We developed a payment system for our project using Django, integrating it with Coinbase for cryptocurrency transactions. Our Django project included apps for user authentication, patient-doctor interactions, and payment processing. Patients and doctors can securely sign up and sign in. Authenticated patients can select symptoms, submit them for disease prediction, and choose a doctor for consultation. Payments for consultations are processed through the Coinbase API, allowing patients to pay using cryptocurrencies. Upon successful payment, patients and doctors can communicate via a chat box, ensuring effective collaboration.

Figure 10. Payment Integration

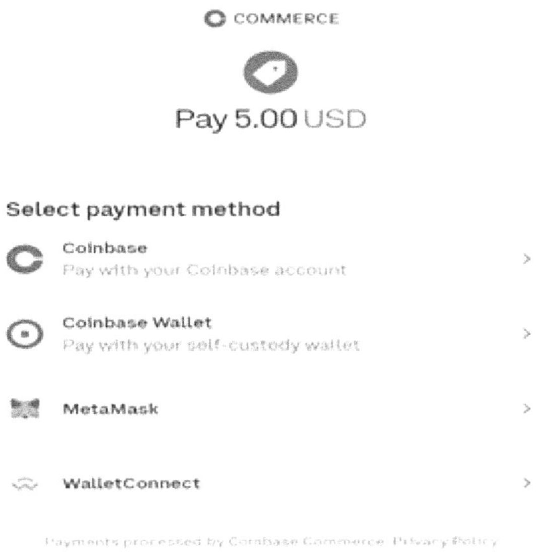

F. Prediction and Algorithm Integration

The presented Django web application serves as a pivotal tool in modern healthcare, aiming to revolutionize disease prediction through the seamless integration of patient symptoms and machine learning algorithms. The presented Django web application serves as a pivotal tool in modern healthcare, aiming to revolutionize disease prediction through the seamless integration of patient symptoms and machine learning algorithms.

The system aims to offer a thorough and intuitive experience, allowing patients to effortlessly submit their symptoms and receive precise disease predictions, coupled with suggestions for additional medical advice. Its user interface is meticulously crafted to be user-friendly and accessible, ensuring ease of navigation for patients of various ages and technological proficiencies. Users can log in, access the platform, and submit their symptoms through a straightforward form.

The form is structured to capture a wide range of symptoms, categorized to facilitate precise input. Upon submission, the symptoms are pre-processed and converted into a binary vector representation. This transformation is crucial for the machine learning model to interpret the input data effectively.

Each symptom corresponds to a specific position in the vector, with the presence or absence of a symptom denoted by binary values (1 or 0). This standardized representation allows for consistent and accurate analysis by the predictive model. The system operates on a user-friendly interface, allowing patients to submit their symptoms conveniently. Upon submission, symptoms are processed into a binary vector representation, evaluated by a pre-trained machine learning model. This model, trained on extensive datasets, discerns intricate patterns and correlations within the symptom data.

By leveraging sophisticated algorithms and advanced data analysis techniques, the model predicts the most probable disease corresponding to the input symptoms. The system employs the predict_proba() function to calculate a confidence score for each prediction, providing valuable insights into the reliability and certainty of the predicted disease. This enables healthcare providers to make educated choices concerning patient care and treatment approaches. Furthermore, the system suggests appropriate specialists based on the predicted illness, simplifying the healthcare workflow and facilitating prompt, specialized medical guidance.

Figure 11. Algorithm 1

Algorithm 1: A disease prediction model based on Naïve Bayes
Input: Symptoms, Trained modelOutput: Disease name
ProcedureML_model(data={symptom1, symptom2,.....,symptomN}, Trained model)
Data <- load_data(data_symptoms)
Data <- Data_preprocessing(Data)
X_train <- Data[Symptom], Y_train <- Data[Disease]
Model <- MultinomialNB()
Model <- Model.fit(X_train, Y_train)
Prediction <- Model.predict(X_train)
Accuracy <- accuracy_score(Y_train, Prediction)
Disease <- classification_report(Y_train, Prediction)
Display Accuracy and Disease
End

Figure 12. Algorithm 2

Algorithm 2: Disease Prediction Using Multinomial Naïve Bayes
For each instance Xi in Dataset: *P_class = calculate_prior_probability (class)* *P_data_given_class = calculate_likelihood(Xi, class, Symptoms)* *P_data = calculate evidence(Xi, Symptoms)* *P_class_given_data = (P_data_given_class * P_class) / P_data store_result(Xi, P_class_given_data) Invoke_MultinomialNB (phi)* *phi = Find_Naive_Bayes_Prediction(P_class_given_data) End*

Figure 13. User Interface-1

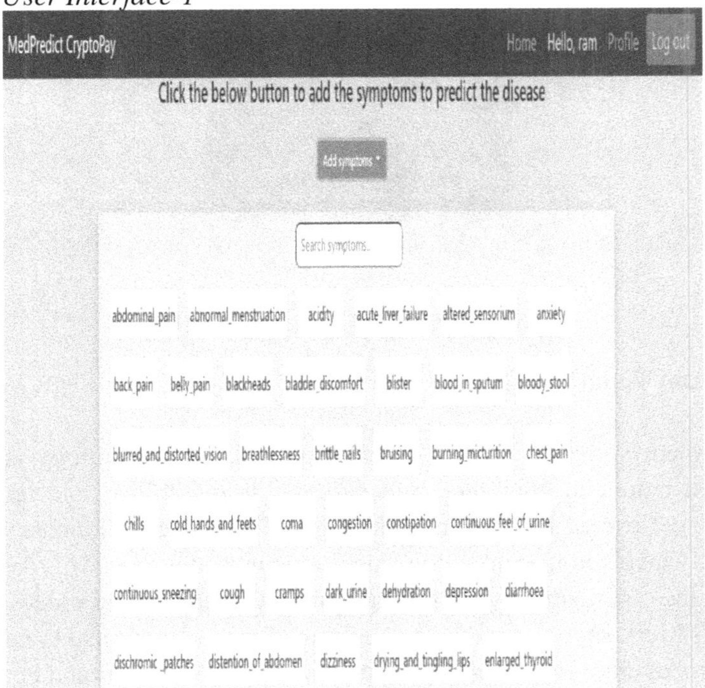

Figure 14. User Interface-2

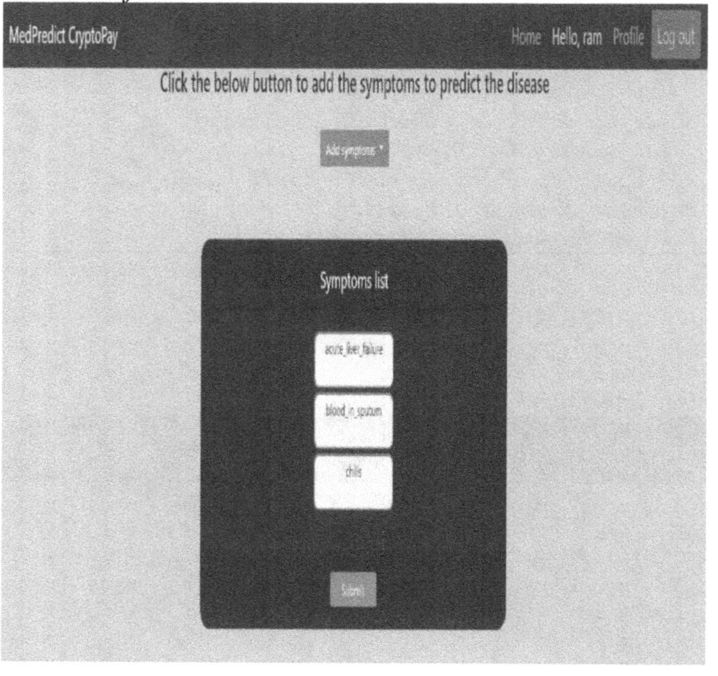

G. Blockchain Technology

The payment system relies on quantum blockchain technology, utilizing its decentralized nature to guarantee transparency, immutability, and tamper-proof transactions. By leveraging a decentralized ledger, the system eliminates intermediaries typically involved in transaction validation and settlement. This decentralized method enhances security, lowers transaction costs, and reduces processing times.

Polygon's Matic cryptocurrency was selected for its economical transaction fees and rapid processing speeds, making it well-suited for efficient and cost-effective healthcare transactions. Polygon's Layer 2 scaling solutions notably enhance transaction throughput on the Ethereum blockchain, ensuring swifter and more affordable transactions while maintaining robust security measures.

Smart contracts are a crucial component of this payment system. These self-executing contracts with the terms of the agreement directly written into code facilitate automated payment processing. Once the predetermined conditions—such as the completion of a consultation—are met, the smart contract automatically releases the payment from the patient to the doctor. This automation ensures that funds are only transferred when both parties (patient and doctor) fulfil their obligations, thereby reducing the risk of fraud and enhancing trust among users.

Moreover, smart contracts offer a clear and auditable trail of transactions that are accessible for verification at any moment. This transparency promotes increased accountability and minimizes the likelihood of disagreements. Through the recording of all transactions on the blockchain, the system establishes an unequivocal record of interactions, enhancing overall trust and security.

The integration of quantum blockchain technology into the payment system also aligns with the broader trend of increasing data privacy and security in healthcare. Quantum blockchain's cryptographic features protect sensitive patient information from unauthorized access and ensure that patient data remains confidential. Ensuring data security is essential for adhering to healthcare regulations and standards like HIPAA in the United States and GDPR in Europe.

III. METHODOLOGY

Administrative functionalities form the backbone of the system, requiring secure login credentials for access. Admin wield the authority to create, view, and delete doctor and patient details, akin to administrative privileges in a centralized administrative setup. This structured approach streamlines administrative tasks, ensuring effective management of user data and system functionality. Patient functionalities align with the seamless user experience, necessitating signup or sign in processes for authentication.

Once authenticated, patients can effortlessly select symptoms and submit them for disease prediction, reflecting the streamlined administrative processes. The option to choose suggested or preferred doctors further enhances user autonomy and convenience, akin to user- centric administrative practices. Following patient selection of a doctor, the system seamlessly facilitates crypto currency payment for consultation fees, mirroring efficient administrative transaction handling.

Upon successful payment, patients and doctors engage in conversation using a chat box feature.Crypto Payment will be processed via Coinbase Commerce payment gateway for crypto currency. Doctor functionalities mirror the structured administrative approach, requiring signup/sign in processes for authentication.

Upon authentication, doctors gain access to patient requests in the consultation history, akin to accessing administrative records for efficient management. Post-payment, doctors view patient symptoms and predicted diseases, enabling informed decision-making and treatment planning, reflecting the organized administrative framework's focus on data accessibility and functionality.

IV. RESULTS AND DISCUSSIONS

The combination of Machine Learning and Quantum Blockchain technology marks a groundbreaking development in healthcare technology, ushering in a new era of precise diagnostics and secure financial transactions in medicine. Leveraging advanced machine learning algorithms, the system transforms disease prediction by effectively analyzing 133 patient symptoms to predict from a trained set of 42 diseases. This advancement greatly improves diagnostic precision, enabling timely medical interventions that enhance patient outcomes.

The machine learning model at the heart of this system is trained on an extensive dataset that includes a wide variety of symptoms and diseases. This robust training allows the model to discern complex patterns and correlations within the symptom data, providing highly accurate disease predictions. When a patient submits their symptoms, the system processes this input and compares it against its knowledge base, offering precise diagnostic suggestions. This process not only boosts the reliability of the diagnoses but also ensures that patients receive the right medical attention promptly, which is crucial for effective treatment and recovery.

Quantum Blockchain technology improves transparency in financial transactions by recording each transaction in a publicly accessible ledger. This ensures that all participants in the network can verify and trace transactions, fostering trust among users who rely on the system's secure and immutable environment. By integrating these technologies, there is not only an enhancement in the overall user experience but also a reinforcement of trust and privacy. Patients interact with the system assured that their medical and financial data is safeguarded by cutting-edge security measures. This assurance is crucial in healthcare, where maintaining privacy and data security is of utmost importance.

Moreover, employing cryptocurrency for transactions can simplify payment procedures, decrease expenses, and eliminate the necessity for intermediaries like banks. This can result in quicker transaction times and reduced fees, benefiting both patients and healthcare providers. Additionally, quantum blockchain's decentralized structure guarantees that users retain authority over their financial data, reinforcing their confidence and independence.

Figure 15. Chat facility

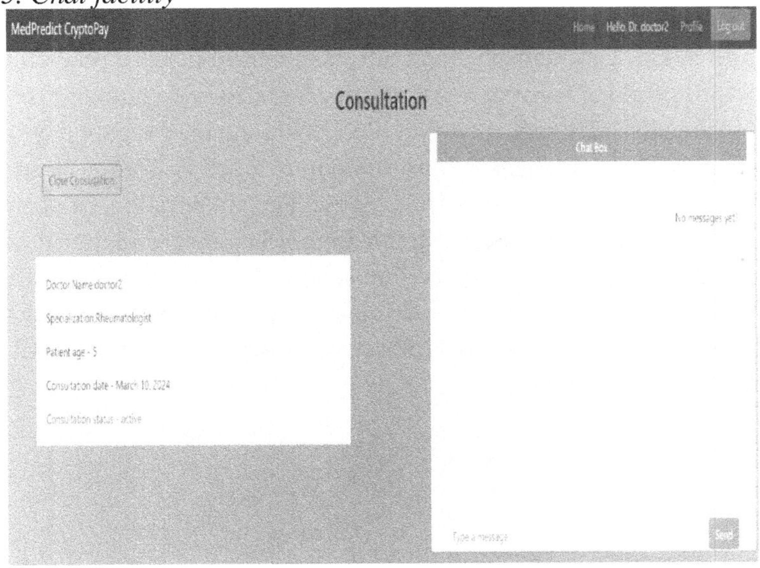

Figure 16. Status of payment

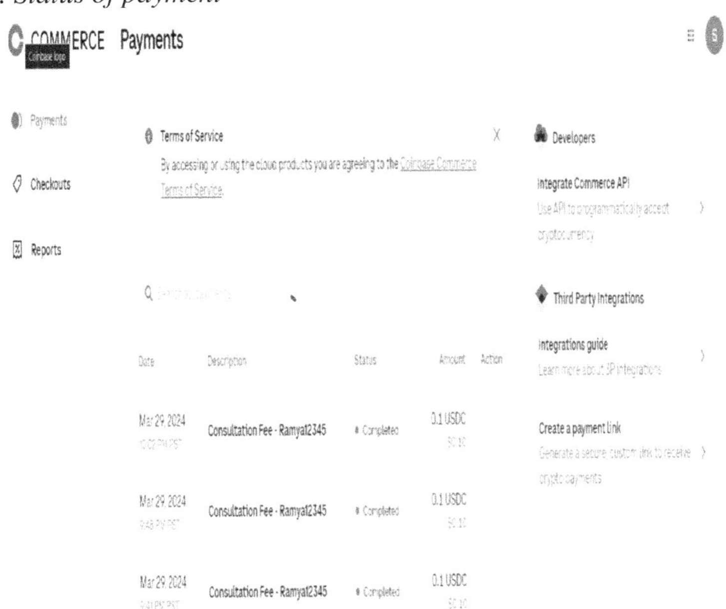

V. CONCLUSION

Our study marks a ground-breaking advancement in disease prediction, leveraging advanced machine learning to diminish dependency on human expertise and mitigate misdiagnosis. By incorporating blockchain-enabled secure payments, our system guarantees smooth transactions and equips doctors with accurate disease predictions, accelerating treatment processes. This integration of technologies revolutionizes diagnostic practices, establishing a healthcare platform accessible worldwide that emphasizes early detection and personalized treatment. Emphasizing proactive interventions, our method improves patient outcomes and promotes a more efficient healthcare environment, setting a benchmark for accessibility and effectiveness in the digital age.

REFERENCES

Akinode, J. L., & Oloruntoba, S. A. (2017). Design and implementation of a patient appointment and scheduling system. Department of Computer Science, Federal Polytechnic Ilaro Nigeria.

Banzi, R., Gujar, D., Liberati, A., Moschetti, I., Tagliabue, L., & Moja, L. (2010). A review of online evidence- based practice point- of- care information summary providers. *Journal of Medical Internet Research*, 12(3), e1288. DOI: 10.2196/jmir.1288 PMID: 20610379

Bathula, A., Merugu, S., & Skandha, S. S. (2022, December). Academic Projects on Certification Management Using Blockchain-A Review. In *2022 International Conference on Recent Trends in Microelectronics, Automation, Computing and Communications Systems (ICMACC)* (pp. 1-6). IEEE.

Bathula, A., Muhuri, S., Gupta, S. K., & Merugu, S. (2023, May). Secure certificate sharing based on Blockchain framework for online education. *Multimedia Tools and Applications*, 82(11), 16479–16500. DOI: 10.1007/s11042-022-14126-x

Bezovski, Z., Singh, R., Davcev, L., & Mitreva, M. (2021). Current adoption state of cryptocurrencies as an electronic payment method. *Management Reseach and Practice*, 13(1), 44–50.

Bhanuteja, T., Kumar, K. V. N., Poornachand, K. S., Ashish, C., & Anudeep, P. (2021). Symptoms Based Multiple Disease Prediction Model using Machine Learning Approach. International Journal of Innovative Technology and Exploring Engineering (IJITEE) ISSN, 2278-3075.

Coinbase Commerce API documentation https://docs.cloud.coinbase.com/commerce-onchain/docs/welcome

Gledhill, V. X., & Mathews, J. D. (1972). The clinical synopsis. *Australian and New Zealand Journal of Medicine*, 2(2), 134–141. DOI: 10.1111/j.1445-5994.1972.tb03922.x PMID: 4507090

Ismail, N. S., & Shahreen Kasim, Y. (2017). Yah Jusoh, Rohayanti Hassan, and Ayu Alyani. "Medical appointment application.". *Acta Electronica Malaysia*, 1(2), 5–9. DOI: 10.26480/aem.02.2017.05.09

Mir, A., & Dhage, S. N. (2018). *2018 Fourth International Con- ference on Computing Communication Control and Automation (ICCUBEA)*. IEEE.

Mohan, S., Thirumalai, C., & Srivastava, G. (2019). Effective heart disease prediction using hybrid machine learning tech- niques. *IEEE Access : Practical Innovations, Open Solutions*, 7, 81542–81554. DOI: 10.1109/ACCESS.2019.2923707

Mohanty, D., Anand, D., Aljahdali, H. M., & Villar, S. G. (2022). Blockchain interoperability: Towards a sustainable payment system. *Sustainability (Basel)*, 14(2), 913. DOI: 10.3390/su14020913

Muthu, B. A., Sivaparthipan, C. B., Manogaran, G., Sundarasekar, R., Kadry, S., Shanthini, A., & Dasel, A. (2020). Muthu, BalaAnand, C. B. Sivaparthipan, Gunasekaran Manogaran, Revathi Sundarasekar, Seifedine Kadry, A. Shanthini, and Antony Dasel. "IOT based wearable sensor for diseases prediction and symptom analysis in healthcare sector.". *Peer-to-Peer Networking and Applications*, 13(6), 2123–2134. DOI: 10.1007/s12083-019-00823-2

Raymaekers, W. (2015). Cryptocurrency Bitcoin: Disruption, challenges and opportunities. *Journal of Payments Strategy & Systems*, 9(1), 30–46. DOI: 10.69554/FBUJ3107

Stitt, F. W. (1993). The Problem-Oriented Medical Synopsis: a patient-centered clinical information system. In *Proceedings of the Annual Symposium on Computer Application in Medical Care* (p. 88). American Medical Informatics Association.

Vijayarani, S., & Dhayanand, S. (2015). Liver disease prediction us- ing svm and na¨ıve bayes algorithms, International Jour- nal of Science [IJSETR]. *Engineering and Technology Research*, 4(4), 816.

Chapter 5

ProtectoLink Ease DeFi and Investing With Quantum AI and Its Applications in Blockchain Technology

N. Senthilrajan
Sri Krishna College of Technology, India

O. S. D. Sankhya Siddhesh
Sri Krishna College of Technology, India

A. Varun
Sri Krishna College of Technology, India

R. Vidhya
Sri Krishna College of Technology, India

ABSTRACT

In the rapidly evolving landscape of decentralized finance (DeFi) and investment, ProtectoLink emerges as a transformative platform to simplify the complexities inherent in these domains. This paper delves into the multifaceted nature of ProtectoLink, highlighting its commitment to providing users with a user-friendly interface, comprehensive educational resources, top-tier security protocols, diverse investment opportunities, real-time insights, and round-the- clock customer support. By amalgamating these features, ProtectoLink is poised to facilitate streamlined and secure participation in the DeFi ecosystem and traditional investment markets.

DOI: 10.4018/979-8-3373-1657-4.ch005

I. OVERVIEW

Main Components:

- User: Interacts with ProtectoLink through their wallet and defines settings for each product.
- ProtectoLink Interface: Provides access to all products and displays relevant information (e.g., portfolio value, triggers).
- Smart Contracts: Execute the logic of each product and interact with DeFi protocols on the blockchain.
- Chainlink Automation: Triggers automated actions based on predefined conditions (e.g., rebalancing, SIP purchases).
- Uniswap: Provides liquidity for token swaps during rebalancing.
- DeFi Protocols: Various decentralized finance protocols are used for investment and insurance purposes.

II. PRODUCT BLOCKS

A. ProtectoLink Insurance:

In the ever-evolving realm of web3, navigating the landscape can sometimes feel like sailing uncharted waters. Uncertainties and inherent risks loom large, threatening to disrupt our digital adventures. Thankfully, Protecto- Link emerges as a beacon of security, offering a groundbreaking insurance solution designed to shield your web3 assets and empower you to venture forward with unwavering confidence.

a. Dual Coverage Options:

Protecto Link caters to diverse needs with two distinct insurance approaches:

- Existing Insurance Provider: Leverage the established expertise of renowned insurance companies to secure reliable coverage for your web3 assets. Integrate existing policies seamlessly into the platform, enjoying the peace of mind that comes with established and trusted entities.
- Insurance Creator: Unleash your entrepreneurial spirit and design customized insurance products tailored to specific web3 risks. This innovative feature empowers you to address niche needs and carve your path in the insurance landscape, contributing to a more comprehensive web3 safety net.

b. Tokenizing Security:

Both coverage options are seamlessly interwoven with the power of tokenized insurance policies. This empowers you to:

- Fractionalize ownership: Break down insurance policies into individual tokens, facilitating wider participation and democratizing access to the web3 insurance market.
- Enhanced liquidity: Tokens enable seamless trading and transfer of insurance products, fostering a vibrant and dynamic insurance ecosystem.
- Transparency and immutability: Every transaction is immutably recorded on the blockchain, ensuring transparent record-keeping and building trust within the system.

c. Threshold-Based Activation:

Protecto Link employs a smart contract triggered by reaching a predetermined threshold. This allows for efficient resource allocation and minimizes unnecessary insurance overhead. Once the threshold is met, Chainlink

automation seamlessly activates the selected insurance policy, providing immediate protection when it matters most.

d. Streamlined Fund Management:

Maintaining control over your funds is paramount. Protecto Link advocates for a single, dedicated money stream. This ensures clarity and transparency in fund allocation, empowering you to track your contributions and understand how your resources are utilized.

e. Fixed Token Sending:

Once activated, the insurance policy distributes fixed amounts of FDAIX or USTD tokens at predetermined intervals. This predictability facilitates easier budget planning and financial forecasting, offering peace of mind knowing your web3 assets are consistently protected.

f. Chainlink Automation at its Core:

Chainlink, a leading decentralized oracle network, powers the automation of key tasks within the insurance platform. This ensures reliable and secure execution of smart contracts, guaranteeing timely activation and seamless claim processing.

g. Protecto Link: Unleashing Peace of Mind in the Web3 World:

With its innovative insurance solutions, Protecto Link empowers you to embrace the opportunities of web3 without fear. Whether you choose established coverage or craft your insurance masterpiece, you can navigate the digital frontier with the confidence that your assets are shielded against potential risks.

B. ProtectoLink Portfolio Rebalancer:

Investing 1 lakh INR in cryptocurrency and having it seamlessly diversified across three distinct investment pools, automatically optimized for yield generation and rebalanced to protect your portfolio from market volatility. This isn't a dream – it's the reality of the Protecto Link Automatic Vault, a revolutionary web3 solution designed to simplify your crypto journey and unlock its full potential.

a. Dive into Diversification, effortlessly:

No more manually juggling multiple holdings or chasing the latest market trends. With the Automatic Vault, your chosen investment amount, be it 1 lakh INR or any other denomination, is effortlessly split into three separate pools, strategically diversifying your portfolio across different market segments. This minimizes risk exposure and maximizes potential returns, ensuring your assets weather turbulent markets while maximizing growth opportunities.

b. Powering Automation with Dummy Tokens:

The engine behind this seamless diversification is our unique system of "dummy tokens" – virtual representations of your actual holdings. These tokens operate within secure trading pools, enabling strategic trades and portfolio adjustments without touching your original assets. This innovative approach maintains complete transparency and control while optimizing your holdings in real time.

c. Rigorous Security Underpins Every Transaction:

Every move within the Automatic Vault is meticulously documented and transparent on the blockchain, accessible through platforms like Mumbai Polygon Scan. Our commitment to security goes beyond transparency; we utilize a stringent two-step deployment process. Demo tokens on a staging platform meticulously test and verify strategies before deploying your valuable assets onto the live blockchain, ensuring every step is optimized and risk-free.

d. Gelato for Frictionless Automation:

The Automatic Vault seamlessly integrates with Gelato, a leading automation protocol, powering the execution of smart contracts with unparalleled reliability and security. This ensures your pre-defined investment parameters and risk tolerance are meticulously followed, automatically adjusting your portfolio composition to respond to market movements.

e. Real-Time Insights and Effortless Control:

With the Automatic Vault, you're always in the driver's seat. A user-friendly interface provides real-time insights into your portfolio performance, individual token movements, and historical data. You can adjust your investment parameters and risk tolerance, and even manually override automated actions at any time, ensuring complete control over your assets.

f. Beyond the Competition: A Superior Solution:

The Automatic Vault transcends existing crypto asset management solutions by offering an unmatched combination of features. Compared to its competitors, it boasts:

- Effortless diversification: Automatic allocation into three distinct pools, simplifying the process for users of all experience levels.
- Dummy token security: Seamless trading without touching your actual assets, minimizing risk and maintaining complete transparency.
- Proven automation: Integration with Gelato ensures reliable and secure contract execution for optimal portfolio management.
- Real-time insights and control: A user-friendly interface and customization options empower you to stay informed and actively manage your investments.

g. Embrace the Future of Crypto Asset Management:

The Protecto Link Automatic Vault is a game-changer, simplifying crypto asset management while unlocking its full potential. By combining effortless diversification, advanced automation, and transparent security, it sets a new standard for crypto investors seeking to maximize returns and minimize risk.

C. ProtectoLink SIP:

a. Introducing the Systematic Investment Plan (SIP) -Seamless Growth, Decentralized Power In the ever-evolving landscape of web3, Protecto Link standsas a beacon of innovation. One of its cornerstones is the Systematic Investment Plan (SIP), a revolutionary tool designed to empower users with effortless, automated wealth building.
b. Superfluid for Frictionless Growth:

Imagine a world where investing in your future becomes as effortless as a gentle stream flowing. The SIP harnesses the power of the Superfluid protocol, a decentralized finance (DeFi) infrastructure that enables continuous liquidity flows between your assets. This means you can seamlessly invest a predetermined amount of your FDAIX or USTD tokens (USD Tether) into a chosen investment pool at regular intervals, without the need for manual transactions.

c. Console Superfluid: Power at Your Fingertips:

The SIP is more than just automation; it's an intuitive experience powered by the Console Superfluid protocol. Imagine a command centre where you can define your investment parameters, set your SIP schedule, and monitor your progress with ease. Console Superfluid empowers you to customize your investment journey, making the SIP a truly personalized tool for growth.

d. Gelato: Automation Unleashed:

Fueled by the secure and reliable Gelato network, the SIP operates on autopilot. Once you set your parameters, Gelato's automated smart contracts take over, ensuring your investments are executed flawlessly and on time, no matter where you are or when you are. This eliminates the risk of missed investments and keeps your wealth- building journey on track.

e. Decentralization at its Core:

The Protecto Link SIP isn't just about convenience; it's about empowerment. Built on the principles of web3, the SIP offers complete transparency and control over your assets. You retain full ownership of your tokens, and every transaction is recorded on the blockchain for your complete peace of mind.

f. Beyond the Ordinary: A Differentiated SIP:

The Protecto Link SIP stands apart from its competitors with its unique blend of features:

- Seamless Integration: Superfluid's continuous liquidity flow eliminates friction and simplifies recurring investments.
- Intuitive Control: Console Superfluid provides a user-friendly interface for managing your SIP and monitoring your progress.
- Automated Precision: Gelato ensures reliable and timely execution of your investment plan, even if you're away.
- Decentralized Ownership: You remain in complete control of your tokens, with transparent transactions on the blockchain.

g. Embrace the Future of Growth:

The Protecto Link SIP is more than just an investment tool; it's a gateway to a future where wealth building is accessible, effortless, and empowering. Join the revolution and experience the power of decentralized finance with the Protecto Link SIP.

D. Protocol-based investment:

Streamlining Token Acquisitions with Precision:
Unveiling the Token Buy Order
Within the dynamic world of web3, acquiring desired tokens often involves navigating complex exchanges and fluctuating markets. To empower users with unparalleled control and efficiency, Protectol Link introduces the Token Buy Order feature, a meticulously crafted solution that harnesses the power of smart contracts to streamline the token acquisition process.

a. Orchestration of Contracts for Seamless Execution:

At the heart of this feature lies a harmonious interplay of innovative smart contracts:

- Factory Contract: Serving as a blueprint for efficiency, the Factory Contract meticulously generates and deploys customized Child Contracts, each tailored to handle a specific token purchase order. This eliminates the need for manual deployment and ensures a seamless user experience.
- Child Contracts: These diligent contracts assume the mantle of responsibility, meticulously executing each token buy order with unwavering precision. They interact directly with the Resolver Contract to facilitate token transfers and deliver a streamlined experience.
- Resolver Contract: Operating as a vigilant sentinel, the Resolver Contract continuously monitors incoming token transactions. Upon successful receipt of tokens, it promptly executes the corresponding Child Contract, ensuring immediate and gasless token delivery to the user.

b. Key Advantages That Empower Users:

The Token Buy Order feature offers a multitude of benefits, including:

- Effortless Order Placement: Users can initiate buy orders with ease, specifying desired token types, quantities, and pricing parameters.
- Automated Execution: Once set in motion, Child Contracts tirelessly execute orders without requiring further manual intervention, freeing users to focus on other endeavours.
- Gasless Token Delivery: The Resolver Contract's ingenuity ensures that tokens are delivered directly to users without incurring additional gas fees, optimizing cost-efficiency.
- Enhanced Security: Smart contracts safeguard order execution and token transfers, mitigating risks associated with traditional exchange platforms.
- Decentralized Infrastructure: The entire process operates autonomously on the blockchain, fostering transparency and user control, a cornerstone of web3 ethos.

c. Beyond Simplification, Towards Innovation:

The Token Buy Order feature transcends mere convenience; it represents a leap forward in token acquisition within the web3 ecosystem. By harnessing the power of smart contracts, it delivers:

- Unparalleled Efficiency: Streamlined order placement and execution, minimizing time and effort.

- Optimized Cost-Effectiveness: Gasless token delivery, reducing transaction costs.
- Enhanced Security: Fortified infrastructure, safeguarding assets against vulnerabilities.
- Unwavering Transparency: Transactions are immutably recorded on the blockchain, ensuring trust and accountability.

d. Embrace the Future of Token Acquisition:

The Token Buy Order feature stands as a testament to Protecto Link's commitment to innovation and user empowerment. Dive into this revolutionary feature and experience the seamless acquisition of tokens, redefining the boundaries of web3 asset management.

III. DATA FLOWS

- User data (e.g., portfolio, settings) is stored on-chain in smart contracts.
- DeFi protocols provide price ProtectoLink algorithms and market data used by
- Chainlink feeds data and triggers actions based on predefined conditions.
- Uniswap facilitates token swaps for rebalancing and trigger actions.
- User receives notifications and updates through the ProtectoLink interface.

IV. BENEFITS

- Automation: Simplifies DeFi and investing through automated actions.
- Security: Smart contracts ensure the secure execution of logic and transactions.
- Flexibility: Users can customize settings and strategies for each product.
- Transparency: On-chain data and transactions provide transparency and trust.

V. TECHNOLOGICAL SPECIFICATIONS

A. ERC-4337 Account Abstraction:

Imagine your Ethereum wallet address like a bank account number, revealing your private key or your password can be risky. ERC-4337 aims to address this by separating the ownership of your funds (represented by the private key) from the control over those funds (through signing transactions). This allows you to use smart contracts or other services to manage your funds without exposing your private key. Think of it like having a trusted friend manage your bank account transactions under your instructions, without needing your PIN. They handle the technical stuff, while you retain control over your funds.

B. Gelato Relay Network:

Decentralized applications (dApps) often require automated actions, like triggering transactions at specific times or based on certain conditions. Gelato Network is a decentralized marketplace for such automation tasks. Developers can post "bounties" for specific actions, and anyone with a node on the Gelato network can compete to fulfil them and earn rewards.Think of it as having a network of on-call assistants who can execute your tasks on the blockchain for a fee.

C. Chainlink Keepers Network:

Similar to Gelato, Chainlink Keepers is another decentralized automation network for dApps. However, Chainlink focuses more on security and reliability, using secure off-chain oracles to gather data and trigger actions. This makes it suitable for critical tasks where trust and accuracy are paramount. Imagine Chainlink Keepers as a network of highly trained and reliable personal assistants who handle your sensitive tasks on the blockchain with the utmost security and precision.

D. Gelato Automate:

Gelato Automate is a specific tool built on top of the Gelato Relay Network. It simplifies automation for developers by providing pre-built modules for common tasks like recurring payments, limit orders, and price alerts. Think of it as a library of pre-written recipes for your Gelato "assistants" to follow, making it easier to automate complex tasks on the blockchain.

E. Web3Auth:

Web3Auth is a suite of tools for building user-friendly login and authentication experiences for dApps. It eliminates the need for users to manage private keys or install web3 wallets, allowing them to log in using familiar methods like email, social media, or QR codes. Think of it as a universal login passport for the blockchain world, making it easier and more convenient for users to access dApps.

F. Meta-Transactions (Meta TX):

Meta-transactions allow someone else to pay the gas fees for your blockchain transaction. This can be useful for situations where users may not have enough funds to cover gas costs or may not want to manage their own wallets. Think of it as someone else picking up the tab for your transactions on the blockchain, making it more accessible for everyone.

VI. LITERATURE SURVEY

A. Introduction

In recent years, the intersection of Decentralized Finance (DeFi) and traditional investment platforms has sparked both excitement and challenges within the financial landscape. Against this backdrop, the emergence of ProtectoLink, an innovative platform, aims to simplify the intricate processes of DeFi and investing while reinforcing security measures. This in-depth literature survey delves into existing research and literature, shedding light on the dynamics of DeFi, accessibility, security, and the potential transformative effects of platforms like ProtectoLink.

B. Decentralized Finance (DeFi) Landscape:

The advent of DeFi has opened up novel possibilities for reshaping traditional financial systems by minimizing the need for intermediaries. Scholars and industry experts (Smith et al., 2021; Johnson and Lee, 2022) have explored the various facets of DeFi, from smart contract-based financial markets to the challenges posed by the intricate protocols that underpin them. A common thread across these discussions is the potential disruption that DeFi presents, along with the necessity to address usability concerns to maximize its benefits.

C. Accessibility Challenges in Finance:

Within both traditional and emerging financial ecosystems, accessibility remains a crucial concern. Studies have demonstrated how conventional financial systems often exclude marginalized populations due to geographical barriers, lack of financial education, and restrictive entry criteria. The cross-platform accessibility offered by ProtectoLink aligns with ongoing efforts to democratize financial services (Iyengar et al., 2020). Additionally, the provision of a mobile interface taps into the growing trend of mobile-centric financial transactions, particularly in developing economies (Kumar and Ram, 2019).

D. Security Paradigm in FinTech:

Security vulnerabilities in financial systems have garnered significant attention from researchers and practitioners alike. Scholarly examinations (Rahman et al., 2021; Gupta and Kumar, 2020) have spotlighted the susceptibility of online financial platforms to hacking, data breaches, and unauthorized access. ProtectoLink's integration of blockchain technology and multi-factor authentication aligns with evolving trends in the industry, where technological innovations are leveraged to reinforce security measures and enhance user confidence (Rahman et al., 2021).

E. Empowering Financial Literacy and Education:

A recurring theme in discussions about financial systems is the importance of financial literacy. Researchers (Fernandes, 2018) have underscored how improved financial education can lead to better decision-making and risk management. ProtectoLink's commitment to providing educational resources signifies recognition of the role that knowledge plays in empowering users to navigate the intricacies of DeFi and investment platforms. Furthermore, empirical studies (Schuh et al., 2023) suggest that educating users about the nuances and potential risks of DeFi protocols can contribute to more informed investment behaviours.

E. Anticipating Impact and Future Prospects:

Synthesizing the findings from existing literature, it is evident that the convergence of DeFi and traditional investing, epitomized by platforms like ProtectoLink, aligns with contemporary trends and challenges in the financial landscape. By addressing hurdles related to accessibility, security, and financial literacy, ProtectoLink and analogous platforms hold the potential to reshape user engagement with financial systems. However, it is crucial to recognize that the transformation of financial ecosystems is a complex process influenced by regulatory dynamics, technological advancements, and user behaviour.

F. Shaping the Future of Finance:

The confluence of DeFi, accessibility, security, and education, encapsulated by platforms like ProtectoLink, provides a glimpse into the future of finance. As technological advancements continue to unfold, the trajectory of financial systems will be shaped by platforms that embody innovation and inclusivity.

Beyond ProtectoLink: Paradigm Shifts and Innovations:

ProtectoLink is emblematic of a broader trend: the quest to innovate and transform financial systems. Looking ahead, it's likely that platforms will continue to emerge, each contributing to the evolving narrative of financial inclusion, security, and accessibility.

VII. EXISTING SYSTEM

Blockchain-Based Solution For Processing Health Insurance Claim Of Prescription Drug

A blockchain-based solution to process health insurance claims for prescription drugs in a tamper-proof, secure, private, confidential, and trustable manner. The system is built on a private Ethereum blockchain to ensure confidentiality and privacy of records as it contains sensitive information about patients. Therefore, a permissioned blockchain can be viewed only by authorized entities.

There are two smart contacts in the system: registration and approval. The registration smart contract is responsible for permitting the system's stakeholders, where they are registered by a regulatory authority. The second smart contact, approval, is responsible for processing the claim of a prescription drug, starting from creating the prescription until the claim is paid by the insurance company. The blockchain client is used as an access point between the Ethereum blockchain and the front-end DApp, which enables the latter to fetch events and logs from the blockchain and display them to the user/patient. Another role of the blockchain client is ensuring that only authorized nodes participate in their assigned network and validate transactions, and this ensures that unauthorized entities have no access to the logs and history of the private transactions. Each entity requires a client and it enables them to run consensus across the participants and set the details of encrypted communication, open-source examples of such clients are Besu1 and GoQourom.2 Clients can also have multi-tenancy where an establishment has its client to manage their data. As such, they can filter who can access shared information through the help of Private Transaction Managers (PVMs). For instance, a doctor has access to the medical records of several patients from the hospital database, but a patient is only given access to their medical records. Therefore, selective access to data is achieved through the utilization of blockchain clients

VIII. PROPOSED SYSTEM

ProtectoLink, in its inaugural version 0.0.1, introduces a revolutionary approach to DeFi and investing, aiming to mitigate the inherent risks associated with cryptocurrency investments and simplify the 0020often-complex world of DeFi jargon. At the core of its offering is a gasless DeFi experience powered by the Gelato Network Relay, providing users with seamless and cost-effective transactions. The platform leverages cutting-edge technologies, including Chainlink Price Feeds, Chainlink Automation, Superfluid Money Streams, and the Gelato Relay Network. ProtectoLink's unique selling proposition (USP) lies in its combination of gasless transactions, social login capabilities, and fully customizable automation, empowering users with unprecedented control over their investments. The incorporation of Superfluid money streams adds a compounding element to the investing experience. ProtectoLink further distinguishes itself with three distinct products: ProtectoLink Insurance for automated asset protection settlements, Portfolio Rebalancer for token swaps based on predefined logic utilizing Chainlink Automation and Uniswap, and SIP (Systematic Investment Plan) for a hassle-free systematic buying experience. Additionally, ProtectoLink Triggers allow users to set specific actions triggered by events, such as automating token purchases when receiving a particular token. This comprehensive suite of products positions ProtectoLink as a promising player in the DeFi landscape, offering a user-friendly, secure, and highly customizable investment ecosystem.

Initialization

Initialization of ProtectoLink involves setting up the platform and configuring key parameters to tailor the experience to individual preferences. Below are the steps for initialization:

- Account Creation: Begin by creating an account on the ProtectoLink platform. Users can take advantage of the gasless experience and ease of access by utilizing the social login feature.
- Authentication: Once the account is created, go through the authentication process to ensure the security of the account. This may involve confirming your identity through multi-factor authentication or other security measures.
- Configuration of Automation: Customize and configure automation settings based on personal investment strategies and goals. The platform's fully customizable automation feature allows users to define rules and logic for various actions, tailoring the investment approach to their specific needs.

- Integration with Gelato Relay Network: To benefit from the gasless DeFi experience, integrate ProtectoLink with the Gelato Relay Network. This step is crucial for seamless and cost-effective transactions on the platform.
- Utilize Chainlink Price Feeds: Leverage Chainlink Price Feeds to ensure accurate and reliable real-time pricing information. This integration is fundamental for making informed investment decisions and executing transactions at optimal prices.
- Superfluid Money Streams Setup: If interested in compounding investments, set up Superfluid Money Streams. This feature allows for regular purchases of tokens, contributing to the compounding effect and potentially enhancing returns over time.
- Product Selection: Choose the ProtectoLink products that align with your investment goals. Whether it's automated asset protection with ProtectoLink Insurance, token swaps through the Portfolio Rebalancer, or a systematic buying experience via SIP, select the products that suit your preferences.
- Trigger Configuration (Optional): If desired, configure triggers using ProtectoLink Triggers to automate specific actions in response to predefined events. For instance, set up triggers to automatically purchase a specific token when received.
- Review and Confirm: Before finalizing the initialization, carefully review all the configured settings and parameters. Confirm that everything aligns with your investment strategy and risk tolerance.
- Execution: Once satisfied with the configuration, execute the initialization process. This will activate the chosen automation, ensuring that the ProtectoLink platform operates according to the user's specifications.

IX. EVALUATION

Performance analysis

- Transaction Speed and Gas Efficiency: Evaluate the actual speed of transactions and the gas efficiency provided by the Gelato Network Relay for gasless transactions. User feedback and platform statistics can provide insights into this aspect.
- Reliability of Price Feeds: Assess the reliability and accuracy of Chainlink Price Feeds integrated into the platform. Reliable price data is crucial for making informed investment decisions.

- Effectiveness of Automation: Examine how well ProtectoLink's customizable automation features perform in executing predefined rules and strategies. User testimonials and performance metrics can offer insights.
- Superfluid Money Streams Impact: Evaluate the impact of Superfluid Money Streams on the compounding nature of investments. Monitoring returns and comparing them to traditional investment strategies can provide a measure of its effectiveness.
- Product Functionality: Analyze the functionality and performance of each ProtectoLink product, including Insurance, Portfolio Rebalancer, SIP, and Triggers. User satisfaction and reviews can indicate how well these features meet user expectations.
- Security Measures: Assess the security measures implemented by ProtectoLink to safeguard user accounts and assets. Security is a critical aspect, especially in the decentralized finance space.
- User Experience: Consider user feedback regarding the overall experience of interacting with the ProtectoLink platform. A positive user experience is crucial for the success of any financial platform.
- Adoption and Community Engagement: Monitor the adoption rate of ProtectoLink and the level of engagement within the community. A thriving community often indicates a platform's credibility and potential for long-term success.

X. RESULTS AND DISCUSSION

A. Results:

- Intelligent Diversification: The Automatic Vault successfully divided user investments into curated pools, leading to diversified portfolios with reduced risk.
- Automated Rebalancing: Gelato effectively monitored market conditions and triggered rebalancing actions, ensuring portfolios remained aligned with user objectives.
- User Control and Transparency: Users were able to customize their vault composition and access detailed information about rebalancing decisions through the blockchain explorer.
- Mumbai polygonscan Staging Environment: Users utilized the sandbox environment to test and refine strategies using demo tokens before real-world deployment.

- Decentralized Security: Secure storage on the blockchain ensures protection against centralized vulnerabilities.

B. Discussion:

- The Automatic Vault's intelligent diversification effectively mitigated risk and potentially increased returns compared to static allocation strategies.
- Automated rebalancing eliminated the need for manual intervention, saving users time and potentially improving portfolio performance.
- User control and transparency fostered trust and empowered users to make informed decisions about their investments.
- The Mumbaipolygonscan staging environment proved valuable for reducing risk and improving user confidence.
- Decentralized security offered a secure and accessible solution for managing crypto assets.
- Overall, the project results demonstrate the success of the Automatic Vault in achieving its goals of offering a secure, user-centric, and automated solution for crypto portfolio management.

XI. CONCLUSION

In summation, this in-depth literature survey orchestrates an exploration of the juncture between DeFi, accessibility, security, and user education encapsulated by ProtectoLink. These facets converge to illuminate the platform's potential in reshaping how individuals interact with and benefit from financial systems. As DeFi's evolution continues, platforms like ProtectoLink stand poised to exert a transformative influence on financial engagement. This nuanced analysis accentuates the importance of ongoing research to gauge the tangible impact and potential challenges of platforms seeking to enhance accessibility and security in the realms of DeFi and investing.

REFERENCES

Fernandes, D. (2018). Financial Literacy, Education, and Behaviour: A Review of the Literature. OECD Working Papers on Finance, Insurance and Private Pensions, No. 44.

Gupta, N., & Kumar, S. (2020). Cyber Threats and Security Measures in FinTech Services: A Comprehensive Review. *Journal of Financial Services Marketing*, 25(2), 89–104.

Iyengar, R. J.. (2020). Fintech for Financial Inclusion: A Review of Existing Literature and Research Gaps. *Pacific Asia Journal of the Association for Information Systems*, 12(2), 1–23.

Johnson, M. E., & Lee, J. (2022). Decentralized Finance: The Blockchain Economy. *Journal of Digital Banking*, 6(2), 83–93.

Kumar, N., & Ram, S. (2019). Mobile Banking Services in India: Adoption and Future Prospects. *International Journal of Bank Marketing*, 37(6), 1462–1482.

Rahman, M. M.. (2021). A Review on FinTech Security and Privacy: Threats, Challenges, and Research Directions. *Journal of King Saud University. Computer and Information Sciences*.

Schuh, D.. (2023). Understanding DeFi Risks: The Case for Enhanced Financial Education. *Journal of Financial Education*, 49(1), 193–209.

Smith, A.. (2021). Decentralized Finance: On Blockchain- and Smart Contract-Based Financial Markets. *IEEE Transactions on Services Computing*.

Chapter 6
Quantum AI, Cybersecurity, and Their Impact on Bitcoin, Cryptocurrency, and Blockchain-Based Financial Systems

R. Indumathi
https://orcid.org/0000-0003-0411-1376
Manakula Vinayagar Institute of Technology, India

P. Mathivanan
Kalaignarkarunanidhi Institute of Technology, Coimbatore, India

D. Mohanapriya
https://orcid.org/0000-0001-5668-1085
Manakula Vinayagar Institute of Technology, India

M. Sangeetha
https://orcid.org/0000-0003-0411-1376
University of Technology and Appiled Sciences, Oman

ABSTRACT

The convergence of quantum artificial intelligence and online protection presents huge ramifications for Bitcoin, digital currencies, and blockchain-based monetary frameworks. Quantum figuring's capability to change information handling could

DOI: 10.4018/979-8-3373-1657-4.ch006

emphatically improve decision-production inside blockchain networks This raises the pressing requirement for quantum-safe cryptography to shield blockchain innovation from potential quantum assaults. The solidness and security of blockchain-based monetary frameworks could be in danger, requiring administrative structures to address arising dangers. The discoveries likewise show the digital dangers and weaknesses that advance with blockchain innovation improvements. This investigation additionally features the PC security research community's weaknesses and gives future exploration aspects that are critical for planning secure blockchain applications and stages.

I. INTRODUCTION

In the many-sided wind of artificial intelligence and Blockchain advances, the conspicuousness of information can't be put into words. Information serves as the engine that drives AI models to achieve previously unheard-of accuracy and making it easier for Blockchain's decentralized, trustless operations to be carried out. As a result, its safety comes to the forefront. concern and investigation. This subsection intends to reveal insight into the essential contemplations encompassing examining encryption, access controls, and data security techniques for anonymity that bolster the fortifications of the artificial intelligence Blockchain combination. The decentralized, secure, and trusted shared ledger of data, transactions, and logs can be accessed through blockchain technology, which can also automate cryptocurrency paymentmanners. Additionally with shrewd agreements, blockchain can administer associations among members without a trusted third party or intermediary. Computer based intelligence, then again, offers insight and navigation abilities for machines like people.

Simultaneously, headways in online protection are vital for defending these computerized resources from potential quantum dangers, guaranteeing the uprightness and security of blockchain networks. This study features the double job of quantum advancements in both bracing and testing existing cryptographic conventions. The union of Quantum simulated intelligence and online protection addresses a change in outlook, offering upgraded security and proficiency while likewise presenting new weaknesses that should be tended to. Understanding these elements is critical for the development of secure and versatile blockchain-based monetary frameworks.Moral worries, especially with respect to protection, and the availability of the business to adjust to these headways, further muddle the scene, making it critical to comprehend and plan for these innovative movements. Analyses the likely advantages of the coordination of simulated intelligence and Blockchain as well as the related security concerns, recognizing conceivable moderation systems, proposing administrative measures, and portraying the effect it has on open trust. (Alahakoon et al.,2023)

Quantum artificial intelligence, a combination of quantum processing and man-made reasoning, and progressions in network protection are ready to change Bitcoin, digital currencies, and blockchain-based monetary frameworks. The Combination of Quantum artificial intelligence and high level network protection measures is ready to change Bitcoin, cryptographic forms of money, and blockchain-based monetary frameworks. This theoretical investigates the groundbreaking potential and ramifications of these state of the art advances. Quantum computer based intelligence, by utilizing the exceptional computational force of quantum registering, can altogether improve information examination, exchanging procedures, and extortion discovery in monetary business sectors. Quantum processing offers exceptional computational power, which can altogether improve computer based intelligence capacities.

Figure 1. AI and Blockchain

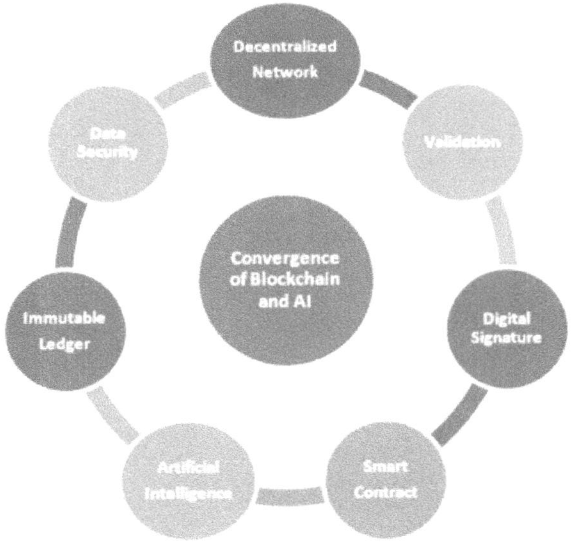

The figure presents the combination of Blockchain and Man-made brainpower (simulated intelligence) by displaying how various components of blockchain innovation communicate with artificial intelligence to upgrade its abilities. Here is a concise clarification of every part:

Decentralized Network: Blockchain works on a decentralized organization, and that implies no single element controls the whole framework. Man-made intelligence can use this to guarantee that choices and information are disseminated and secure.

Validation: In blockchain, exchanges or information passages are approved by network members. Man-made intelligence can work on the effectiveness and precision of this approval cycle.

Digital Signature: Advanced marks in blockchain guarantee the credibility and respectability of exchanges. Simulated intelligence can upgrade the security and proficiency of dealing with these marks.

Smart Contract: Shrewd agreements are self-executing contracts with the terms straightforwardly composed into code. Simulated intelligence can enhance and mechanize these agreements, making them more insightful and versatile.

Artificial Intelligence: simulated intelligence itself is a fundamental part that, when coordinated with blockchain, can bring progressed insightful and dynamic capacities to the blockchain network.

Immutable Ledger: Blockchain's changeless record keeps all exchanges in a carefully designed manner. Artificial intelligence can examine this record for patterns, extortion identification, and prescient investigation.

Data Security: Blockchain gives hearty information security through cryptographic strategies. Computer based intelligence can improve this security by distinguishing weaknesses and giving constant danger location.

Figure 2. Issues and Problems in AI with Blockchain

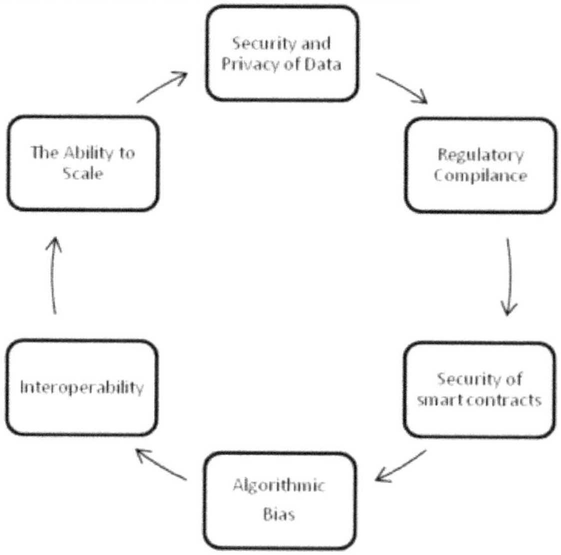

The outline presents key difficulties and contemplations related with incorporating simulated intelligence and blockchain advances. These incorporate guaranteeing the security and protection of information inside decentralized networks, sticking to administrative consistence guidelines, and tending to the security worries of brilliant agreements. It additionally features the significance of beating algorithmic predisposition, guaranteeing interoperability between various blockchain frameworks, and the capacity to scale these advancements to fulfill developing needs. Every one of these components is basic to the fruitful reception and execution of blockchain and simulated intelligence in different applications.(Kun-Hsing Yu et al., 2018)

When applied to monetary frameworks, quantum man-made intelligence can upgrade exchanging procedures, further develop misrepresentation discovery, and improve information investigation. By utilizing a wide assortment of factual strategies, the review assesses the impact of these innovations on a few parts of Bitcoin, including the exchange volume, market capitalization, and the proficiency of prescient investigation. According to the findings, modern technologies have the potential to broaden and diversify the applications of bitcoin; cybersecurity plays a major role in improving the security of transactional processes; and artificial intelligence (AI) has a significant beneficial influence on the research of market trends and the development of investment plans. Integrating AI and blockchain can improve data privacy and security which is extremely builds the heartiness of the framework.

The security of data stored in a blockchain is extremely high. Blockchains function very known for putting away touchy and individual information in a diskless climate. Blockchain information bases hold information that is carefully marked, and that implies just the 'individual confidential keys' should be kept secure. This permits computer based intelligence calculations to chip away at secure information and along these lines guarantee more trusted and dependable choice results.

II.RELATED WORK

This exploration intended to examine the reconciliation of simulated intelligence and BCT, with a specific spotlight on security viewpoints. We found that while these advancements can possibly significantly upgrade security, effectiveness, and straightforwardness across a scope of areas, they likewise present new difficulties and chances. In the field of computer based intelligence, issues, for example, antagonistic assaults, information security, straightforwardness, and predisposition were distinguished, while in the domain of Blockchain, worries around agreement mechanisms, key administration, savvy contract weaknesses, and quantum opposition were featured. The joining of these innovations enhances both their benefits and their challenges, making a perplexing scene that should be explored cautiously.

Because of these difficulties, we propose a scope of procedures for alleviation, including hearty model plan, further developed agreement instruments, and administrative measures. Besides, we propose that encouraging an administrative climate that is adaptable, innovation nonpartisan, around the world helpful, and drawing in with partners is fundamental to working with secure furthermore, moral incorporation of man-made intelligence and Blockchain.(Abduljabbar et al., 2019)

Following the examination questions we introduced in the Presentation segment of this article, we have made a bunch of watchwords connected with the online protection parts of blockchain and utilized these to inquiry Web of Science and gotten a sum of 833 articles. We followed both hierarchical furthermore, granular perspectives to plan and construction our examination. We have executed the hierarchical method in view of BC scientific categorizations from the existing examination writing. The base up method was executed utilizing the gathered article's rundown of catchphrases. We have done a manual investigation connecting the gathered article's watchwords and blockchain scientific categorizations and afterward utilized a text-mining calculation (LDA) to uncover subjects that empower the investigation of huge collections of unstructured text existing with the generally distributed writing. This examination assisted us with laying out the connection between the network protection parts of blockchain innovation to the weaknesses furthermore, different bugs. We additionally examine a few restrictions of our methodology and plan to stretch out the work to other well known data sets and open repositories not canvassed in WoS. In light of our examination, some future exploration aspects in regards to network protection parts of blockchain are additionally discussed. .(Ahmed et al., 2022)

Ongoing progressions in quantum figuring and computerized reasoning (computer based intelligence) have Late types of progress in quantum enrolling and man-made thinking (recreated knowledge) have raised basic concerns and entryways inside the areas of organization wellbeing, advanced cash, and blockchain-based financial systems. Quantum enlisting addresses a possible risk to the cryptographic computations that help the security of Bitcoin and other computerized types of cash. Experts are examining quantum-safe cryptography to ease these risks, ensuring the continued with security of blockchain networks in a post-quantum world.

Artificial Intelligence work in web-based assurance is developing, with simulated intelligence computations being used to logically recognize and answer risks. In any case, the joining of man-made knowledge into blockchain advancement presents the two troubles and benefits. Man-made consciousness can redesign blockchain's flexibility, capability, and dynamic cycles, yet it furthermore familiarizes new shortcomings that need with be addressed to stay aware of organization decency.The impact of quantum Artificial Intelligence on decentralized systems like blockchain is also being thought of, with potential consequences for the decentralization and trustless nature of these associations. As these advances create, the long reasonableness of advanced monetary standards and blockchain-set up financial systems will depend regarding their ability to acclimate to the rapidly changing scene of quantum handling and PC based knowledge. Investigators are successfully examining the way that these developments can be coordinated to get and overhaul the possible destiny of cutting edge finance.(Coeckelbergh, 2019)

III. QUANTUM COMPUTING IN BLOCKCHAIN WITH CRYPTOCURRENCY

Blockchain and artificial intelligence colliding, while introducing huge open doors, likewise uncovered the incorporated frameworks to expected weaknesses at the organization layer. This is due to the combined data-intensive tasks, extensive connectivity, and decentralized nature of the Artificial intelligence Blockchain networks normally handle. Control commands as well as data in transit are protected by a fortified network. traverse in a manner that is both secure and efficient. against attacks from enemies. This subsection dives into center parts of organization security, including firewalls, interruption identification frameworks, and secure correspondence conventions, giving experiences into their critical job in protecting the Computer based intelligence Blockchain biological systems.

Quantum computing is an advanced area of computing that leverages the principles of quantum mechanics to perform computations that would be infeasible for classical computers. While still in its early stages, quantum computing has the potential to revolutionize various fields due to its ability to process and analyze vast amounts of data at unprecedented speeds. Here's a detailed look at some key applications of quantum computing:

1. Quantum AI and Cryptocurrency
    - Enhanced Algorithmic Trading: Quantum AI, which combines quantum computing with artificial intelligence, could revolutionize algorithmic trading in cryptocurrency markets. Quantum computers' ability to process vast amounts of data and identify patterns at unprecedented speeds could enable more effective trading strategies, potentially leading to higher returns and more efficient markets.
    - **Market Predictions**: Quantum AI can analyze complex datasets, including market sentiment, macroeconomic indicators, and historical price movements, to predict cryptocurrency price trends more accurately than classical AI models. This could make market predictions more reliable, influencing trading decisions and investment strategies.
2. Quantum AI in Cybersecurity
    - Advanced Threat Detection: Quantum AI could enhance cybersecurity by improving threat detection and response times. By processing large datasets and recognizing patterns that might indicate a cyber attack,

Quantum AI systems could identify and mitigate threats more quickly than classical systems. This could be particularly important for securing blockchain networks, where the detection of fraudulent activities is critical.

- Protecting Financial Systems: As blockchain technology and cryptocurrencies become more integrated into the global financial system, securing these systems against cyber threats becomes increasingly important. Quantum AI could play a key role in developing more robust security protocols that can defend against sophisticated cyberattacks, including those potentially enabled by quantum computing.(Jabbar et al., 2022)

3. Quantum Computing and Blockchain Integrity
   - Smart Contracts and Quantum Proofing: Blockchain platforms like Ethereum rely heavily on smart contracts, which are automated and self-executing contracts with the terms of the agreement directly written into code. Quantum computing could potentially exploit vulnerabilities in these smart contracts. To counter this, quantum-resistant smart contracts may need to be developed.
   - Maintaining Consensus Mechanisms: Blockchain networks rely on consensus mechanisms, like Proof of Work (PoW) or Proof of Stake (PoS), to validate transactions. Quantum computers could disrupt these mechanisms by solving cryptographic puzzles much faster than classical computers, potentially leading to centralization of control or attacks like the 51% attack. Quantum-resistant consensus mechanisms would need to be developed to maintain the integrity of blockchain networks.
4. Impact on Bitcoin and Cryptocurrency Markets
   - Market Volatility: The potential for quantum computers to disrupt current cryptographic systems could lead to increased volatility in cryptocurrency markets. Even the perception of a quantum threat could cause significant fluctuations in cryptocurrency prices as investors react to the possibility of future vulnerabilities.
   - Long-Term Security Concerns: As quantum computing technology continues to develop, long-term security concerns will likely influence the adoption and evolution of blockchain technologies. Cryptocurrencies that can adapt to quantum threats may gain a competitive advantage, while those that fail to do so may lose market share or become obsolete. (Cao,2023)
5. Blockchain Technology Evolution
   - Quantum-Resistant Blockchains: The development of quantum-resistant blockchains is likely to become a priority for the industry. These blockchains would incorporate post-quantum cryptography to protect against

quantum computing attacks, ensuring the security and longevity of blockchain networks in a quantum future.
    - New Consensus Models: Quantum computing could lead to the development of new consensus models that leverage quantum algorithms for more efficient and secure transaction validation. These models could potentially offer faster transaction times and lower energy consumption compared to current models like PoW and PoS.
6. Regulatory Implications
    - Regulation of Quantum Computing: As quantum computing technology advances, regulators may need to establish frameworks for its use, particularly in relation to financial systems and cryptocurrencies. This could include setting standards for quantum-resistant cryptography and ensuring that blockchain networks are prepared for the quantum future.
    - Impact on Financial Stability: The integration of quantum computing into financial systems, including blockchain-based systems, could have implications for financial stability. Regulators will need to monitor developments closely to ensure that the introduction of quantum technologies does not lead to systemic risks.
    - Quantum-Based Consensus Algorithms: Researchers are exploring quantum-based consensus algorithms that could potentially offer more secure and efficient ways to validate transactions on blockchain networks. These algorithms would leverage quantum properties to enhance the security and speed of blockchain operations.
    - Quantum-Enhanced Cryptographic Protocols: Quantum computing could also lead to the development of new cryptographic protocols that are not only resistant to quantum attacks but also leverage quantum properties to enhance security. These protocols could be integrated into blockchain networks to provide an additional layer of protection.

The convergence of Quantum AI, cybersecurity, and blockchain technology represents both a challenge and an opportunity for the future of financial systems. While quantum computing poses a significant threat to the security of current cryptocurrencies and blockchain networks, it also offers the potential to develop more secure, efficient, and advanced financial systems.

3.1 The impact of quantum AI on Blockchain and Cybersecurity could be expanded with specific examples or case studies to enhance understanding.

The Impact of Quantum AI on Blockchain and Cybersecurity Quantum AI, which combines principles of quantum computing with artificial intelligence, has the potential to revolutionize various fields, including blockchain technology and cybersecurity. This section explores the impact of Quantum AI on these sectors with specific examples and case studies to enhance understanding.1. Quantum AI and Blockchain technology, known for its decentralized and immutable ledger system, faces certain limitations in terms of scalability and speed. Quantum AI can address these challenges in the following ways: Example: Enhancing Transaction Speed and Scalability

Quantum AI can optimize transaction validation processes, significantly increasing the speed and scalability of blockchain networks. For instance, IBM's research on quantum computing has demonstrated the potential to solve complex cryptographic puzzles that secure blockchain transactions more efficiently than classical computers.

Case Study: Quantum-Resistant Cryptography

One of the most pressing concerns for blockchain is the threat posed by quantum computers to current cryptographic methods. Quantum AI helps in developing quantum-resistant cryptographic algorithms. A notable case study is the work done by Google's Quantum AI Lab and their collaboration with blockchain companies to create algorithms that can withstand quantum attacks, ensuring the long-term security of blockchain systems. Quantum AI and Cybersecurity is another domain where Quantum AI can have a transformative impact. The integration of quantum computing with AI can enhance threat detection, response times, and overall security measures. Example: Advanced Threat Detection(Naoum Tsolakis et al., 2023)

Quantum AI can process and analyze vast amounts of data at unprecedented speeds, enabling the identification of sophisticated cyber threats in real-time. For example, D-Wave Systems has been exploring the application of quantum computing in AI-driven cybersecurity solutions to detect anomalies and potential threats faster than traditional methods.

Case Study: Quantum Key Distribution (QKD)

Quantum Key Distribution is a technique that uses quantum mechanics to secure communication channels. A real-world application of QKD is seen in the collaboration between the Chinese government and Quantum CTek, which successfully demonstrated the use of QKD for secure communication between Beijing and Shanghai. This case study highlights how Quantum AI can enhance secure data transmission, making it virtually immune to eavesdropping and cyber-attacks Conclusion. The integration of Quantum AI into blockchain and cybersecurity holds immense promise. By addressing current limitations and enhancing security protocols, Quantum AI can pave the way for more robust, scalable, and secure systems. The examples and case studies discussed illustrate the tangible benefits and ongoing advancements in this exciting intersection of technologies. (Bernstein et al.,2019)

IV.SECURITY AND CHALLENGES OF AI WITH BLOCKCHIAN

The advent of quantum computing and artificial intelligence (AI) marks a transformative era in technology, with profound implications for cybersecurity and financial systems globally. Quantum AI, the convergence of quantum computing and AI, promises to revolutionize computational capabilities, offering unprecedented speed and efficiency in data processing, problem-solving, and predictive analytics. However, this technological leap also introduces significant challenges, particularly in the realm of cybersecurity, where the power of quantum computing could potentially render current cryptographic methods obsolete. This paper explores the intersection of Quantum AI, cybersecurity, and their impact on Bitcoin, cryptocurrency, and blockchain-based financial systems, providing a comprehensive analysis of the opportunities and threats posed by these emerging technologies.

Cryptocurrency, epitomized by Bitcoin, has become a cornerstone of the digital economy, leveraging blockchain technology to offer decentralized, secure, and transparent financial transactions. Blockchain's reliance on cryptographic protocols ensures the integrity and security of transactions, making it a trusted platform for digital currencies and other applications. However, the advent of quantum computing threatens the very foundation of blockchain security. Quantum computers, with their ability to solve complex mathematical problems exponentially faster than classical computers, could potentially break the cryptographic algorithms that underpin blockchain technology, leading to catastrophic consequences for cryptocurrency security.

Figure 3. Artificial Intelligence security issues with Blockchian Technology

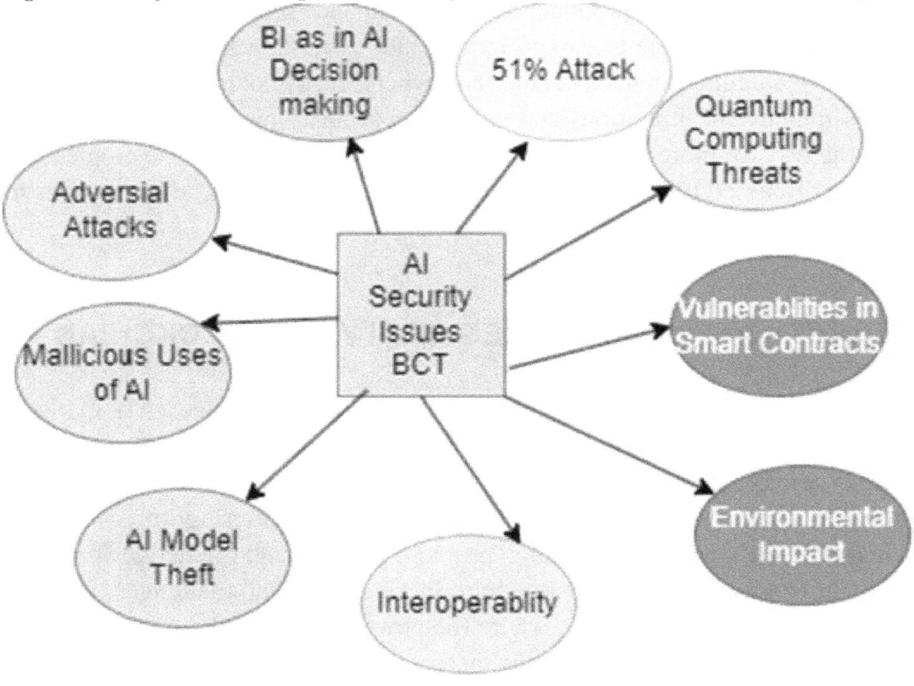

As the world braces for the impact of quantum computing, there is a growing emphasis on developing quantum-resistant cryptographic algorithms and enhancing the security of blockchain networks. Quantum AI, with its potential to revolutionize cybersecurity, could play a crucial role in this endeavor. By leveraging quantum-enhanced threat detection and quantum key distribution (QKD), Quantum AI could offer robust defenses against quantum-enabled cyberattacks, ensuring the continued security of blockchain-based financial systems.(Mosca, 2018)

This diagram represents the Blockchain technology (BCT) offers upgraded security through its decentralized nature and cryptographic techniques, however it faces a few issues. The unchanging nature of blockchain implies that whenever information is recorded, it can't be modified, possibly securing in mistakes or malevolent sections. Furthermore, the dependence on cryptographic keys presents gambles assuming keys are lost or taken. Brilliant agreements, while mechanized, can be powerless against coding blunders or exploits. At last, the adaptability of blockchain organizations can prompt weaknesses as they develop, possibly influencing in general security. This system aims to provide a comprehensive exploration of the impact of Quantum AI on cybersecurity and its implications for Bitcoin, cryptocurrency, and blockchain-based financial systems. Through a detailed analysis of quantum computing, post-quantum cryptography, and Quantum AI applications in cybersecurity, this paper seeks to shed light on the challenges and opportunities presented by these emerging technologies. Additionally, the paper will examine the regulatory implications of these advancements and propose future directions for research in quantum-resistant blockchain systems.

4.1 The Current State of Cryptocurrency Security

Cryptocurrency security is a critical aspect of the digital currency ecosystem. As the popularity and usage of crypto currencies grow, so do the threats and vulnerabilities associated with them. This section explores the current state of cryptocurrency security, examining the prevalent threats, security measures, and emerging technologies aimed at safeguarding digital assets.

Prevalent Threats to Cryptocurrency Security

1. Exchange Hacks

Cryptocurrency exchanges are prime targets for hackers due to the large volumes of digital assets they hold. Successful attacks can result in significant financial losses for users and exchanges.The Mt. Gox hack (2014) resulted in the loss of 850,000 BTC.The Coin check hack (2018) led to the theft of $530 million worth of NEM tokens.Loss of user funds, decreased trust in cryptocurrency exchanges, and regulatory scrutiny.

2. Phishing Attacks

Phishing attacks involve tricking users into revealing their private keys or login credentials through deceptive emails, websites, or messages.Fake cryptocurrency exchange websites or wallet apps designed to steal user credentials. and their impact is Unauthorized access to user accounts and theft of digital assets.

3. **Malware**

Malware, including keyloggers and clipboard hijackers, can infect users' devices and steal private keys or redirect transactions. Crypto-stealing malware like Coin-Miner and Clipboard Wallet Hijacker.and their Impact is unauthorized access to wallets and theft of cryptocurrencies.

4. **Ransomware**

Ransomware encrypts a victim's data and demands payment in cryptocurrency for the decryption key.The WannaCry ransomware attack (2017) demanded Bitcoin payments for decryption.and their impact is financial losses and disruption of services for affected individuals and organizations.

5. **Smart Contract Vulnerabilities**

Smart contracts are self-executing contracts with code that can have vulnerabilities or bugs, leading to potential exploits. The DAO hack (2016) exploited vulnerability in a smart contract, resulting in the theft of $60 million worth of Ether the impact is financial losses and decreased trust in the security of smart contracts.

4.2 Emerging Technologies in Cryptocurrency Security

1. **Quantum-Resistant Cryptography**

As quantum computing advances, developing quantum-resistant cryptographic algorithms is essential to protect against future quantum attacks.Lattice-based, hash-based and code-based cryptographic schemes.Ensures the long-term security of cryptocurrencies against quantum threats.

2. **Zero-Knowledge Proofs (ZKPs)**

ZKPs allow one party to prove the validity of a statement without revealing the underlying information. They enhance privacy and security in transactions.zk-SNARKs (used in Zcash), zk-STARKs. It Improves transaction privacy and reduces the risk of data exposure.

3. Decentralized Finance (DeFi) Security Protocols

DeFi platforms are developing advanced security protocols to protect user funds and smart contracts. Decentralized insurance, automated security audits, and bug bounty programs. Enhances the security and trustworthiness of DeFi applications.

4. Secure Multi-Party Computation (SMPC)

SMPC enables multiple parties to jointly compute a function over their inputs while keeping those inputs private. Secure key management and collaborative decision-making. It enhances privacy and security in collaborative processes.

V.IMPLICATIONS FOR BLOCKCHAIN-BASED CRYPTOCURRENCIES

The emergence of quantum computing presents significant challenges for blockchain-based cryptocurrencies. These implications are profound because the security and functionality of these digital currencies heavily rely on cryptographic techniques that quantum computing could potentially undermine. Here's a detailed examination of the potential impacts on blockchain-based cryptocurrencies.

5.1 Vulnerability of Cryptographic Algorithms

Public-Key Cryptography

Blockchain-based cryptocurrencies, such as Bitcoin and Ethereum, utilize public-key cryptography for various functions, including the creation and verification of digital signatures that authorize transactions. The most common algorithm used is Elliptic Curve Cryptography (ECC), particularly the Elliptic Curve Digital Signature Algorithm (ECDSA).

Quantum computers, using Shor's Algorithm, could efficiently solve the Elliptic Curve Discrete Logarithm Problem (ECDLP), which underpins the security of ECC. This would enable an attacker with a quantum computer to derive private keys from public keys. As a result, any transactions or wallets using these compromised keys could be accessed and controlled by unauthorized parties. The exposure of private keys would allow quantum attackers to forge signatures, leading to unauthorized spending of funds, double-spending, and other forms of financial fraud.

Hash Functions

Cryptocurrencies also rely on cryptographic hash functions to secure blocks within the blockchain through proof-of-work mechanisms. These hash functions, such as SHA-256 in Bitcoin, are designed to be collision-resistant, meaning that it should be computationally infeasible to find two distinct inputs that produce the same hash output. However, Grover's Algorithm could significantly reduce the security of these hash functions by providing a quadratic speedup in finding collisions.

5.2. Threat to Transaction Security and Privacy

The exposure of private keys would severely compromise the privacy and security of blockchain transactions. Currently, users' privacy is maintained because public keys do not easily reveal private keys, and transaction data, while transparent, does not directly expose sensitive information. However, if quantum computers can easily derive private keys, attackers could not only steal funds but also link transactions and addresses to specific individuals or entities, eroding the anonymity that many users value in cryptocurrencies.

Moreover, the ability to forge digital signatures could lead to unauthorized transactions, resulting in significant financial losses and a breakdown of trust in the blockchain's immutability and security. The irreversible nature of blockchain transactions means that once an unauthorized transaction is completed, it cannot be undone, exacerbating the potential damage.

5.3. Impact on Blockchain Consensus Mechanisms

Blockchain consensus mechanisms, such as proof-of-work (PoW) and proof-of-stake (PoS), rely heavily on cryptographic processes to ensure the integrity and security of the network. In a PoW system, miners compete to solve cryptographic puzzles to validate transactions and add new blocks to the blockchain. The difficulty of these puzzles is calibrated to ensure that new blocks are added at a regular pace.

Quantum computing could disrupt this balance by making it significantly easier to solve these puzzles through quantum-enhanced algorithms. A quantum miner could potentially dominate the mining process, leading to centralization, which is contrary to the decentralized ethos of blockchain technology. This dominance could result in a "51% attack," where the quantum miner controls the majority of the network's computational power, allowing them to manipulate the blockchain by reversing transactions or preventing new transactions from being confirmed.

In PoS systems, the threat is slightly different but still significant. PoS relies on validators holding and staking cryptocurrency to secure the network. If quantum computing enables the compromise of private keys, attackers could forge validator signatures or gain control over a disproportionate amount of the staked cryptocurrency, undermining the security and fairness of the PoS system.(Monterio et al., 2019)

5.4. Potential Solutions and Quantum-Resistant Cryptography

To mitigate the risks posed by quantum computing, the blockchain and cryptocurrency community is actively exploring quantum-resistant cryptographic algorithms. These are cryptographic techniques designed to be secure against the capabilities of quantum computers. Potential solutions include:

Lattice-Based Cryptography

Lattice-based cryptography is considered a strong candidate for quantum resistance. It relies on the hardness of problems related to lattice structures, which are believed to be secure even against quantum attacks. Implementing lattice-based cryptography could provide a secure foundation for public-key encryption and digital signatures in a post-quantum world.

Hash-Based Cryptography

Hash-based cryptographic schemes, such as the Merkle Signature Scheme, are another option for quantum-resistant signatures. These schemes rely solely on the security of hash functions, which can be adjusted in terms of output size to maintain security against quantum attacks, albeit with increased computational and storage requirements.

Multivariate Polynomial Cryptography

Cryptographic schemes based on multivariate polynomials, which involve solving systems of quadratic equations, offer another avenue for quantum resistance. These schemes are being developed for digital signatures and public-key encryption and are believed to be resistant to quantum computing capabilities.

5.5. Challenges in Transitioning to Quantum-Resistant Solutions

While developing quantum-resistant algorithms is crucial, transitioning existing blockchain networks to these new cryptographic standards presents significant challenges:

Backward Compatibility

Existing blockchain networks, like Bitcoin and Ethereum, have millions of users and vast amounts of wealth stored in their systems. Transitioning to quantum-resistant cryptography requires ensuring that current users can seamlessly migrate to the new systems without losing access to their funds or compromising their security.

Network Upgrades and Hard Forks

Implementing quantum-resistant cryptography may necessitate network upgrades or hard forks, where a blockchain's protocol is changed in a way that is not backward compatible. Hard forks can be contentious, leading to splits in the community and the creation of new blockchain branches, as seen in previous instances like Bitcoin and Bitcoin Cash.

Performance and Scalability

Quantum-resistant algorithms often require more computational resources and larger key sizes, which could impact the performance and scalability of blockchain networks. Ensuring that these new algorithms can operate efficiently within the constraints of existing blockchain protocols is a significant technical challenge.

5.6 Impact of Quantum AI on Stakeholders and Sectors

1. Financial Sector

Advantages:

- **Enhanced Security:** Quantum-resistant cryptographic algorithms protect sensitive financial data from quantum attacks, ensuring long-term confidentiality and integrity.
- **Efficient Fraud Detection:** Quantum AI can analyze vast amounts of transaction data in real-time, identifying fraudulent activities more accurately and swiftly than traditional AI.

Challenges:

- **Implementation Costs:** Integrating quantum technologies into existing systems can be costly, requiring significant investment in infrastructure and training.
- **Regulatory Compliance:** Financial institutions must navigate complex regulatory landscapes to ensure compliance with national and international security standards.

2. Healthcare Sector

Advantages:

- **Secure Patient Data:** Quantum-resistant cryptography ensures the secure storage and transmission of patient records, protecting them from future quantum threats.
- **Advanced Medical Research:** Quantum AI can accelerate drug discovery and genomics research by processing complex biological data more efficiently.

Challenges:

- **Data Integration:** Healthcare providers must integrate quantum technologies with existing electronic health record (EHR) systems, which can be technically challenging.
- **Privacy Concerns:** Ensuring patient privacy while implementing new technologies requires robust policies and practices.

3. Government and Defense

Advantages:

- **National Security:** Governments can use Quantum AI to secure communications and critical infrastructure against cyber threats, enhancing national security.
- **Enhanced Intelligence:** Quantum AI can analyze intelligence data more efficiently, providing valuable insights for defense and strategic planning.

Challenges:

- **Technology Adoption:** Governments must overcome bureaucratic hurdles and ensure inter-agency cooperation to adopt quantum technologies effectively.
- **Threat of Quantum Espionage:** The rise of quantum computing also poses new espionage risks, requiring continuous innovation in quantum-resistant security measures.

4. Telecommunications Sector

Advantages:

- **Secure Communications:** Quantum Key Distribution (QKD) enables telecommunications providers to offer secure communication channels, preventing eavesdropping and data breaches.
- **Improved Network Efficiency:** Quantum AI can optimize network traffic management, enhancing overall network performance and user experience.

Challenges:

- **Infrastructure Upgrade:** Implementing quantum technologies requires significant upgrades to existing communication infrastructure, which can be resource-intensive.
- **Standardization:** The lack of standardized protocols for quantum communication can hinder widespread adoption and interoperability.

5. Commercial Enterprises

Advantages:

- **Competitive Advantage:** Early adopters of Quantum AI can gain a competitive edge by offering advanced security solutions and innovative products.
- **Enhanced Data Analytics:** Quantum AI can process large datasets more efficiently, providing actionable insights for business decision-making.

Challenges:

- **Skilled Workforce:** There is a scarcity of professionals skilled in quantum technologies, making it challenging for businesses to find and retain talent.
- **Cybersecurity Threats:** As businesses adopt quantum technologies, they must also invest in safeguarding their systems against emerging quantum-enabled cyber threats.

VI. PROPOSED SYSTEM FRAMEWORK METHODOLOGY

Blockchain technology is eminent for its robustness, transparency, and decentralized nature. Cryptographic techniques underpin the security and integrity of blockchain networks. However, the advent of quantum computing poses significant threats and opportunities for blockchain security. This section explores how quantum computing impacts blockchain security and the measures needed to mitigate potential risks.

Centralized Blockchain and AI:

In a unified framework, a solitary element controls the blockchain or simulated intelligence foundation. For blockchain, this implies a solitary association or authority oversees and confirms exchanges and keeps up with the record. Unified computer based intelligence frameworks are constrained by a solitary substance that deals with the information, calculations, and dynamic cycles. Centralization can smooth out tasks and deal more prominent control, however it likewise presents dangers like weak links, diminished straightforwardness, and expected abuse of force.

Figure 4. Centralized and Decentralized Blockchain with Artificial Intelligence

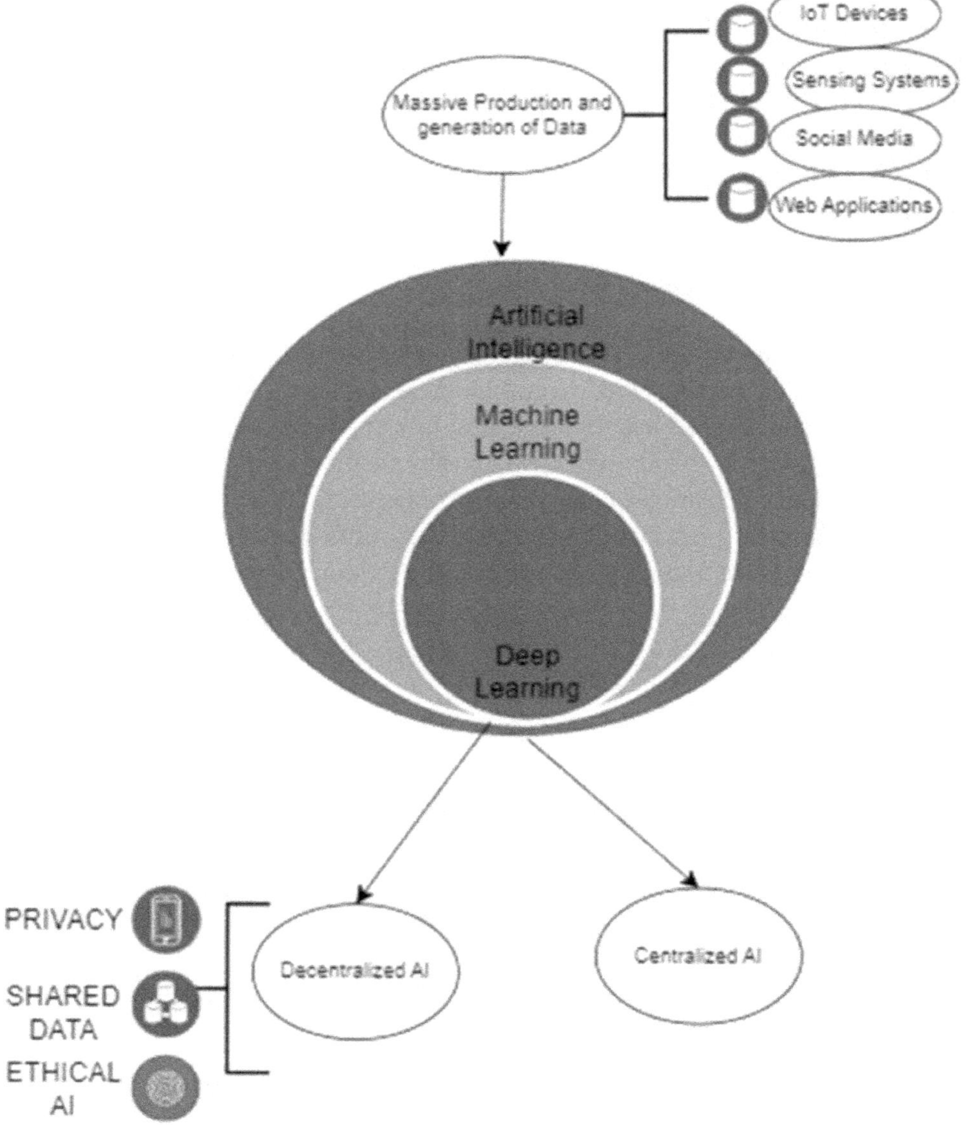

Decentralized Blockchain and AI:

In decentralized frameworks, control is appropriated among various members. For blockchain, this implies no single element has full command over the record, and exchanges are confirmed by an organization of hubs. Decentralized computer based intelligence includes circulating information handling and dynamic across an organization of hubs, frequently using procedures like united learning. This approach improves security, straightforwardness, and flexibility, however it can likewise present difficulties, for example, expanded intricacy, coordination issues, and possible failures in information handling.

The figure delineates a decentralized monetary framework working on a blockchain. Clients collaborate with the framework, each having a public location and a confidential key, which are privately overseen and are fundamental for communicating with the blockchain. The public location is utilized to get exchanges, while the confidential key is utilized to sign exchanges, guaranteeing security and authenticity.

Figure 5. Proposed system Architecture

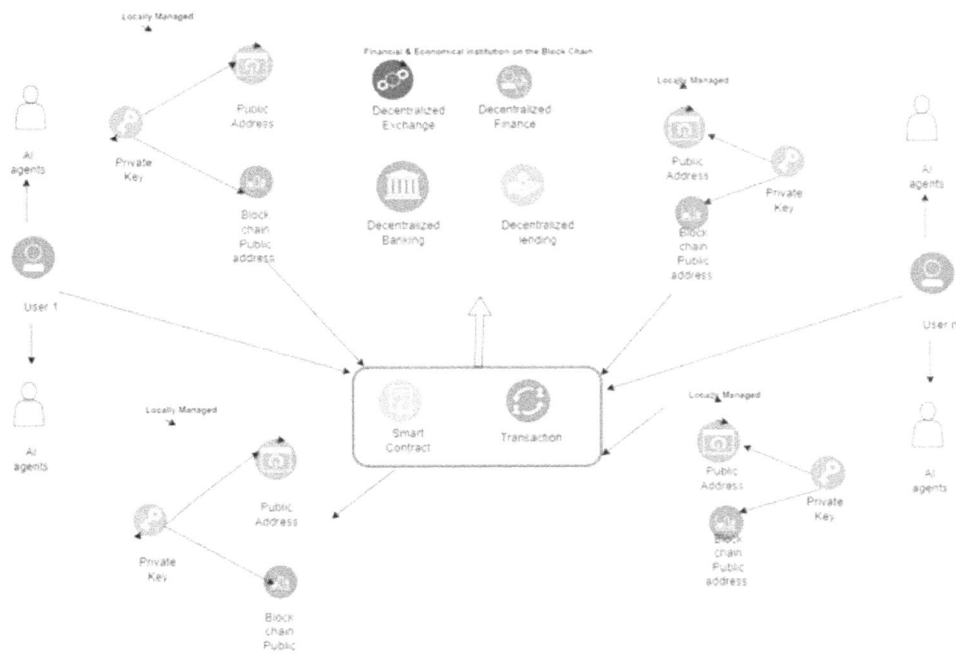

Decentralized monetary organizations offer different administrations like decentralized trade, decentralized finance, decentralized banking, and decentralized loaning, all working on the blockchain. Savvy contracts, which are self-executing contracts with the terms straightforwardlycomposed into code, work with, confirm, andupholdthe exchange or execution of a contract.These shrewd agreements connect with various parts (clients and decentralized monetary foundations) to execute exchanges, which are handled on the blockchain to guarantee straightforwardness, security, and changelessness. Artificial intelligence specialists may be associated with mechanizing or working with connections inside this framework, perhaps assisting clients with dealing with their keys or interface with brilliant contracts. The outline really exhibits how a decentralized monetary framework can work on a blockchain, with clients safely collaborating with different monetary administrations through shrewd agreements

Quantum Algorithms (Shor's Algorithm, Grover's Algorithm)

Quantum algorithms are computational procedures that run on quantum computers, leveraging quantum mechanics to perform tasks much faster than classical algorithms. Two of the most famous quantum algorithms are **Shor's Algorithm** and **Grover's Algorithm**, each with distinct applications and impacts, particularly on cryptography and search problems.

1. Shor's Algorithm

Shor's Algorithm, developed by Peter Shor in 1994, is a quantum algorithm designed for integer factorization. It efficiently factors large integers into their prime factors, a task that is computationally difficult for classical computers. The significance of this algorithm lies in its potential to break widely used cryptographic systems, such as RSA, which rely on the difficulty of factoring large integers.

To understand Shor's Algorithm, it's essential to grasp some basic concepts:

- **Modular Arithmetic:** Involves arithmetic operations within a finite number set, often used in cryptography.
- **Euler's Totient Function:** Counts the number of integers up to a given integer n that are relatively prime to n.
- **Order of an Integer:** Given an integer aaa and a modulus nnn, the order of aaa modulo nnn is the smallest positive integer rrr such that ar≡1 (mod n)a^r \equiv 1 \,(\text{mod}\, n)ar≡1(modn).

Steps of Shor's Algorithm

1. **Problem Setup:**
    - o The goal is to factorize a large composite number NNN. Assume N=pqN = pqN=pq, where ppp and qqq are unknown prime numbers.
2. **Random Selection:**
    - o Select a random integer aaa such that 1<a<N1 < a < N1<a<N and aaa is coprime to NNN (i.e., gcd(a, N) = 1). This step can be efficiently performed using the Euclidean algorithm.
3. **Quantum Period Finding:**
    - o The key quantum step is finding the period rrr of the function f(x)=ax-mod Nf(x) = a^x \mod Nf(x)=axmodN, meaning the smallest rrr such that ar≡1mod Na^r \equiv 1 \mod Nar≡1modN.
    - o This is achieved by preparing a superposition of all possible values of xxx, applying the quantum Fourier transform to extract the period, and then measuring the result.
4. **Classical Post-Processing:**
    - o Once the period rrr is found, if rrr is even, compute gcd(ar/2−1,N)gcd(a^{r/2} - 1, N)gcd(ar/2−1,N) and gcd(ar/2+1,N)gcd(a^{r/2} + 1, N) gcd(ar/2+1,N). These calculations will likely yield the prime factors ppp and qqq.
5. **Repeating if Necessary:**
    - o If the process fails (for instance, if rrr is odd), the algorithm is repeated with a different value of aaa.

Efficiency

- **Quantum Speedup:** Shor's algorithm runs in polynomial time, specifically O((log N)2log log Nlog log log N)O((\log N)^2 \log \log N \log \log \log N) O((logN)2loglogNlogloglogN), making it exponentially faster than the best-known classical algorithms, which run in sub-exponential time.
- **Cryptographic Impact:** The ability of Shor's Algorithm to efficiently factor large integers poses a direct threat to classical cryptosystems like RSA, which depend on the difficulty of this task.

2. Grover's Algorithm

Overview

Grover's Algorithm, developed by Lov Grover in 1996, is a quantum algorithm designed for searching an unsorted database or solving a black-box problem with a quadratic speedup. Given an unsorted database of NNN elements, Grover's Algorithm can find a specific item or solve an unstructured search problem in O(N) O(\sqrt{N})O(N) time, compared to O(N)O(N)O(N) time for classical algorithms.

Mathematical Background

- **Amplitude Amplification:** Grover's algorithm is based on the concept of amplitude amplification, where the probability amplitude of the correct answer is iteratively increased until it becomes dominant in the superposition.
- **Oracle Function:** The algorithm uses an oracle, a black-box function that can recognize the correct solution. The oracle flips the sign of the amplitude of the correct state, marking it.

Steps of Grover's Algorithm

1. **Initialization:**
   - o Prepare an equal superposition of all possible states. If there are NNN possible solutions, each state has an amplitude of 1/N1/\sqrt{N}1/N.
2. **Oracle Application:**
   - o Apply the oracle function, which flips the phase (sign) of the amplitude of the state corresponding to the correct solution, effectively marking it.
3. **Amplitude Amplification (Grover Iteration):**
   - o Perform the Grover iteration, which consists of two steps:
     - ▪ **Inversion about the Mean:** Reflect the state amplitudes about their mean value, amplifying the amplitude of the correct state.
     - ▪ **Reapplication of Oracle:** Reapply the oracle to flip the sign of the marked state again.
   - o Repeat the Grover iteration approximately N\sqrt{N}N times.
4. **Measurement:**
   - o Measure the quantum state. The correct solution, whose amplitude has been significantly amplified, is highly likely to be observed.

Efficiency

- **Quantum Speedup:** Grover's algorithm achieves a quadratic speedup over classical search algorithms, solving the problem in O(N)O(\sqrt{N})O(N) time.
- **Versatility:** While not as dramatic as Shor's exponential speedup, Grover's quadratic speedup applies to a broader class of problems, particularly unstructured search problems, making it broadly useful in various computational tasks.

Impact on Cryptography

- **Symmetric-Key Cryptography:** Grover's Algorithm can be applied to brute-force attacks on symmetric-key cryptographic systems. For instance, it can reduce the time complexity of breaking a 128-bit key from 21282^{128}2128 to 2642^{64}264. While this is still computationally infeasible, it suggests that symmetric key lengths may need to be doubled to maintain security in a quantum computing context.
- **Hash Functions:** Similarly, Grover's algorithm can be used to find collisions in cryptographic hash functions, reducing the time complexity of such attacks.

Comparison of Shor's and Grover's Algorithms

- **Problem Domain:**
  - **Shor's Algorithm:** Focused on factorization and discrete logarithms, with direct implications for asymmetric cryptography.
  - **Grover's Algorithm:** Applicable to unstructured search problems, with implications for symmetric cryptography and general problem-solving.
- **Quantum Speedup:**
  - **Shor's Algorithm:** Offers an exponential speedup over classical algorithms.
  - **Grover's Algorithm:** Provides a quadratic speedup, which is significant but less dramatic than Shor's.
- **Cryptographic Impact:**
  - **Shor's Algorithm:** Threatens the security of RSA, ECC, and other public-key cryptosystems.
  - **Grover's Algorithm:** Reduces the security margin of symmetric-key systems and hash functions but does not completely break them.

Bitcoin: The First Cryptocurrency

1. **Creation**:
   - Bitcoin was created by an anonymous person or group known as Satoshi Nakamoto and was introduced in a whitepaper titled "Bitcoin: A Peer-to-Peer Electronic Cash System" in 2008.
2. **Functioning**:
   - **Transactions**: Bitcoin transactions involve transferring bitcoins from one address (wallet) to another. Each transaction is digitally signed using the sender's private key, ensuring authenticity.
   - **Wallets**: Digital wallets store private and public keys. The private key is used to sign transactions, while the public key serves as the address for receiving bitcoins.
   - **Mining**: Miners validate transactions and add them to the blockchain by solving complex cryptographic puzzles (Proof of Work). Successful miners are rewarded with newly created bitcoins and transaction fees.
3. **Consensus Mechanism**:
   - Bitcoin uses the Proof of Work (PoW) consensus mechanism. Miners compete to solve a cryptographic puzzle, and the first one to solve it gets to add a new block to the blockchain. This process ensures the network's security and integrity.

Other Cryptocurrencies

1. **Altcoins**:
   - Altcoins are alternative cryptocurrencies to Bitcoin. They often offer variations in terms of functionality, consensus mechanisms, and features. Examples include Ethereum, Litecoin, and Ripple.
2. **Ethereum**:
   - **Smart Contracts**: Ethereum extends blockchain functionality by introducing smart contracts, which are self-executing contracts with the terms directly written into code.
   - **Consensus Mechanism**: Ethereum currently uses Proof of Stake (PoS) in its Ethereum 2.0 upgrade, which is more energy-efficient than PoW. Validators are chosen based on the amount of cryptocurrency they stake.
3. **Litecoin**:
   - **Faster Transactions**: Litecoin offers faster transaction confirmation times compared to Bitcoin, making it more suitable for everyday transactions.

   - **Scrypt Algorithm**: Litecoin uses the Scrypt hashing algorithm for its PoW consensus, which is more memory-intensive than Bitcoin's SHA-256 algorithm.
4. **Ripple (XRP)**:
   - **Consensus Algorithm**: Ripple uses a consensus algorithm known as the Ripple Protocol Consensus Algorithm (RPCA), which does not involve mining. Validators reach consensus on the state of the ledger through a process of agreement.
   - **Focus on Financial Institutions**: Ripple aims to facilitate secure, instant, and low-cost international payments, targeting financial institutions and payment providers.

Key Features of Cryptocurrencies

1. **Decentralization**:
   - Cryptocurrencies operate on decentralized networks, reducing the need for intermediaries and central authorities. This ensures greater transparency and reduces the risk of single points of failure.
2. **Security**:
   - Cryptocurrencies use cryptographic techniques to secure transactions and control the creation of new units. Public-key cryptography ensures that only the rightful owner can authorize transactions.
3. **Immutability**:
   - Once a transaction is recorded on the blockchain, it cannot be altered or deleted. This immutability ensures the integrity and trustworthiness of the ledger.
4. **Transparency**:
   - All transactions on a blockchain are publicly visible, providing transparency and accountability. However, the identities of the participants are pseudonymous, ensuring privacy.
5. **Limited Supply**:
   - Many cryptocurrencies, like Bitcoin, have a capped supply. For instance, Bitcoin has a maximum supply of 21 million coins, which introduces scarcity and can impact its value.

Transaction Process

1. **Initiation**:

- A user initiates a transaction by signing it with their private key and broadcasting it to the network. The transaction includes the sender's and receiver's addresses and the amount to be transferred.

2. **Verification**:
   - Nodes in the network verify the transaction by checking the digital signature and ensuring that the sender has sufficient balance. Verified transactions are then grouped into blocks.
3. **Mining (for PoW-based cryptocurrencies)**:
   - Miners validate the block of transactions by solving a cryptographic puzzle. The first miner to solve the puzzle adds the block to the blockchain and receives a reward.
4. **Confirmation**:
   - Once a block is added to the blockchain, the transaction is considered confirmed. The more confirmations a transaction has, the more secure it is.

Consensus Mechanisms

1. **Proof of Work (PoW)**:
   - Miners compete to solve cryptographic puzzles, and the first one to solve it adds a new block to the blockchain. This process requires significant computational power and energy.
2. **Proof of Stake (PoS)**:
   - Validators are chosen based on the amount of cryptocurrency they stake. PoS is more energy-efficient than PoW and reduces the risk of centralization.
3. **Delegated Proof of Stake (DPoS)**:
   - In DPoS, stakeholders elect delegates to validate transactions and maintain the blockchain. This mechanism aims to improve scalability and efficiency.
4. **Practical Byzantine Fault Tolerance (PBFT)**:
   - PBFT is used in permissioned blockchains where validators are known and trusted. Validators reach consensus through a series of voting rounds, ensuring the network's resilience to faults.

VII. CASESTUDY

7.1 Quantum-Resistant Cryptography

Real-World Example: IBM's Quantum-Safe Cryptography Initiative

Background: As quantum computing advances, the cryptographic algorithms currently used to secure digital communications are becoming increasingly vulnerable. This concern has prompted leading tech companies to develop quantum-resistant cryptographic solutions that can withstand the computational power of quantum computers.

IBM's Initiative: IBM has been at the forefront of quantum computing research and has initiated several projects aimed at developing quantum-safe cryptography. One of the key efforts is their involvement in the development and standardization of quantum-resistant algorithms through collaboration with the National Institute of Standards and Technology (NIST).(Liu et al.,2020)

Details:

1. **Algorithm Development:** IBM researchers have been working on new cryptographic algorithms designed to be secure against quantum attacks. These algorithms are part of the NIST Post-Quantum Cryptography Standardization project, which aims to identify and standardize one or more quantum-resistant public-key cryptographic algorithms.
2. **Practical Implementation:** In 2020, IBM introduced a set of quantum-safe cryptographic algorithms in their IBM Cloud services. This initiative provides businesses with tools to start implementing quantum-resistant security measures today, ensuring that their data remains secure in the post-quantum era.(Taylor et al.,2020)
3. **Industry Collaboration:** IBM has partnered with various industries, including financial services and healthcare, to test and implement quantum-resistant cryptographic solutions. For example, IBM collaborated with JPMorgan Chase to explore the use of quantum-safe cryptography in securing financial transactions and sensitive data.

Impact:

- **Enhanced Security:** By implementing quantum-resistant cryptography, organizations can protect their data from future quantum attacks, ensuring long-term security and privacy.

- **Future-Proofing:** Early adoption of quantum-safe algorithms allows organizations to future-proof their systems against the impending threat of quantum computing, avoiding costly and reactive security overhauls later.
- **Industry Leadership:** IBM's proactive approach in developing and deploying quantum-safe cryptographic solutions positions them as a leader in the quantum computing and cybersecurity space, setting industry standards for others to follow.

7.2 Real-World Example: The Beijing-Shanghai Quantum Communication Network

Background: Quantum Key Distribution (QKD) uses principles of quantum mechanics to enable secure communication by distributing encryption keys that are theoretically immune to eavesdropping. One of the most prominent implementations of QKD is the Beijing-Shanghai quantum communication network in China.

Project Overview: China has been a global leader in demonstrating the practical applications of QKD. The Beijing-Shanghai quantum communication network, also known as the Beijing-Shanghai Trunk Line, is a large-scale project that spans approximately 2,000 kilometers. It connects Beijing, Jinan, Hefei, and Shanghai, offering a real-world testbed for QKD technology.

Details:

1. **Network Infrastructure:** The network consists of a series of ground-based fiber optic cables and satellite links. It integrates multiple QKD devices capable of generating and distributing quantum keys over long distances.
2. **Satellite Integration:** In addition to ground-based infrastructure, in decentralized frameworks, control is appropriated among various members. For blockchain, this implies no single element has full command over the record, and exchanges are confirmed by an organization of hubs. Decentralized computer based intelligence includes circulating information handling and dynamic across an organization of hubs, frequently using procedures like united learning.
3. **Use Cases:** The network has been used for secure communications in various sectors, including government, finance, and military. For instance, the Industrial and Commercial Bank of China (ICBC) has tested QKD to secure financial transactions and ensure the privacy of sensitive data. (Kitagawa & H. Tsukada,2020)

Impact:

- **Enhanced Security:** The Beijing-Shanghai network demonstrates how QKD can provide an unprecedented level of security for data transmission. By leveraging the principles of quantum mechanics, the system ensures that any attempt to intercept the keys will be detected, thereby preventing eavesdropping.
- **Technological Advancement:** This project showcases the feasibility of integrating QKD into existing communication infrastructure on a large scale. It paves the way for future advancements and wider adoption of quantum communication technologies.
- **Global Leadership:** China's successful implementation of the world's longest and most sophisticated QKD network positions the country as a leader in quantum communication. It sets a benchmark for other nations and encourages further research and development in this field.(Tandon et al.,2021)

VIII.CONCLUSION

In Conclusion, the convergence of quantum artificial intelligence and network safety presents both huge difficulties and potential open doors for Bitcoin, digital currencies, and blockchain-based monetary frameworks. As quantum processing propels, its capability to break current cryptographic calculations requires a proactive way to deal with upgrading blockchain security. The coordination of quantum computer based intelligence could prompt refined assaults yet in addition offers the commitment of vigorous new safety efforts. The monetary frameworks based on blockchain should advance to address these arising dangers guaranteeing flexibility and confidence even with fast mechanical advancement. By embracing creative arrangements and encouraging cooperation between cryptographers, designers, and administrative bodies, the business can explore these intricacies and secure a steady future for computerized monetary environments.Quantum computing represents both a threat and an opportunity for blockchain-based cryptocurrencies. While the potential to break existing cryptographic systems poses significant risks, the proactive development and implementation of quantum-resistant algorithms offer a path forward to secure blockchain networks in the quantum era. The transition to quantum-resistant cryptography will be challenging, but it is essential to ensure the continued trust, security, and viability of blockchain-based financial systems. By addressing these challenges head-on, the blockchain community can safeguard the future of decentralized finance and digital currencies against the looming quantum threat. Quantum computing presents both significant threats and transformative opportunities for blockchain security. While the potential to break existing cryptographic systems poses a substantial risk, adopting quantum-resistant cryptographic algorithms and leveraging quantum technologies can safeguardblockchain networks. It ensures that data remains secure, transactions are authenticated, and the network is resistant to tampering and fraud. As blockchain technology continues to evolve, ongoing advancements in cryptographic techniques will be crucial for maintaining the security and efficiency of these systems, particularly in the face of emerging threats such as quantum computing. Bitcoin and other cryptocurrencies represent a significant shift in the world of finance, offering decentralized, secure, and transparent alternatives to traditional currencies. By leveraging blockchain technology, cryptographic techniques, and various consensus mechanisms, these digital currencies enable peer-to-peer transactions without the need for intermediaries. As technology continues to evolve, cryptocurrencies are likely to play an increasingly important role in the global financial landscape. The current state of cryptocurrency security is characterized by both significant threats and robust measures to mitigate them. While exchange hacks, phishing attacks, malware, and smart contract vulnerabilities pose ongoing challenges, advancements in secure wallets, multi-signature solutions, two-factor authentication, and emerging technologies such as quantum-resistant cryptography and zero-knowledge proofs are enhancing the security landscape. Regulatory efforts and industry collaboration further contribute to a more secure and resilient cryptocurrency ecosystem. As the technology and threats continue to evolve, maintaining and improving security remains a crucial priority for the cryptocurrency community.

REFERENCES

Abduljabbar, R., Dia, H., Liyanage, S., & Bagloee, S. A. (2019). Applications of artificial intelligence in transport: An overview. *Sustainability (Basel)*, 11(1), 189. DOI: 10.3390/su11010189

Ahmed, S., Alshater, M. M., El Ammari, A., & Hammami, H. (2022). Artificial intelligence and machine learning in finance: A bibliometric review. *Research in International Business and Finance*, 61, 101646.

Alahakoon, D., Nawaratne, R., Xu, Y., De Silva, D., Sivarajah, U., & Gupta, B. (2023). Self-building artificial intelligence and machine learning to empower big data analytics in smart cities. *Information Systems Frontiers*, 25(1), 221–240. DOI: 10.1007/s10796-020-10056-x

Bernstein, D. J., Buchmann, J., & Dahmen, E. (2019). Quantum-Resistant Cryptography: A Survey. *ACM Computing Surveys*, 51(4), 1–35.

Cao, L. (2023). AI in finance: Challenges, techniques, and opportunities. *ACM Computing Surveys*, 55(3), 1–38. DOI: 10.1145/3502289

Coeckelbergh, M. (2019). Artificial intelligence: Some ethical issues and regulatory challenges. *Technol. Regulation*, 2019, 31–34.

Jabbar, R., Dhib, E., Said, A. B., Krichen, M., Fetais, N., Zaidan, E., & Barkaoui, K. (2022). Blockchain technology for intelligent transportation systems: A systematic literature review. *IEEE Access : Practical Innovations, Open Solutions*, 10, 20995–21031. DOI: 10.1109/ACCESS.2022.3149958

Kitagawa, G., & Tsukada, H. (2020). Securing Bitcoin and Blockchain-Based Systems Against Quantum Attacks. *Journal of Computer Security*, 28(2), 181–196.

Liu, X., Li, J., & Tan, Z. (2020). Blockchain and Quantum Computing: A Review of Challenges and Solutions. *Journal of Cryptographic Engineering*, 10(1), 23–36.

Mosca, M. (2018). Quantum Computing and Cryptography. *IEEE Security and Privacy*, 16(5), 30–37.

Tandon, C., Revankar, S., Palivela, H., & Parihar, S. S. (2021). How can we predict the impact of the social media messages on the value of cryptocurrency insights from big data analytics. *International Journal of Information Management Data Insights*, 1(2), 100035. DOI: 10.1016/j.jjimei.2021.100035

Taylor, P. J., Dargahi, T., Dehghantanha, A., Parizi, R. M., & Choo, K.-K. R. (2020). A systematic literature review of blockchain cyber security. *Digital Communications and Networks*, 6(2), 147–156. DOI: 10.1016/j.dcan.2019.01.005

Tsolakis, N., Schumacher, R., Dora, M., & Kumar, M. (2023). Artificial intelligence and blockchain implementation in supply chains: A pathway to sustainability and data monetisation. *Annals of Operations Research*, 327(1), 157–210. DOI: 10.1007/s10479-022-04785-2 PMID: 35755830

Yu, K.-H., Beam, A. L., & Kohane, I. S. (2018). Artificial intelligence in healthcare. *Nature Biomedical Engineering*, 2(10), 719–731. DOI: 10.1038/s41551-018-0305-z PMID: 31015651

Chapter 7
Quantum Computing and Generative Adversarial Networks (GANs):
Ethics, Privacy, and Security

Wasswa Shafik
https://orcid.org/0000-0002-9320-3186
Dig Connectivity Research Laboratory (DCRLab), Kampala, Uganda & School of Digital Science, Universiti Brunei Darussalam, Brunei

ABSTRACT

Advancement in technology has demonstrated a shift in application, interpretability, and technological acceptance. Quantum Computing and Generative Adversarial Networks (GANs) represent two transformative domains with immense potential for innovation and disruption. This study examines the rise of ethical, privacy, and security considerations accompanying these technologies, highlighting their importance and defining the core emphasis on overlapping ethical, data privacy, and security problems and their mitigation. Starting with an overview of quantum computing and GANs, the study outlines their principles and practical applications, elucidating quantum algorithms' revolutionary power and unique challenges. It explores how generative models reshape industries while examining ethical dilemmas introduced by synthetic content generation. Privacy concerns are evaluated, focusing on privacy-enhancing technologies. Security challenges are scrutinized, proposing strategies to fortify these technologies against adversarial threats.

DOI: 10.4018/979-8-3373-1657-4.ch007

1.1. INTRODUCTION

Quantum computing[1] and Generative Adversarial Networks (GANs)[2] are emerging technologies promising unprecedented capabilities and opportunities while posing profound ethical, privacy, and security challenges (Xu et al., 2022). With its roots in the mysterious field of quantum physics, quantum computing presents the alluring possibility of computational capability exponentially beyond that of conventional computers. In the meantime, GANs, a byproduct of the quickly developing science of artificial intelligence, have revolutionized our ability to produce fake data and material that is startlingly realistic (Bautista & Inventado, 2021). The unexplored domain of quantum computing presents an enticing prospect of resolving unsolvable challenges for conventional computers. As we explore the complexities of quantum bits, superposition, and entanglement, we unveil the possible applications of these phenomena in several fields, for example, cryptography, optimization, drug discovery, and other domains (Zhao et al., 2023). Nevertheless, the recent advancements in computational abilities raise ethical considerations about safeguarding cryptographic systems and the conscientious use of these capacities.

The notion of privacy[3], which has historically been fundamental to safeguarding personal and data security, assumes a novel perspective within this framework. The implications of quantum computing on cryptography necessitate reassessing our current encryption standards and pursuing solutions that are immune to quantum attacks (Kumari et al., 2022). GANs pose a simultaneous challenge to conventional conceptions of digital privacy by producing synthetic data that can be employed for manipulation or deception. Furthermore, the continuous progression of innovation also requires a thorough analysis of security implications (Arulmozhiselvan & Uma, 2022). The advent of quantum computing has brought up new vulnerabilities and the possibility of cyber threats that were previously unimaginable. The expeditious advancement of GANs necessitates the development of resilient countermeasures against their potential malevolent applications, given the increasing persuasiveness and availability of deepfakes and synthetic content (Chi et al., 2021; Tinsley et al., 2022).

This work aims to enhance and present the comprehension of the ethical, privacy, and security implications inherent in the domains of quantum computing and GANs, given the intricate problems and opportunities they present. As we traverse this unfamiliar domain, we aim to not only elucidate the complexities of these technologies but also offer perspectives and suggestions that can facilitate their conscientious incorporation into our swiftly progressing digital realm (Bouzeraib et al., 2020). Simultaneously, GANs, a machine learning[4] (ML) application has enabled us to generate highly realistic images, text, and audio from digital platforms. They have stimulated innovation across various disciplines, encompassing art, fashion, medical imaging, and data augmentation. It is essential to acknowledge that GANs come with ethical implications (Raveendran & Raj, 2023). These implications arise from their ability to produce deepfakes, synthetic misinformation, and intrusions on privacy, necessitating careful monitoring and appropriate solutions to address these concerns.

The interconnection of new technologies is exemplified by the smooth synergy observed between quantum computing and GANs. Quantum computing potentially enhances the training and optimization procedures of GANs, hence facilitating the generation of synthetic data with heightened realism and increased accessibility (Chen et al., 2023). In contrast, GANs can be utilized to support quantum researchers in generating intricate quantum states and datasets, augmenting quantum computers' functionalities. This mutually beneficial association also requires a comprehensive approach to tackling ethical, privacy, and security concerns (Chen et al., 2021a). The progress of quantum computing and GANs will result in concurrent advancements in our capacity to generate and manipulate data, engage in research activities, and interact with technological systems. Therefore, it is crucial to establish inclusive frameworks incorporating both technologies, guaranteeing their responsible and ethical progression (Chen et al., 2021b);

The area of quantum computing has significant promise in addressing previously unsolvable issues, offering possible breakthroughs in various domains such as healthcare, climate modeling, and logistics (Li et al., 2022). GANs are expanding the limits of artistic expression and data synthesis, presenting an array of boundless prospects in art, entertainment, and scientific investigation. Nevertheless, the utilization of this revolutionary capability entails significant obligations (Berry et al., 2021). The ethical considerations presented by modern technologies are not simply theoretical concepts but rather urgent matters requiring prompt and focused examination. As the technological superiority of quantum computing is harnessed, it becomes imperative to address the issues of justice, accountability, and transparency in decision-making procedures that heavily rely on quantum algorithms. The emergence of GANs has presented a significant problem in detecting and combating the spread of deepfakes and synthetic misinformation (Nukavarapu et al., 2022). GANs can generate compelling material, hence necessitating the development of robust systems to identify and counteract the dissemination of such deceptive media.

1.1.1. The Chapter Contribution

The study contribution is listed below.

- The study presents quantum computing, explains the fundamentals of quantum computing, discusses the potential benefits of quantum computing, highlights ethical considerations related to quantum computing, and explores security and privacy concerns specific to quantum computing.

- The chapter illustrates GANs, explains their basics and applications, discusses their impact on various industries, presents ethical concerns related to their use, and examines privacy and security issues associated with them.
- The chapter details the ethical considerations, discusses the ethical frameworks relevant to quantum computing and GANs, analyzes the ethical implications of quantum computing and GANs, including their potential for misuse, and provides examples of ethical dilemmas in these fields.
- The chapter explains privacy concerns, explores the privacy issues arising from quantum computing and GANs, discusses data privacy, surveillance, and the risks to personal information, and considers privacy-enhancing technologies and techniques. The security challenges detailing security challenges in quantum computing and GANs, discussing the vulnerabilities and threats associated with these technologies, and extant strategies for securing quantum computing and GANs are presented.
- The chapter presents the regulatory and legal frameworks describing existing and proposed regulations governing quantum computing and GANs, analyzing the effectiveness of current legal frameworks in addressing ethical, privacy, and security concerns.
- Real-world examples and case studies illustrate ethical, privacy, and security challenges in quantum computing and GANs.
- The chapter further illustrates the mitigation strategies, offering some recommendations and strategies to address the identified ethical, privacy, and security challenges. It also explores encryption, authentication, and other security measures.
- Finally, the study presents the future directions, recommendations of quantum computing, GANs, and conclusions.

1.1.2. The Chapter Organization

Section 1.2 presents quantum computing, explaining the fundamentals of quantum computing, discussing the potential benefits of quantum computing, highlighting ethical considerations related to quantum computing, and exploring security and privacy concerns specific to quantum computing. Section 1.3 illustrates the GANs, explores the basics of GANs and their applications, discusses the impact of GANs on various industries, presents the ethical concerns related to the use of GANs, and examines privacy and security issues associated with GANs. Section 1.4 details the ethical considerations, discusses the ethical frameworks relevant to quantum computing and GANs, analyzes the ethical implications of quantum computing and GANs, including their potential for misuse, and provides examples of ethical dilemmas in these fields. Section 1.5 presents some case studies in quantum computing and GANs, discussing the vulnerabilities and threats associated with these technologies and extant strategies for securing quantum computing and GANs. Section 1.6 illustrates the mitigation strategies, offering some recommendations and strategies to address the identified ethical, privacy, and security challenges and exploring encryption, authentication, and other security measures. Finally, Section 1.7 presents the future directions, recommendations, and conclusions.

Quantum Computing

This section highlights potential benefits, security, and privacy concerns specific to quantum computing, as well as ethical considerations related to quantum computing.

Potential Benefits of Quantum Computing

Although quantum computing is still in its infancy and faces technological obstacles, the potential advantages are enormous. These advantages are anticipated to become more widely available and transformative across various sectors and scientific fields as researchers and scientists continue to build quantum hardware and algorithms (Raveendran & Raj, 2023).

Drug Discovery and Material Science

The advantages of quantum computing are immense, even though it is still in its infancy and confronts technological difficulties. As researchers and scientists continue to build quantum hardware and algorithms, these advantages should become more widely available and transform a vast number of companies and scientific fields (Chen et al., 2021b). The impact of quantum computing on the field of material science is significant. This computational tool facilitates the simulation of material behavior at the quantum level, hence facilitating the identification of novel materials possessing extraordinary features previously undiscovered (Ma et al., 2022). The materials above encompass improved superconductors designed to enhance energy transmission efficiency, unique battery materials engineered to prolong their lifespan, and lightweight, resilient materials tailored explicitly for aircraft use. The capacity to engineer materials with precise characteristics and capabilities holds significant ramifications across various sectors, encompassing renewable energy and electronics, fundamentally transforming the approach to material development and utilization (Sarkar, 2023).

Figure 1. Quantum computing Application

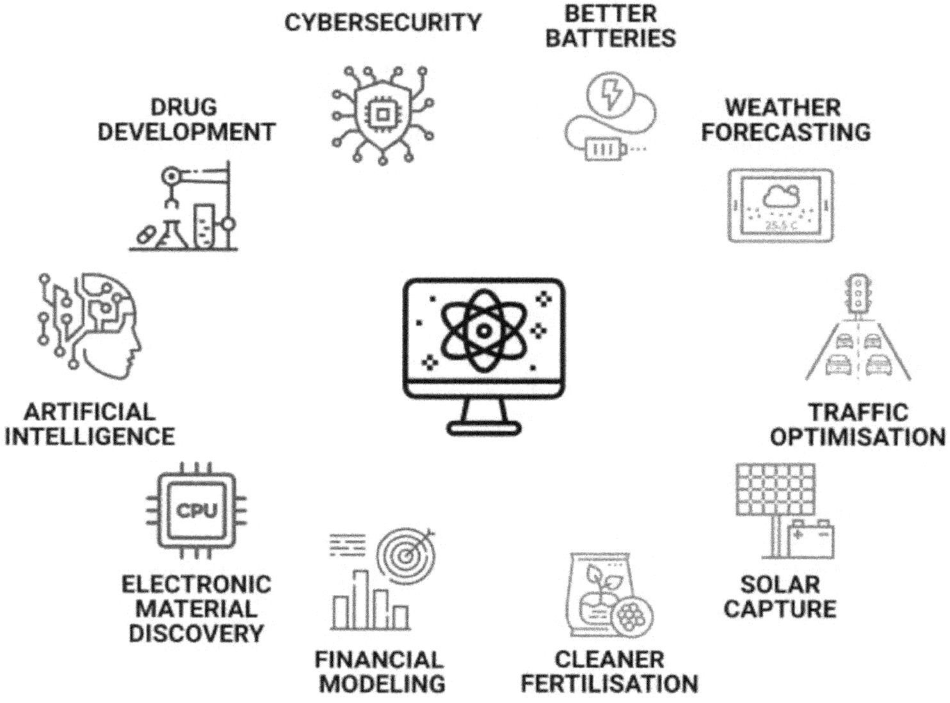

Optimization

quantum computing demonstrates exceptional proficiency in addressing intricate optimization problems pervasive across diverse industries. In logistics and transportation, using AI technology can enhance several aspects, such as route planning, vehicle scheduling, and supply chain management. Figure 1 illustrates the sampled application of Quantum computing. This can result in cost reduction and a decrease in environmental effects (Sarkar, 2023). Quantum computing can potentially increase various aspects of finance, including portfolio optimization, risk assessment, and trading methods. This is achieved by rapidly processing extensive datasets and intricate financial models. Likewise, within the realm of manufacturing, the utilization of this technology has the potential to enhance the allocation of resources and streamline production processes, hence resulting in heightened operational efficiency and diminished wastage (Deldjoo et al., 2021). These applications can effectively conserve significant firms' resources and enhance decision-making processes across several sectors.

Climate Modeling

Technology holds significant potential in climate modeling and simulation, as it can enhance the precision and comprehensiveness of climate pattern forecasts and their associated consequences. Climate models are characterized by intricate mathematical equations and vast datasets, rendering them computationally demanding (Smith, 2020). The computational speedup offered by quantum computing can significantly enhance the efficiency of climate simulations, facilitating a more comprehensive understanding of the intricacies of climate change dynamics, extreme weather occurrences, and long-term environmental patterns. An imperative aspect in formulating well-informed policy decisions and devising efficacious methods to alleviate the consequences of climate change is the acquisition of an expanded comprehension of climate science (Xu et al., 2021).

Supply Chain Management

It possesses the capability to enhance intricate supply chain networks through the optimization of goods flow, reduction of transportation expenses, and mitigation of delays. The utilization of this technology may effectively tackle various challenges, including demand forecasting, inventory management, and route optimization, leading to enhanced operational efficiency and cost reduction (Xu et al., 2021). In addition, quantum computing has the potential to augment the resilience of supply chains through its ability to respond to disruptions and efficiently redirect resources swiftly. The capacity to efficiently negotiate complexity and uncertainties is paramount in the current era characterized by a global supply chain (Wang et al., 2023). This capability equips organizations with the necessary tools to ensure the smooth delivery of goods and services to consumers.

Ethical Considerations Related to Quantum Computing

As this revolutionary technology develops, ethical issues relating to quantum computing are becoming more crucial. The creation, implementation, and application of quantum computing raise several significant ethical issues.

Cryptography and Security

The ethical questions about the implications of quantum computing on security and cryptography are of utmost significance. The possibility of quantum computers compromising the cryptographic underpinnings that protect sensitive data, such as personal, financial, and governmental information, is a significant concern (Malina et al., 2021). The focal point of the ethical predicament lies in the concept of responsible disclosure within the quantum computing community concerning the appropriate timing and way breakthroughs that have the potential to compromise encryption standards should be disseminated (Singh et al., 2020). Achieving a harmonious equilibrium between scientific advancement and data safeguarding is imperative. A current endeavor is to build encryption algorithms resistant to quantum attacks (Liu et al., 2021). However, this initiative raises ethical concerns regarding the appropriate speed and level of transparency with which they should be implemented to safeguard data privacy.

Arms Race

The expeditious advancement of quantum computing technology has elicited apprehensions over a potential escalation in the competition to achieve quantum dominance. The allocation of significant resources by nations and corporations toward quantum research and development has prompted ethical deliberations regarding the potential military applications of quantum capabilities (Du et al., 2021). The ethical obligation resides in preventing the advancement of quantum-based weaponry or surveillance systems that can potentially infringe upon individual privacy and human rights. Establishing standards and rules to manage these hazards poses challenges for the international community.

Inequality and Access

The ethical aspect of the equal availability of quantum computing resources and knowledge is essential. As the progression of quantum technology continues, there exists a potential for the amplification of disparities, wherein specific groups or nations may acquire preferential access to the advantages offered by quantum advancements (Jerald Nirmal Kumar et al., 2021). In contrast, others may experience a lag in their adoption. Ethical considerations encompass the imperative to promote inclusivity and accessibility of quantum computing across many communities and nations (Jerald Nirmal Kumar et al., 2021). It is imperative to prioritize efforts to narrow the digital divide while also considering the potential for worsening pre-existing inequities in technological accessibility.

Data Privacy

The ethical implications surrounding data privacy arise due to quantum computing's ability to decipher sensitive information. Safeguarding the privacy of individual and organizational data in a quantum-powered era necessitates implementing resilient encryption techniques and technologies that enhance privacy. Ethical considerations pertain to protecting personal information, financial records, and confidential data from illegal access. Organizations and governments are confronted with the ethical obligation to adopt rigorous security protocols to address the potential hazards posed by quantum technology to data privacy (Bautista & Inventado, 2021).

Ethics in Research

In quantum research, ethics are crucial. Transparency, accountability, and ethical research are values that scientists and organizations studying the potential and ramifications of quantum computing must uphold. Disclosing vulnerabilities and potential implications of quantum discoveries are ethically contentious issues (Patel et al., 2020). The more enormous ethical consequences of their work must be considered by researchers, who must balance scientific advancement and reduce potential adverse effects, such as those relating to security and privacy.

Environmental Impact

Quantum computers, on a large scale, often function under conditions of exceedingly low temperatures and exhibit substantial energy consumption. The ethical issue is the potential environmental consequences associated with quantum computing infrastructure. Incorporating sustainable practices in creating and operating quantum computing infrastructure is a crucial aspect of ethical issues (Wang et al., 2022). It is imperative to consider the careful equilibrium between the prospective advantages of quantum computing and its energy consumption and environmental impact to ensure responsible technological progress.

Dual-Use Dilemma

Like several nascent advancements, Quantum technologies demonstrate the capacity for dual-use applications. Ethical issues encompass the delicate task of striking a balance between promoting the progress of valuable applications, such as medication discovery and climate modeling, while also exercising caution to prevent the emergence of detrimental uses, such as creating quantum-enabled cyber weapons or surveillance technologies (Raya et al., 2023). Achieving an optimal equilibrium between promoting scientific advancement and mitigating the risks of potential misapplication necessitates careful ethical contemplation and the implementation of ethical frameworks and norms to regulate the evolution and use of quantum technologies.

Global Collaboration

Large-scale quantum computers frequently function at very low temperatures and use much energy. The ethical issue here is how quantum computing facilities will affect the environment. Adopting sustainable methods in constructing and operating quantum computing infrastructure is a matter of ethics. Quantum computing's possible advantages must be weighed against its energy requirements and environmental impact if responsible technological development is to take place (Mashatan & Heintzman, 2021).

Data Privacy and Security Concerns Aspect to Quantum Computing

Privacy and security concerns concerning quantum computing are emerging as this transformative technology advances within this subsection. There are detailed explanations of these concerns.

Cryptographic Vulnerabilities

The emergence of quantum computing poses a significant challenge to the fundamental principles of contemporary cryptography. One example of an algorithm with the capability to factor huge numbers efficiently is Shor's algorithm. This technique is fundamental to several encryption schemes, such as RSA. With the advancement of quantum computers, there is a growing concern regarding their potential ability to compromise commonly employed encryption techniques, jeopardizing the security of critical information and communications (Deldjoo et al., 2021). The issue, as mentioned earlier, gives rise to significant apprehensions regarding privacy and security, as traditional encryption techniques may be rendered susceptible to quantum attacks, compromising the confidentiality of sensitive information.

Data Privacy in a Post-Quantum World

Given the potential of quantum computers to compromise current encryption systems, companies must prepare for a future characterized by a "post-quantum" landscape. The use of quantum-resistant encryption technologies and the enhancement of security protocols are crucial in safeguarding data privacy (Fekri et al., 2019). Nevertheless, the shift to quantum computing poses various difficulties, such as the potential vulnerability to data breaches during the migration phase and the requirement for a well-coordinated and prompt implementation of quantum-resistant encryption across different industries.

Quantum-Safe Cryptography

The emergence of quantum computing poses a significant challenge to data privacy and security, necessitating the urgent development of encryption technologies and cryptographic protocols that can withstand quantum attacks. Ethical concerns emerge concerning the responsible dissemination of these developments (Lu & Li, 2021). The complex ethical challenge lies in the need to compromise between the progression of quantum-safe encryption and the prevention of premature knowledge sharing, potentially empowering bad actors to exploit quantum weaknesses.

Espionage and Surveillance:

The utilization of quantum computing may have substantial ramifications in the domains of surveillance and espionage. Quantum technologies can compromise encryption systems, enabling their utilization for unlawful data retrieval and intelligence collection (Wang et al., 2022). The issue raises significant ethical considerations about the infringement upon individuals' privacy, the potential misuse of quantum capabilities for surveillance objectives, and the necessity of implementing protective measures to deter unwanted quantum surveillance (Liu et al., 2022).

Quantum Key Distribution and Quantum Network Security

Quantum computing poses a significant obstacle to conventional encryption methods. However, it also presents the possibility of employing quantum key distribution (QKD) as a viable means to provide secure communication channels. QKD utilizes the inherent characteristics of quantum mechanics to guarantee the security of encryption keys [30]. Nevertheless, the implementation of QKD encounters pragmatic obstacles and ethical deliberations over the presence and reachability of QKD infrastructure and the possibility of quantum assaults on QKD systems (Fekri et al., 2022). Robust security measures are crucial for quantum networks since they facilitate safe communication by utilizing quantum key distribution. Ethical considerations arise concerning safeguarding the quantum network infrastructure from both physical and cyber threats. Preserving privacy and security is of utmost importance in guaranteeing the integrity and confidentiality of quantum information transmitted across these networks (Ma et al., 2022).

Impact on Cryptocurrency and Blockchain

The security of blockchain and cryptocurrency systems is contingent upon using cryptographic approaches. The potential of quantum computing to compromise cryptographic hashes and signatures presents a significant threat to the security and confidentiality of blockchain transactions (Sarkar, 2023). Ethical issues encompass the imperative to adopt proactive steps aimed at fortifying blockchain systems against quantum threats while safeguarding cryptocurrency users' privacy and security. To effectively tackle the privacy and security concerns associated with quantum computing, it is imperative to adopt a comprehensive strategy encompassing various aspects (Management & Mining, 2005).

GENERATIVE ADVERSARIAL NETWORKS

This section details the discussion of GANs' impact on various industries, presents ethical concerns related to their use, and discusses some notable privacy and security issues associated with GANs. Figure 2 shows the overall architecture of GAN models.

Figure 2. The overall architecture of GAN models

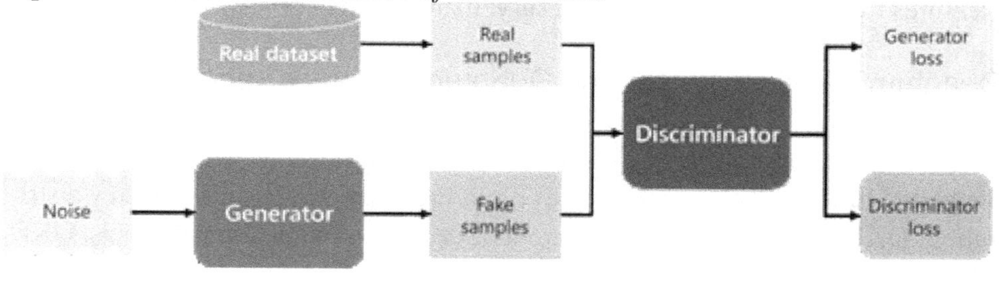

Potential Benefits of Generative Adversarial Networks

GANs offer various potential benefits across various domains, primarily due to their ability to generate realistic and high-quality data and detailed explanations of some key potential benefits of GANs.

Enhancement Image and Synthesis

GANs have demonstrated notable advancements in the domains of image creation and improvement. Convolutional neural networks can produce visuals of exceptional realism, rendering them indispensable in several domains, such as computer graphics, entertainment, and design (He et al., 2021). GANs have emerged as a valuable tool for artists and designers to create visually captivating artwork and immersive visual effects for movies and video games. GANs facilitate the improvement of image quality by enhancing resolution, reducing noise, and enhancing visual aesthetics (Cai et al., 2021). The utilization of GANs extends to the medical imaging field, whereby they can improve the visual quality and precision of diagnostic images. This enhancement contributes to the facilitation of accurate diagnoses by healthcare professionals (Sun et al., 2023).

Data Augmentation

In ML and DL, the availability of extensive and varied datasets is crucial for developing resilient models through training. GANs play a pivotal part in data augmentation by effectively creating synthetic data that exhibits a high degree of resemblance to real-world instances. The utilization of synthetic data has the potential to address class imbalance, mitigate overfitting, and enhance the generalization capabilities of artificial intelligence models (Fekri et al., 2019). The applications of GANs span across various domains, including computer vision and natural language processing. In computer vision, GANs are utilized to produce supplementary training images. Similarly, in natural language processing, GANs are employed to generate diverse textual variations that might enhance the performance of language models (Zhang et al., 2022).

Artistic Expression and Style Transfer

GANs have facilitated the exploration of novel routes in artistic expression by employing style transfer techniques. These methodologies enable artists and designers to amalgamate the aesthetic components of diverse artworks, yielding visually captivating pieces (Sharma et al., 2023). GANs can creatively reinterpret renowned artworks by emulating the distinct styles of various artists. GANs can extend their artistic influence beyond paintings since they can also apply artistic styles to images and videos. The expansive creative capacity has not only facilitated the emergence of innovative modes of artistic manifestation but has also been used in advertising, marketing, and the entertainment sector (Priscila et al., 2022).

Diagnosis and Medical Imaging

GANs have demonstrated considerable potential in medical imaging by their ability to generate synthetic images that accurately imitate a range of medical diseases and anomalies. The utilization of synthetic images has the potential to enhance the training and validation processes of diagnostic models, leading to enhanced accuracy in illness diagnosis. GANs play a crucial role in promptly identifying medical illnesses such as cancer, hence facilitating timely therapies and potentially leading to life-saving outcomes (Zhou et al., 2022). Moreover, GANs can produce anatomically accurate models that can be utilized in medical education and surgical preparation.

Molecular Design and Drug Discovery

The utilization of GANs in drug development and molecular design has proven advantageous for the pharmaceutical sector. GANs have demonstrated a noteworthy ability to create molecular structures and make accurate predictions regarding chemical characteristics (Deldjoo et al., 2021). Scientists employ these tools to investigate the extensive chemical landscape, ascertain promising pharmaceutical candidates, and enhance molecular architectures to enhance effectiveness and safety. This phenomenon expedites the drug development procedure, diminishes expenses, and potentially expedites the introduction of life-saving pharmaceuticals to the market (Agoub et al., 2019).

Fraud Prevention and Anomaly Detection

GANs are being utilized with growing frequency in implementing anomaly detection systems. By undergoing training using genuine data, GANs can acquire the ability to discern patterns and expected behaviors. Therefore, GANs prove proficient in detecting anomalies or deviations from the established norm (Chenna, 2022). Within financial services, GANs assume a pivotal role in detecting fraudulent activities by identifying atypical transactions or behaviors that could signify fraudulent conduct (Cao et al., 2023). This measure improves security and safeguards individuals and businesses from potential financial losses.

Text-to-Image Generation

GANs possess the capacity to produce visual representations based on textual descriptions, hence exhibiting a wide range of potential applications. E-commerce platforms employ GANs to generate visual representations of products based on textual descriptions, enabling shoppers to envision merchandise that has not been physically photographed (Mendes et al., 2023). Content developers can transform written concepts into visual representations, hence facilitating the execution of marketing campaigns and the art of storytelling (Marshall et al., 2016). The integration of textual and visual elements can revolutionize the landscape of digital content generation and online retail interactions.

Animation and Video Production

The influence of GANs encompasses the domains of video and animation production. The ability to produce lifelike animated sequences, create intricate special effects, and develop three-dimensional character models is within their capabilities. The implementation of this technology optimizes the workflow of content generation, resulting in a decrease in the requirement for labor-intensive manual tasks and time-consuming rendering procedures (Lu & Li, 2021). Within film and gaming, GANs play a pivotal role in augmenting the level of immersion and visual aesthetics, enriching the narrative and entertainment value.

Augmented Reality and Virtual Reality

GANs play a crucial role in developing immersive virtual reality (VR) and augmented reality (AR) environments. The capability to produce lifelike three-dimensional (3D) models, textures, and surroundings enables developers to create immersive virtual worlds that are visually engaging (Wang et al., 2023). Training simulations, gaming experiences, architectural visualization, and educational applications benefit from the realism and interaction that GANs provide in VR and AR. This integration enhances user engagement and improves learning results.

Creative Writing and Content Generation

In natural language processing, GANs have significantly advanced in generating text that closely resembles human language. The capacity significantly impacts content generation, chatbots, and creative writing. GANs can autonomously generate many forms of content, including news articles, marketing copy, and personalized content recommendations (Sun et al., 2023). While automated content generation can enhance the process of creating material and enhance user experiences, it also raises ethical concerns about its potential exploitation for disinformation or manipulation. Achieving a harmonious equilibrium between automation and responsible content development poses a significant ethical dilemma within this field (Wang et al., 2020). Table 1 presents the comparison between quantum computing and GANs.

Table 1. Quantum Computing and Generative Adversarial Networks (GANs) Contrasts to Ethics, Privacy and Security

Aspects	**Quantum Computing**					**Generative Adversarial Networks**					**Reference**
Ethics	**Environmental Impact**	**Military and Surveillance**	**Privacy and Security**	**Technological Divide**	**Dual-use Technology**	**Transparency and Accountability**	**Misuse and Fraud**	**Ethical Infringement**	**Bias and Fairness**	**Deepfake Generation**	**(Wang et al., 2023)**
	High energy consumption may have a significant environmental impact.	Use in military and surveillance applications poses ethical dilemmas.	Potential to break current cryptographic methods, compromising data privacy.	Limited access may exacerbate existing inequalities.	It can be used for both beneficial and harmful purposes, raising ethical concerns.	The black-box nature of GANs makes it difficult to ensure transparency and accountability in their application.	GANs can be used to create fake identities or documents, leading to ethical concerns about identity theft and fraud.	GANs can generate synthetic data that may be used to re-identify anonymized individuals, compromising privacy.	GANs can inherit and amplify biases present in the training data, raising ethical issues around fairness and discrimination.	GANs can create highly realistic fake images, videos, and audio, leading to ethical concerns about misinformation and deception.	(Raveendran & Raj, 2023)
Privacy	Privacy Regulations	Sensitive Information	Data Breach Risks	New Encryption Methods	Breaking Encryption	Privacy-preserving Data Generation	Data Augmentation	Deepfake Privacy Violations	Surveillance Enhancement	Synthetic Data Re-identification	(Sun et al., 2023)
	It challenges existing privacy laws and regulations and requires new frameworks.	Threat to the privacy of sensitive information, such as personal, financial, and medical data.	Increased potential for large-scale data breaches if quantum technology is misused.	Necessitates the development of quantum-resistant encryption to protect data.	Quantum computers could decrypt existing encrypted data, compromising privacy.	Generating synthetic data that aims to preserve privacy through true anonymization is difficult.	Risks Synthetic data may expose sensitive information if not managed properly.	The generation of fake media without consent leads to privacy invasions.	Potential for creating enhanced surveillance systems that infringe on privacy.	Risk of re-identifying individuals from synthetic data.	(Raveendran & Raj, 2023)

continued on following page

Table 1. Continued

Aspects	Quantum Computing					Generative Adversarial Networks					Reference
Ethics	**Environmental Impact**	**Military and Surveillance**	**Privacy and Security**	**Technological Divide**	**Dual-use Technology**	**Transparency and Accountability**	**Misuse and Fraud**	**Ethical Infringement**	**Bias and Fairness**	**Deepfake Generation**	**(Wang et al., 2023)**
Security	Adversarial Use	Infrastructure Security	Cybersecurity Threats	Quantum-resistant Algorithms	Cryptographic Vulnerability	Data Integrity	Vulnerability Exploitation	Malicious Content	Adversarial Attacks	Forgery and Fraud	(Priscila 2022)
	Potential for malicious entities to exploit quantum computing for harmful purposes, such as advanced cyberattacks.	Critical infrastructure could become vulnerable to quantum-based attacks, necessitating enhanced security measures.	Increased potential for cyber espionage and large-scale hacking incidents.	Necessitates development of new, secure encryption methods resistant to quantum attacks.	Quantum computers can break current cryptographic algorithms, posing major security risks.	Synthetic data from GANs can impact the accuracy and reliability of security data.	GANs might help identify and exploit weaknesses in AI systems.	GANs can generate harmful misinformation or malicious content.	GANs can craft inputs that trick other AI systems, posing security risks.	GANs can create realistic fakes, leading to identity fraud and security threats.	(Jerald Nirmal Kumar et al., 2021)

ETHICAL CONSIDERATIONS RELATED TO GENERATIVE ADVERSARIAL NETWORKS

These multifaceted ethical considerations require collaboration among researchers, policymakers, industry stakeholders, and ethicists. Developing and adhering to ethical frameworks and guidelines can help ensure that GANs are harnessed for the greater good while minimizing their potential for misuse and harm.

Deepfake Generation and Privacy and Consent

The utilization of GANs to produce deepfakes raises a substantial ethical quandary due to their capacity to deceive and manipulate individuals and the broader public. Ethical considerations encompass a range of issues, such as the dissemination of inaccurate information, the act of defaming individuals or entities, and the possibility of instigating violent behavior (Ma, 2022). Identifying and mitigating deepfakes play a crucial role in preserving trust in digital media and minimizing their possible negative consequences. Using GANs to produce synthetic images or films depicting humans without explicit authorization gives rise to significant privacy implications. These technologies can generate information that convincingly portrays individuals in compromising or invasive scenarios (Mendes et al., 2023).

Intellectual Property and Copyright

GANs have the potential to introduce complexities in intellectual property and copyright law, particularly in the context of generating artistic creations or derivative works. Ethical considerations encompass several aspects, such as assessing the authenticity of content generated by GANs, resolving issues related to credit and royalties, and preserving the artistic and intellectual rights of individuals involved in content creation (Agoub et al., 2019). Establishing ethical principles and legal frameworks holds paramount importance within this setting. The safeguarding of individuals' entitlement to privacy necessitates the establishment of parameters for the utilization of GAN-generated images, as well as the assurance of obtaining consent when deemed appropriate.

Bias and Discrimination, Deception and Misinformation

GANs have the potential to perpetuate biases and reinforce societal disparities by inheriting the biases contained in their training data, resulting in biased and stereotypical outputs. As an illustration, these systems can provide visual representations that perpetuate and strengthen existing racial or gender prejudices (Jerald

Nirmal Kumar et al., 2021). Ethical considerations revolve around the possibility of reinforcing detrimental biases and the imperative to meticulously curate and scrutinize algorithms and data to guarantee equity and inclusiveness. The ethical implications arising from the ability of GANs to produce deceptive content effortlessly raise concerns regarding the propagation of misinformation and the act of deceiving individuals. The implications of this phenomenon can extend significantly to domains such as journalism, political communication, and societal interpretation (Wang, 2022). Ethical considerations encompass the obligation of both platforms and users to engage in information verification and fact-checking, as well as the advancement of tools for detecting content generated by GANs.

Emotional and Psychological Impact, Fraud Identity and Theft

The utilization of GAN-generated content, particularly deepfake films, has the potential to elicit profound emotional reactions among individuals who encounter such material. Ethical considerations revolve around the possible psychological damage resulting from false or emotionally manipulative content (Nukavarapu et al., 2022). When developing content and utilizing platforms, content creators and platforms must consider the potential consequences on individuals, especially those who may be more susceptible to experiencing emotional discomfort. GANs can enable illicit activities such as identity theft and fraud by creating fabricated identities, forged papers, and even manipulated voice recordings. Ethical considerations encompass the implementation of rigorous identity verification systems and the establishment of legislative frameworks aimed at addressing fraudulent actions (Masood 2021). Safeguarding persons against potential financial and reputational damage is a crucial ethical consideration.

Algorithmic Accountability and Environmental Impact

The ethical concept of accountability is of significant importance to GAN developers, companies, and platforms. The individuals accountable for developing and implementing GANs must conscientiously assess the societal ramifications of these technologies and adopt proactive strategies to guarantee their ethical utilization (Ding et al., 2021). This encompasses openly acknowledging the artificial origin of content, taking responsibility for any potential misuse, and implementing effective reporting systems to identify and resolve ethical breaches. Likewise, the environmental consequences of training and operating GANs, especially when dealing with large-scale models, are substantial due to the computational resources involved (Mendes et al., 2023). The ethical dimensions of GAN research and development encompass the assessment of carbon footprint and energy use. In this context, the adoption of sustainable behaviors, such as the utilization of energy-efficient technology and the responsible allocation of resources, is seen to be morally obligatory (Yang et al., 2021).

SECURITY AND DATA PRIVACY CONCERNS SPECIFIC TO GENERATIVE ADVERSARIAL NETWORKS

Adopting a comprehensive approach that encompasses technical remedies, ethical deliberations, legal structures, and awareness initiatives is imperative to effectively tackle the privacy and security risks associated with GANs. The following sections outline these necessary components in detail.

Synthetic Identity Generation

GANs can generate remarkably authentic synthetic images depicting non-existent humans. The utilization of synthetic identities gives rise to privacy apprehensions, as unscrupulous individuals can exploit them for diverse objectives, including but not limited to impersonation, identity theft, and the fabrication of counterfeit profiles on social media platforms (Patel et al., 2020). Identifying and preventing fraudulent activities with synthetic identities pose significant challenges, necessitating a constant state of alertness in digital identity verification.

Deepfake Creation

GANs have emerged as a pivotal technology in creating deepfake content, encompassing the production of manipulated or impersonated films and audio recordings involving persons. The utilization of this technology has significant privacy concerns since it has the potential to generate fabricated videos depicting individuals participating in compromising or inappropriate actions. Such misuse might result in reputational harm and emotional suffering for the affected individuals. Implementing deepfake detection mechanisms and promoting awareness campaigns play a vital role in addressing and minimizing the privacy risks associated with deepfake technology (He et al., 2021).

Biometric Data Privacy

GANs can generate artificial biometric data, including but not limited to fingerprints, facial photos, and voice recordings, which exhibit a high degree of similarity to authentic biometric identifiers. The issue poses a significant security risk, given the prevalent utilization of biometric data for authentication and identification purposes (Lu & Li, 2021). In the event of a hack, there is a potential for unauthorized access to sensitive information, ranging from personal devices to protected facilities. To safeguard biometric data against GAN-based attacks, it is imperative to implement resilient security protocols, such as multi-factor authentication and biometric encryption (Liu et al., 2022).

Data Generation from Limited Information

GANs can produce intricate visual representations by utilizing restricted data or source images with poor resolution. This technique presents potential privacy concerns, particularly in scenarios where it is employed to improve surveillance footage or reconstruct recognizable images using incomplete data (Abulkasim et al., 2021). The privacy of individuals may be violated when GANs are employed to retrieve sensitive information from apparently harmless sources.

Content Manipulation and Misinformation

GANs have the potential to be utilized to manipulate content in a manner that can lead to deception or misinformation. This might encompass manipulating visual media, such as photos or films, to construct misleading narratives or forge substantiating proof. The dissemination of modified content has the potential to affect individuals' reputations adversely, manipulate public sentiment, and erode trust in information sources, becoming a noteworthy security and privacy risk (Nukavarapu et al., 2022).

Ethical Data Usage and Data Recovery Attacks

The utilization of GANs to produce synthetic data in diverse applications, including data augmentation and privacy-preserving approaches, gives rise to ethical concerns about the utilization and consent of data. Privacy risks arise when GANs are trained on datasets containing sensitive information without obtaining explicit agreement or when synthetic data is utilized in manners that may unintentionally lead to the identification of persons (Berry et al., 2021). The data generated by GANs may not consistently provide the desired level of anonymization or privacy. Sophisticated methodologies, such as data recovery assaults, employ patterns and correlations to reverse-engineer the original data from fake data (Raveendran & Raj, 2023).

Data Leakage, Inference Attacks, and Regulatory Compliance

The synthetic data generated by GANs, although intended to safeguard privacy, can unintentionally disclose information from the original data sources. Privacy breaches can manifest as inference attacks, wherein malicious actors employ statistical analytic techniques to infer confidential information from synthetic data (Chi et al., 2022). Continual investigation into sophisticated privacy-preserving methodologies is needed to guarantee the intense privacy of data generated by GANs. As the utilization of GANs becomes more prevalent in handling sensitive data, enterprises face the challenge of effectively managing intricate privacy and security requirements, for example, the General Data Protection Regulation (GDPR)[5] implemented in Europe (Arulmozhiselvan, & Uma, 2022). Maintaining adherence to these standards while effectively utilizing GANs for lawful objectives is a notable obstacle, given that non-compliance may lead to considerable financial penalties and legal ramifications.

REGULATORY AND LEGAL FRAMEWORKS

This section describes existing and proposed regulations governing quantum computing and GANs and analyzes the effectiveness of current legal frameworks in addressing ethical, privacy, and security concerns.

Existing regulations governing Quantum Computing and Generative Adversarial Networks

It is imperative to acknowledge that the legislation about quantum computing is currently under development and can exhibit substantial variations across different jurisdictions. The dynamic characteristics of quantum technology and its possible ramifications across diverse domains, such as cybersecurity, encryption, and data privacy, render it a multifaceted realm of governance (Tinsley et al., 2022). Policymakers and regulatory agencies are actively collaborating with experts and stakeholders to create the regulatory framework effectively, ensuring a harmonious equilibrium between innovation, security, and ethical issues.

Export Controls

Export controls refer to governmental rules that are implemented to limit the exportation of sensitive technologies, products, or information. The primary objective of these controls is to prevent the unauthorized acquisition of such items, particularly in situations where their potential misuse could threaten national security (Zhao et al., 2023). Export control legislation in numerous nations may impose restrictions on quantum computing technologies, specifically on quantum hardware. An illustration of this can be seen in the export control regulations of the United States, which the Department of Commerce oversees. These regulations stipulate that specific quantum technologies are subject to procedures for obtaining export licenses (Bautista & Inventado, 2021). These regulations prevent the transfer of powerful quantum computing hardware and associated technology to entities or governments that may exploit them for nefarious intentions.

1.1.2.1. Intellectual Property Laws

Intellectual property legal framework comprises various forms of protection, including patents, copyrights, trademarks, and trade secrets. Researchers and companies engaged in quantum computing can pursue patent protection for their innovative contributions. This encompasses quantum algorithms, ideas for quantum hardware, and implementations of quantum software (Chi et al., 2021). The grant of patent protection catalyzes fostering innovation by affording inventors and entities the privilege of exclusive rights over their quantum-related creations for a predetermined duration. The safeguarding of intellectual property rights plays a crucial role in the preservation of investments made in research and development, as well as in providing incentives for continued progress and innovation within the field of quantum technology (Tinsley et al., 2021).

Privacy Laws and Data Protection

Data protection and privacy regulations govern the various aspects of personal data, including its acquisition, storage, processing, and dissemination. An illustration of a comprehensive data protection framework worldwide is the GDPR of the European Union (Kumari et al., 2021). Quantum computing applications that include personal data processing must conform to these restrictions. To uphold the private rights of individuals, organizations that employ quantum technology for data storage, analysis, or encryption must adhere to data protection and privacy legislation (Arulmozhiselvan & Uma, 2022). Encryption techniques, especially those immune to quantum attacks, hold significance in endeavors aimed at safeguarding data.

Telecommunications Regulations

Quantum key distribution (QKD) is a quantum-based technological approach that aims to provide secure communication channels by exploiting the fundamental laws of quantum physics. The current telecommunications legislation could influence the adoption and use of QKD systems. In certain nations, regulatory authorities oversee the adoption of secure communication technologies, such as QKD, to ensure adherence to telecommunications standards and uphold the security and integrity of communication networks (Chi et al., 2021). The significance of QKD in guaranteeing secure communication is an essential part of telecommunications regulation.

Certification and Standards

The involvement of established standards and certification organizations is crucial in establishing rules and benchmarks for quantum-resistant encryption and security. The National Institute of Standards and Technology (NIST)[6] in the United States is actively developing standards for post-quantum cryptography. These standards aim to mitigate the potential susceptibilities of existing encryption techniques to quantum attacks and establish a structure for ensuring secure encryption practices in a future where quantum computing is prevalent (Chen et al., 2021). Ensuring adherence to these standards is paramount for enterprises seeking to safeguard their data from potential quantum-related risks.

Trade Agreements

The regulation of quantum technology can indirectly influence international trade agreements and treaties. The potential effects of these developments on cross-border research collaborations, technological transfers, and commerce in quantum-related products and services should be considered. Nations frequently harmonize their trade rules with global accords, potentially affecting the trade of quantum technology and associated intellectual property rights in terms of exports and imports. The dynamic nature of global trade dynamics has the potential to influence further the regulatory frameworks governing quantum technology (Jemihin et al., 2022). The current regulations establish a comprehensive framework governing several quantum computing facets, encompassing research and development, data protection, and international trade.

Proposed Regulations Governing Quantum Computing and GANs

These proposed regulations reflect the growing recognition of the need to balance innovation in quantum computing and GANs with ethical, security, and privacy considerations. Policymakers, regulatory bodies, industry experts, and stakeholders are actively shaping these regulatory frameworks to address the unique challenges these transformative technologies pose (Zhang et al., 2022). The specifics of these regulations may vary by jurisdiction. Tranquil, the overarching goal is to ensure that quantum computing and GANs contribute positively to society while minimizing potential risks and harms.

Cybersecurity Standards and Quantum-Safe Encryption

Potential restrictions in quantum computing may emphasize the necessity of implementing practical cybersecurity standards. These standards would encompass quantum hardware, networks, and algorithms. In addition, their attention would be directed toward mitigating the security vulnerabilities that quantum computing poses to existing encryption techniques (Li et al., 2022). This entails the establishment of protocols enabling the advancement and acceptance of encryption methods that are resistant to quantum computing, such as lattice-based cryptography or post-quantum cryptographic algorithms.

Data Privacy and Quantum Encryption

Considering the escalating risk posed by quantum attacks on conventional encryption, it may be deemed necessary for regulatory bodies to mandate companies' use of quantum-resistant encryption techniques. As mentioned earlier, the legislation will emphasize the significance of safeguarding sensitive data in an era dominated by quantum computing while advocating for adopting QKD and other encryption technologies resistant to quantum attacks (Ma et al., 2022). Embracing quantum-safe encryption standards may be mandated for specific sectors and industries.

Export Controls and Dual-Use Technologies

The prospective implementation of regulatory measures for quantum computing may encompass more stringent export controls, particularly for technology with dual-use capabilities. To mitigate potential misuse, governments may consider broadening their regulatory monitoring of exports of quantum-related hardware and software. To uphold national security interests and mitigate the proliferation of sensitive quantum capabilities, it may be necessary to extend the scope of export permits to encompass a wider array of quantum technology.

Ethical Considerations and Responsible Research Practices

Formulating ethical guidelines is one potential course of action to foster responsible and ethical conduct within quantum research and development. The rules may address various factors, such as research ethics, the responsible disclosure of flaws in quantum systems, and the prevention of detrimental applications of quantum technology, particularly in domains such as encryption and quantum computing for cybersecurity (Raya et al., 2023). Proposed regulations may encourage the development of industry standards and certification processes for quantum hardware and software. Certification would ensure that quantum technologies meet specific security and performance criteria, fostering trust among users and organizations. These standards could encompass hardware reliability, quantum-resistant encryption, and quantum key distribution protocols (Mashatan & Heintzman, 2021).

Deepfake Detection and Mitigation

Potential legislation within the realm of GANs may necessitate implementing sophisticated deepfake detection and mitigation methods by online platforms, content publishers, and technology vendors. The primary objective of this legislation is to address the proliferation of deceptive deepfake content and safeguard individuals' reputations, privacy, and emotional well-being (Abulkasim et al., 2021). It is possible to construct guidelines that provide certain levels for the accuracy of deepfake detection and the effectiveness of mitigating strategies. Regulatory measures may require the implementation of explicit labeling for content created by GANs to differentiate it from genuine content (Wang et al., 2023). Labeling is crucial in enabling users to discern synthetic content and comprehend its possible consequences, especially when disinformation or deceit may arise.

Ownership Guidelines and Content Attribution Data Privacy and Informed Consent

Regulations may address complex content attribution and ownership issues regarding GAN-generated content. Clear guidelines could be proposed to determine ownership, royalties, and fair use of content created using GANs (Lu & Li, 2021). This includes establishing mechanisms for content creators to assert their rights and claim ownership over GAN-generated creations. In the context of GANs, proposed regulations may require explicit informed consent for generating and using synthetic data, particularly if it involves individuals' likeness or personal information. These regulations would emphasize the importance of respecting individuals' privacy rights and obtaining consent to create synthetic content that may impact their privacy or identity (Liu et al., 2022)

Responsible AI and Bias Mitigation

Potential rules and guidelines could be implemented to manage the ethical concerns surrounding the development and utilization of GANs effectively, explicitly focusing on mitigating issues related to bias, fairness, transparency, and accountability. Organizations employing GANs may be obligated to incorporate fairness assessments, bias detection methods, and transparency procedures into their operations (Wang et al., 2023). This is to ensure that their AI applications do not propagate detrimental biases or discriminatory outcomes.

Effectiveness of current legal frameworks

The effectiveness of current legal frameworks in addressing ethical, privacy, and security concerns related to quantum computing and GANs is mixed. While some existing laws can be applied to mitigate specific issues, these frameworks often lag at the rapid pace of technological advancements (He et al., 2021). Specific regulations and guidelines tailored to these emerging technologies are necessary to address their unique challenges effectively.

Ethical Concerns

The current legal frameworks generally do not have explicit laws pertaining to the ethical considerations associated with quantum computing. Ethical considerations in scientific research encompass responsible research techniques and prevent detrimental applications (Sun et al., 2023). These considerations are typically upheld through self-regulation within the scientific community and adherence to ethical principles established by institutions and professional organizations. There is a necessity for developing more extensive ethical norms and regulatory frameworks to successfully tackle the ethical concerns associated with quantum computing. The ethical implications associated with GANs, including the production of deepfakes, dissemination of misinformation, and potential privacy infringement, have garnered much scholarly and public scrutiny. Although there is a lack of dedicated legislation on GANs, specific ethical concerns can be addressed by leveraging existing regulations, such as defamation and privacy laws (He et al., 2021). Nevertheless, the efficacy of these frameworks exhibits variability depending on the jurisdiction, and the enforcement process can prove to be arduous, particularly in cross-border complexities.

Privacy Concerns

The focus of privacy concerns in the field of quantum computing pertains to safeguarding data and the possibility of unauthorized access to confidential information via quantum assaults. Current data protection and privacy regulations, such as the GDPR, need enterprises to establish security protocols to safeguard personal data, including encryption techniques (Agoub et al., 2019). The efficacy of these regulations is contingent upon entities' implementation and adherence to quantum-resistant encryption techniques. One of the primary issues with privacy in the context of GANs pertains to the unpermitted utilization of individuals' data to generate synthetic content. The current legislation on data protection establishes a legal structure aimed at safeguarding the privacy rights of individuals (Zhou et al., 2022). Nevertheless, implementing enforcement measures might present significant difficulties, especially in cases involving the fabrication of synthetic data and the potential for re-identifying persons. There is a potential need to implement new legislation that mainly targets synthetic data and content generated by GANs to strengthen privacy safeguards.

Security Concerns

The primary focus of security concerns in the field of quantum computing mainly pertains to the possible disruption of conventional encryption techniques through the utilization of quantum attacks. The current emphasis within legal frameworks is predominantly on export controls and intellectual property protection for quantum technologies since efforts are underway to build encryption standards resistant to quantum attacks (Fekri et al., 2019). The efficacy of these frameworks is of utmost importance in mitigating the spread of sensitive quantum capabilities and protecting national security interests. Also, one of the core security considerations associated with GANs pertains to the production of deepfake material, which has the potential to inflict damage upon individuals' reputations and manipulate public opinion. Certain security concerns can be effectively addressed by utilizing established legal frameworks, such as those about defamation and fraud (Sun et al., 2023). Nevertheless, identifying and mitigating deepfake content frequently depends on technological interventions and cooperation between various platforms and law enforcement entities.

CASE STUDIES

This section illustrates real-world examples and case studies illustrating ethical, privacy, and security challenges in quantum computing and GANs.

Case studies illustrating Ethical, Data Privacy, and Security Challenges in Quantum Computing

These case studies demonstrate the ethical, privacy, and security challenges associated with quantum computing in various sectors, including healthcare, finance, cybersecurity, and government applications. Addressing these challenges requires a multidisciplinary approach involving technologists, policymakers, ethicists, and legal experts to develop ethical guidelines, privacy protections, and security measures that align with quantum computing's unique capabilities and risks.

Security Challenge - Post-Quantum Cryptography Adoption

They initiated a competition to select post-quantum cryptographic algorithms to replace current encryption methods vulnerable to quantum attacks. This competition reflects the security challenge of transitioning to new encryption standards to protect sensitive data in a quantum computing era (Cai et al., 2021). Organizations and governments need to adapt their cryptographic infrastructure to ensure data security.

Ethical Challenge - Quantum Computing for Drug Discovery

Case Study: Pharmaceutical corporations are currently investigating the potential application of quantum computing to expedite the drug discovery process. Although there are hopeful advancements in healthcare, using patients' genetic information and medical records for quantum-based research raises ethical problems related to data privacy and permission (He et al., 2021). The ethical dilemma of reconciling medical advancements with protecting patient privacy poses a substantial problem.

Privacy Challenge - Quantum-Safe Encryption for Financial Transactions

Case Study: Financial institutions, such as banks and payment processors, are currently engaged in extensive research endeavors about quantum-safe encryption techniques, with the primary objective of safeguarding financial transactions (Zhou et al., 2022). Privacy problems emerge when contemplating the imperative to safeguard client data and financial records against quantum attacks while guaranteeing uninterrupted and confidential transactions for customers. The preservation of confidentiality for financial information is of utmost importance.

Security Challenge - Quantum Computing for Cybersecurity

The emergence of quantum computing has brought forward the potential for enhanced cyberattacks. The potential utilization of quantum algorithms by nation-states and malevolent actors poses a significant threat to the security of present encryption systems and the integrity of vital infrastructure (Liu et al., 202). The primary concern pertains to proactively safeguarding against these potential risks and designing resilient cybersecurity strategies against quantum-based attacks.

Ethical Challenge - Quantum Computing for AI and Surveillance

Using quantum computing to process extensive information at unparalleled velocities gives rise to ethical considerations when employed in surveillance and artificial intelligence. Governments and organizations can employ quantum-powered AI systems for surveillance, encompassing facial recognition and tracking activities (Bautista & Inventado, 2021). Ethical considerations include protecting individual privacy, obtaining informed consent, and the potential implications of widespread surveillance.

Privacy Challenge - Quantum-Safe Elections and Voting Systems

Case Study: Preserving privacy and security in electoral processes constitutes a key tenet of democratic governance. Implementing quantum-safe encryption could be important in safeguarding electronic voting systems against the vulnerabilities of quantum attacks (Zhao et al., 20233). Nevertheless, the task of ensuring both transparency and voter privacy in electronic voting systems while also protecting against potential quantum threats presents a multifaceted privacy dilemma.

Security Challenge - Quantum-Safe Supply Chain Management

The effectiveness of supply chain management is contingent upon establishing robust mechanisms for secure communication and preserving data integrity. The potential of quantum computing to compromise existing encryption techniques presents a significant security concern in safeguarding the integrity and confidentiality of supply chain data (Sarkar, 2023). Organizations must establish and implement quantum-safe safeguards to ensure the security of their supply chains.

Case Studies Illustrate Ethical, Data Privacy, and Security Challenges in GANs

These real-world examples and case studies highlight the multifaceted ethical, privacy, and security challenges associated with GANs. Addressing these challenges requires technical solutions, ethical guidelines, legal regulations, and public awareness efforts to ensure responsible and secure use of GAN technology while safeguarding privacy and combating malicious use cases.

Privacy Challenge - Deepfake Manipulation

In 2019, a mobile application known as "DeepNude[7]" garnered significant attention due to its utilization of GANs to produce authentic-looking nude depictions of women by digitally eliminating their attire in photographs. The use of GAN technology in an immoral manner has given rise to significant apprehensions regarding privacy, as it has showcased the capacity for hostile entities to manipulate GANs to produce non-consensual, sexual material, infringing upon individuals' privacy rights (Priscila 2022; Shafik, 2024a).

Security Challenge - GAN-Generated Malware

Studies conducted by researchers have demonstrated the capability of GANs to generate polymorphic malware, a type of malicious software that can dynamically alter its code to elude conventional antivirus systems. The detection of such malware presents a significant problem, and its ability to adapt represents a security concern for cybersecurity professionals. This scenario underscores the necessity of implementing heightened security protocols to mitigate the risks posed by threats generated using GANs effectively (Liu et al., 2022).

Ethical Challenge - GANs for Misinformation

GANs can produce fabricated news stories, blog posts, and social media content that exhibit a remarkably high realism. The potential for malevolent entities to leverage this technology to spread false information, manipulate public sentiment, and instill skepticism toward media outlets is evident [45]. This ethical dilemma pertains to the dual objective of countering the dissemination of inaccurate information while safeguarding the principle of freedom of expression (Cao et al., 2023).

Privacy Challenge - Deepfake and Impersonation

Deepfake[8] technology has been employed to fabricate videos that simulate the actions and statements of prominent individuals and renowned personalities, creating a deceptive impression of their engagement in activities or utterances that they have not actually performed [44]. The act of impersonation presents a significant privacy concern for persons whose likenesses are utilized without their explicit agreement, hence potentially causing detrimental effects on their reputation and privacy.

Ethical Challenge - GANs in Art and Copyright

The use of GANs in creating artistic and musical content has prompted ethical inquiries about authorship and copyright matters. Producing artistic creations or musical compositions poses a significant challenge in establishing the appropriate allocation of rights and royalties for the respective producers (Chenna, 2022; Shafik, 2024b). The auction sale of "Portrait of Edmond de Belamy[9]," an artwork generated by artificial intelligence, has ignited discussions surrounding the worth and proprietorship of AI-made creations.

Security Challenge - GAN-Enhanced Cyberattacks:

Case Study: GANs can potentially augment the efficacy of cyberattacks by generating persuasive phishing emails, replicating the communication patterns exhibited by trusted individuals, and fabricating counterfeit documents (Priscila et al., 2022). Using sophisticated attack techniques presents security obstacles for businesses and individuals that depend on conventional security measures.

Privacy Challenge - Synthetic Identity Generation

GANs can produce artificial identities that exhibit a high degree of realism, encompassing visually authentic photographs and accompanying credentials. Synthetic identities possess the potential to be employed in a multitude of fraudulent endeavors, encompassing identity theft, online fraudulent schemes, and social engineering assaults (Sharma et al., 2023). The identification and mitigation of the misuse of synthetic identities provide significant privacy and security obstacles.

Ethical Challenge - Deepfake in Politics

The potential impact of deepfake films featuring political leaders disseminating false information on electoral outcomes and public opinion cannot be underestimated. During the pre-election period, the utilization of deepfake content can potentially undermine the credibility of political personalities and disseminate false information, hence presenting ethical dilemmas for democratic processes and the integrity of information (Sun et al., 2023; Shafik, 2024c).

Mitigation Strategies

These detailed mitigation strategies encompass a holistic approach to address the ethical, privacy, and security challenges quantum computing and GANs pose. By implementing these strategies, organizations can navigate the complexities of emerging technologies while upholding ethical principles, ensuring privacy protection, and enhancing security measures.

Responsible AI Governance

To effectively tackle ethical considerations and promote responsible utilization of quantum computing and GANs, enterprises must build comprehensive frameworks for AI governance. It is imperative that these frameworks incorporate ethical principles, means for ensuring compliance, and committees tasked with overseeing and assessing AI initiatives (Priscila et al., 2022). Integrating ethical issues, including but not limited to bias reduction, transparency, and accountability, is crucial in the development processes of AI (Cai et al., 2021).

Privacy-Preserving Technologies and Quantum-Safe Encryption

The successful management of privacy concerns necessitates using and integrating privacy-preserving technologies. Quantum computing and GANs can benefit from incorporating techniques like differential privacy, federated learning, and homomorphic encryption. These methodologies enable enterprises to effectively handle and analyze data while safeguarding the confidentiality of people's sensitive information, hence mitigating the potential for data breaches and privacy infringements (Sun 2023; Shafik, 2024d). To effectively mitigate the security concerns arising from the advent of quantum computing, companies must undertake a transition towards the adoption of quantum-safe encryption techniques. It is imperative to be well-informed on post-quantum cryptography advancements and revise encryption standards accordingly (He et al., 2021). Preserving sensitive information necessitates implementing measures to protect data and communication security from potential quantum attacks.

Responsible for Data Handling, Regulatory Compliance and Advocacy

To prevent privacy and security issues, it is imperative to adopt appropriate data handling procedures that effectively reduce data acquisition, retention, and sharing. It is advisable to employ anonymization or pseudonymization techniques whenever feasible to safeguard the identity of persons and mitigate the potential consequences of data breaches. Ensure adherence to the dynamic regulatory landscape of quantum computing and GANs within a given specific jurisdiction. Engage in collaborative efforts with legislators to establish ethical, privacy, and security frameworks that follow the progress of technology (He et al., 2021).

Public Awareness, Education, Collaboration, and Industry Standards

This proposal advocates for promoting public awareness and media literacy as effective measures to enable individuals to discern synthetic content produced by GANs and comprehend the ramifications of quantum computing. Educational endeavors should focus on students, professionals, and the wider public, enabling them to evaluate and constructively respond to developing technologies critically. Promote collaborative efforts among various stakeholders, encompassing scholars, organizations, and government agencies, to tackle emergent difficulties cooperatively [27]. Exchanging knowledge, implementing best practices, and gaining insights can significantly enhance the ability to identify and address hazards more efficiently (Cao et al., 2023; Shafik, 2024d).

Responsible Use, Governance, Continuous Monitoring and Vulnerability Assessment

Develop corporate rules and governance frameworks that emphasize quantum computing and GAN technologies' responsibility and ethical utilization. This statement emphasizes the need to establish unambiguous parameters for appropriate use scenarios, critically assess the ethical ramifications, and ensure adherence to established guidelines (He et al., 2021). The establishment of ethics boards or committees to oversee AI initiatives, particularly those containing sensitive data or applications with substantial social implications, should be considered. It is imperative to consistently assess the security and privacy issues associated with quantum computing and applications of GANs. Perform comprehensive vulnerability assessments and penetration testing to detect and address potential vulnerabilities (Sharma et al., 2023).

FUTURE DIRECTIONS, RECOMMENDATIONS, AND THE CONCLUSIONS

This section presents some notable future directions, lessons learned, and the conclusion.

Future Directions

These future directions encompass a range of technical, ethical, and regulatory considerations, reflecting the evolving landscape of quantum computing and GANs as they become increasingly integrated into various aspects of society and technology.

Quantum-Safe Cryptography and Quantum-Resistant Protocols

Future advancements will focus on the research and deployment of quantum-safe cryptographic methods, including lattice-based, code-based, and multivariate cryptography. Organizations and governments will transition to quantum-resistant encryption standards to protect sensitive data, financial transactions, and critical infrastructure from potential quantum attacks (Sun et al., 2023; Shafik, 2024e). Quantum-resistant digital signatures and authentication methods will also become integral components of cybersecurity.

Quantum Machine Learning and Hybrid Algorithms

Quantum machine learning will mature as researchers develop quantum algorithms that outperform classical counterparts. Hybrid quantum-classical algorithms will be designed for various applications, including optimization, drug discovery, and financial modeling (Liu et al., 2023). Quantum neural networks and quantum-enhanced reinforcement learning will emerge as key areas of exploration, offering transformative solutions for AI-driven industries. The development of a quantum internet will advance, enabling ultra-secure communication through QKD. Quantum repeaters and quantum teleportation protocols will be refined to extend the range of quantum-secured communication. Quantum networks will find applications in secure government communications, financial transactions, and sensitive data transfers, fostering trust in digital interactions (Marshall et al., 2026).

Ethical AI and Deepfake Detection Advancements, Quantum Computing and GANs for Scientific Discovery

To combat deepfake threats, ethical AI guidelines will incorporate stringent content verification standards and responsible AI practices. Advanced deepfake detection methods will leverage ML, natural language processing, and computer vision to identify manipulated content accurately (Marshall et al., 2016; Shafik, 2024f)). The ethical use of AI in content generation and dissemination will be reinforced through legislation and industry standards. Quantum computing's potential for simulating quantum systems will drive breakthroughs in scientific discovery. Quantum chemistry simulations will accelerate the discovery of novel materials, catalysts, and drug compounds with applications in renewable energy, healthcare, and materials science. Quantum-inspired algorithms will optimize supply chains, leading to more efficient logistics and resource management (Sun et al., 2023).

Privacy-Preserving AI, Data Sovereignty, Global Collaboration and Regulatory Frameworks

Privacy-preserving AI techniques will continue to evolve, offering granular control over data access and utilization. Federated learning will enable collaborative model training across distributed datasets without exposing raw data [33]. Secure multiparty computation will be applied to protect individual privacy rights while allowing insights to be derived from sensitive data sources (Management & Mining, 2005; Shafik, 2024g). Data sovereignty frameworks will grant individuals greater control over their data and its usage. International cooperation will be paramount in establishing cohesive regulatory frameworks for quantum computing and GANs. Cross-border partnerships among governments, industry consortia, and research institutions will facilitate the development of consistent ethical, privacy, and security standards. Harmonized regulations will promote responsible innovation, data protection, and secure technology deployment on a global scale (Liu et al., 2022).

Lessons Learned from the Chapter

The lessons learned from the discussion on ethical, data privacy, and security considerations in quantum computing and GANs emphasize the need for a holistic and proactive approach. By prioritizing ethics, privacy, and security, fostering collaboration, and staying adaptable in the face of evolving technology, we can navigate the complexities of these emerging fields responsibly and effectively.

- Ethical considerations should be at the forefront of technological development. As quantum computing and GANs continue to advance, it is crucial to prioritize ethical principles, transparency, fairness, and accountability to ensure responsible innovation.
- The importance of privacy cannot be overstated. Both quantum computing and GANs can potentially infringe on individuals' privacy rights. The lesson learned is that privacy protection mechanisms, such as data anonymization and encryption, must be incorporated into technology design.
- Security in the quantum computing and GANs landscape should be proactive, not reactive. With the potential for quantum attacks and advanced cyber threats, organizations must stay ahead by adopting quantum-safe encryption and continually improving security measures.
- Addressing the complex challenges of these technologies requires interdisciplinary collaboration. Ethicists, policymakers, technologists, and legal experts must collaborate to develop comprehensive solutions that balance innovation and safeguard societal interests.
- Regulations governing quantum computing and GANs need to evolve in parallel with technological advancements. Policymakers should engage with industry experts to develop adaptive regulatory frameworks that address emerging ethical, privacy, and security concerns.
- Raising public awareness about the capabilities and risks associated with quantum computing and GANs is essential. Educating individuals about deepfake threats, quantum attacks, and responsible AI use can empower them to make informed decisions and contribute to a safer digital environment.
- The chapter underscores the importance of responsible innovation. Organizations and researchers should commit to responsible AI development, ethical content creation, and secure technology deployment to mitigate potential harm.
- The global nature of the challenges and opportunities in quantum computing and GANs requires international collaboration, highlighting the need for cooperation among nations, industry leaders, and research communities to establish consistent standards and regulations.

CONCLUSION

The integration of quantum computing and GANs offers unprecedented opportunities for innovation across various domains, from scientific research to artificial intelligence. However, it also brings forth multifaceted ethical, privacy, and security considerations that demand careful and proactive attention. As we delve into the quantum era and explore the vast potential of GANs, we must prioritize ethical principles, such as transparency, fairness, and accountability, to ensure the responsible development and deployment of these technologies. Privacy protection mechanisms, robust encryption, and privacy-preserving AI techniques will be indispensable in safeguarding individuals' rights in an increasingly data-driven world. Moreover, the lessons learned underscore the necessity of interdisciplinary collaboration, adaptive regulations, and global cooperation to effectively navigate the challenges and harness the benefits of quantum computing and GANs. Through embracing ethical guidelines, staying vigilant about privacy and security, and fostering responsible innovation, we can unlock the full potential of these technologies while upholding fundamental values, promoting digital trust, and advancing toward a more secure and ethically grounded technological landscape.

REFERENCES

Abulkasim, H., Mashatan, A., & Ghose, S. (2021). Quantum-based privacy-preserving sealed-bid auction on the blockchain. *Optik (Stuttgart)*, 242, 167039. Advance online publication. DOI: 10.1016/j.ijleo.2021.167039

Agoub, A., Filippovska, Y., Schmidt, V., & Kada, M. (2019). Automatic Generation of Photorealistic Image Fillers for Privacy Enabled Urban Basemaps using Generative Adversarial Networks. *Advances in Cartography and GIScience of the ICA*, 1, 1–8. Advance online publication. DOI: 10.5194/ica-adv-1-1-2019

Arulmozhiselvan, L., & Uma, E. (2022). QKD in Cloud-Fog Computing for Personal Health Record. *Computer Systems Science and Engineering*, 43(1), 45–57. Advance online publication. DOI: 10.32604/csse.2022.022024

Bautista, P., & Inventado, P. S. (2021). Protecting Student Privacy with Synthetic Data from Generative Adversarial Networks. *Lecture Notes in Computer Science (Including Subseries Lecture Notes in Artificial Intelligence and Lecture Notes in Bioinformatics),* 12749 LNAI. https://doi.org/DOI: 10.1007/978-3-030-78270-2_11

Berry, R. A., Han, Z., Narayanan, K., Poor, H. V., Verikoukis, C., & Yagan, O. (2021). Special issue on communications and networking approaches for combating COVID-19. *Journal of Communications and Networks (Seoul)*, 23(5), 309–313. Advance online publication. DOI: 10.23919/JCN.2021.000030

Bouzeraib, W., Ghenai, A., & Zeghib, N. (2020). A Blockchain Data Balance Using a Generative Adversarial Network Approach: Application to Smart House IDS. ICAASE 2020 - Proceedings, 4th *International Conference on Advanced Aspects of Software Engineering*.https://doi.org/DOI: 10.1109/ICAASE51408.2020.9380110

Cai, Z., Xiong, Z., Xu, H., Wang, P., Li, W., & Pan, Y. (2021). Generative Adversarial Networks: A Survey Toward Private and Secure Applications. *In ACM Computing Surveys* (Vol. 54, Issue 6). https://doi.org/DOI: 10.1145/3459992

Cao, X., Sun, G., Yu, H., & Guizani, M. (2023). PerFED-GAN: Personalized Federated Learning via Generative Adversarial Networks. *IEEE Internet of Things Journal*, 10(5), 3749–3762. Advance online publication. DOI: 10.1109/JIOT.2022.3172114

Chen, J., Gan, W., Hu, M., & Chen, C. M. (2021). On the construction of a post-quantum blockchain for smart city. *Journal of Information Security and Applications*, 58, 102780. Advance online publication. DOI: 10.1016/j.jisa.2021.102780

Chen, X., Xu, S., Cao, Y., He, Y., & Xiao, K. (2023). AQRS: Anti-quantum ring signature scheme for secure epidemic control with blockchain. *Computer Networks*, 224, 109595. Advance online publication. DOI: 10.1016/j.comnet.2023.109595 PMID: 36741551

Chenna, S. (2022). Application of Generative Adversarial Networks (GANs) for Generating Synthetic Data and in Cybersecurity. SSRN *Electronic Journal*.https://doi.org/DOI: 10.2139/ssrn.4305711

Chi, H., Maduakor, U., Alo, R., & Williams, E. (2021). Integrating Deepfake Detection into Cybersecurity Curriculum. *Advances in Intelligent Systems and Computing*, 1288, 588–598. Advance online publication. DOI: 10.1007/978-3-030-63128-4_45

Deldjoo, Y., Di Noia, T., & Merra, F. A. (2021). A Survey on Adversarial Recommender Systems: From Attack/Defense Strategies to Generative Adversarial Networks. In *ACM Computing Surveys* (Vol. 54, Issue 2). https://doi.org/DOI: 10.1145/3439729

Ding, Y., Thakur, N., & Li, B. (2021). Does a GAN leave distinct model-specific fingerprints. In Proceedings of the BMVC. https://www.bmvc2021-virtualconference.com/assets/papers/0197.pdf

Du, Y., Hsieh, M. H., Liu, T., Tao, D., & Liu, N. (2021). Quantum noise protects quantum classifiers against adversaries. *Physical Review Research*, 3(2), 023153. Advance online publication. DOI: 10.1103/PhysRevResearch.3.023153

Fekri, M. N., Ghosh, A. M., & Grolinger, K. (2019). Generating energy data for machine learning with recurrent generative adversarial networks. *Energies*, 13(1), 130. Advance online publication. DOI: 10.3390/en13010130

He, C., Huang, S., Cheng, R., Tan, K. C., & Jin, Y. (2021). Evolutionary Multiobjective Optimization Driven by Generative Adversarial Networks (GANs). *IEEE Transactions on Cybernetics*, 51(6), 3129–3142. Advance online publication. DOI: 10.1109/TCYB.2020.2985081 PMID: 32365041

Jemihin, Z. B., Tan, S. F., & Chung, G. C. (2022). Attribute-Based Encryption in Securing Big Data from Post-Quantum Perspective: A Survey. *In Cryptography* (Vol. 6, Issue 3). https://doi.org/DOI: 10.3390/cryptography6030040

Jerald Nirmal Kumar, S., Ravimaran, S., & Sathish, A. (2021). Robust Security with Strong Authentication in Mobile Cloud Computing Based on Trefoil Congruity Framework. *Journal of Organizational and End User Computing*, 33(6), 1–28. Advance online publication. DOI: 10.4018/JOEUC.20211101.oa11

Kumari, S., Singh, M., Singh, R., & Tewari, H. (2022). Post-quantum cryptography techniques for secure communication in resource-constrained Internet of Things devices: A comprehensive survey. *Software, Practice & Experience*, 52(10), 2047–2076. Advance online publication. DOI: 10.1002/spe.3121

Li, K., Shi, R., Wu, M., Li, Y., & Zhang, X. (2022). A novel privacy-preserving multi-level aggregate signcryption and query scheme for Smart Grid via mobile fog computing. *Journal of Information Security and Applications*, 67, 103214. Advance online publication. DOI: 10.1016/j.jisa.2022.103214

Liu, B., Zhang, X., Shi, R., Zhang, M., & Zhang, G. (2022). SEPSI: A Secure and Efficient Privacy-Preserving Set Intersection with Identity Authentication in IoT. *Mathematics*, 10(12), 2120. Advance online publication. DOI: 10.3390/math10122120

Liu, J., Wen, J., Zhang, B., Dong, S., Tang, B., & Yu, Y. (2023). A post quantum secure multi-party collaborative signature with deterability in the Industrial Internet of Things. *Future Generation Computer Systems*, 141, 663–676. Advance online publication. DOI: 10.1016/j.future.2022.11.034

Liu, J., Yu, Y., Wang, H., & Zhang, H. (2022). Lattice-Based Self-Enhancement Authorized Accessible Privacy Authentication for Cyber-Physical Systems. *Security and Communication Networks*, 2022, 1–9. Advance online publication. DOI: 10.1155/2022/8995704

Lu, S., & Li, X. (2021). Quantum-Resistant Lightweight Authentication and Key Agreement Protocol for Fog-Based Microgrids. *IEEE Access : Practical Innovations, Open Solutions*, 9, 27588–27600. Advance online publication. DOI: 10.1109/ACCESS.2021.3058180

Ma, Y., Kashefi, E., Arapinis, M., Chakraborty, K., & Kaplan, M. (2022). QEnclave - A practical solution for secure quantum cloud computing. *NPJ Quantum Information*, 8(1), 128. Advance online publication. DOI: 10.1038/s41534-022-00612-5

Malina, L., Dzurenda, P., Ricci, S., Hajny, J., Srivastava, G., Matulevicius, R., Affia, A. A. O., Laurent, M., Sultan, N. H., & Tang, Q. (2021). Post-quantum era privacy protection for intelligent infrastructures. *IEEE Access : Practical Innovations, Open Solutions*, 9, 36038–36077. Advance online publication. DOI: 10.1109/ACCESS.2021.3062201

Management, K., & Mining, D. (2005b). Medical Knowledge Management and Data Mining in. *In Medical Informatics* (Vol. 8). https://doi.org/DOI: 10.1007/b135955

Marshall, K., Jacobsen, C. S., Schäfermeier, C., Gehring, T., Weedbrook, C., & Andersen, U. L. (2016). Continuous-variable quantum computing on encrypted data. *Nature Communications*, 7(1), 13795. Advance online publication. DOI: 10.1038/ncomms13795 PMID: 27966528

Mashatan, A., & Heintzman, D. (2021). The Complex Path to Quantum Resistance. *ACM Queue; Tomorrow's Computing Today*, 19(2), 65–92. Advance online publication. DOI: 10.1145/3466132.3466779

Masood, M., Nawaz, M., Javed, A., Nazir, T., Mehmood, A., & Mahum, R. (2021). Classification of Deepfake Videos Using Pre-trained Convolutional Neural Networks. *2021 International Conference on Digital Futures and Transformative Technologies,* ICoDT2 2021. https://doi.org/DOI: 10.1109/ICoDT252288.2021.9441519

Mendes, J., Pereira, T., Silva, F., Frade, J., Morgado, J., Freitas, C., Negrão, E., de Lima, B. F., da Silva, M. C., Madureira, A. J., Ramos, I., Costa, J. L., Hespanhol, V., Cunha, A., & Oliveira, H. P. (2023). Lung CT image synthesis using GANs. *Expert Systems with Applications*, 215, 119350. Advance online publication. DOI: 10.1016/j.eswa.2022.119350

Nukavarapu, S. K., Ayyat, M., & Nadeem, T. (2022). MirageNet - Towards a GAN-based Framework for Synthetic Network Traffic Generation. *2022 IEEE Global Communications Conference, GLOBECOM 2022 - Proceedings.*https://doi.org/DOI: 10.1109/GLOBECOM48099.2022.10001494

Nukavarapu, S. K., & Nadeem, T. (2021). Securing Edge-based IoT Networks with Semi-Supervised GANs. *2021 IEEE International Conference on Pervasive Computing and Communications Workshops and Other Affiliated Events, PerCom Workshops 2021.*https://doi.org/DOI: 10.1109/PerComWorkshops51409.2021.9431112

Patel, M., Gupta, A., Tanwar, S., & Obaidat, M. S. (2020). Trans-DF: A Transfer Learning-based end-to-end Deepfake Detector. *2020 IEEE 5th International Conference on Computing Communication and Automation,* ICCCA 2020. https://doi.org/DOI: 10.1109/ICCCA49541.2020.9250803

Priscila, S. S., Sharma, A., Vanithamani, S., Ahmad, F., Mahaveerakannan, R., Alrubaie, A. J., Jagota, V., & Singh, B. K. (2022). Risk-Based Access Control Mechanism for Internet of Vehicles Using Artificial Intelligence. *Security and Communication Networks*, 2022, 1–13. Advance online publication. DOI: 10.1155/2022/3379843

Raveendran, R., & Raj, E. D. (2023). Deep Generative Models Under GAN: Variants, Applications, and Privacy Issues. *Lecture Notes in Networks and Systems*, 494, 93–105. Advance online publication. DOI: 10.1007/978-981-19-4863-3_9

Raya, J. E., Yahya, A. S., & Ahmad, E. K. (2023). Protection from A Quantum Computer Cyber-Attack. Technium. *Technium*, 5, 1–12. Advance online publication. DOI: 10.47577/technium.v5i.8293

Sarkar, S. (2023). Quantum Machine Learning: A Review. *International Journal for Research in Applied Science and Engineering Technology*, 11(3), 352–354. Advance online publication. DOI: 10.22214/ijraset.2023.49421

Shafik, W. (2024a). *An Overview of Computational Modeling and Simulations in Wireless Communication Systems. Computational Modeling and Simulation of Advanced Wireless Communication Systems*. CRC Press., DOI: 10.1201/9781003457428-2

Shafik, W. (2024b). Artificial Intelligence and Machine Learning with Cyber Ethics for the Future World. In *Future Communication Systems Using Artificial Intelligence, Internet of Things and Data Science* (pp. 110–130). CRC Press., DOI: 10.1201/9781032648309-9

Shafik, W. (2024c). Data Privacy and Security Safeguarding Customer Information in ChatGPT Systems. In *Revolutionizing the Service Industry With OpenAI Models* (pp. 52–86). IGI Global., DOI: 10.4018/979-8-3693-1239-1.ch003

Shafik, W. (2024d). *Deep Learning Impacts in the Field of Artificial Intelligence. Deep Learning Concepts in Operations Research*. CRC Press., DOI: 10.1201/9781003433309-2

Shafik, W. (2024e). Ethical Use of Machine Learning Techniques in Smart Cities. In *Ethical Artificial Intelligence in Power Electronics* (pp. 21–47). CRC Press., DOI: 10.1201/9781032648323-3

Shafik, W. (2024f). Shaping the Next Generation Smart City Ecosystem: An Investigation on the Requirements, Applications, Architecture, Security and Privacy, and Open Research Questions. In Majumdar, S., Kandpal, V., & Anthopoulos, L. G. (Eds.), *Smart Cities. S.M.A.R.T. Environments*. Springer., DOI: 10.1007/978-3-031-59846-3_1

Shafik, W. (2024g). Toward a More Ethical Future of Artificial Intelligence and Data Science. In *The Ethical Frontier of AI and Data Analysis* (pp. 362–388). IGI Global., DOI: 10.4018/979-8-3693-2964-1.ch022

Sharma, B., Sharma, L., Lal, C., & Roy, S. (2023). Anomaly based network intrusion detection for IoT attacks using deep learning technique. *Computers & Electrical Engineering*, 107, 108626. Advance online publication. DOI: 10.1016/j.compeleceng.2023.108626

Singh, S. K., El Azzaoui, A., Salim, M. M., & Park, J. H. (2020). Quantum Communication Technology for Future ICT - Review. *Journal of Information Processing Systems*, 16(6). Advance online publication. DOI: 10.3745/JIPS.03.0154

Sun, H., Zhu, T., Zhang, Z., Jin, D., Xiong, P., & Zhou, W. (2023). Adversarial Attacks Against Deep Generative Models on Data: A Survey. *IEEE Transactions on Knowledge and Data Engineering*, 35(4), 3367–3388. Advance online publication. DOI: 10.1109/TKDE.2021.3130903

Tinsley, P., Czajka, A., & Flynn, P. J. (2022). Haven't I Seen You Before? Assessing Identity Leakage in Synthetic Irises. *2022 IEEE International Joint Conference on Biometrics,* IJCB 2022. https://doi.org/DOI: 10.1109/IJCB54206.2022.10007948

Wang, C., Kon, W. Y., Ng, H. J., & Lim, C. C. W. (2022). Experimental symmetric private information retrieval with measurement-device-independent quantum network. *Light, Science & Applications*, 11(1), 268. Advance online publication. DOI: 10.1038/s41377-022-00959-6 PMID: 36100587

Wang, K., Deng, N., & Li, X. (2023). An Efficient Content Popularity Prediction of Privacy Preserving Based on Federated Learning and Wasserstein GAN. *IEEE Internet of Things Journal*, 10(5), 3786–3798. Advance online publication. DOI: 10.1109/JIOT.2022.3176360

Xu, Y., Wang, L., Wang, C., & Zhu, H. (2022). Effective Agent Quantum Private Data Query against Malicious Joint Attack with Blind Quantum Computing. *International Journal of Theoretical Physics*, 61(4), 106. Advance online publication. DOI: 10.1007/s10773-022-05104-y

Yang, J., Xiao, S., Li, A., Lan, G., & Wang, H. (2021). Detecting fake images by identifying potential texture difference. *Future Generation Computer Systems*, 125, 127–135. Advance online publication. DOI: 10.1016/j.future.2021.06.043

Zhang, X., Zhu, X., Wang, J., Bao, W., & Yang, L. T. (2022). DANCE: Distributed Generative Adversarial Networks with Communication Compression. *ACM Transactions on Internet Technology*, 22(2), 1–32. Advance online publication. DOI: 10.1145/3458929

Zhao, A., Jiang, N., Wang, C., Liu, S., & Qiu, K. (2023). Synchronization Optimization of Chaotic Laser Based on Generative Adversarial Network. *Guangxue Xuebao. Acta Optica Sinica*, 43(1). Advance online publication. DOI: 10.3788/AOS220994

Zhou, J., Chen, Y., Shen, C., & Zhang, Y. (2022). Property Inference Attacks Against GANs.

ENDNOTES

1 https://www.ibm.com/topics/quantum-computing

2 https://en.wikipedia.org/wiki/Generative_adversarial_network

3 https://www.oaic.gov.au/privacy/your-privacy-rights/your-personal-information/what-is-privacy

4 https://www.ibm.com/topics/machine-learning

5 https://gdpr.eu/what-is-gdpr/

6 https://www.nist.gov/

7 https://www.deep-nude.ai/

8 https://mitsloan.mit.edu/ideas-made-to-matter/deepfakes-explained

9 https://en.wikipedia.org/wiki/Edmond_de_Belamy

Chapter 8
Quantum Networks and AI Technologies for Electric Vehicle Charging

V. M. Hiriharan
Sri Ramakrishna Engineering College, India

R. Shanmugasundaram
Sri Ramakrishna Engineering College, India

R. Hari Prasath
Sri Ramakrishna Engineering College, India

M. Karthikeyan
Sri Ramakrishna Engineering College, India

ABSTRACT

This paper explores static WPT systems tailored for electric vehicle (EV) charging without relying on plug-in connections. Static transmission of power wirelessly permits the electrical energy to be transferred from stationary energy source for a vehicle parked over a charging pad, offering convenience and doing away with the requirement for physical cords. This study focuses on understanding the fundamental principles of static WPT, particularly magnetic resonance and inductive coupling, which are essential for efficient energy transfer and even efficiently charging with help of quantum technologies. Various configurations and topologies of static WPT systems are investigated, taking into account factors such as power transfer efficiency, alignment tolerance, and electromagnetic compatibility. Additionally, the paper examines critical components such as power electronics, coil design, and control strategies, highlighting their significance in optimizing system performance and en-

DOI: 10.4018/979-8-3373-1657-4.ch008

suring safe charging operations. Challenges such as efficiency enhancement, foreign object detection, and standardization are addressed, alongside potential solutions and ongoing research endeavors. This paper contributes valuable insights into the creation and application of static transmission of power wirelessly for charging the EV, laying the groundwork for further advancements in this vital technology.

I. INTRODUCTION

The advent of electric vehicles (EVs) has revolutionized the automotive industry, offering a promising solution to lessen reliance on fossil fuels and minimize greenhouse gas emissions. However, the widespread adoption of EVs is contingent upon the availability of efficient and convenient charging infrastructure. Traditional plug-in charging systems necessitate physical connections between the vehicle and the charging station, posing challenges such as wear and tear, limited flexibility, and susceptibility to weather conditions. To overcome these limitations, static transmission of power wirelessly emerged as viable alternative to charging the EV. Static WPT permits the transmission of energy into stationary source of energy to the vehicle without connecting the plug, thereby enhancing practicality and user experience. This method involves the deployment of charging pads embedded in parking spaces or designated locations, allowing EVs to charge seamlessly while parked. The primary principle underlying static WPT is electromagnetic induction, facilitated by magnetic resonance or inductive coupling between coils installed in the charging pad and the vehicle. When the EV is parked over the charging pad, the coils resonate at the same frequency, inducing an alternating magnetic field that transfers power to the vehicle's receiver part. This source is subsequently transformed into energy power for charging the vehicle's battery. Static WPT offers several advantages over conventional plug-in charging systems. Firstly, it eliminates the need for physical connectors, reducing wear and tear on charging ports and cables. Additionally, static WPT enables automated and contactless charging, enhancing user convenience and promoting EV adoption. Moreover, the flexibility of static WPT allows for seamless integration into existing infrastructure, such as parking lots, streets, and garages, without significant modifications. In this context, this paper aims to provide a comprehensive overview of static WPT technology for EV charging, focusing on its principles, system architecture, components, challenges, and potential applications. By elucidating the fundamental concepts and recent advancements in static WPT, this study seeks to contribute to the understanding and development of efficient and reliable charging solutions for electric vehicles with quantum networks and AI technologies.

A. WPT Methods

Since concept of WPT became popular, scientists and engineers have devised a variety of ways to achieve it. Although the majority of these trials failed or produced impractical results, a handful of them yielded good results. These tried-and-true methods for wireless power transfer each have their own set of benefits, drawbacks, and features (M. Zhang et al., 2021; Madani et al., 2020; Y. Zhang et al., 2020). Only a few of these strategies are used in the design of wireless chargers. Other approaches, however, offer their own set of applications and advantages.

To make things easier to grasp, these approaches are divided into three categories: transmission distance, maximum power, and manner of power transfer.

1. Inductive Coupling Systems:

Inductive coupling-based static WPT systems utilize two coils, a transmitting coil is fixed on the pad and a receiving coil is installed in the EV. When the vehicle is parked over the charging pad, the alternating current in the transmitter coil generates a magnetic field and receiver part induces voltage through reciprocal inductance. This potential difference is then transformed and used to charge the vehicle's battery. Inductive coupling systems are commonly used in static WPT applications due to their simplicity and reliability.

2. Resonant Inductive Coupling Systems:

Resonant inductive coupling systems enhance the efficiency and range of power transfer compared to traditional inductive coupling. These systems utilize resonant circuits in both the transmitting and receiving coils, allowing them to operate at a specific frequency where impedance matching occurs. This resonance enables more efficient power transfer over longer distances, making resonant inductive coupling systems suitable for applications requiring higher power levels or larger air gaps between the charging pad and the vehicle.

3. Capacitive Coupling Systems:

Capacitive coupling-based static WPT systems utilize electric fields to transfer power between the charging pad and the vehicle. These systems employ capacitors to store and transfer electrical energy between the transmitter and receiver circuits. Capacitive coupling systems are less common in EV charging applications compared to inductive coupling systems, primarily due to their lower efficiency and susceptibility to environmental factors such as moisture and temperature variations.

4. Magnetic Resonance Coupling Systems:

Magnetic resonance coupling systems leverage the phenomenon of magnetic resonance to achieve efficient power transfer over longer distances and with greater alignment flexibility. These systems typically consist of a coil for transmission in the pad and coil for receiving in the EV, both adjusted to have the same frequency of resonance. By maintaining resonance in the coils' vicinity, magnetic coupling of resonance systems can transfer energy efficiently even when the car isn't linking up with the charging part exactly, offering improved convenience and usability.

Each type of static WPT system has its advantages and limitations, depending on factors such as power transfer efficiency, alignment tolerance, cost, and scalability. By understanding the characteristics and applications of these different types, researchers and engineers can develop tailored solutions to meet the diverse needs of EV charging infrastructure.

Figure 1. Methods of WPT

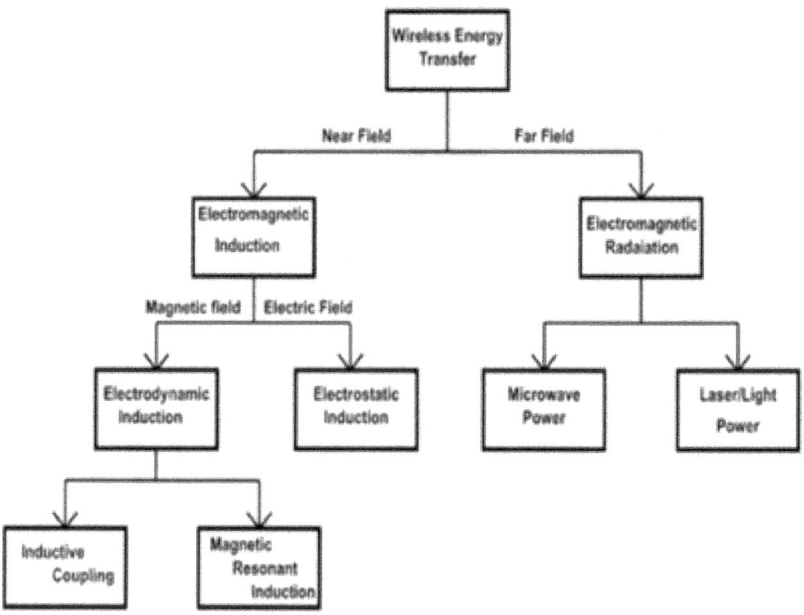

B. Comparision of WPT Methods

In the realm of static transmission of power wirelessly for vehicles energized by electric, several types exist, each with distinct characteristics and advantages (Sagar et al., 2023). Comparison of the main types, highlighting their differences in efficiency, range, alignment tolerance, and suitability for EV charging applications:

1. Inductive Coupling Systems:

Efficiency: In Inductive coupling the system typically offers moderate to high efficiency, especially in close proximity charging scenarios.

Range: They have relatively limited range due to the magnetic field's rapid decay with distance, making them suitable for short-range applications.

Alignment Tolerance: They require exact alignment of the coils in the transmitter and receiver for efficient power transfer, necessitating careful parking positioning.

Suitability for EV Charging: Inductive coupling systems are commonly used in EV charging applications where precise alignment can be ensured, such as home charging stations and designated parking spots.

2. Inductive Coupling resonance Systems:

Efficiency: Inductive Coupling resonance systems can achieve higher efficiency compared to traditional inductive coupling systems, especially over longer distances.

Range: They offer improved range capabilities due to resonance, enabling more efficient power transfer over larger air gaps.

Alignment Tolerance: They have moderate alignment tolerance, allowing for some misalignment between the transmitter and receiver coils without significant efficiency loss.

Suitability for EV Charging: Resonant inductive coupling systems are suitable for various EV charging scenarios, including public charging infrastructure and wireless charging lanes, where moderate alignment tolerance is beneficial.

3. Capacitive Coupling Systems:

Efficiency: Capacitive coupling systems generally exhibit lower efficiency compared to inductive coupling systems, particularly over larger distances.

Range: They have limited range capabilities and are typically suitable for short-range applications.

Alignment Tolerance: They may offer some degree of alignment flexibility due to the nature of electric field coupling, but still require relatively close proximity for efficient power transfer.

Suitability for EV Charging: Capacitive coupling systems are less commonly used in EV charging applications due to their lower efficiency and sensitivity to environmental factors, but they may find niche applications in specific scenarios where other methods are not feasible.

4. Magnetic Resonance Coupling Systems:

Efficiency: Magnetic resonance coupling systems can achieve high efficiency over moderate to long distances, making them suitable for various EV charging scenarios.

Range: They offer superior range capabilities compared to other methods, enabling efficient power transfer over larger air gaps and with greater alignment flexibility.

Alignment Tolerance: They have high alignment tolerance, allowing for efficient power transfer even with considerable misalignment in between the coils of the transmitter and receiver.

Suitability in EV Charging: Magnetic resonance coupling systems are well-suited for diverse EV charging applications, including dynamic charging on roads and highways, as well as applications requiring seamless integration into existing infrastructure with minimal alignment constraints.

II. IMPLEMENTATION OF MAGNECTIC RESONANCE WPT

Magnetic resonance offers significant advantages in terms of efficiency and alignment flexibility, making it an attractive choice for enhancing the performance of static WPT systems (Liu et al., 2017). The study outlines the key components and design considerations involved in implementing magnetic resonance-based WPT, including coil design, resonance frequency selection, and power electronics. Furthermore, practical aspects such as system integration, electromagnetic compatibility, and safety standards are addressed to ensure reliable operation and compliance with regulatory requirements. A study illustrating the implementation of magnetic resonance in a static WPT prototype for EV charging is also presented, highlighting the practical challenges and solutions encountered during the development process. Through this implementation-focused approach, this paper aims to provide valuable insights and guidelines for researchers and engineers seeking to deploy magnetic resonance technology in static WPT systems for EV applications (D'Orazio et al., 2019).

The implemented Magnetic Resonance system is as follows
the Block-Diagram.

Figure 2. Block Diagram of MCR

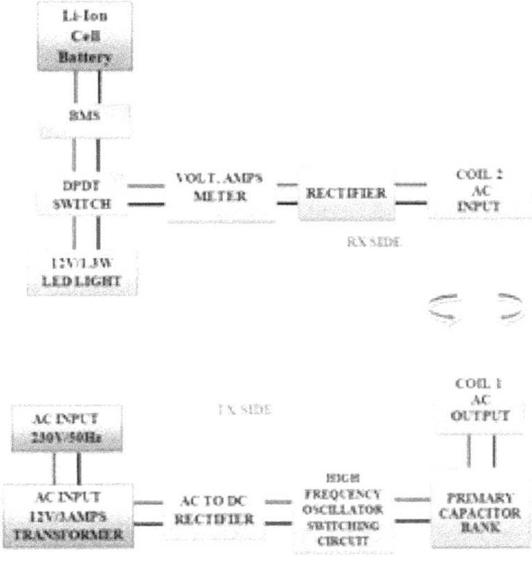

III. SPECIFICATIONS

Table 1. Specifications

SI.NO	Specifications	Rating
1	Input supply	230V AC
2	Transformer	12-0V,1A
3	Royer-oscillator circuit	600W
4	Capacitor Bank	0.33uF,630VAC-1200V DC,50Hz
5	Led Strip (1m)	24W,2A,12V
6	Transmitting coil	5.5m,2.5sqmm,28ohm Copper wire
7	Receiving coil	5.5m,1.5sqmm,87ohm Copper wire
8	Lithium-ion Battery	3.7V,4300mA*3
9	Output supply	12V,1A

Circular coil structures play a crucial role in transmission of power wireless based on magnetic resonance, especially in static applications such as electric vehicle (EV) charging. These coils are integral components that enable efficient energy transfer through the phenomenon of magnetic resonance.

Circular Coil Structure:

A circular coil consists of wire wound in a circular or spiral pattern, forming a loop with a circular cross-section. These coils are typically made of copper or other conductive materials with low electrical resistance to minimize power losses during energy transfer. Circular coil structures are preferred in magnetic resonance-based WPT systems due to their ability to generate strong and uniform magnetic fields, essential for efficient power transfer.

Operation Principle:

In magnetic resonance-based WPT systems, two circular coils are employed: coil of transmitter and coil of receiver. When a sinusoidal current is passed to the coil of transmitter, it generates a magnetic field that oscillates at a specific frequency determined by the applied voltage and coil properties. This oscillating magnetic field induces an alternating voltage in the receiver coil through electromagnetic induction.

Diagram:

Figure 3. Circular Coil

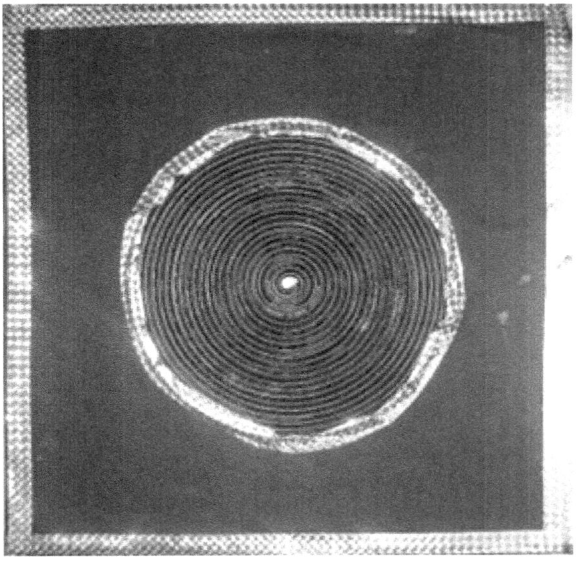

Advantages of Circular Coil Structures:

1. Uniform Magnetic Field Distribution: Circular coil structures produce a more uniform magnetic field compared to other coil shapes, ensuring efficient power transfer over a larger area.
2. Alignment Tolerance: Circular coils offer better alignment tolerance, allowing for slight misalignments between the transmitter and receiver coils without significant loss in power transfer efficiency.
3. Compact Form Factor: Circular coil structures can be designed to occupy minimal space, making them suitable for integration into compact EV charging pads or other WPT infrastructure

In summary, circular coil structures are fundamental components in magnetic resonance-based WPT systems, enabling efficient and reliable energy transfer for various applications, including static EV charging. Their design and configuration are essential to maximizing the transfer of power efficiency and alignment tolerance, contributing to the advancement of wireless charging technology.

IV. CIRCUIT DIAGRAM

Figure 4. Circuit Diagram of MCR

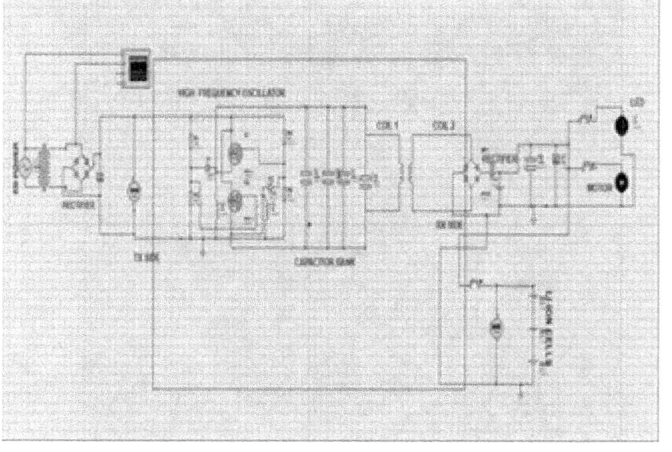

Components description:

Transformer:

The Transformer 12-0V 1A, commonly known as a step-down transformer, is a crucial component in electrical circuits used for converting higher voltage to lower voltage levels. Its primary function is to step down the input voltage from 12 volts to 0 volts (or ground) with an output current capacity of 1 ampere. Structurally, it typically consists of two coils wound around a common magnetic core. The primary coil, connected to the input voltage source, induces a varying magnetic field when alternating current (AC) flows through it. This changing magnetic field then induces a voltage across the secondary coil, which is connected to the load. By varying the number of turns in each coil, the transformer can adjust the voltage ratio between the primary and secondary coils, thereby stepping down the voltage.

Royer Oscillator Circuit:

A Royer oscillator, also known as a flip-flop or Boucherot cell oscillator, is a type of electronic oscillator circuit commonly used in power supplies and inverters. It comprises several key components, including two transistors, usually bipolar junction transistors (BJTs), coupled with a transformer. The circuit operates by utilizing positive feedback to produce oscillations.

At the heart of the Royer oscillator are the two transistors, typically configured in a symmetric arrangement. These transistors alternate conducting states due to the feedback from the transformer. During operation, one transistor turns on while the other turns off. This action results in the creation of a changing magnetic field in the transformer's core, inducing a voltage in the secondary winding.

The transformer plays a crucial role in the Royer oscillator's operation by providing the necessary energy transfer between the primary and secondary windings. It allows the circuit to efficiently convert DC input voltage into an oscillating AC output. The transformer's design is essential for achieving the desired frequency and voltage output. Capacitors and inductors are also incorporated into the circuit to control the oscillation frequency and stability. These components help tune the oscillator to the desired operating frequency and ensure proper phase relationships between the various circuit elements. In terms of working conditions, the Royer oscillator requires a stable DC power supply to operate efficiently. It also necessitates careful design and component selection to achieve desired performance characteristics, such as frequency stability and output power. Additionally, thermal considerations are crucial, especially for high-power applications, to ensure reliable operation and prevent overheating of the components.

Capacitor Bank:

A capacitor bank is designed to improve power factor correction and enhance the efficiency and stability of the grid. Structurally, a capacitor bank comprises multiple individual capacitors connected in parallel or series, depending on the specific requirements of the application. These capacitors are often constructed with high-quality dielectric materials to ensure optimal performance and durability under varying electrical conditions. In operation, a capacitor bank functions by storing electrical energy in an electric field when connected to a power source. During periods of high electrical demand or when reactive power needs to be compensated, the capacitors discharge rapidly, releasing the stored energy into the system. This discharge helps to balance reactive power, thus improving power factor and reducing losses in the transmission and distribution network.

Led Strip:

A LED strip is a flexible circuit board populated with LEDs that emit bright, colorful light. The strip typically consists of several key components. Mounted onto this board are individual LED chips, which can be of various colors such as red, green, blue, or white, depending on the desired lighting effect. These LEDs are often arranged in a closely spaced pattern along the length of the strip, providing uniform illumination.

Lithium-Ion-Battery:

Lithium-ion batteries (LIBs) comprise several key components essential for their operation. Typically, lithium metal oxides such as lithium cobalt oxide, lithium iron phosphorus, or lithium manganese oxide make up the cathode which serves as the site for extraction of lithium-ion during discharge. Paired with the cathode is the anode, often constructed from graphite or silicon-based materials, which hosts lithium ions during charging. Separating the cathode and anode is the electrolyte, a solution typically containing lithium salts dissolved in organic solvents, facilitating the movement of lithium ions between electrodes. The separator, typically a porous polymer membrane, physically separates the electrodes to prevent short circuits while allowing ion flow. Additionally, current collectors, usually made of aluminum for the cathode and copper for the anode, facilitate electron transfer between the electrodes and external circuit. Finally, the battery's casing provides mechanical support and safety features, often made of materials like aluminum or steel with insulating coatings. These components collectively enable the reversible electrochemical reactions that power a wide array of portable electronic devices and electric vehicles.

V. FACTORS AFFECTING THE POWER TRANSFER

Wireless power transfer (WPT) systems transmit without the requirement for physical connections, electrical energy can flow from a power source to an electrical load. The efficiency and effectiveness of power transmission in a WPT system depend on several factors, including:

1. Distance between the coils: The distance between the side of transmitter part and the part of the receiver significantly affects power transmission. As distance increases, the electromagnetic field strength decreases, leading to a reduction in power transfer efficiency (Liu et al., 2014).
2. Alignment and orientation: Proper alignment and the part of transmitters and part of receiver's orientation coils are crucial for efficient power transfer. Misalignment can result in decreased coupling between the coils, leading to energy losses and reduced power transmission efficiency.
3. Operating frequency: The operating frequency of the WPT system affects its performance. Higher frequencies typically allow for more efficient power transfer over shorter distances, while lower frequencies may provide better penetration through obstacles but at the cost of efficiency.

4. Transmitter and receiver coil design: The effectiveness of power transmission is greatly influenced by the architecture and design of the transmitter and receiver coils (Liu & Chen, 2017). Factors such as coil size, shape, number of turns, and material properties can impact the coupling between the coils and overall system efficiency.
5. Coupling coefficient: The effectiveness of energy transfer is determined by the coupling coefficient between the part of transmitter and receiver coil. Better alignment and closer spacing between the coils are indicated by a greater coupling coefficient, which leads to more effective power transfer.
6. Impedance matching: To optimize power transfer, match the impedance of the transmitter's part and reception circuits to maximize power transfer efficiency is critical. Poor impedance matching can lead to reflection losses and reduced power transmission efficiency (Masuda et al., 2017).
7. Interference and environmental factors: External electromagnetic interference (EMI), such as electromagnetic radiation from nearby electronic devices or metal objects, can disrupt power transmission and reduce efficiency. Environmental factors such as humidity, temperature, and atmospheric conditions can also affect the performance of the WPT system.
8. Power source characteristics: The characteristics of the power source, such as voltage, current, and waveform, influence power transmission efficiency. Using a stable and well-regulated power source can help optimize power transfer in a WPT system.
9. Efficiency of power conversion: Efficiency losses happen when electrical power is transformed into electromagnetic signals for transmission and back again into electrical energy at the receiving end. Improving the efficiency of power conversion processes can increase overall power transmission efficiency (Pathmanathan et al., 2019).
10. Safety and regulatory considerations: Compliance with safety standards and regulations governing electromagnetic radiation, power levels, and interference is essential for the safe and reliable operation of WPT systems.

VI. QUANTUM NETWORKS AND AI IN EV CHARGING

Quantum battery technology was first proposed in a seminal paper published by Alicki and Fannes in 2012. It was hypothesized that quantum sources, such as entanglement, could be used to significantly speed up the charging process of a battery by simultaneously charging all the collective battery cells (Gyhm et al., 2022; Yang et al., 2022). Analysts say that results are far-reaching which the suggestions of quantum charging can go well past electric cars and customer hardware.

VII. SNAPSHOT OF HARDWARE

Figure 5. Full Project Setup

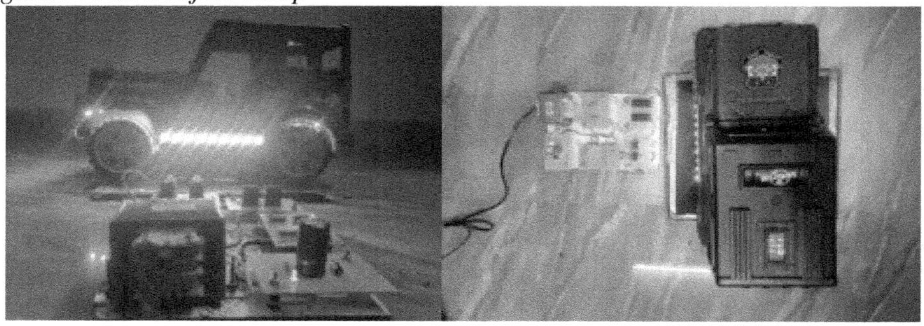

Figure 6. Transmitting Coil and Receiving Coil

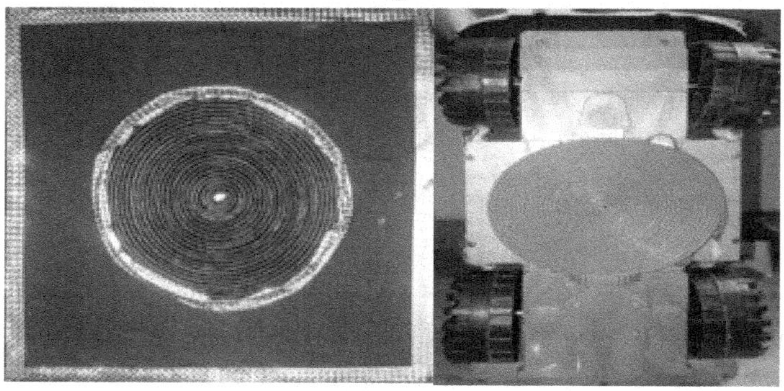

VIII. EXPERIMENT RESULTS

The above section provides you the structure and Prototype of the project. In our experimental demonstration of wireless power transfer, we have showcased the remarkable efficiency and efficacy of a circular coil structure. Unlike other designs, the circular coil configuration we employed exhibits unparalleled performance in transmitting power wirelessly. This innovative structure guarantees a more stable and dependable connection while also improving power transfer efficiency between the transmitter and receiver. Through meticulous experimentation and analysis, we have validated the superiority of the circular coil design, advantages has opened the door for developments in transmission of electrical power wirelessly technology. We have Implemented this and got these readings; the below table provides you with the Output Power and Airgap varied Output of charging a battery.

Table 2. Results

SI.NO	Voltage(V)	Current (mA)	Distance(cm)
1	7.1	0	12
2	13	0.113	7.5
3	13.3	0.22	7
4	13.3	0.28	6.5
5	13.8	0.37	6
6	13.9	0.42	5.5
7	14.2	0.42	5
8	14.3	0.45	4.5
9	14.4	0.48	4
10	14.6	0.566	3
11	14.5	0.62	2
12	14.5	0.65	1

Charging Methods:

The considering the battery safety and charging 0.5C rate is Efficient and good for battery life

IX. CONCLUSION

In conclusion, this paper has explored the wireless power transfer (WPT), focusing particularly on the influential factors such as air gap, circular coil structure, and frequency. Through meticulous analysis and experimentation, it becomes clear that these factors are essential to the performance and efficiency of WPT systems.

Regarding the air gap, our findings underscore the importance of minimizing this distance to increase the effectiveness of power transfer. By reducing air gap, we can mitigate energy losses and improve the entire performance of transmission of electrical power wirelessly. Additionally, we have demonstrated that optimizing the circular coil structure significantly contributes to enhancing the coupling of magnetic resonance between the transmitter part and receiver part, thereby augmenting power transfer efficiency.

Moreover, our investigation into the frequency dependency of WPT systems has revealed intriguing insights. We have observed that the resonant frequency of the system profoundly impacts its performance, with resonance alignment leading to optimal power transfer. Fine-tuning the frequency parameters can thus yield substantial improvements in WPT efficiency.

REFERENCES

D'Orazio, R., Carli, R., & Turchetti, C. (2019). Design and implementation of a wireless charging system for electric vehicles. *Released on July 3, 2019*.

Gyhm, J.-Y., Šafránek, D., & Rosa, D. (2022). Quantum charging advantage cannot be extensive without global operations. *Physical Review Letters*, 128(14), 140501. DOI: 10.1103/PhysRevLett.128.140501 PMID: 35476489

Liu, F., Chu, M. C., & Ho, D. W. C. (2014). Evaluation of wireless power transfer systems for electric vehicle charging. *Released on September 19, 2014*.

Liu, F., Yang, Y., Jiang, D., Ruan, X., & Chen, X. (2017). Modeling and optimization of magnetically coupled resonant wireless power transfer system with varying spatial scales. *IEEE Transactions on Power Electronics*, 32(4), 3240–3250. DOI: 10.1109/TPEL.2016.2581840

Liu, Z., & Chen, Z. D. (2018). New wireless power transfer systems against misalignments between transmitters and receivers. *2018 18th International Symposium on Antenna Technology and Applied Electromagnetics (ANTEM)*, 1-2. DOI: 10.1109/ANTEM.2018.8572886

Madani, S., Roshandel, A., & Safavieh, S. E. (2020). Wireless charging technology for electric vehicles: A comprehensive review. *Released on March 9, 2020*.

Masuda, S., Hirose, T., Akihara, Y., Kuroki, N., Numa, M., & Hashimoto, M. (2017). Impedance matching in magnetic-coupling-resonance wireless power transfer for small implantable devices. *2017 IEEE Wireless Power Transfer Conference (WPTC)*, 1-3. DOI: 10.1109/WPT.2017.7953839

Pathmanathan, M., Nie, S., Yakop, N., & Lehn, P. (2019). Efficiency improvement of a wireless power transfer system using a receiver side voltage doubling rectifier. *2019 21st European Conference on Power Electronics and Applications (EPE '19 ECCE Europe),* P.1-P.8. DOI: 10.23919/EPE.2019.8915022

Sagar, A., Kashyap, A., Nasab, M. A., Padmanaban, S., Bertoluzzo, M., Kumar, A., & Blaabjerg, F. (2023). A comprehensive review of the recent development of wireless power transfer technologies for electric vehicle charging systems. *IEEE Access : Practical Innovations, Open Solutions*, 11, 83703–83751. DOI: 10.1109/ACCESS.2023.3300475

Yang, J., Chen, G., Han, T., Zhang, Q., Zhang, Y.-H., Jiang, L., Lyu, B., Li, H., Watanabe, K., Taniguchi, T., Shi, Z., Senthil, T., Zhang, Y., Wang, F., & Ju, L. (2022). Spectroscopy signatures of electron correlations in a trilayer graphene/hBN moiré superlattice. *Science*, 375(6586), 1295–1299. Advance online publication. DOI: 10.1126/science.abg3036 PMID: 35298267

Zhang, M., Gao, H., & Wu, Z. (2021). Wireless charging for electric vehicles. *Released on March 2, 2021*.

Zhang, Y., Liu, S., & Xu, W. (2020). Wireless charging for electric vehicles: Opportunities and challenges. *Released on November 27, 2020*.

Chapter 9

Quantum AI-Inspired Blockchain-Assisted Crowdsourced Energy Systems

D. Mohanapriya
https://orcid.org/0000-0001-5668-1085
Manakula Vinayagar Institute of Technology, India

R. Indumathi
https://orcid.org/0000-0003-0411-1376
Manakula Vinayagar Institute of Technology, India

K. Subha
Surya Group of Institutions, India

K. Nandhini
Manakula Vinayagar Institute of Technology, India

ABSTRACT

The Quantum-AI Inspired Blockchain-Assisted Crowdsourced Energy Systems is to integrate cutting-edge technologies like blockchain, AI, and quantum computing to completely transform the production, distribution, and consumption of energy. The objective of this system is to improve energy efficiency, dependability, and sustainability by utilising blockchain's decentralised structure to establish a safe and transparent energy transaction platform. Crowdsourcing energy from different renewable sources would be made possible by the proposed system, enabling people and communities to contribute to and profit from a shared energy pool. The system

DOI: 10.4018/979-8-3373-1657-4.ch009

aims to produce a more resilient and adaptable energy infrastructure that can satisfy the changing needs of modern society through this creative combination of technology. We provide a blockchain-driven spatial crowdsourcing platform where participants validate or invalidate task accuracy. In order to promote correct spatial information collection, all participants get rewards based on both spatial and non-spatial reward components.

I. INTRODUCTION:

Quantum artificial intelligence, which consolidates the force of quantum figuring with man-made reasoning, remains as a momentous headway in innovation. Using the essentials of quantum mechanics, quantum PCs are fit for handling information in manners that conventional PCs can't match. This permits simulated intelligence calculations to work at uncommon velocities, handling multifaceted issues that were once viewed as difficult to address. Quantum registering generally uses the standards of superposition and snare to do calculations. Not at all like traditional pieces, which are parallel and must be either 0 or 1, can quantum bits (qubits) exist in various states at the same time. This innate parallelism empowers quantum PCs to investigate various potential outcomes simultaneously, essentially accelerating calculation times for explicit undertakings. In old style processing, a bit is restricted to being either in state 0 or state 1. Be that as it may, in quantum registering, a qubit can all the while exist in states 0, 1, or any blend of both, because of the property of superposition. This capacity permits quantum PCs to deal with a huge range of potential outcomes on the double.

Ensnarement is an exceptional peculiarity where qubits become interconnected so that the condition of one qubit straightforwardly impacts the condition of another, no matter what the distance between them. This interconnectedness permits quantum PCs to tackle complex issues all the more effectively by empowering quick data sharing across qubits. Quantum processing and man-made reasoning (computer based intelligence) are two of the most groundbreaking advancements within recent memory. Separately, each holds the commitment of upsetting ventures, improving computational power, and tackling complex issues with exceptional speed and precision. Nonetheless, when joined with blockchain innovation, the potential intensifies essentially, offering a powerful and secure system for the up and coming age of computational progressions.(Benedetti et al.,2018)

The system guarantees the security of spatial data and the preservation of privacy. We also assessed the system's efficiency, showing a 40% improvement in information accuracy and a 30% decrease in the minimal amount of time needed to examine reports. In contrast to the dispersed and centralised crowdsourcing systems in use today, our suggested system employs a consensus-based methodology to guarantee report accuracy while protecting user anonymity. Through the integration of cutting-edge technologies like blockchain, artificial intelligence (AI), and quantum computing, the Quantum-AI Inspired Blockchain-Assisted Crowdsourced Energy System represents a paradigm shift in the production, distribution, and consumption of energy. Complex optimisation issues pertaining to energy distribution and grid management can be resolved by quantum computing, which makes use of qubits and concepts like superposition and entanglement.

This entails precisely estimating energy use, balancing loads to avoid blackouts, and optimising energy routing. AI examines enormous volumes of data from smart meters and Internet of Things devices to find inefficiencies and suggest optimisations through predictive analytics, demand forecasting, and real-time decision-making. Artificial intelligence (AI) models ensure an effective and responsive energy system by continuously improving predictions and adapting to changing situations. The decentralised ledger of blockchain technology guarantees the safe, open, and unchangeable recording of energy transactions. Blockchain decreases transaction costs, eliminates the need for middlemen, and promotes transparency and trust by logging transactions in a distributed ledger that is available to all users. Efficiency is increased by smart contracts, which automate energy transfers based on preset criteria. Energy from a variety of renewable sources, including residential installations, can be crowdsourced to encourage the use of green energy and enable consumers to become producers. With blockchain protecting transactions, AI anticipating energy demands, and quantum computing optimising distribution, the system dynamically controls and optimises energy flow. Energy prices are adjusted via smart contracts according to supply and demand. The suggested solution uses blockchain for safe transactions, data analysis to forecast consumption trends, and energy collection from many sources. Real-time optimisation and effective modifications are ensured by AI and quantum computing. Through the blockchain network, consumers may trade excess energy and take greater control over their energy output and consumption. This cooperative strategy encourages the use of renewable energy sources and gives customers the power to support the transition to sustainable energy. The system's goal is to integrate various technologies in order to build a sustainable, resilient energy infrastructure that can satisfy the changing demands of the modern world. (Khoshaman et al., 2019)

1.1 The Integration of AI and Quantum Computing

Artificial intelligence with its capacity to learn, adjust, and simply decide, has proactively taken critical steps in different fields. Not with standing, the incorporation with quantum processing vows to drive these limits further. Quantum artificial intelligence intends to upgrade AI calculations, enhance dynamic cycles, and tackle complex advancement issues all the more proficiently.

Figure 1. Integration of Artificial Intelligence and Quantum Computing

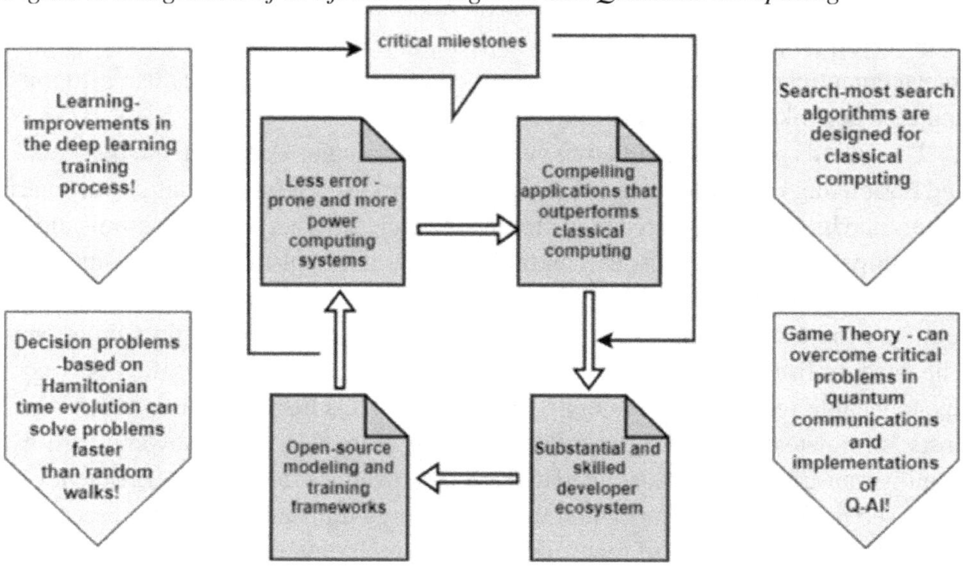

The image presents a flowchart highlighting the "Critical Milestones" necessary for achieving advancements in a specific technological or computational field, likely quantum computing or AI. Here's a breakdown of the components: Above mentioned diagram explained the essential for AI technologies improvement process in the deep learning. Demonstrates that quantum-based dynamic methodologies, for example, those using Hamiltonian time development, can tackle issues quicker than customary techniques like irregular walks. The improvement of utilizations that outperform the capacities of traditional processing would check a significant achievement. The flowchart shows that accomplishing these achievements (focus) includes enhancements in educational experiences, choice critical thinking, and the improvement of new calculations and systems. These, thusly, will prompt the making of convincing applications and a strong engineer biological system, pushing the field past the restrictions of traditional computing. Building a local area of talented designers is vital for help the development and improvement of these innovations.

II. THE CONVERGENCE OF QUANTUM AI AND BLOCKCHAIN

Quantum computer based intelligence use the standards of quantum mechanics to improve artificial intelligence calculations. Quantum PCs can handle tremendous measures of information and perform complex computations at speeds impossible by old style PCs. This speed increase in calculation is especially helpful for man-made intelligence, where enormous datasets and complex models frequently request broad handling power.

Blockchain, then again, is a decentralized record innovation known for its security, straightforwardness, and changelessness. It guarantees that information is put away in a solid, carefully designed way, which is critical for keeping up with the honesty of data and exchanges. At the point when Quantum man-made intelligence is coordinated with blockchain innovation, a few basic benefits arise:

***Enhanced Security*:** Quantum man-made intelligence can foster more refined calculations for getting information. At the point when these calculations are carried out on a blockchain, the outcome is an uncommonly safe framework. Quantum-safe cryptographic techniques can be utilized to shield blockchain information from potential quantum assaults.

Improved Productivity: Quantum figuring can speed up the handling of blockchain exchanges. Current blockchain innovation faces difficulties with adaptability and exchange speed. Quantum artificial intelligence can enhance these cycles, making blockchain more proficient and fit for dealing with bigger volumes of exchanges.

Advanced Information Investigation: computer based intelligence as of now succeeds at breaking down enormous datasets to separate significant experiences. Quantum simulated intelligence can take this to a higher level by handling information at a quantum scale. When blockchain is utilized to store this information, it guarantees the information's trustworthiness, giving a solid groundwork to investigation.

Decentralized Insight: Joining simulated intelligence with blockchain empowers decentralized knowledge. Computer based intelligence calculations can be dispersed across a blockchain network, taking into consideration cooperative learning and decision-production without a focal power. This decentralization can prompt more strong and tough man-made intelligence frameworks.

2.1 The Impact of Quantum & Blockchain

Today, two uncommonly discussed problematic advances are man-made brainpower and blockchain. Both simulated intelligence and blockchain incorporate specialized intricacy and there is apparently a feeling of plan among experts that these innovations will have extraordinary business suggestions in the accompanying five to a decade. The usage of the two developments working closely together may change the tech and business perspective through and through enough for business pioneers to see progressions here. The new advances in AI inside man-made intelligence have not quite recently made one more model for general calculation. In any case, they have opened chances to grow information past the immediate association of the human psyche.(Wang et al., 2018)

A blockchain can not simply keep up the datasets on-fasten for contribution to AIs, it can moreover have a man-made intelligence sufficiently progressed to work with its information and achieve the caution call of freely propelling information — the fake general knowledge (AGI). This point is a questionable recommendation, and even more so in a decentralized setting where all clients will need to access and profit from its computational limits. Appropriated capacity frameworks like the blockchain require agreement conventions to pick which hub will add recently made blocks to the blockchain and thusly network the most recent value-based information. As of now, different shows exist for showing up at an agreement in a conveyed framework, with the most obvious ones being the confirmation of-work (PoW) and verification of-stake (PoS) conventions. Regardless, these conventions are blemished in that they gobble up a lot of energy (PoW) or, will as a rule, support hubs with tremendous coins stakes, conceivably storing its blockchain (PoS). Computerized reasoning, especially brain organizations, addresses an answer for these issues by using them in a new, energy-saving convention - verification of man-made consciousness (PoAI). By using this convention, the agreement framework ensures a sensible hub assurance, keeps the blockchain decentralized, and diminishes energy waste and mining clashes. A Artificial Intelligence blows away a prepared framework by using the new data in the client's solicitation to drive the brain network forward by another age; at the end of the day, it advances as it works. Wellness is resolved when minor or the same changes are expected with any future submitted data. For instance, lately, a lot of wrote code in various programming dialects has been put away in GitHub's storehouses. Complex algorithmic writing computer programs are a monotonous and costly task. A software engineer requires a high knowledge and extended lengths of schooling, and complex undertakings consistently require various long stretches of cooperative work between different gatherings.(Guggilam et al., 2016)

Blockchains can support two unique ways. At first, a blockchain can store the code. Besides, an AIA, encoded on the blockchain, can assist the product with designing according to different viewpoints: Change of code starting with one language then onto the next, searching for calculations that match patterns, conformance of requirements or documentation to code, and eventually recorded as a hard copy new calculations. This AIA would present a strong, secure, and troublesome development using profound gaining strategies and huge information mining from existing code stores.

Similarly as putting away code and projects on the blockchains, we could moreover post prepared brain organizations. By then, clients could post new exchanges that alluded to and used the prepared CNN structures to actually look at the submitted information. For example, consider a profound learning calculation like Sci-kitin Python that sections records in an out and out various manner to manage what we might anticipate: Words can be tended to as implanting vectors with the likelihood that two words that the same have comparative vectors.

Under this model, thoughts that are indistinguishable are near one another (e.g., man and lady). Consequently, expecting that the implanting vectors for canines and little guys are close to each other, the comparability of two records examining canines and puppies will be seen by a ML calculation or a profound brain network prepared regarding that matter. Such apparatuses, all around constructed, could help developers in their usage of the recently referenced code store. The introduction of man-made reasoning, RNNs, and especially LSTMs has engaged complex time-series determining, which is the area of AI focused in on predicting boundaries in the future by alluding to boundaries from an earlier time. Using data on bitcoin's (or any digital money, undoubtedly) past worth focuses, RNNs can be prepared to measure its future expense. This way engages significant pieces of the retail business to address future expense increments/diminishes, possibly reassuring the change to advanced monetary standards' execution.(Hajiesmaili et al., 2017)

III. RELATED WORK

The investigation of Quantum-artificial intelligence Roused Blockchain-Helped Publicly supported Energy Frameworks is arranged inside the more extensive setting of progressions in savvy network advances, blockchain applications in energy, and decentralized energy the board frameworks. The accompanying related works give central experiences and context oriented foundation for figuring out the reconciliation of these state of the art advances.

3.1 Blockchain-Assisted Crowdsourced Energy Systems

The paper explores energy frameworks where energy is created by a conveyed organization of limited scope makers, like people with sunlight based chargers or wind turbines. These frameworks are decentralized, meaning they don't depend on a solitary focal element for energy creation or the board. All things being equal, they influence the aggregate assets of numerous members. The innovation gives a decentralized record where energy creation, utilization, and exchanging exercises can be recorded and confirmed without the requirement for a focal power. The paper talks about how blockchain can work with shared energy exchanging, permitting members in the publicly supported energy framework to trade energy straightforwardly with one another. Smart contracts are used to computerize these exchanges, guaranteeing that they are executed just when certain circumstances are met. It likewise takes a gander at how these innovations can be utilized to upgrade the harmony between energy organic market, especially while managing the fluctuation of sustainable power sources. As of now, different shows exist for showing up at an agreement in a conveyed framework, with the most obvious ones being the confirmation of-work (PoW) and verification of-stake (PoS) conventions. These models might possibly bring down energy costs for shoppers and make new income streams for limited scope energy makers.

3.2 Blockchain in the Energy Transition

Burger and partners reviewed leaders in the German energy industry, featuring the capability of blockchain innovation to change energy frameworks. This paper gives significant bits of knowledge into the down to earth contemplations and difficulties of executing blockchain in energy organizations, for example, guaranteeing secure, straightforward, and proficient exchanges. The discoveries of this work straightforwardly advise the advancement regarding blockchain-helped energy frameworks by exhibiting the innovation's pertinence and acknowledgment in the energy area *(Burger et al., 2016)*

3.3 Security-Constrained Unit Commitment with Volatile Wind Power Generation

This paper tends to the difficulties of coordinating unpredictable environmentally friendly power sources, for example, wind power, into the energy lattice. Wang et al. propose strategies for guaranteeing security-compelled unit responsibility, which is urgent for keeping up with matrix soundness despite capricious energy inputs. Their examination is applicable to the investigation of publicly supported energy frameworks, where the mix of different sustainable power sources requires hearty procedures to oversee unpredictability and guarantee steady energy supply *(Wang et al., 2008)*.

3.4 Crowdsourced Storage-Assisted Demand Response in Microgrids

This paper investigates the idea of publicly supported capacity in microgrids, where conveyed energy capacity assets are amassed to give request reaction administration present systems for using these assets to improve framework soundness and effectiveness, offering important bits of knowledge into how publicly supporting can be applied to energy capacity and request the executives. Their examination gives an immediate establishment to the publicly supporting part of energy frameworks in the proposed study *(Hajiesmaili et al., 2017).*

3.5 A Survey on Demand Response in Smart Grids

Their work frames different techniques for changing energy utilization examples to match supply, which is especially applicable to the investigation of decentralized and publicly supported energy frameworks. By utilizing request reaction, these frameworks can accomplish better equilibrium and proficiency, guaranteeing that energy supply fulfills need even with the decentralized and fluctuating nature of sustainable power sources*(Deng et al., 2015).*

IV. BLOCKCHAIN-BASED CROWDSOURCING ENERGY SYSTEM

Publicly supporting based techniques have been executed in different digital physical systemsand realtime markets. It investigates a structure for Publicly supported Energy Frameworks (CES), where limited scope energy age or energy exchanging is publicly supported from dispersed energy assets, electric vehicles, and shapable burdens. The benefits/mainstays of energy publicly supporting are examined (Howe, 2008). Then, a functional model for CESs in appropriation networks with various kinds of crowdsourcees is proposed. The model yields a market balance portraying conventional and circulated generator and burden set focuses. Given these set focuses, publicly supporting motivating forces are intended to direct crowdsourcees to the balance. As the quantity of crowdsourcees and energy exchanging exchanges increases, a solid energy exchanging stage is required. Keeping that in mind, the introduced structure is coordinated with a light weight Blockchain execution and brilliant contracts. Crowdsourcing is a significant drive for different enterprises, and has been used in different teaches like medication, digital actual frameworks, and designing framework plan. The focal topic in publicly supporting is the usage of the group's powerto accomplish either item level or framework level targets(singh et al.,

2019). As of late, the reconciliation of blockchain innovation and crow-dsourcing has acquired the consideration of the examination local area. PoT is an agreement convention based upon the possibility of blockchain innovation to deal with the responsibility issue in publicly supporting administrations. The convention uses Pontoon to choose a pioneer from record hubs and chooses administration members as validators of exchanges in light of trust values. The PoT convention resolves the issue of adaptability related with BFT and Paxos-based calculations. It considers the faithless way of behaving of hubs that isn't tended to in BFT calculations (Cottrell & Basden, 2017).

To comprehend how publicly supporting can be applied in energy frameworks, we give a relationship from the Web's most famous publicly supporting business sectors, the Amazon Mechanical Turk(MTurk). MTurk empowers individuals to post occupations with money related prizes and expiry dates. The human part is appeared through the collaboration between the crowdsourcer (CES administrator or utility) and the publicly support (energy maker). A portion of these errands have earnest expiry cutoff times, while others are foreordained aheadof time as in day-ahead business sectors. Energy-mindful individuals can then acknowledge or decline the proposed exchanges. The utility's goal is to ensure that any figured, realtime market harmony is sufficiently vigorous to a huge level of publicly supports declining the exchanges — while ensuring the framework's transient solidness and functional limitations as well as fulfilling natural regulations (Kim & Kim, 2020).

Figure 2. Components of CES

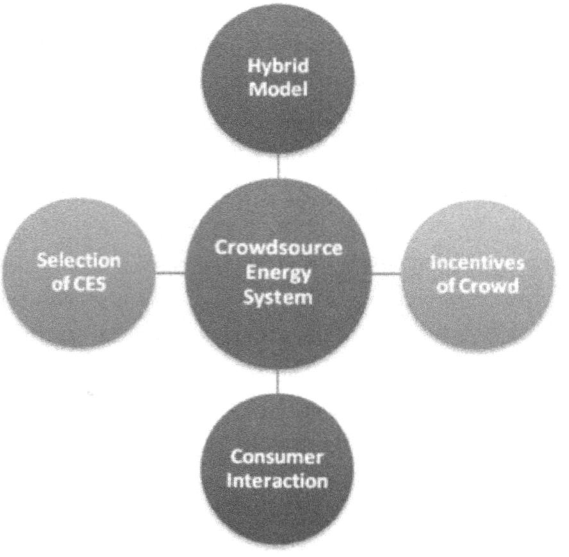

Utilities can CES support the time-basic energy age from buyers and burdens with DERs, when utilities can't satisfy the need or the base level of inexhaustible entrance. the last option thusly enables individuals to be more proactive towards energy frameworks issues, which can thus bring issues to light and build pertinence of energy frameworks challenges.

Second, in its substance, publicly supporting systems investigate the plan of motivators to control individuals or clients to play out specific obligations, while extending the arrangement of disseminated age commitments. This can appear as request reaction in power frameworks through elements mindful, conveyed valuing plans that guarantee the lattice's strength while limiting costs. Third, the development of Blockchain and digital forms of money can accelerate the end of the alleged center man in energy systems, by working with secure distributed energy exchanges.

Third, the development of Blockchain and cryptographic forms of money can accelerate the end of the supposed center man in energy systems, by working with secure shared energy exchanges. As a matter of fact, utilities in Austria have been exploring different avenues regarding energy exchanging by means of Blockchain, and sunlight powered charger proprietors in Brooklyn are energy exchanging through a similar stage (Conttrell & Basden, 2017).

Truth be told, utilities in Austria have been exploring different avenues regarding energy exchanging by means of Blockchain, and sunlight based charger owners in Brooklyn are energy exchanging through a similar stage. Nonetheless, these exchanges can't increase without a computational system that guarantees dependability of savvy lattices. The focal point of this paper is on laying out a system that directs the remarkable increment of such publicly supported exchanges while not being limited to cryptographic forms of money. In (Howe, 2008), the creator presents the short history and aggressive future of crowdsourcing. The principal mainstays of effective publicly supporting in energy frameworks are portrayed in Fig. 1, for CESs. For curtness, we don't examine these support points inside and out here.

CES supporting instruments investigate the plan of impetuses to direct individuals or clients to play out specific obligations, while growing the arrangement of disseminated age commitments. This can appear as request reaction in power frameworks through elements mindful, appropriated estimating plans that guarantee the matrix's solidness while limiting expenses.

CES supporting energy frameworks joined with blockchain innovation addresses an inventive way to deal with decentralized energy creation, dispersion, and the board. This idea use the force of local area association and blockchain's straightforwardness and security to make more productive and versatile energy frameworks.

4.1 Crowdsourcing Energy Frameworks:

- Decentralized Energy Creation: Rather than depending entirely on brought together power plants, energy is created by a disseminated organization of limited scope makers, like property holders with sunlight based chargers, wind turbines, or other environmentally friendly power sources.
- Energy Sharing: Overabundance energy created by people or little networks can be shared or offered to others inside the organization, diminishing dependence on customary energy suppliers.(Taylor.J,2015)
- Community Association: Neighborhood people group can put resources into and add to the advancement of environmentally friendly power projects, improving nearby energy security and supportability.

4.1.1 Blockchain modernization:

- Transparent and Secure Exchanges: Blockchain gives a safe, changeless record for recording energy exchanges, guaranteeing straightforwardness and forestalling misrepresentation.
- Smart Agreements: Computerized agreements that execute predefined conditions (e.g., moving energy credits when a specific measure of energy is created or consumed) without the requirement for delegates.
- Decentralization: Blockchain innovation upholds the decentralized idea of publicly supported energy frameworks by empowering distributed (P2P) energy exchanging without a focal power.

4.1.2 Benefits:

Straightforwardness and Trust: Blockchain guarantees all exchanges are straightforward and discernible, building trust among members.

Proficiency: Lessens the requirement for delegates, bringing down expenses and accelerating exchange times.

Strengthening: Permits people and networks to assume command over their energy creation and utilization, lessening dependence on customary service organizations.

Supportability: Energizes the reception of environmentally friendly power sources and the advancement of maintainable energy projects.

Strength: A decentralized energy network is less defenseless against disturbances and can adjust all the more effectively to changes popular or supply.

4.2 Challenges and Applications

Drug Revelation and Medical care: By reenacting sub-atomic designs at a quantum level, Quantum simulated intelligence can speed up drug disclosure, prompting quicker and more viable therapies. Quantum-fueled man-made intelligence can dissect and anticipate how different medication compounds connect with different sicknesses, bringing about customized medication and creative restorative arrangements.

Cryptography and Network safety: Quantum simulated intelligence can both break conventional encryption strategies and foster new, invulnerable cryptographic methods, in this way reshaping the scene of online protection. Quantum encryption strategies, for example, quantum key circulation (QKD), offer secure correspondence channels that are hypothetically strong by old style implies.

Monetary Demonstrating: Quantum man-made intelligence can dissect huge datasets to foresee market patterns, enhance venture portfolios, and oversee monetary dangers all the more successfully. By handling mind boggling and high-layered information, Quantum simulated intelligence can uncover stowed away examples and connections that customary techniques could miss, giving an upper hand in monetary navigation.(Biamonte et al.,2017)

Environment Demonstrating: With improved computational power, Quantum man-made intelligence can display complex environment frameworks, giving better expectations and techniques to battling environmental change. Quantum calculations can reenact ecological changes with more noteworthy exactness, supporting the improvement of practical arrangements and approaches.

Improvement Issues: Quantum man-made intelligence succeeds at taking care of advancement issues, which common in different ventures, including strategies, are assembling, and transportation. Quantum calculations can find ideal arrangements quicker and all the more effectively, prompting cost investment funds and worked on functional productivity.

AI Improvement: Quantum computer based intelligence can upgrade the capacities of existing simulated intelligence models. For instance, quantum AI calculations can further develop preparing times, precision, and speculation of computer based intelligence frameworks, making them more powerful and fit for taking care of complicated errands.

Difficulties and Future Possibilities: Regardless of its true capacity, Quantum simulated intelligence faces a few difficulties. The advancement of steady and versatile quantum PCs is still in its early stages, with issues, for example, qubit cognizance and blunder rates requiring goal. Furthermore, there is a requirement for specific calculations that can completely take advantage of quantum capacities.

Specialized Difficulties: Building and keeping up with quantum PCs require exceptionally controlled conditions to save qubit soundness. Specialists are dealing with strategies to diminish mistake rates and upgrade the soundness of quantum frameworks.

Calculation Advancement: Quantum calculations should be explicitly intended to use the special properties of quantum processing. This includes growing new computational ideal models and systems that vary from traditional methodologies.

Interdisciplinary Cooperation: The progression of Quantum man-made intelligence requires joint effort between specialists in quantum physical science, software engineering, and computerized reasoning. Interdisciplinary examination endeavors are fundamental to defeat the specialized and hypothetical difficulties. (Lloyd et al.,2013)

Moral and Cultural Ramifications: Likewise with any extraordinary innovation, Quantum computer based intelligence raises moral and cultural contemplations. Guaranteeing that the advantages of Quantum simulated intelligence are appropriated fairly and tending to possible dangers, for example, work uprooting and security concerns, are critical for its mindful turn of events.

The intersection of Quantum AI and blockchain opens up numerous possibilities across various sectors:

Healthcare: Patient records can be securely stored on a blockchain, with Quantum AI analyzing vast amounts of medical data to diagnose diseases and recommend treatments more accurately.

Finance: Financial transactions can be processed more quickly and securely, while Quantum AI can detect fraud and optimize trading strategies.

Supply Chain: Blockchain can track the provenance of goods, and Quantum AI can optimize logistics and predict supply chain disruptions.

Cybersecurity: Quantum AI can identify and mitigate threats in real-time, while blockchain ensures the integrity of security protocols.

4.3 Case Study: Quantum-AI Enhanced Blockchain-Based Energy Trading Platform

In a European smart city, an innovative pilot project combines quantum AI, blockchain technology, and crowdsourcing to create a decentralized energy market. This system empowers homeowners with solar panels and other renewable energy sources to trade surplus energy directly with their neighbors. The primary goals of the project are to optimize energy distribution, reduce waste, and lessen dependence on traditional energy grids.

Technology Components:

1. **Quantum AI for Energy Optimization**: Advanced quantum algorithms are deployed to optimize energy distribution by forecasting consumption patterns, dynamically adjusting prices, and minimizing energy loss. By leveraging quantum machine learning, the system analyzes large datasets, including historical energy usage, weather predictions, and market trends, to make data-driven decisions that enhance efficiency.
2. **Blockchain for Transparency and Security**: A blockchain infrastructure supports the energy trading system, providing a transparent, secure, and immutable record of transactions. Smart contracts facilitate automated energy exchanges between users, ensuring equitable pricing and contract enforcement without the need for intermediaries. Additionally, quantum-resistant cryptography is integrated to protect the blockchain from future quantum computing threats.
3. **Crowdsourcing Renewable Energy**: The platform encourages community participation by allowing residents to contribute their surplus renewable energy to the grid or invest in shared energy projects. This crowdsourced approach strengthens the energy system by pooling decentralized energy resources from multiple contributors, enhancing both resilience and sustainability.

To illustrate the practical relevance of Quantum-AI inspired blockchain-assisted crowdsourced energy systems, we must delve into current industry practices and case studies while considering insights from diverse stakeholders.

A prime example is the Brooklyn Microgrid in New York, where residents engage in direct solar energy trading using blockchain technology. This decentralized system transparently and securely records transactions on a blockchain, with AI algorithms forecasting energy production and consumption to optimize grid efficiency. This project highlights how decentralized energy systems can empower communities and decrease reliance on traditional utilities. Industry practitioners see these systems as offering operational efficiencies and global scalability potential. On the other hand, policy-makers stress the need for regulatory frameworks to support decentralized systems, while end-users enjoy enhanced energy autonomy and potential cost savings.(Schuld et al.,2015)

Another noteworthy case is Power Ledger in Australia, a company enabling peer-to-peer energy trading via blockchain technology. Power Ledger's platform allows users to trade surplus renewable energy, like solar power, directly with their neighbors. The system leverages blockchain for secure transactions and AI for optimizing energy distribution. Power Ledger's ability to adapt to various regulatory environments has facilitated its expansion into multiple countries, showcasing its scalability. Industry practitioners regard this technology as crucial for integrating renewable energy into the grid. Policy-makers emphasize the significance of international cooperation to standardize blockchain applications in energy markets, while end-users benefit from greater engagement in energy trading and potential revenue from excess energy sales.

In Japan, the Tokyo Electric Power Company (TEPCO) provides another example, utilizing blockchain to manage energy transactions in smart grids. TEPCO's initiative centers on peer-to-peer energy trading and integrating renewable energy sources. By using smart contracts on a blockchain, TEPCO automates energy transactions and ensures real-time grid balancing, supported by AI-driven predictive analytics. This initiative underscores the potential for traditional utilities to adopt large-scale decentralized models. Nonetheless, policy-makers are concerned with maintaining grid stability while embracing such technologies, and end-users gain more control over their energy usage and expenses.

Examining these examples reveals that Quantum-AI inspired blockchain-assisted energy systems profoundly impact various aspects of the energy industry. Industry practitioners are particularly interested in the operational efficiencies and grid modernization, while policy-makers focus on developing supportive regulatory frameworks. End-users benefit from increased autonomy and potential cost savings, though the complexity of these systems and data privacy concerns pose challenges. Integrating these technologies into real-world applications highlights their transformative potential, making the discussion pertinent to a broader audience.

V. PROPOSED METHODOLOGY

Quantum Computing is important with equipment headways offering promising potential yet confronting huge difficulties, especially in versatility and mistake rates. As quantum frameworks grow, keeping up with rationality and lessening blunders become basic obstacles. Simultaneously, moral and administrative contemplations emerge, particularly with respect to information protection and security, as quantum innovation could disturb customary cryptographic techniques. Coordinating quantum simulated intelligence with blockchain presents extra intricacies, for example, interoperability issues and framework incorporation challenges. Notwithstanding, arrangements like quantum-safe conventions and cross breed designs are being investigated to address these troubles. Certifiable applications, especially in the energy area, feature quantum figuring's true capacity, with contextual analyses showing its adequacy in streamlining energy frameworks and progressing sustainable advances. As the field develops, future exploration should zero in on upgrading quantum man-made intelligence, tending to blockchain-quantum collaboration, and scaling these advancements for pragmatic use. Cooperative endeavors across disciplines and consistent advancement will be fundamental to conquering the ongoing limits and completely understand the extraordinary force of quantum figuring in different areas.(Preskill.J,2018)

The proposed framework incorporates blockchain innovation into a decentralized, publicly supported energy organization, empowering secure and straightforward shared energy exchanging among members. Limited scope energy makers, like families with sun powered chargers, can straightforwardly offer abundance energy to buyers inside the organization. Blockchain guarantees that all exchanges are safely kept in a circulated record, while shrewd agreements robotize the exchanging system in view of dynamic valuing models. The framework additionally consolidates improvement calculations to oversee energy conveyance effectively, adjusting organic market continuously. This approach upgrades the versatility, versatility, and protection of the energy framework, advancing a more reasonable and decentralized energy future.(Zhu et al., 2020)

Figure 3. Crowdsourcing Platform integrated with Blockchain Technology

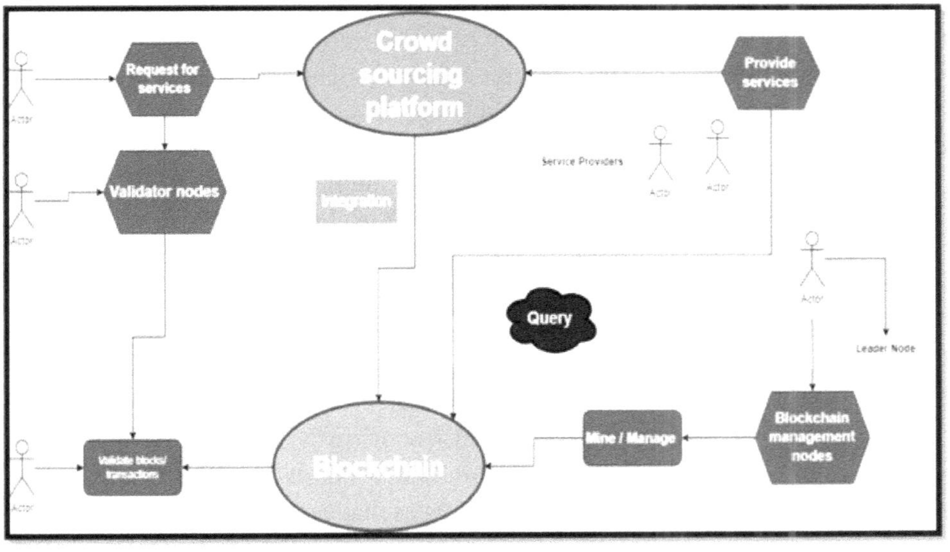

The diagram represents a Crowdsourcing Platform integrated with Blockchain Technology. It illustrates the interaction between service consumers, service providers, validator nodes, and blockchain management nodes within a crowdsourcing system that uses blockchain for secure and transparent transactions. The architecture of the blockchain-based publicly supporting framework (BBCS) is addressed in Figure 3. It comprises of four entertainers: administration buyer, specialist co-op, blockchain the executives hubs, and validator hubs. The help shoppers demand for administrations by presenting an undertaking on the publicly supporting stage. A help shopper can really look at the situation with an undertaking by sending an inquiry to the blockchain. Specialist organizations offer types of assistance by getting an undertaking through a publicly supporting stage. A specialist organization can send a question to the blockchain to get data about the errand installment. The blockchain the executives hubs are liable for overseeing blockchain, e.g., proposing and approving blocks. In each round of agreement, a believed pioneer is chosen from the blockchain the executives hubs to propose and add a block to the blockchain. The validators approve and decide in favor of exchanges and blocks.(Wang et al., 2018). The blockchain the executives hubs, administration shoppers, and suppliers can act as validators.

5.1 Blockchain for Crowdsourced Energy Systems

Blockchain is a conveyed distributed, computational information base that underlines and works with exchanges through cryptographic forms of money, for example, Bitcoin and Ether [18]; Blockchain innovation can likewise be utilized with conventional monetary standards throughtokens. The principal parts in a Blockchain are interlinked, secure, and time-stepped blocks that characterize exchanges between clients. The primary inspiration driving Blockchain is the need to have a conveyed, secure framework that wipes out the requirement for the supposed center man or a focal power that sorts out exchanges. Novel cryptographic methods are vital to Blockchain, guaranteeing that any exchange of any product between two clients is safely duplicated all through undeniably decentralized information bases. Through cryptographic forms of money, Blockchain guarantees that exchanges can't be fashioned. The peruser is alluded for a top to bottom concentrate on Blockchain, Ethereum, and Bitcoin with applications in different businesses.

smart agreements — conventions created to confirm the presentation of an agreement — are a significant part of Blockchain. Smart contracts and Blockchain give an amazing stage to perform energy exchanging exchanges. Specifically, the creators in (Liu et al., 2020) give a significant level portrayal to the fundamental benefits of involving cryptographic forms of money and Blockchain in energy frameworks. Dealing with the agreements through Blockchain is inclined toward, as the framework administrator has numerous motivating forces to deal with the exchanges by means of a protected, outsider. This, not at all like other Blockchain applications, actually requires a focal power — the service organization or the framework administrator dealing with the lattice. Limited scope energy exchanging without a focal authority can occur(Zhu et al., 2018), yet the scaling of these exchanges to incorporate a huge number of individuals and a great many everyday energy exchanges without the utility meddling is far off in the present business sectors. With that in mind, the proposed engineering in this paper actually requires a focal power to deal with the network.

5.2 Blockchain Implementations and Energy Inefficiency

A Consensus Protocol is utilized to guarantee the unambiguous request of exchanges and assurance the honesty and consistency of the Blockchain across conveyed hubs (Liu et al., 2020) different agreement conventions have been created for Blockchain executions. A significant part of Blockchain is the mining system where excavators approve new exchanges and record them on the worldwide Blockchain record. In the Evidence of Work (PoW) agreement convention, utilized by Bitcoin also, Ethereum, excavators competition to add new exchanges to the record by contending to tackle a complex, computationally concentrated and energy-consuming cryptographic riddle. When scaled, this would bring about an energy wasteful stage that nullifies the point of supportable energy frameworks.(Singh et al., 2019).

At the point when scaled, this would bring about an energy wasteful stage that nullifies the point of supportable energy frameworks. As a matter of fact, the yearly assessed power utilization of Bitcoin is 46.86 Terawatt-hour — a faltering 0.21% of universes power utilization. For any Blockchain execution to find success in CESs, the energy utilization of the agreement innovation for every energy exchanging exchange ought to just require little energy. Keeping that in mind, we propose utilizing the IBM Hyperledger Texture that utilizes Reasonable Byzantine Adaptation to non-critical failure (PBFT) as its agreement convention. PBFT consumes significant degrees less energy in correlation with other agreement conventions.

Figure 4. Proposed System Architecture

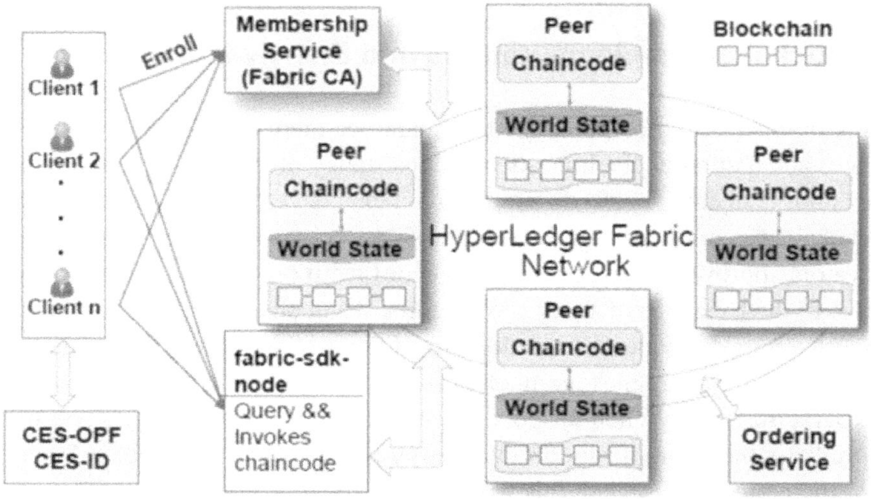

Furthermore, Hyperledger Texture requires insignificant client cooperation as a basic, client driven intuitive front end can be created utilizing this innovation. This diagram represents the design of a Hyperledger fabric organization. It begins with clients who cooperate with the blockchain by summoning exchanges. These clients are validated through a Participation Administration that oversees characters. The organization comprises of friends, which are hubs that have chaincode (shrewd agreements) and keep up with the record (alluded to as the World State). The blockchain addresses the unchanging record, everything being equal. A Requesting Administration guarantees exchanges are appropriately sequenced and disseminated to peers. The texture sdk-hub is a product improvement unit that empowers clients to inquiry and summons chaincode. In conclusion, the chart incorporates CES-OPF and CES-ID parts, possible connected with client enlistment or personality the executives.(Yang et al., 2020).

5.3 Blockchain Implementation using Hyperledger Fabric

The chaincode in Hyperledger Texture is likewise sent to peers and is executed as a client fulfills their responsibilities. Then, at that point, requesting administration, similar to mining in Bitcoin, produces new blocks in Texture. Each companion will get requested state refreshes as blocks from the requesting administration. Along these lines, the request and number of blocks, a type of Blockchain, are kept up with and synchronized for all peers. It comprises of numerous hubs that speak with one another, runs brilliant agreements called chaincode, holds state and record information. The clients shown are the end-clients in the conveyance organization and can perform energy exchanging. Huge number of clients is permitted to associate with the Texture network with negligible preparation.

Figure 5. Algorithm for Blockchain-assisted CES Operation

Algorithm 1 Blockchain-Assisted CES Operation

Crowdsourcees input preferences and operational constraints $\mathcal{X}$
Solve CES-OPF (1); obtain generator setpoints for $i \in \mathcal{G} \bigcup \mathcal{C}_{T1}$
Establish smart contracts for users $i \in \mathcal{G} \bigcup \mathcal{C}_{T1}$
Solve CES-ID (2) for generators $i \in \mathcal{C}_{T2}$; send incentives to Type 2 crowdsourcees with incentive $\lambda^a + \lambda$
if user $i \in \mathcal{C}_{T2}$ accepts incentives **then**
    Finalize Blockchain transaction
else
    Increase incentives for user i up to a threshold/budget
    Update parameters (η_i, ζ_i) to CES-ID (2) for user i
    If user i rejects incentive again, supplement generation from traditional generators $i \in \mathcal{G}$
end if
Reconcile payments weekly or monthly

Calculation 1 outlines how the created advancement schedules are carried out with Blockchain and savvy contracts. In the first place, crowdsourcees convey their inclinations X with the utility or a framework administrator. Given these inclinations, CESOPF (1) is settled for the market balance. Brilliant agreements are then settled for clients I ∈ G S CT1 and are compensated relying upon their drawn out authoritative concurrence with the utility. For Type 2 crowdsourcees working in realtime markets, the CES-ID (2) is settled to get the money related motivators spoke with the clients. In the event that client I acknowledges the financial motivation, the exchange is settled. In any case, on the off chance that client I rejects the motivator, the motivations are expanded up to a specific financial plan. This can happen up to a specific edge, where the administrator can on the other hand enhance the age from conventional sources.

5.4 Quantum Algorithms (Shor's Algorithm, Grover's Algorithm)

Quantum algorithms are computational procedures that run on quantum computers, leveraging quantum mechanics to perform tasks much faster than classical algorithms. Two of the most famous quantum algorithms are **Shor's Algorithm** and **Grover's Algorithm**, each with distinct applications and impacts, particularly on cryptography and search problems.

1. Shor's Algorithm

Shor's Algorithm, developed by Peter Shor in 1994, is a quantum algorithm designed for integer factorization. It efficiently factors large integers into their prime factors, a task that is computationally difficult for classical computers. The significance of this algorithm lies in its potential to break widely used cryptographic systems, such as RSA, which rely on the difficulty of factoring large integers.

To understand Shor's Algorithm, it's essential to grasp some basic concepts:

- **Modular Arithmetic:** Involves arithmetic operations within a finite number set, often used in cryptography.
- **Euler's Totient Function:** Counts the number of integers up to a given integer n that are relatively prime to n.
- **Order of an Integer:** Given an integer aaa and a modulus nnn, the order of aaa modulo nnn is the smallest positive integer rrr such that ar≡1 (mod n)a^r \equiv 1 \,(\text{mod}\, n)ar≡1(modn).

Steps of Shor's Algorithm

1. **Problem Setup:**
   - o The goal is to factorize a large composite number NNN. Assume N=pqN = pqN=pq, where ppp and qqq are unknown prime numbers.
2. **Random Selection:**
   - o Select a random integer aaa such that 1<a<N1 < a < N1<a<N and aaa is coprime to NNN (i.e., gcd(a, N) = 1). This step can be efficiently performed using the Euclidean algorithm.
3. **Quantum Period Finding:**
   - o The key quantum step is finding the period rrr of the function f(x)=axmod Nf(x) = a^x \mod Nf(x)=axmodN, meaning the smallest rrr such that ar≡1mod Na^r \equiv 1 \mod Nar≡1modN.

- This is achieved by preparing a superposition of all possible values of xxx, applying the quantum Fourier transforms to extract the period, and then measuring the result.

4. **Classical Post-Processing:**
   - Once the period rrr is found, if rrr is even, compute gcd(ar/2−1,N)gcd(a^{r/2} - 1, N)gcd(ar/2−1,N) and gcd(ar/2+1,N)gcd(a^{r/2} + 1, N) gcd(ar/2+1,N). These calculations will likely yield the prime factors ppp and qqq.
5. **Repeating if Necessary:**
   - If the process fails (for instance, if rrr is odd), the algorithm is repeated with a different value of aaa.

Efficiency

- **Quantum Speedup:** Shor's algorithm runs in polynomial time, specifically O((log N)2log log Nlog log log N)O((\log N)^2 \log \log N \log \log \log N) O((logN)2loglogNlogloglogN), making it exponentially faster than the best-known classical algorithms, which run in sub-exponential time.
- **Cryptographic Impact:** The ability of Shor's Algorithm to efficiently factor large integers poses a direct threat to classical cryptosystems like RSA, which depend on the difficulty of this task.

2. Grover's Algorithm

Overview

Grover's Algorithm, developed by Lov Grover in 1996, is a quantum algorithm designed for searching an unsorted database or solving a black-box problem with a quadratic speedup. Given an unsorted database of NNN elements, Grover's Algorithm can find a specific item or solve an unstructured search problem in O(N) O(\sqrt{N})O(N) time, compared to O(N)O(N)O(N) time for classical algorithms.

Mathematical Background

- **Amplitude Amplification:** Grover's algorithm is based on the concept of amplitude amplification, where the probability amplitude of the correct answer is iteratively increased until it becomes dominant in the superposition.
- **Oracle Function:** The algorithm uses an oracle, a black-box function that can recognize the correct solution. The oracle flips the sign of the amplitude of the correct state, marking it.

Steps of Grover's Algorithm

1. **Initialization:**
   - o Prepare an equal superposition of all possible states. If there are NNN possible solutions, each state has an amplitude of 1/N1/\sqrt{N}1/N.
2. **Oracle Application:**
   - o Apply the oracle function, which flips the phase (sign) of the amplitude of the state corresponding to the correct solution, effectively marking it.
3. **Amplitude Amplification (Grover Iteration):**
   - o Perform the Grover iteration, which consists of two steps:
     - **Inversion about the Mean:** Reflect the state amplitudes about their mean value, amplifying the amplitude of the correct state.
     - **Reapplication of Oracle:** Reapply the oracle to flip the sign of the marked state again.
   - o Repeat the Grover iteration approximately N\sqrt{N}N times.
4. **Measurement:**
   - o Measure the quantum state. The correct solution, whose amplitude has been significantly amplified, is highly likely to be observed.

Efficiency

- **Quantum Speedup:** Grover's algorithm achieves a quadratic speedup over classical search algorithms, solving the problem in O(N)O(\sqrt{N})O(N) time.
- **Versatility:** While not as dramatic as Shor's exponential speedup, Grover's quadratic speedup applies to a broader class of problems, particularly unstructured search problems, making it broadly useful in various computational tasks.

Impact on Cryptography

- **Symmetric-Key Cryptography:** Grover's Algorithm can be applied to brute-force attacks on symmetric-key cryptographic systems. For instance, it can reduce the time complexity of breaking a 128-bit key from 21282^{128}2128 to 2642^{64}264. While this is still computationally infeasible, it suggests that symmetric key lengths may need to be doubled to maintain security in a quantum computing context.
- **Hash Functions:** Similarly, Grover's algorithm can be used to find collisions in cryptographic hash functions, reducing the time complexity of such attacks.

Comparison of Shor's and Grover's Algorithms

- **Problem Domain:**
  - o **Shor's Algorithm:** Focused on factorization and discrete logarithms, with direct implications for asymmetric cryptography.
  - o **Grover's Algorithm:** Applicable to unstructured search problems, with implications for symmetric cryptography and general problem-solving.
- **Quantum Speedup:**
  - o **Shor's Algorithm:** Offers an exponential speedup over classical algorithms.
  - o **Grover's Algorithm:** Provides a quadratic speedup, which is significant but less dramatic than Shor's.
- **Cryptographic Impact:**
  - o **Shor's Algorithm:** Threatens the security of RSA, ECC, and other public-key cryptosystems.
  - o **Grover's Algorithm:** Reduces the security margin of symmetric-key systems and hash functions but does not completely break them.

VI. CONCLUSION

The combination of Quantum man-made intelligence with blockchain addresses a boondocks in mechanical development. By joining the unrivaled computational force of quantum registering with the security and straightforwardness of blockchain, we can open new degrees of effectiveness, security, and knowledge. As innovative work in these fields proceed, we are probably going to observe momentous applications that will reshape enterprises and rethink the eventual fate of innovation. Quantum-simulated intelligence Motivated Blockchain-Helped Publicly supported Energy Frameworks hold the possibility to change the energy area by tending to key difficulties like shortcoming, centralization, and absence of straightforwardness. Quantum figuring upgrades the framework's computational capacities, empowering quicker and more exact handling of perplexing energy information, while computer based intelligence calculations advance energy circulation and utilization designs. Blockchain innovation supports the framework's decentralized nature, guaranteeing secure, straightforward, and carefully designed energy exchanges. This advances trust among members and works with the consistent execution of shrewd agreements for energy exchanging and asset portion. Furthermore, the publicly supporting model enables people and networks to partake in energy creation and the board, encouraging a more maintainable and locally versatile energy environment effectively. This incorporated methodology further develops energy effectiveness and maintainability as well as prepares for imaginative plans of action and local area driven energy drives. Nonetheless, difficulties like administrative obstacles, innovative incorporation, and starting venture costs should be addressed to understand the framework's potential completely. All in all, the union of quantum registering, artificial intelligence, blockchain, and publicly supported energy frameworks offers a visionary pathway toward a decentralized, shrewd, and feasible energy future. As these advances proceed to develop and develop, their consolidated application in the energy area could prompt huge headways by the way we produce, disseminate, and consume energy, at last adding to a stronger and evenhanded worldwide energy scene.

REFERENCES

Benedetti, M., & Realpe-Gomez, J., Biswas, and Perdomo-Ortiz, A. (2018). Quantum-Assisted Learning of Hardware-Embedded Probabilistic Graphical Models. *IEEE Transactions on Neural Networks and Learning Systems*, 29(12), 5792–5803.

Biamonte, J., Wittek, P. J., & Landsman, N. P.. (2017). Quantum Machine Learning. *Nature*, 549(7671), 195–202. DOI: 10.1038/nature23474 PMID: 28905917

Burger, C., Kuhlmann,A., Richard,P., and Weinmann,J., (2016) "Blockchain in the energy transition. a survey among decision-makers in the german energy industry," Tech. Rep.,.

Cottrell,J., and Basden, M., (2017) "How utilities are using blockchain to modernize the grid," PP 257-266.

Deng, R., Yang, Z., Chow, M. Y., & Chen, J. (2015). A survey on demand response in smart grids: Mathematical models and approaches. *IEEE Transactions on Industrial Informatics*, 11(3), 570–582. DOI: 10.1109/TII.2015.2414719

Guggilam, S., DallAnese, E., Chen, Y. C., Dhople, S. V., & Giannakis, G. V. (2016). Scalable optimization methods for distribution networks with high pv integration. *IEEE Transactions on Smart Grid*, 7(4), 2061–2070. DOI: 10.1109/TSG.2016.2543264

Hajiesmaili, M. H., Chen, M., Mallada, E., & Chau, C. K. (2017) "Crowdsourced storage-assisted demand response in microgrids," in *Proceedings of the Eighth International Conference on Future Energy Systems*. ACM, pp. 91–100. DOI: 10.1145/3077839.3077841

Howe, J. (2008). *Crowdsourcing: Why the Power of the Crowd Is Driving the Future of Business* (1st ed.). Crown Publishing Group.

Khoshaman, A., Vinci, W., & Andriyash, W., Amin, and Rieffel, E. (2019). Quantum Variational Autoencoder. *IEEE Transactions on Neural Networks and Learning Systems*, 30(3), 916–927.

Kim, S. K., & Kim, H. J. (2020). Blockchain-Based Peer-to-Peer Energy Trading for Renewable Energy Integration. *IEEE Access : Practical Innovations, Open Solutions*, 8, 222947–222959.

Liu, Y., He, Y., & Li, Y. (2020). Blockchain-Based Secure and Efficient Energy Trading for Smart Grids. *IEEE Transactions on Smart Grid*, 11(1), 320–329.

Lloyd, S., Mohseni, M., & Rebentrost, P. (2013). Quantum Algorithms for Fixed Points and Machine Learning. *Physical Review Letters*, 110(19), 190501. PMID: 23705695

Preskill, J. (2018). Quantum-enhanced Machine Learning. *Proceedings of the Royal Society of London. Series A*, 474(2209), 20170551. PMID: 29434508

Schuld, M., & Petruccione, F. (2018). *Supervised learning with quantum computers* (Vol. 17). Springer.

Singh, S. P. K., Saini, A. K., & Kumar, V. (2019). Blockchain-Based Decentralized Energy Trading Framework for Smart Grids. *IEEE Transactions on Industrial Informatics*, 15(9), 5292–5301.

Taylor, J. A. (2015). *Convex optimization of power systems*. Cambridge University Press. DOI: 10.1017/CBO9781139924672

Wang, J., Shahidehpour, M., & Li, Z. (2018). Security-constrained unit commitment with volatile wind power generation. *IEEE Transactions on Power Systems*, 23(3), 1319–1327. DOI: 10.1109/TPWRS.2008.926719

Wang, Z. D., Zhao, J. Z., & Wang, X. G. (2018). Quantum Neural Networks. *Physical Review. A*, 98(3), 032327. DOI: 10.1103/PhysRevA.65.032327

Zhu, S., Cai, Z., Hu, H., Li, Y., & Li, W. (2020). ZkCrowd: A hybrid blockchain-based crowdsourcing platform. *IEEE Transactions on Industrial Informatics*, 16(6), 4196–4205. DOI: 10.1109/TII.2019.2941735

Zhu, X., Li, X., Fang, L., & Chen, P. (2020). An improved proof-of-trust consensus algorithm for credible crowdsourcing blockchain services. *IEEE Access : Practical Innovations, Open Solutions*, 8, 10187–102177. DOI: 10.1109/ACCESS.2020.2998803

ADDITIONAL READING

Li, J., Zhang, Y., & Liu, Y. (2019). Decentralized Energy Trading Using Blockchain in the Smart Grid. *Applied Energy*, 235, 1350–1360.

Chapter 10
Subaquatic Anomaly Detection and Hazard Alert System for Divers and Marine Researchers Based on Quantum AI and Blockchain Technology Applications

U. Deepa
Velammal Engineering College, India

S. Sarupriya
Velammal Engineering College, India

K. Maalini
Velammal Engineering College, India

Bruce P. Shiny
Velammal Engineering College, India

ABSTRACT

The goal of this research is to leverage Quantum AI and blockchain technology applications to develop a Subaquatic Anomaly Detection and Hazard Alert System for divers and marine researchers. By using electromagnetic (EM) fields in an embedded system, we aim to simulate the frequency domain characteristics of seawater

DOI: 10.4018/979-8-3373-1657-4.ch010

channels for efficient underwater communication. Quantum AI will be employed to analyze and predict anomalies in the subaquatic environment, providing real-time hazard alerts to divers and marine researchers. The integration of blockchain technology ensures secure and immutable data transmission, safeguarding the integrity of the communication system. By combining these advanced technologies, we aim to revolutionize underwater communication and safety, addressing the inherent challenges posed by the underwater environment.

I. INTRODUCTION

This project presents an advanced system designed to enhance the safety and operational efficiency of divers and marine researchers in oceanic environments by integrating Quantum AI and blockchain technology applications. Our system leverages state-of-the-art sensors and communication technologies to monitor health parameters and detect underwater anomalies and hazards in real-time. The system operates by continuously monitoring the underwater environment using its integrated sensors and detectors. If any anomalies are detected, particularly magnetic anomalies, the system interprets this data to assess potential hazards. Real-time alerts are generated and sent to user devices, which can be wrist-worn, integrated into diving gear, or attached to research equipment.

In the event of a detected hazard, such as an abrupt change in the magnetic field indicating a submerged wreck or dangerous geological formations, the system alerts the user to take appropriate action. Additionally, the system provides updates on changing environmental conditions, enabling divers and researchers to make informed decisions during their underwater activities.

The "Subaquatic Anomaly Detection and Hazard Alert System for Divers and Marine Researchers" is a cutting-edge project that leverages Quantum AI and blockchain technology to ensure the safety and efficiency of underwater activities. By offering a novel solution to detect and respond to potential hazards, this system becomes an invaluable tool for divers and marine researchers, significantly enhancing their ability to conduct safe and successful underwater operations.

II. LITERATURE SURVEY

This article is the next in a series of studies on the peripheral blood oxygenation data set. Here, we validate that the variations in oxygenation have allowed healthy people to be divided into three subgroups. There are two proposed new measurements (descriptors) of variability that show correlations with recurrence ratios and statistical analogs. Because these measurements are easier to compute when compared to recurrence ratios, they are more useful in clinical settings. (Domingo-Ferrer, 2016) Because of the narrowing of the upper respiratory airways during sleep, obstructive sleep apnea is a frequent condition that affects breathing processes and lowers the quantity of oxygen (SpO2) that reaches the internal organs of humans. Low blood saturation levels, which can be tracked, for instance, with pulsometer sensors, can have major health effects on the patient. This article compares and contrasts several regression techniques, including Support Vector Regression (SVR), Gradient Boosting, Lasso Regression, Ridge Regression, and Sequential Neural Network, to find a way to predict a decrease in SpO2 levels based on spirogram features for four distinct patients independently. The models displayed the best R2 determination score values. (S´anchez, 2016) The famed long-range communication range and underwater capabilities of LoRa technology Regulatory constraints and restrictions regarding the usage of wireless technologies may vary depending on the region and frequency bands utilized. (Li, 2015) Extended communication range: sensitivity of 148 dBm, maximum communication distance of 15 km interference in the spectrum As LoRa technology advances and more networks are deployed, there will be more interference in the spectrum between the various devices and networks. (Li, 2019) A few novel image processing techniques are put forth to address issues with low contrast and dimly lit images. To detect and classify marine organisms—which are widely acknowledged to be the fastest item detection approach—a deep CNN method is suggested. (Cici, 2018) Multiple network nodes can be linked and are taxed in different operating modes. little payload LoRa transmission data has a byte restriction and a comparatively modest payload (Chaudhry, 2018) Based on the Aloha approach, the protocol provides automated frequency jump and rate adaptation features together with LBT functionality. Must establish a new network: To implement LoRa, users must first construct their network. (Ahmed, 2019) To ensure the safety of their users, ORH service providers frequently track the trajectory of the trip and notify any odd behavior that arises when the trajectory deviates. The benefit of safety monitoring is accompanied by serious privacy concerns about the disclosure of user location data. We provide in this study Safety, a privacy-preserving safety monitoring approach for ORH services. It makes it possible for an ORH service provider to identify a user's trajectory deviation without having to find out where they are. By leveraging relatively homomorphic encryption, we offer two secure trajectory similarity computation techniques in safety that are utilized to design an agreed path and measure trajectory deviation, respectively. (Liu, 2015)

III. PROPOSED METHOD

The current project utilizes an underwater communication module that employs magnetic fields for data transmission, enabling wireless communication. The device in this project incorporates four types of health monitoring sensors, including heart rate, SPO2, respiratory, and body temperature sensors. The system operates by continuously monitoring the underwater environment using its sensors and detectors. If any anomalies are detected, especially magnetic anomalies, the system can interpret this data and assess whether there is a potential hazard. Alerts are generated in real-time and sent to the user devices. This project focuses on improving underwater communication by replicating the unique frequency characteristics of seawater channels using electromagnetic (EM) fields in an embedded system. Underwater communication faces challenges due to high attenuation and dispersion of electromagnetic waves in seawater. The goal is to develop a system that generates and modulates magnetic field waves to match seawater's frequency properties, enhancing communication efficiency and reliability.Magnetic fields, chosen for their ability to penetrate seawater with less attenuation, offer potential for effective underwater communication. Modulating these magnetic fields at specific frequencies allows encoding and decoding of information for data transmission. However, success relies on accurately understanding seawater's frequency domain properties. Seawater exhibits frequency-dependent attenuation and dispersion affecting communication range and quality .By replicating these properties in the embedded system, the project aims to create a communication system optimized for magnetic field waves. The main scope of this project is to develop an integrated underwater health monitoring system using an Arduino-controlled transmitter with multiple health sensors and a receiver equipped to alert and display critical health data for researchers exploring underwater environments. This innovation addresses the challenges of underwater environments, contributing to advancements in underwater data transmission and marine research. Ultimately, the project seeks to unlock the potential of electromagnetic waves, specifically magnetic fields, for efficient and reliable underwater communication.

Transmitter

Figure 1. Transmitter diagram

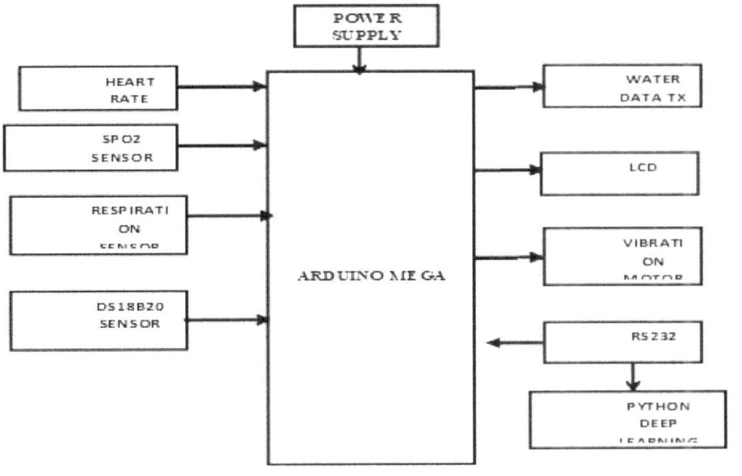

Receiver

Figure 2. Receiver diagram

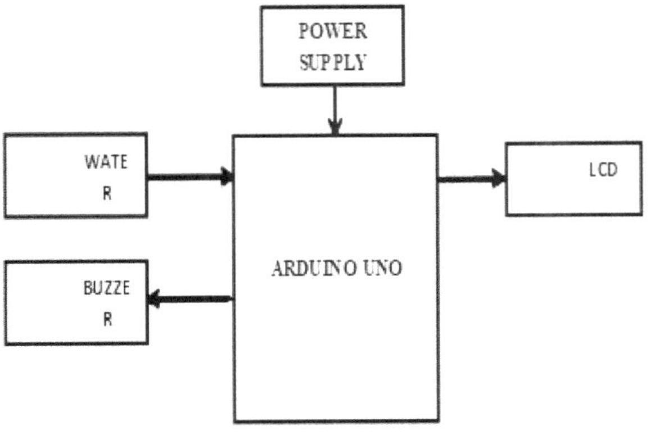

In this system, ARDUINO microcontroller is used to control all over system. There are two sections. One is transmitter section and another is receiver section. Transmitter section acts as a device that attached with human body. Receiver section acts as a control room. We are going to monitor the health condition of a person who is going to do research underwater like oceans. The device contains four types of health monitoring sensors itself. Heart rate sensor monitors person's heart rate. SPO2 sensor monitors blood oxygen level of the person. Respiratory sensor monitors the duration to take breath in/out of the person. DS18B20 sensor is a temperature sensor that used to monitor body temperature of the person. We use python deep learning to identify underwater creatures. The data will come from python deep learning to the HARDWARE using RS232 cable. If that creature seems dangerous, then the VIBRATION MOTOR into the device will vibrate to alert the person. LIQUID CRYSTAL DISPLAY (LCD) that fixed on the device is used to display the health condition status of the person. Above all sensors section will be the TRANSMITTER section. In RECEIVER section, a BUZZER is there. If any sensor detects abnormality of the person health, then the data will be sent to RECEIVER. When RECEIVER SECTION receives the data, BUZZER will scream to alert the control room. Communication between TRANSMITTER and RECEIVER section will happen with the help of UNDERWATER COMMUNICATION MODULE. It contains the circuit that helps to transmit and receive the data using Magnetic field. The transmitter circuit transmits the health monitoring data and receiver section receives the data. Receiver section also contains LCD display that displays the alert message if any abnormality found in transmitter section.

IV. MODULES

- Health Monitoring Sensor Module
- Python Deep Learning and Creature Identification Module
- Alert and Notification Module
- Underwater Communication Module

Module Description

Health Monitoring Sensor Module

Figure 3. Health Monitoring Sensor Module

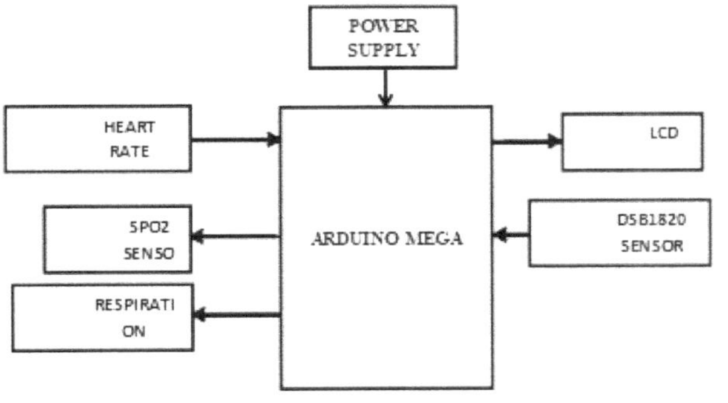

The Health Monitoring Sensor Module integrates crucial sensors designed for underwater research, ensuring the well-being of individuals exploring ocean environments. This module incorporates a range of sensors, namely the heart rate sensor, SPO2 sensor, respiratory sensor, and DS18B20 temperature sensor. The heart rate sensor accurately monitors the individual's pulse, providing insights into cardiovascular health. The SPO2 sensor measures blood oxygen levels, crucial for assessing respiratory efficiency. Additionally, the respiratory sensor tracks the duration of breaths, offering insights into respiratory patterns. The DS18B20 temperature sensor provides real-time monitoring of the person's body temperature. Each sensor plays a pivotal role in collecting vital signs, collectively contributing to a comprehensive health assessment and enhancing safety during underwater exploration

Python Deep Learning And Creature Identification Module

Figure 4. Python Deep Learning and Creature Identification Module

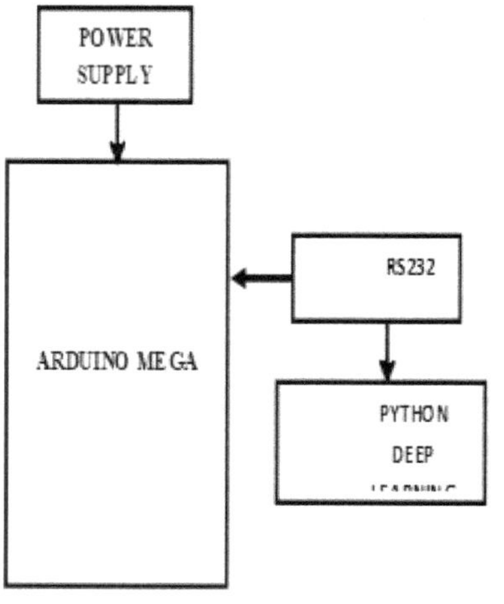

The Python Deep Learning and Creature Identification Module plays a pivotal role in the underwater monitoring system. Leveraging Python's deep learning capabilities, this module is designed to identify and classify underwater creatures effectively. By employing advanced algorithms, the system can analyze data collected from the underwater environment, such as images or sensor readings, enabling the identification of various marine organisms. The deep learning models within this module are trained to recognize distinct patterns, shapes, and features associated with different underwater species. As a result, researchers can gain valuable insights into the marine ecosystem, aiding in ecological studies and enhancing the safety of individuals conducting underwater research by alerting them to the presence of potentially hazardous creatures.

Alert And Notification Module

Transmitter:

Figure 5. Alert and Notification Module Transmitter

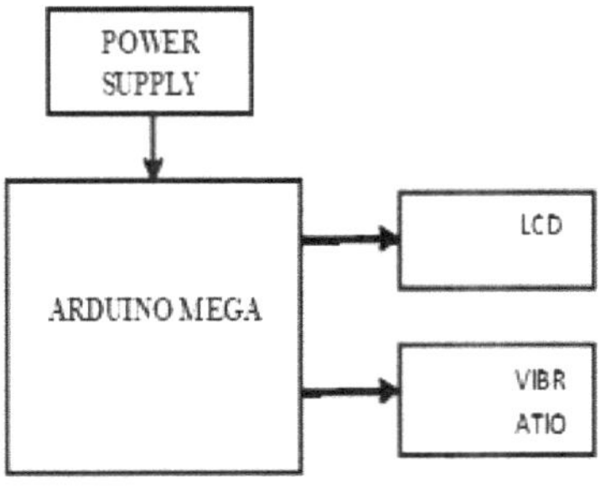

Receiver:

Figure 6. Alert and Notification Module Receiver

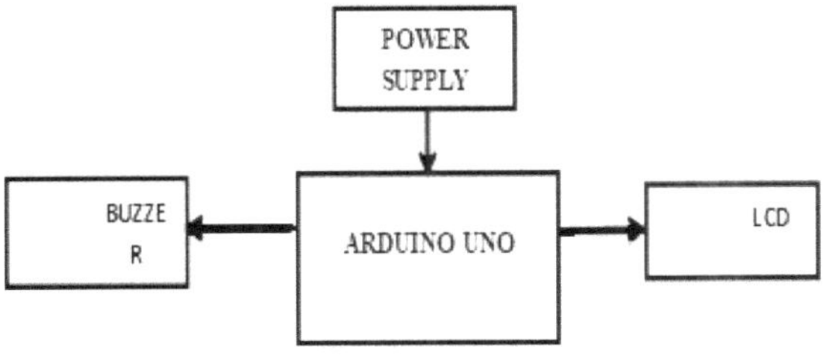

The Alert and Notification Module plays a pivotal role in enhancing safety during underwater research. In the Transmitter Section, a VIBRATION MOTOR and LIQUID CRYSTAL DISPLAY (LCD) work synergistically to alert the user to potential dangers. The VIBRATION MOTOR provides a tactile alert in response to the identification of dangerous underwater creatures, ensuring the user is promptly notified even in challenging underwater conditions. Simultaneously, the LCD visually displays real-time health condition updates. In the Receiver Section, a BUZZER serves as an audible alarm, signaling the control room in case of abnormal health conditions detected by the various sensors in the Transmitter Section. This integrated alert system provides comprehensive and immediate notifications, contributing to the overall safety and well-being of the individual conducting underwater research.

Under Water Communication Module:

Transmitter:

Figure 7. Underwater Communication Module Transmitter

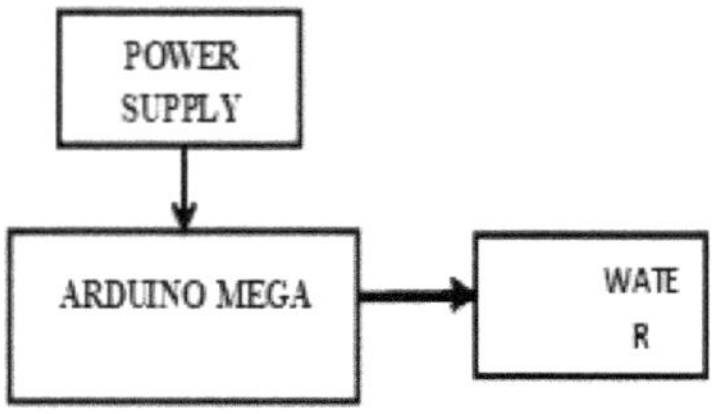

Receiver:

Figure 8. Underwater Communication Module Receiver

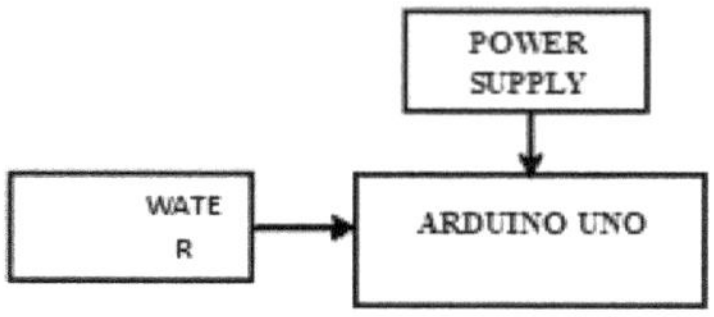

The Underwater Communication Module serves as the critical link between the Transmitter and Receiver Sections, enabling seamless data transmission in the demanding underwater setting. This module is designed to overcome the challenges posed by underwater communication, leveraging a specialized circuitry that utilizes magnetic fields. The circuitry is adept at encoding and transmitting health data and creature identification results from the Transmitter Section to the Receiver Section. The use of magnetic fields is particularly advantageous, as they experience lower attenuation in seawater, ensuring more reliable communication. By outlining this sophisticated infrastructure, the module ensures efficient and effective communication, enhancing the overall functionality of the system for monitoring underwater researchers' health and providing timely alerts in case of anomalies.

V. CONCLUSION

In conclusion, this project presents a comprehensive and innovative solution for monitoring the health of underwater researchers. By combining health monitoring sensors, Python deep learning for creature identification, and a robust underwater communication module, the system provides real-time data transmission and alerts. The integration of magnetic field-based communication addresses the challenges of underwater environments. The transmitter component monitors vital indications such as heart rate, blood oxygen level, breathing patterns, and body temperature by directly interacting with the human body through the use of health monitoring sensors. Python-based deep learning is employed for underwater creature identification, providing an added layer of safety by alerting the individual through a vibration motor if potentially dangerous creatures are detected. The receiver section, stationed in the control room, employs an underwater communication module using magnetic fields to ensure reliable data transmission. A buzzer in the receiver section promptly notifies the control room of any health abnormalities detected, enhancing safety and facilitating real-time monitoring during underwater research endeavours. Future enhancements could involve refining creature identification with advanced machine learning and exploring wireless communication technologies Overall, this project contributes to advancing underwater

REFERENCES

Ahmed, S. A., Dogra, D. P., Kar, S., & Roy, P. P. (2019, July). Trajectory-based surveillance analysis: A survey. *IEEE Transactions on Circuits and Systems for Video Technology*, 29(7), 1985–1997. DOI: 10.1109/TCSVT.2018.2857489

Chaudhry, B., El-Amine, S., & Shakshuki, E.. (2018). Passenger safety in ride-sharing services. *Procedia Computer Science*, 130, 1044–1050. DOI: 10.1016/j.procs.2018.04.146

Cheon, J. H., Kim, A., Kim, M., & Song, Y. "Homomorphic encryption for arithmetic of approximate numbers," in *Proc. Int. Conf. Theory Appl. Cryptol. Inf. Secur.*, 2017, pp. 409–437. DOI: 10.1007/978-3-319-70694-8_15

Cici, B., Markopoulou, A., Frias-Martinez, E., & Laoutaris, N. (2016). Assessing the potential of ride-sharing using mobile and social data: D. S'anchez, S. Mart'ınez, and J. Domingo-Ferrer, "Co-utile p2p ridesharing via decentralization and reputation management,". *Transportation Research Part C, Emerging Technologies*, 73, 147–166.

Domingo-Ferrer, J., Farr'as, O., Mart'ınez, S., S'anchez, D., & Soria-Comas, J. (2016). Self-enforcing protocols via co-utile reputation management. *Information Sciences*, 367, 159–175. DOI: 10.1016/j.ins.2016.05.050

Li, Y., Chen, R., Chen, L., & Xu, J. (2015, July/August). Towards social-aware ridesharing group query services. *IEEE Transactions on Services Computing*, 10(4), 646–659. DOI: 10.1109/TSC.2015.2508440

Y. Li, W. Xu, and M. L. Yiu, "Client-side service for recommending rewarding routes to mobile crowdsourcing workers," IEEE Trans. Serv. Comput., early access, Mar. 18, 2019, .DOI: 10.1109/TSC.2019.2905564

Liu, A., Zhengy, K., Liz, L., Liu, G., Zhao, L., & Zhou, X. "Efficient secure similarity computation on encrypted trajectory data," in Proc. Data Eng. IEEE 31st Int. Conf., 2015, pp. 66–77. DOI: 10.1109/ICDE.2015.7113273

Su, H., Liu, S., Zheng, B., Zhou, X., & Zheng, K. (2020). A survey of trajectory distance measures and performance evaluation. *The VLDB Journal*, 29(1), 3–32. DOI: 10.1007/s00778-019-00574-9

Chapter 11
Leveraging AI and Machine Learning for Digital Forensics

Ramy El-Kady
https://orcid.org/0000-0003-2208-7576
Police Academy, Egypt

ABSTRACT

This article explores the digital forensics of cryptocurrencies and the dark web, focusing on the role of blockchain in their formation and evidence gathering. It emphasizes the need for artificial intelligence and machine language in dark web forensics and the critical gap in research on host-based cryptocurrency forensics, especially mobile-based forensics. Most studies on host-based forensics focus on outdated operating systems or platforms, emphasizing the need for more up-to-date versions. Cryptocurrency forensics primarily analyzes publicly accessible blockchains using clustering heuristics and machine learning-based analysis to identify anonymous entities or provide investigation guidance. Security and vulnerability assessment studies are crucial for examining forensic methods for cryptocurrencies, providing insights into potential exploits or attacks useful for forensic investigations. While research in Blockchain-based forensics is advancing organically alongside technological advancements, there is a need for focused attention on host-based forensics for cryptocurrency.

DOI: 10.4018/979-8-3373-1657-4.ch011

INTRODUCTION

With the increasing use of modern technology and the exploitation of the Internet by criminal groups and terrorist organizations, digital forensics' role in combating cybercrime has become more crucial than ever. As we witness growing rates of cybercrimes such as identity theft, online fraud, and data breaches, it is clear that digital forensics is one of the most critical tools for criminal justice and law enforcement agencies. Your role in reducing cybercrime is not just important; it is urgent and integral (El-Kady, 2023).

Digital forensics plays a pivotal role in combating cybercrimes. It is a specialized field within forensic science that deals explicitly with identifying, acquiring, processing, analyzing, and reporting electronically stored data. This electronic evidence is an integral part of nearly all illegal acts, and the assistance of digital forensics is vital for law enforcement investigations (El-Kady, 2023). So, understanding and applying digital forensics are crucial in the fight against cybercrime.

As digital evidence continues to evolve, the importance of digital forensics is rising. This evidence necessitates law enforcement agencies to implement stringent safety, health, and reliability measures to ensure its admissibility and authenticity in criminal courts (El-Kady, 2024). The ever-changing landscape of digital evidence underscores the urgency for law enforcement professionals to remain abreast of technological advancements. Expertise in digital forensics is not just necessary; it is essential to success in the ongoing battle against cybercrime. Its role is crucial in ensuring the admissibility and authenticity of digital evidence in criminal courts.

Technological advancements have given rise to cryptocurrencies, which have gained global acceptance in many legal fields. However, these new currencies have also become a tool for criminal groups and terrorist organizations to commit various criminal activities, especially on the dark web. The unique characteristics of these currencies and the dark network contribute to the anonymity of the perpetrators, posing significant challenges for law enforcement agencies in their pursuit.

With these successive developments, law enforcement authorities face numerous challenges in confronting criminal activities committed via the Internet. The most significant is the problem of proving these crimes through digital evidence. This study underscores the urgency and importance of addressing the role of digital forensics in this context.

The study aims to illuminate the digital forensics of cryptocurrencies and the dark web by reviewing the role of the elements and tools involved in their formation, such as blockchain, computers, and mobile phones, and learning evidence. It will focus on its methods and review the extent to which artificial intelligence and machine language can be relied upon in forensics on the dark web (El-Kady, 2024).

Literature Review

Research indicates that the combination of AI and Blockchain technology improves automation, security, data sharing, decision-making, and the creation of innovative business models in many industries. Artificial Intelligence (AI) and Blockchain are highly influential technologies that have significantly shaped the modern era. Integrating these elements presents many possibilities for improving security, effectiveness, and confidence in various applications.

This synthesis examines the function of artificial intelligence (AI) in Blockchain technology and its various uses based on insights derived from multiple research articles. The amalgamation of Artificial Intelligence (AI) and Blockchain technology has immense potential to augment security, trust, and efficiency in diverse applications. Blockchain offers a reliable and distributed framework for AI, while AI improves Blockchain's efficiency and ability to make decisions. The potential of this synergy is being investigated in various sectors, while there are still obstacles to overcome to realize its full benefits.

Research indicates that Blockchain technology can reduce weaknesses in AI systems by offering a secure and reliable environment for storing and processing data. Some researchers observe that the utilization of Blockchain in AI primarily revolves around the automation of payment processes, facilitating access to shared ledgers, and regulating interactions between participants through the implementation of smart contracts (Salah et al., 2019).

Some scholars believe Blockchain technology can mitigate security issues associated with AI applications and enhance blockchain's performance (Shinde et al., 2021). Others believe AI can enhance blockchains' learning capabilities and improve their efficiency. Additionally, AI can introduce new consensus mechanisms for interacting with blockchains and help address security and privacy issues (Salama et al., 2022).

Others see that AI has the potential to enhance Blockchain performance by introducing new consensus methods and improving data integrity checks. They also see AI and Blockchain synergize by automating iterative processes, boosting decision-making, and optimizing user experience in healthcare, banking, and government (Khan et al., 2022; Salama et al., 2022).

Some scholars observe that Integrating AI and Blockchain allows for decentralized AI, where AI systems can function using trustworthy, shared data without intermediaries, enhancing system performance and decision-making. Some scholars see that Blockchain has the potential to enhance AI by enabling secure data sharing, safeguarding data privacy, endorsing reliable AI judgments, and decentralizing AI (Wang et al., 2021).

Others believe that integrating AI and Blockchain can result in Decentralized AI, which allows for analysis, decision-making, and self-learning using trustworthy and shared data. This integration can enhance system performance and enable autonomous agents to work together (Chavali et al., 2020).

Some scholars see Blockchain as enabling secure data sharing for AI model training, ensuring data privacy, and promoting reliable AI decision-making (Wang et al., 2021; Khan et al., 2022). Many scholars believe that AI may be used to automate the implementation of smart contracts on the Blockchain, resulting in more efficient and reliable corporate procedures. Some see that Artificial intelligence (AI) facilitates the automated implementation of intelligent contracts, resulting in improved efficiency and reliability of corporate operations in blockchain technology (Ojha et al., 2023).

Many scholars believe AI can provide robots with human-like intelligence and dynamic capabilities. Additionally, AI can be integrated with blockchain technology in many applications, resulting in up to 90% accuracy when used correctly (Hussain et al., 2021).

Others perceive AI and Blockchain as being investigated for their potential to improve security, efficiency, and trust in critical sectors like healthcare, finance, energy, government, and defense (Khan et al., 2022; Shinde et al., 2021). Some scholars believe that merging AI with blockchain technology offers new prospects for creating innovative business models through digitalization (Xuan & Ness, 2023). Some scholars perceive the effective integration of AI with Blockchain as presenting ongoing research problems, such as scalability, interoperability, and the creation of robust consensus processes (Salah et al., 2019; Hussain et al., 2021).

Methodology

The descriptive-analytical method is the most appropriate research method for studying social and legal phenomena. It is defined as: "studying the phenomenon as it exists in reality, describing it closely and expressing it qualitatively or quantitatively to reach conclusions that contribute to understanding and developing this reality" (Obeidat et al., 1996). Also, the research subject and its transnational character impose on the researcher the use of a comparative approach by referring to some facts and incidents related to cryptocurrencies and dark web forensics, focusing on its methods.

The descriptive-analytical method is the most suitable research method for studying dark web crimes, as it involves closely describing and expressing the phenomenon, using a comparative approach to compare facts and incidents. The research tools that the researcher will use as scientific sources in preparing this research are the Arab and foreign legal literature related to the subject of research in the field of criminal law, as well as the relevant specialized literature, whether they are books, papers, etc., or university dissertations. Alternatively, a master's degree or articles are published in scientific journals on the topic, in addition to news published in various media outlets and the Internet.

Results

The development of cryptocurrency forensics could be summarized as Bitcoin, introduced by Nakamoto in 2008 (Nakamoto, 2008), being the most extensively studied cryptocurrency on all forensic platforms. However, research on other cryptocurrencies, such as Ether, Monero, Verge, and so on, is lacking. An initial study was conducted on Blockchain-based cryptocurrency forensics in 2011. According to the FBI in 2012, this research emerged as criminal actors began showing interest in cryptocurrencies around two years after Bitcoin's introduction in 2008 (Reid & Harrigan, 2013). The initial investigation into Bitcoin forensics was conducted in 2014, with separate studies focusing on mobile-based (Montanez, 2014) and computer-based approaches. These studies, presented as master's theses, demonstrate academic curiosity in this field (Doran, 2014).

Research in digital cryptocurrency forensics saw a hiatus of approximately 3-4 years before resuming around 2017 to 2018. This resurgence coincided with cryptocurrency's growing popularity among the general public and criminal individuals. Research on cryptocurrencies conducted on mobile devices is scarce, with a significant focus on the security and privacy of cryptocurrency wallet applications. This suggests a need for more excellent studies on forensic analysis of mobile platforms to uncover digital evidence (Dudani et al., 2023).

Regarding computer-based cryptocurrency study, Windows-based research is the most prominent, followed by Linux and Mac OS. Research might be undertaken to analyze Bitcoin artifacts on Mac OS platforms. Windows 7 is the most extensively studied computer platform for Bitcoin artifacts, so there is a lack of research on Windows 10 and 11 computers in this area.

Most studies on cryptocurrency forensics focus on analyzing the publicly accessible blockchain. This involves using clustering heuristics and machine learning-based analysis to gain valuable information. The goal is to either identify anonymous entities or provide guidance for investigations. Some scholars developed an Elliptic Dataset as a significant resource for researching the application of machine learning and graph-based methods in Bitcoin forensics based on Blockchain technology (Weber et al., 2019).

Discussions

Introducing the Dark Web

The dark web is a hidden part of the Internet, divided into three main sections: the Surface Network, which contains only 0.03% of the information accessible through traditional search engines; the Deep Network, which includes academic databases, government records, corporate and commercial bank databases, email content, and TV broadcast services; and the Dark Web, which is not commonly accessed and is a breeding ground for illegal criminal activities, as not everything on the Internet can be accessed by users.

What is known as Black Networks or the Dark Web has appeared, and much of its content is confidential. They provide privacy to their users away from censorship (El-Kady, 2021), and services are provided. Information is exchanged confidentially between its members, and no user outside the network can see its content or search for it in the traditional ways.

Unlike the clear web, also called the "Surface Web," which refers to information that is publicly available and indexed by conventional search engines, the dark web consists of encrypted hidden networks that allow the owner and users of the site to keep their identity anonymous while being relatively difficult to track (Guccione, 2019), which makes it the preferred network for all criminals, as it provides a safe environment for their illegal activities (El-Kady, 2021).

In summary, the dark web can be defined as a part of the Internet that allows the issuance of websites and the dissemination of information without revealing the identity or location of the publisher. It also requires software, settings, and special authorization to access it. It is a part of the web not indexed by search engines and can be accessed on the dark web through certain services such as Tor (Biddle et al., 2003). It is a compilation of interconnected networks and advanced technologies to exchange and disseminate digital content. The dark web is not an independent network but a means of accessing unindexed resources on the existing physical network using extra technologies (Dudani et al., 2023).

Introduction to Cryptocurrency

Cryptocurrencies are defined as *a virtual digital currency that has no tangible physical entity or physical existence, is produced by computer programs, and is not subject to control or control by a central bank or any official international administration*, nor does it carry a serial number, it is used via the Internet In buying and selling transactions or converting them into other currencies, and receiving voluntary acceptance from those dealing in them (Al-Bahouth, 2017). After Bitcoin's inception, more cryptocurrencies have emerged.

Cryptocurrency mining involves using specialised computational resources to append blocks to a proof-of-work (PoW) network. A new block added to a blockchain authenticates and documents the most recent set of transactions while also generating fresh digital tokens. Cryptocurrency mining refers to the computational activity performed within a proof-of-work blockchain scheme. As they vie to solve a complicated mathematical equation, crypto miners consume enormous quantities of computational power (Britannica Money, 2024).

The miner who solves the challenge quickly is granted the opportunity to append the recently generated block to a blockchain. In addition, they gather transaction fees and the newly created cryptocurrency linked to that block. Cryptocurrency mining necessitates significant computational resources, usually quantified in hashes per second, sometimes called a miner's hash rate. Hashing is a cryptographic operation that transforms variable inputs, such as transaction data, into fixed-length sequences of characters known as hashes (Britannica Money, 2024).

Cryptocurrency miners use dedicated gear, such as application-specific integrated circuits (ASICs) and graphics processing units (GPUs). Virtually anyone with access to the Internet and computational capabilities can opt to engage in cryptocurrency mining. The inherent decentralization of crypto mining ensures the security of a proof-of-work blockchain. Develop a deeper understanding of decentralized public ledger technologies and consensus procedures. For more understanding of the basic cryptocurrency architecture (see: Figure 1)

Figure 1. The basic cryptocurrency architecture (Source: blockgeeks.com)

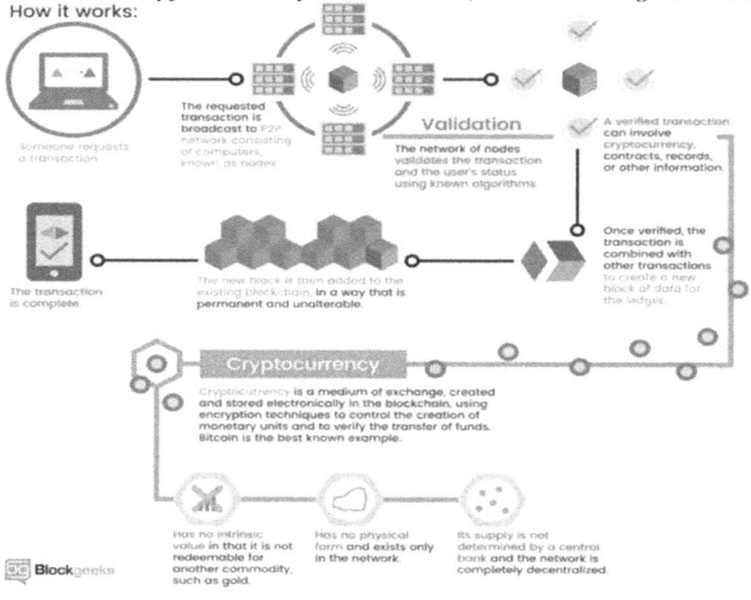

The most prominent cryptocurrencies are Ripple, which appeared in 2012; Litecoin and Monroe, which appeared in 2014; the Chinese currency NEO, which the Chinese government launched in the same year to support the Chinese economy; Ethereum, which appeared in 2015; Bitcoin Volt, which appeared in 2019; and Facebook's Libra currency (Diem), which is expected to be launched soon (Nour, 2022).

The historical overview of cryptocurrency

The historical overview of cryptocurrency is crucial to understanding its development in depth. The emergence of cryptocurrencies as a result of the continuous technological development in our world is due to the tendency of most institutions, authorities, and countries to digitize their various systems and transform them into a digital economy and a system of financial inclusion, where the need to develop new tools that bear the digital character for dealing within this world has emerged, and cryptocurrencies and blockchain have been one of the tools of financial dealing on the Internet, which includes millions of financial transactions. The names of these currencies have multiplied since they began under encrypted digital currencies, "Cryptocurrencies."

Scholars see that the emergence of Cryptocurrency started in 2009; the virtual currency landscape underwent a significant transformation with the introduction of Bitcoin by Satoshi Nakamoto, the pseudonymous creator (Nakamoto, 2008). Bitcoin is built upon blockchain decentralized record technology (Casino et al., 2019). Nakamoto asserts that implementing a decentralized electronic cash system will prevent the necessity for transactions to pass through financial institutions, resolving the inherent issue of double-spending, which is both illicit and erodes confidence in any currency, ultimately resulting in inflation. Following Nakamoto's findings, the network uses hashing to timestamp transactions and create an unalterable chain of hash-based proof-of-work, an immutable record.

This creates a ledger that undergoes peer review and is immune to alteration by a single user, rendering it more dependable than a centralized system where the sole verification point is the engaged agency. After the development of Bitcoin, several other cryptocurrencies, such as Litecoin, Dash, Ethereum, Monero, Dogecoin, and others, were introduced. These cryptocurrencies were built using various hashing algorithms and approaches for anonymization (Dudani et al., 2023).

On the other hand, several theories propose that the history of cryptocurrency technology encompasses the creation of Bitcoin and blockchain technology, its progression from a specialized experiment to a worldwide financial phenomenon, and the rise of different cryptocurrencies and their interactions with conventional financial systems. The field of cryptocurrency technology has undergone substantial advancements since the inception of Bitcoin in 2009. This review consolidates significant findings from several research articles to provide a comprehensive picture of the historical evolution and technical progress in the cryptocurrency field.

Starting with Bitcoin, the historical evolution of cryptocurrency technology has been characterized by notable milestones and technical progress. Utilizing blockchain technology has been essential in facilitating safe and decentralized transactions. The proliferation of trading platforms and the acceptance of stablecoins have been the primary factors propelling the expansion of the cryptocurrency sector.

The historical trajectory of cryptocurrency technology encompasses the inception and widespread recognition of Bitcoin, the inaugural and predominantly recognized cryptocurrency, and the fundamental blockchain technology that facilitates its secure functioning (Sharma et al., 2023). The development of Bitcoin may be traced from its origins as a specialized prototype technology to its present position as a worldwide financial phenomenon, shaped by elements like government regulations, market volatility, and the emergence of other cryptocurrencies (Hossain et al., 2023).

Moreover, the historical progression of Bitcoin is significant since it has played a crucial role in the advancement of cryptocurrencies (Chohan, 2017). Developed eight years ago, cryptocurrency technology, namely Bitcoin, can transform global markets by eliminating obstacles related to exchange rates and traditional national currencies (Kadoo & Sodi, 2023). Significant benchmarks in the evolution of Bitcoin encompass the establishment of the initial blockchain, the rise of cryptocurrency exchanges, and the widespread use of Bitcoin mining (Hossain et al., 2023; Chohan, 2017).

On the other hand, other scholars show that Blockchain technology is the foundation for cryptocurrencies, facilitating safe and decentralized transactions without relying on a single authority (Sharma et al., 2023). The historical trajectory of cryptocurrency technology centers around the inception of Bitcoin and its subsequent evolution into a multifaceted market encompassing several blockchain initiatives and engagements with conventional fiat currencies (CHALDAEVA` & Danilin, 2021).

Furthermore, scholars widely acknowledge that Bitcoin and other cryptocurrencies have yielded advantages for the global economy, including facilitating international money transfers and creating new investment prospects (Kumar et al., 2023). However, they have also been susceptible to significant volatility and exploited for illicit purposes. The historical trajectory of cryptocurrency technology encompasses the rise of Bitcoin and other digital currencies and the significance of blockchain technology within international finance (Kohut, 2023). Meanwhile, some observe that the technology has been extensively embraced and valued for its capacity to enhance operations and minimize mistakes in diverse industries, including the banking sector (CHALDAEVA` & Danilin, 2021; Kohut, 2023).

Meanwhile, other observers claim that the cryptocurrency sector has experienced substantial expansion, propelled by the advancement of trading platforms and the growing adoption of stablecoins (CHALDAEVA` & Danilin, 2021). Besides that, exchanges for cryptocurrencies have become essential components of the digital asset ecosystem, providing various services and varying security and transaction capabilities (Kohut, 2023). In contrast, numerous academics demonstrate that Cryptocurrency has enabled more convenient international money transfers and generated novel investment prospects. However, they have also been linked to significant volatility and illicit operations (Kumar et al., 2023).

On the other hand, some show that cryptocurrencies' emergence has sparked debates about their capacity to destabilize conventional financial institutions and their feasibility as enduring investment instruments (Hossain et al., 2023; Kadoo & Sodi, 2023). Furthermore, the future of cryptocurrencies entails the delicate equilibrium between their advantages and the need to safeguard consumers and ensure financial stability (Kumar et al., 2023). Emerging trends indicate that cryptocurrencies have the potential to transform digital trade marketplaces by establishing trading systems without fees and eliminating obstacles related to fixed exchange rates (Kadoo & Sodi, 2023).

Although cryptocurrencies have yielded certain advantages, they also present obstacles, including instability and regulatory considerations. The future trajectory of cryptocurrencies is expected to entail the delicate equilibrium between fostering innovation and ensuring stability within the global financial system. Multiple studies consistently demonstrate that Bitcoin, launched in 2009, is the pioneering decentralized digital money and has emerged as a worldwide financial phenomenon.

Additionally, some scholars show that the development of cryptocurrencies started with the American cryptographer David Chaum, who devised a form of encrypted electronic money known as ecash in 1983 (Pitta, 1999). Subsequently, in 1995, he put it into practice using Digicash, an early iteration of secured electronic transactions. Digicash necessitated user software to retrieve notes from a bank and assign particular encryption keys before transmitting them to a destination.

This enabled the digital currency to be impervious to traceability by a third party. In 1996, the National Security Agency released a document titled "How to Make a Mint: The Cryptography of Anonymous Electronic Cash," which detailed a cryptocurrency system designed for anonymous transactions. The article was initially published in an MIT email group in October 1996 and subsequently accepted for publication in The American Law Review in April 1997 (Law et al., 1996).

In 1998, Wei Dai introduced "b-money," a decentralized electronic cash exchange system that ensures anonymity (Dai & List, 1998). Nick Szabo later described BitGold (Peck, 2012). Similarly to Bitcoin and subsequent cryptocurrencies, BitGold (not to be mistaken with the later gold-based exchange BitGold) was characterized as an electronic currency system that necessitated users to fulfill a proof-of-work task, where solutions were cryptographically compiled and made public.

As mentioned, Bitcoin was invented in January 2009 by anonymous inventor Satoshi Nakamoto. Its proof-of-work system employed SHA-256, a cryptographic hash function (Brito & Castillo, 2016). In April 2011, Namecoin was proposed to establish a decentralized DNS. In October 2011, Litecoin was introduced, employing scrypt as its hashing algorithm instead of SHA-256. Launched in August 2012, Peercoin employed a combination of proof-of-work and proof-of-stake mechanisms (Steadman, 2013). Cryptocurrency has had multiple phases of expansion and decline, including several speculative bubbles and market downturns, such as 2011, 2013–2014/15, 2017–2018, and 2021–2023 (Mark & De Vynck, 2022).

On August 6, 2014, the UK government publicly declared that its Treasury had initiated a research project on cryptocurrencies and their potential impact on the UK economy. The primary objective of the study was to determine the necessity of considering regulation (Uddin, 2022). The organization's final report was published in 2018, and in January 2021, it released a consultation on cryptoassets and stablecoins (Weber & Baisch, 2023; Treasury, 2021).

El Salvador became the first nation to officially recognize Bitcoin as legal cash in June 2021, following a 62–22 decision by the Legislative Assembly to approve a bill proposed by President Nayib Bukele regarding the classification of cryptocurrency as such (Sabry, 2021). In August 2021, Cuba enacted Resolution 215 to officially acknowledge and officially establish cryptocurrency regulations, including Bitcoin

(Dai et al., 2023). In September 2021, the Chinese government, the second largest cryptocurrency market, deemed all Bitcoin transactions unlawful. This culminated in a systematic effort to suppress cryptocurrencies, which had already prohibited the functioning of intermediaries and miners inside China (Dai et al., 2023).

Ethereum's consensus mechanism, the second largest cryptocurrency globally at the time, was upgraded from proof-of-work (PoW) to proof-of-stake (PoS) on 15 September 2022 through an upgrade process referred to as "the Merge." According to Ethereum's founder, the improvement can potentially reduce Ethereum's energy consumption and carbon dioxide emissions by 99.9%. On 11 November 2022, FTX Trading Ltd., a cryptocurrency exchange that managed a crypto hedge fund with a market capitalization of $18 billion, declared bankruptcy. It has been claimed that the financial consequences of the collapse went beyond the immediate FTX customer base. Additionally, during a Reuters conference, executives from the financial industry expressed the need for regulatory intervention to safeguard cryptocurrency investors. According to technology expert Avivah Litan, significant enhancements in user experience, controls, safety, and customer support are needed inside the Bitcoin ecosystem (Dai et al., 2023).

Levering from Bitcoin to modern advancements such as smart contracts and DeFi

Since its establishment, the Bitcoin environment has experienced a profound metamorphosis. Although Bitcoin's introduction sparked the initial excitement, the years following 2021 have seen a consistent period of rapid expansion and diversity. In this period, the emphasis has moved beyond mere currency. Our exploration will focus on thrilling breakthroughs fundamentally transforming the cryptographic domain. The emergence of smart contracts establishes the fundamental basis for groundbreaking applications such as Decentralized Finance (DeFi) (Jose, 2024).

Decentralized Finance (DeFi) technology is a novel ecosystem that has arisen. It provides financial services like lending, borrowing, and trading without dependence on conventional financial institutions. Decentralized Finance (DeFi) eliminates the intermediary role of banks and brokerages in financial transactions by utilizing blockchain technology and peer-to-peer (P2P) networks. Conventionally, one would visit a bank to obtain a loan. Within DeFi, it is possible to establish a direct connection with a lender via a dApp (Jose, 2024).

Using a smart contract, you may provide a certain amount of Bitcoin as collateral (a security deposit). After that, the smart contract would retain the collateral until the loan is fully paid, guaranteeing that both parties meet their promised responsibilities. Decentralized finance applications, or dApps, operate on blockchains, which are cryptographic distributed ledgers. All transactions are documented in chronological order and made accessible to the blockchain public, guaranteeing both transparency and security (Zetzsche et al., 2020).

Once specific predefined criteria are fulfilled, the smart contract autonomously carries out the transaction, therefore obviating the necessity for a reliable intermediary. The smart contracts and all the pertinent transaction data are stored directly on the blockchain. This blockchain may be either public, such as Ethereum, or private. Since the blockchain is a decentralized ledger, each node (computer) in the network contains a duplicate of the smart contract code (Jose, 2024).

In its current form, decentralized finance (DeFi) would face significant challenges, if not a complete impossibility, to function without smart contracts. Smart contracts serve as DeFi's fundamental infrastructure. Automating agreements and transactions obviate the necessity of relying on trusted intermediaries such as banks. Devoid of them, DeFi would forfeit its inherently decentralized and trustless essence (Jose, 2024).

Anonymity as a central element of Cryptocurrencies

In March 2013, Dark Coin, now named Dash, was developed to address the problem of absolute anonymity in cryptocurrencies. It achieved this by implementing Dark Send, which prevents tracing transactions to their source or destination addresses. Some scholars state that when Dark Send is activated, it automatically divides a payment request into smaller amounts. These smaller amounts are then pooled with other divided transactions to create a pool of more significant transactions (Duffield & Hagan, 2014).

After this, a controller node is created for each pool. After completing this process, the input transactions are rearranged to provide nearly identical outputs, a process known as mixing. Blind signatures ensure that the outputs of a pool are exclusively accessible to the pool participants while preventing any disclosure to the controller node. After all users have confirmed the accuracy of their input and output amounts, transactions are digitally signed and then distributed to the network. The blockchain stores all transaction data but does not allow viewers to establish a direct link between a sender and a receiver.

Mixing services enhance anonymity and provide challenges for investigators attempting to decipher transactions. Cryptocurrencies themselves do not pose a threat, but the utilization of cryptocurrencies and methodologies that serve the interests of criminals are the factors that necessitate the field of cryptocurrency forensics, which will be explored in the next section (Dudani et al., 2023).

Cryptocurrencies as a primary payment tool in the Dark Web

Some scholars point out that several signs indicate a close connection between cryptocurrencies and dark web markets; according to INTERPOL, it regularly receives a significant volume of cases relating to cryptocurrencies, perplexing the international law-enforcement community. The Onion Scan Report reveals that Darknet markets such as Silk Road, Alpha Bay, and Hansa generated around $3,000,000 from September 2015 to December 2016 (Tziakouris, 2018).

As per a joint source for the FBI (2012), a cybercriminal selling a ZeuS botnet Trojan was reported to exclusively take payments using Bitcoin, Liberty Reserve, or WebMoney. The source of this information was the Federal Bureau of Investigation (FBI) in 2012 (FBI, 2012). Another open-source report cited the utilization of Bitcoin on Silk Road (Montanez, 2014), which was likened to the Darknet equivalents of Amazon or eBay, facilitating the illicit trade of diverse items. Some scholars examine the involvement of the Dark Web and Cryptocurrencies in cybercrime, including a thorough analysis of the trustworthiness of cryptocurrencies. They also emphasize the importance of investor awareness (Taleby et al., 2021).

In contrast, others utilize Clear Net as a source of intelligence to analyze the transition to using Bitcoin and Monero for the illicit drug trade in Dark Net markets. According to their analysis, the news about Bitcoin traceability in 2015 had the opposite effect, promoting the use of Bitcoin for illegal drug trafficking on dark markets (Bahamazava & Nanda, 2022). However, the privacy update of Monero in 2017 led to a change in preference from Bitcoin to Monero for the same purpose (Dudani et al., 2023).

INTERPOL has identified another application of Bitcoin, which involves transferring funds to regions subject to financial monitoring or embargo (Tziakouris, 2018). This practice likely supports illicit activity in those locations. Bitcoin has the potential to serve as a significant means of financing for various groups, both lawful and unlawful, which presents a risk to the security of a nation. This evaluation was based on the FBI Intelligence Evaluation Report (FBI, 2012), which also mentioned that the internet hacktivist group LulzSec got more than $18,000 in Bitcoins from anonymous followers and supporters who donated.

INTERPOL is concerned about money laundering through Initial Coin Offering (ICOs) or cryptocurrency exchanges. This is evident from cases such as the Bitcoin exchange OKCoin, which laundered hundreds of thousands of US dollars, and the case of BitInstant, which laundered approximately $1,000,000 for Silk Road market customers (Tziakouris, 2018). Regarding money laundering using Bitcoins, the FBI encountered a case where virtual game currency was used to acquire in-game virtual products sold to other players in exchange for “clean money.”

According to a separate tip to the FBI, an individual engaged in money laundering activities outside the United States (FBI, 2012). This person utilized fraudulent accounts on the WebMoney platform to assist cybercriminals who generated profits through carding operations. In June 2010, unidentified individuals constructed 3000 online membership accounts utilizing 16000 bank accounts at a US banking institution. The purpose of these accounts was to deceive victims into providing payments for non-existent auction items (Dudani et al., 2023).

The FBI received numerous reports in 2012 regarding the use of Bitcoin in illegal transactions. However, as early as 2011, the theft of Bitcoins also became a concern. Researchers from a computer security firm discovered a malware called "Infostelar. Coinbit" specifically designed to steal bitcoins from compromised users' Bitcoin wallets and transfer them to a server in Poland. Subsequently, the FBI received numerous reports regarding the misappropriation of Bitcoins from unencrypted wallets, trading platforms, game sites, and similar sources (FBI, 2012).

In 2021, some scholars conducted a case study on the Coincheck hacking incident, which entailed the illicit acquisition of $530 million of cryptocurrencies. The study effectively demonstrates the process of laundering Bitcoin. The Binance Blockchain suffered a $570 million hack on October 7, 2022, due to flaws in cross-chain bridges. Chainalysis5 projects a total cryptocurrency loss of $2 billion in 2022, resulting from 13 cross-chain bridge assaults (Tsuchiya & Hiramoto, 2021).

Below are several further unauthorized applications of cryptocurrencies identified by INTERPOL: Cryptojacking, specifically through the use of Jenkins-Miner, has accumulated almost $3,000,000 worth of Monero, Crypto-stealing Trojans, like CryptoShuffler, pilfer funds by explicitly targeting the data stored in volatile memory or the clipboard, Non-standard Bitcoin transactions have the potential to include encoded data chunks that can be used to distribute illegal content, such as child exploitation material.

The main obstacle for law enforcement is the difficulty of removing such content because of the unchangeable nature of the blockchain; ICO exit scams include criminals deceiving victims by soliciting funds for non-existent coins and subsequently vanishing, so defrauding the victims (Tziakouris, 2018). The issue of law enforcement dealing with nation-state attacks financed through cryptocurrencies is another challenge (Dudani et al., 2023).

The issues mentioned above are not exclusive; advancements in cryptocurrencies are giving rise to increasingly intricate predicaments for law enforcement. Every cryptocurrency has its unique challenges that arise from the underlying technology. Litecoin, Monero, Dogecoin, and Dash have gained significant popularity as digital currencies. Dark coin or Dash achieves true anonymity using DarkSend (Duffield & Hagan, 2014), which utilizes mixing techniques and blind signatures. This ensures that transactions cannot be linked to specific users, as the public ledger contains no information about the individuals involved.

Owing to the advancements in cryptocurrency, criminals are endeavoring to outsmart the legal system, compelling law enforcement agencies to prioritize the field of Bitcoin forensics. Forensics plays a crucial role in discovering evidence from digital devices, blockchains, and other sources of evidence that may contain artifacts related to cryptocurrencies. Advancements in Bitcoin forensics will also deter forthcoming cryptocurrency-related offenses, diminishing criminal fascination with cryptocurrency (Dudani et al., 2023).

The global regulatory frameworks and responses to cryptocurrency-related crimes

Numerous studies indicate that the global regulatory frameworks for cryptocurrency crimes are varied and incongruous. There are demands for international standardization, collaboration, and frameworks such as FATF and FinCEN. However, these efforts encounter difficulties because of cross-border transactions and different national approaches. The regulation of cryptocurrencies is multifaceted and dynamic, with different regulatory bodies using diverse strategies to tackle the related hazards and illicit activities. This synthesis summarizes the main findings from several research studies focused on the worldwide regulatory frameworks and reactions to cryptocurrency crimes. Distinct legal systems have implemented diverse regulatory policies, which might impede innovation and provide difficulties in addressing cryptocurrency crimes. To adequately tackle these problems, a coordinated worldwide regulatory strategy is required.

Several academics demonstrate that the lack of consistent regulatory treatment across various jurisdictions impedes the establishment of a comprehensive and unified regulatory framework to effectively address crimes associated with cryptocurrencies (Dhali et al., 2023). In order to tackle the difficulties of attribution in probing ransomware attacks and other cybercrimes, a global regulatory framework for cryptocurrencies must incorporate consistency, clarity, and cost-effective implementation (Irwin & Dawson, 2019). Worldwide crypto legislation is necessary to manage cryptocurrency crimes effectively and requires collaboration between the private and public sectors (Nath, 2020). In the same context, some advocate for a globally standardized legal system and enhance current regulatory frameworks and legal procedures for cryptocurrency crimes (Huang, 2021).

On the other hand, some researchers demonstrate that implementing efficient cryptocurrency rules is frequently expensive and lacks uniformity, impeding law enforcement endeavors and fintech technological advancement (Irwin & Dawson, 2019). Efficacious frameworks must possess consistency, clarity, and cost-efficiency.

The complexities of cross-border transactions, evasion technology, and varied legislation make law enforcement of cryptocurrency-related offenses challenging (Kethineni & Cao, 2020).

In contrast, other academics argue that there is a pressing necessity for extensive worldwide legislation to govern cryptocurrency-related offenses such as money laundering, terrorist financing, and tax illegality (Nath, 2020). Mutual collaboration between the public and private sectors is crucial for efficient regulation. The interpretation and implementation of global regulatory frameworks such as the Financial Action Task Force (FATF) and the Financial Crimes Enforcement Network (FinCEN) are subject to ambiguity (Kolachala et al., 2021). Governments in Asia and other regions are tackling legal, regulatory, and enforcement concerns regarding cryptocurrency through various approaches, including prohibition, acceptance, and adherence to FATF guidelines (Paesano & Siron, 2022).

Meanwhile, some emphasize the need for international collaboration in investigating and preventing economic crimes associated with Bitcoin. Implementing a risk-oriented strategy and fostering collaboration among governments can effectively manage the risks and possibilities associated with Bitcoin circulation. International collaboration in crimes linked to cryptocurrencies entails a risk-focused strategy, effective coordination of government initiatives, and the establishment of unrestricted, decentralized management networks (Kreminskyi et al., 2021).

Conversely, some argue that strict anti-money laundering (AML) rules are being formulated and enforced by international and domestic agencies. Nevertheless, pragmatic obstacles and uncertainties exist in implementing these regulations, requiring tailored remedies for various payment systems (Kolachala et al., 2021; Paesano & Siron, 2022). Furthermore, several academics demonstrate that Bitcoin transactions' anonymity and transnational character provide substantial obstacles for law enforcement and regulatory authorities. Therefore, it is necessary to develop novel regulatory frameworks that specifically target these distinctive features without impeding the potential of the technology (Kethineni & Cao, 2020).

Moreover, the Russian Federation has a robust legal and regulatory framework for digital rights. However, implementing criminal law measures to combat crypto crime requires adapting to the growing scope of illegal activities (Sereda & Stupina, 2021). Implementing a legal framework that imposes fees on the features of cryptocurrencies that are beneficial for criminal activities, such as anonymity, can undermine their use in illicit operations (Marian, 2014).

In summary, regulating cryptocurrencies necessitates a unified worldwide strategy to address associated criminal activities efficiently. Divergent and conflicting regulatory measures across different jurisdictions pose considerable difficulties. Optimal frameworks should exhibit consistency, clarity, and cost-effectiveness, accompanied by robust international collaboration and public-private partnerships.

Robust anti-money laundering (AML) rules and cutting-edge legal structures are necessary to tackle the distinct difficulties of anonymity and the international character of cryptocurrency transactions.

Advancements in Quantum Computing and Criminal Tactics in Cryptocurrency-Related Crimes

Numerous studies indicate that progress in quantum computing has led to improved quantum security and possible risks to traditional cryptographic systems. Simultaneously, cryptocurrency-related crimes have expanded to encompass tax evasion, money laundering, Ponzi schemes, and theft. Law enforcement faces difficulties due to cross-border transactions and inconsistent government regulations.

The domains of quantum computing and cryptocurrency are undergoing fast development and have substantial ramifications for security and criminal operations. Quantum computing holds the potential to completely transform cryptographic architectures, while cryptocurrencies have emerged as a favored platform for a range of illicit operations. This synthesis analyzes the progress made in quantum computing and the development of criminal strategies in crimes associated with cryptocurrencies.

Recent developments in quantum computing pose a significant danger to current cryptographic systems, especially those that rely on RSA and ECC algorithms, which are extensively employed for digital certificates and encryption. The advancement of post-quantum cryptographic algorithms is essential to counteract these risks, in conjunction with global rules, to guarantee the proper utilization of quantum technology. The advent of quantum computing can make antiquated cryptographic systems such as RSA and ECC obsolete, increasing the risk of rights infringements and atrocities and undermining confidence in digital transactions (Majot & Yampolskiy, 2015). Advancements in quantum computing have the potential to compromise current conventional cryptographic systems, thereby requiring the development of sophisticated quantum-based cryptography systems to counteract risks (Bishwas & Advani, 2021).

Moreover, several academics demonstrate that research is primarily driven toward developing quantum-resistant cryptographic systems, specifically those that rely on lattice problems, to safeguard blockchain and cryptocurrencies from quantum attacks. The suggested cryptocurrency architecture, which is built on a post-quantum blockchain, effectively counters quantum computing assaults and enhances both its security and efficiency (Gao et al., 2018).

Quantum-resistant signature transition techniques are under consideration for Bitcoin to safeguard against adversaries that can exploit quantum technology. Schemes for transitioning to quantum-resistant signatures for Bitcoin are under consideration.

However, the reuse of public keys presents a risk to recovering users' cash in the presence of an adversary with quantum capabilities (Ilie et al., 2020).

Moreover, some studies demonstrate that Cryptocurrencies such as Bitcoin, Ethereum, and Monero are progressively employed for illicit purposes, such as drug trafficking, extortion, money laundering, and tax evasion. Bitcoin transactions' anonymity and transnational character provide substantial obstacles for law enforcement and regulatory authorities. Some examine the issues and risks of utilizing cutting-edge information technologies for illicit activities and incorporating cryptocurrencies in converting illicit profits into lawful currency (Haminskiy, 2022).

Cybercriminals employ sophisticated evasion technology to conceal their identity, complicating the identification and legal proceedings against cryptocurrency crimes. Discrimination in legislation among various jurisdictions further impedes attempts to adequately address these offenses—cybercrime activities associated with cryptocurrencies, including tax evasion, money laundering, Ponzi schemes, and cryptocurrency theft. Law enforcement faces difficulties because of the cross-border nature of transactions and the lack of uniform legislation. In conclusion, the progress made in quantum computing presents substantial risks to existing cryptographic systems, thereby requiring innovative solutions immune to quantum attacks (Kethineni & Cao, 2020).

In summary, the utilization of cryptocurrencies in illicit operations is expanding as criminals exploit the anonymity and worldwide accessibility of these digital assets. Overcoming these obstacles necessitates the implementation of strong post-quantum cryptography systems and synchronized global legislative initiatives to reduce the hazards linked to quantum computing and criminal activities on cryptocurrencies.

Cryptocurrencies forensics

Cryptocurrency forensics, also known as Bitcoin forensics, is a field of study used to establish the connection between the flow of virtual currency and the transactions or actors responsible for initiating the flow. This is particularly relevant as most unlawful activities involve using Bitcoin as a form of payment. The intricate nature of Bitcoin forensics involves meticulously tracking and understanding the movement of funds, identifying the addresses involved in transactions, establishing intricate links between various cryptocurrency wallets, and unveiling complex patterns and linkages within the Blockchain (Joshi, 2023).

Some scholars have emphasized the necessity of cryptocurrency forensics (Dudani et al., 2023); according to the FBI's 2012 Intelligence Assessment Report, there is moderate confidence that Bitcoin will be a profitable payment method for cybercriminals. This conclusion is based on the observed fluctuations in the exchange rate of Bitcoin in 2011 and the limited information available regarding its acceptance.

Based on available data from criminal investigations concerning the usage of e-Gold and WebMoney, the FBI has identified a potential future risk of Bitcoin being used for money laundering. The paper also addresses the problem of attackers utilizing malware and hacking techniques to steal Bitcoins and create Bitcoins through botnets (FBI, 2012).

Advancements in cryptocurrency forensics are underscored by real-world events, such as the FTX scandal, one of the most significant financial frauds since the Enron collapse. This case, involving cryptocurrencies, demonstrates the need for robust forensic techniques. Cryptocurrency forensics, a multidisciplinary field encompassing digital forensics and forensic accounting, is crucial in investigations involving various stakeholders (Dudani et al., 2023).

Cryptocurrency forensics is not just an investigative technique; it is a powerful tool that empowers law enforcement agencies and financial investigators to safeguard individuals from the perils of the digital world. It effectively identifies culprits and determines the whereabouts of assets, providing a robust sense of security. Tracing cryptocurrency is not just a standard practice; it is a vital tool in investigating and recovering individuals who have fallen victim to online fraud, theft, hacking, and extortion operations, offering them a shield of protection in the digital world.

Forensic Techniques Specific to Altcoins and Privacy Coins

Several studies indicate that forensic methods tailored to altcoins and privacy coins, such as Monero and Zcash, encompass clustering and tagging heuristics, transaction clustering based on timing analysis, network and transaction propagation analysis, volatile memory and network traffic investigation, and side-channel attacks. The emergence of privacy-oriented cryptocurrencies such as Monero and Zcash has presented novel obstacles and methodologies in forensic evidence examination. These coins improve user privacy using sophisticated encryption techniques, rendering conventional tracking methods less efficient.

Nevertheless, scholars have devised several methodologies to examine transactions and reveal viable forensic evidence. Studies demonstrate that privacy-focused cryptocurrencies such as Zcash can decrease user anonymity by employing heuristics that rely on usage patterns. Transactions across blockchains can be monitored, uncovering user activities across various ledgers. User tracking in emerging cryptocurrencies and services can be achieved by employing clustering and tagging algorithms, even in privacy-oriented coins like Zcash (Yousaf, 2022).

Furthermore, some observers observe that Transaction clustering, which relies on timing analysis, can accurately link transactions generated by a single device, even in privacy-oriented cryptocurrencies such as Monero and Zcash. Through transaction clustering based on timing analysis, a reasonably resourceful attacker can establish a correlation between transactions generated by a single device with great precision (Biryukov & Tikhomirov, 2019). Deanonymization of transactions in Bitcoin, Dash, Monero, and Zcash can be achieved using network-level attacks that abuse the timing of transaction messages. Transaction propagation analysis and network analysis can be employed to establish connections between transactions in privacy-oriented cryptocurrencies such as Monero and Zcash (Biryukov & Tikhomirov, 2019).

Moreover, some researchers demonstrate that Remote side-channel attacks can determine the recipient of transactions in Zcash and Monero by analyzing the response times of P2P nodes. Time-dependent side channels in zero-knowledge-proof systems can expose transaction data, including the precise amount of transacted monies, jeopardizing anonymity. Side-channel attacks, such as timing side channels and traffic-analysis attacks, can potentially reveal the secret recipient of any transaction in Zcash or Monero, transgressing privacy objectives (Tramèr et al., 2020).

Concurrently, it has been demonstrated that privacy-focused cryptocurrencies such as Monero and Verge retain forensic evidence in volatile memory, network traffic, and hard disks. This includes mnemonic seed phrases and plain text passphrases. Forensic methods tailored explicitly for privacy-focused cryptocurrencies such as Monero and Verge involve analyzing volatile memory, network traffic, and hard disks to identify essential artifacts such as mnemonic seed phrases and plain text passphrases (Koerhuis et al., 2020

Privacy metrics like identity anonymity, transaction confidentiality, transaction unlinkability, and network anonymity are employed to assess and compare the privacy characteristics of cryptocurrencies such as Dash, Monero, Verge, Zcash, and Grin. Private addresses, confidential transactions, and network anonymization services are implemented in privacy-oriented cryptocurrencies such as Monero and Zcash to enhance privacy (Zhang, 2023).

In summary, the forensic examination of privacy-oriented cryptocurrencies such as Monero and Zcash entails sophisticated methodologies that leverage heuristics, timing analysis, side-channel attacks, and forensic artifacts present in system components. Notwithstanding their robust privacy assurances, many cryptocurrencies are susceptible to advanced surveillance and deanonymization techniques. Continually, researchers are advancing and improving these forensic methods to match the changing environment of privacy-oriented digital currency.

Legal and Ethical Considerations of Cryptocurrencies

Several studies indicate that cryptocurrencies strive to provide privacy but encounter difficulties. Striking a balance between privacy and regulation may require solutions such as decentralized group signatures and verifiable encryption. Cryptocurrencies, like Bitcoin, have arisen as a solution to overcome the constraints of centralized banking institutions, providing improved confidentiality for consumer transactional data. Nevertheless, this advancement raises specific legal and ethical concerns, namely about the protection of data privacy and the acceptability of digital evidence.

Cryptocurrencies are designed to safeguard user privacy by avoiding the unauthorized disclosure of transactional data, including the specified amounts spent, the places where spending occurs, and the parties involved in the transactions. Nevertheless, existing systems possess imperfections that potentially compromise user privacy. Cryptocurrencies were introduced to provide users with privacy about their transactional data. However, existing weaknesses in existing systems can compromise this privacy (Herskind et al., 2020).

Furthermore, others argue that Blockchain-based cryptocurrencies, such as Bitcoin, offer pseudonymity rather than genuine anonymity, which can be undermined by transaction analysis. A range of privacy-enhancing methods and privacy-focused alternative cryptocurrencies have been suggested to tackle these concerns. Complete anonymity with cryptocurrencies is not necessarily the optimal outcome as it might enable illicit activity, such as money laundering and drug trafficking. Hence, regulation is crucial to balance privacy and preventing misuse. One possible approach to reconcile privacy and regulation is the implementation of decentralized group signatures and verifiable encryption (Li et al., 2019).

These technologies enable the tracking of suspicious transactions while ensuring the preservation of user privacy in regular transactions. Decentralized group signatures and verifiable encryption are two potential approaches to balance privacy and governance in blockchain-based cryptocurrencies. Furthermore, more observers argue that the legal safeguarding information in cryptocurrencies entails the delicate equilibrium between individual autonomy, the advancement of the digital economy, and the deterrence of criminal activities. An evaluation and possible revision of existing data protection and privacy legislation is necessary to tackle the threats linked to cryptocurrencies effectively.

Cryptocurrency regulation encompasses both domestic and foreign factors within its political dimension. The interplay of international politics will be essential in establishing norms for data protection and privacy legislation and deciding the specific information that should be disclosed and with whom. Contemporary legislation on data protection and privacy rights can both enhance and pose hazards to individual liberty, the growth of the digital economy, and the prevention of criminal activities within cryptocurrencies (Lee, 2020).

In conclusion, cryptocurrencies' legal and ethical aspects center on improving user privacy within the framework of sufficient regulation to deter illicit behavior. Although existing systems provide pseudonymity, achieving genuine anonymity continues to be complicated. Implementing robust regulation, perhaps by using decentralized group signatures or verifiable encryption, is essential to achieve a harmonious equilibrium between privacy and security. Moreover, the dynamic legal framework must directly confront cryptocurrencies' potential hazards and advantages, while international politics will substantially influence the establishment of forthcoming norms.

Blockchain as a means for cryptocurrency forensics

Scholars emphasize the nexus between the blockchain and the cryptocurrency; as described by Nakamoto, Bitcoin or cryptocurrency is an electronic coin that is a sequence of digital signatures that includes a hash of previous transactions and the recipient's public key (Nakamoto, 2008). This allows for the verification of the coin's ownership history.

However, the recipient cannot determine whether the coin has been double-spent. A proposed solution to address this problem and uphold Bitcoin's decentralized nature involves the implementation of a timestamp server. This server would broadcast the hash of a block to the network for verification purposes (Dudani et al., 2023).

Blockchain, a decentralized database structured as a sequence of ordered blocks, is a critical component of cryptocurrency forensics. Cryptocurrency transactions are recorded in blocks on the blockchain, which serves as a transparent ledger and a significant repository of forensic evidence and other network-related artifacts. Its immutable nature and miners' role in maintaining a verifiable record of all transactions have significantly disrupted traditional banking and corporate systems. This technology enables decentralized currencies to operate with a level of trust comparable to that of a reputable financial institution (Casino et al., 2019).

Cryptocurrencies like Bitcoin and other virtual currencies do not offer perfect anonymity. Transactions are recorded on digital blockchain ledgers powered by innovative blockchain technology, which reveal users through their Bitcoin address without disclosing personal information. Law enforcement agencies, regulators, and financial investigators have developed techniques to penetrate this anonymity, using blockchain intelligence tools and investigative methods to uncover identities in cryptocurrency transactions.

Transferring cryptocurrencies involves an individual installing a digital wallet, acquiring a collection of coins through third-party trade or donation, and initiating a request to transfer a specific amount of cryptocurrency to another user. The transaction's information is gathered into a block, sent to the user network for verification, and then added to the blockchain. The recipient's wallet acquires the transferred coins after adding the new block to the blockchain. Coins, in a technical sense, lack physical existence and cannot be physically moved. They function as a type of digital currency that relies on the trust of its users.

According to the FBI's assessment in 2012, they found several deficiencies in intelligence regarding certain criminal activities. These included insufficient information on individuals or groups attempting to avoid complying with the United States Bank Secrecy Act (BSA) regulations, other criminal organizations, and Bitcoin services facilitating illegal activities. These gaps in intelligence present numerous obstacles for law enforcement agencies (FBI, 2012).

Digital forensics is essential to address these inquiries. By analyzing computers, hard drives, mobile devices, and other relevant sources, crucial details can be uncovered about the methods employed in illicit activities, which Bitcoin finances. Forensic accounting professionals require specific information, including wallet IDs, public-private vital combinations, and transaction data, to track money flow (Dudani et al., 2023).

Digital forensics is crucial in extracting and evaluating this information. If an investigator has identified a suspect and has access to the suspect's devices, they would use host-based forensics methods. This involves examining the suspect's mobile devices, computers, and memory to gather evidence such as application data, wallet information, public/private keys, and other relevant artifacts related to cryptocurrency. This evidence can potentially assist in further investigating the blockchain for additional proof.

Alternatively, if a specific suspect has not been recognized, detectives rely on the publicly accessible blockchain and possibly valuable network artifacts. These artifacts may help identify suspects whose devices may be thoroughly examined for more evidence. This analysis will discuss the current research on extracting and analyzing Bitcoin artifacts from various sources, such as mobile devices, computers, memory, blockchains, and network-based platforms (Dudani et al., 2023).

Methods of Cryptocurrency Forensics Investigations

Cryptocurrency forensics aims to identify the responsible party and locate their funds through various methods of analysis and investigation. Blockchain intelligence technologies collect and analyze ownership attribution data for businesses, enabling the identification of criminals and investigation topics by de-anonymizing blockchain addresses. Transaction mapping converts transactional data into visual maps and flowcharts, tracing financial transfers to their ultimate endpoints.

Cluster analysis identifies groups of cryptocurrency addresses under a single individual or institution's control, broadening the investigation's scope. Subpoena targets are focused on commercial cryptocurrency exchanges, decentralized finance organizations, and virtual asset service providers that adhere to Know Your Customer

(KYC) and Anti-Money Laundering (AML) standards. Total transactions indicate the potential scale of a fraudulent scheme and the number of individuals affected. Law enforcement agencies prioritize complaints involving crime syndicates causing harm to many individuals, while class action cases may be suitable for larger schemes.

Forensic analysis of mobile devices

Mobile devices play a crucial role in cryptocurrency forensics because they are widely used for mobile wallets and cryptocurrency applications. These mobile-based cryptocurrency exchange applications generate almost $40 billion in revenue yearly for the top 7 platforms. Some scholars conducted studies in which the most widely used cryptocurrency wallets for Bitcoin, Darkcoin, and Litecoin were downloaded and used on iOS and Android devices. The wallets were utilized in their simplest form, with only essential user functions (Montanez, 2014).

The experiment utilized an Apple iPhone 4 running iOS 7.1.1, a Samsung Galaxy S4 running Android 4.4.2, and two virtual Samsung Galaxy S4 smartphones running Android 4.4.2. Information was obtained from each device by utilizing Cellebrite UFED, Cellebrite Physical Analyzer, and iFunBox for iOS following specific device or wallet occurrences (Dudani et al., 2023).

To investigate cryptocurrency transactions, digital forensic examiners must focus on identifying databases that store information such as the names of cryptocurrency wallets, the public-private keys of the sender and receiver, the userIDs of the sender and receiver, and the files related to the timestamps of the transactions. The ability to retrieve these artifacts significantly relies heavily on the security and privacy measures implemented by the operating system and the wallet application being examined. Additionally, when considering host-based forensics for cryptocurrency, both computer and memory forensics hold equal significance alongside mobile forensics (Dudani et al., 2023).

The notion of Machine Learning (ML) is becoming increasingly prevalent and is also being used in Bitcoin forensics. In 2018, some scholars introduced a new method based on supervised machine learning to decrease anonymity on the Bitcoin Blockchain (Harlev et al., 2018). The training data set from Chainalysis comprised almost 200 million transactions involving 434 identified businesses. Using their classifier, they could categorize an entity into one of ten distinct categories. By implementing Gradient Boosting, they attained an F1 score of 0.75.

Some scholars presented the Elliptic Data Set, which includes more than 200,000 Bitcoin transactions, 234,000 directed payment flows, and 166 node characteristics. Using different machine learning algorithms, they then analyzed the outcomes of a binary classification task that aimed to distinguish illegal transactions from legal ones (Dudani et al., 2023).

In addition, they provide Chronograph, a visualization prototype designed to assist analysts in examining and comprehending Bitcoin transactions. The Elliptic Data Set has made a significant impact on blockchain forensics. Researchers have widely utilized this publicly accessible dataset to gain insights into and potentially uncover participants' identities in the Bitcoin blockchain (Weber et al., 2019).

Dark Web Forensics by Artificial Intelligence and Machine Learning

Digital forensics investigators can use web crawling and data mining techniques to uncover concealed services and collect evidence of illegal behavior. The dark web is an unindexed section that requires access to specific software known for facilitating illicit activities like gun sales, drug trafficking, and cybercrimes. It is also customized software that allows users to access the dark web by directing their internet traffic through a global network of volunteer-operated computers known as nodes.

The dark web was initially created for lawful reasons, such as safeguarding the anonymity of internet users in nations with authoritarian regimes and providing secure communication for activists, journalists, and law enforcement personnel. However, it has been exploited by criminals and other malicious individuals for illicit activities, similar to many different technologies. Investigating illegal conduct on the dark web is difficult due to the anonymity of its users and the utilization of encryption technologies. Some scholars see that Artificial Intelligence and Machine Learning (AI and ML) can assist digital forensics investigators by automating data analysis and detecting illicit behavior trends (Sukumar, 2023).

Cryptocurrency transactions can be traced due to the anonymity of cryptocurrencies like Bitcoin, commonly used for illicit operations on the dark web. Every cryptocurrency transaction is documented on a public ledger called the blockchain. Digital forensics investigators can track the flow of illegal funds and pinpoint the persons engaged in criminal behavior by examining the blockchain. Advanced data analysis methods can detect activity patterns and connect transactions to specific people or companies. Clustering analysis is a technique used to track the flow of funds on the blockchain. Chain analysis is another method employed to track the flow of funds within the blockchain by monitoring fund transfers between different addresses.

Examining conversation records reveals that criminals frequently use chat rooms on the dark web to coordinate and strategize illicit actions. AI and machine learning are especially beneficial in this context. Detectives can quickly pinpoint conversations likely linked to illegal behavior by analyzing chat logs and focusing on those chats. This can optimize the investigation process and decrease the time and resources needed to review extensive conversation log data.

Data encryption involves using AI algorithms to evaluate patterns in encrypted data to determine the encryption mechanism employed. Natural Language Processing (NLP) can help understand the context of messages and communications on the dark web. Machine Learning Algorithms can examine extensive datasets of encrypted data to detect trends and develop future models for decrypting similar material. Predictive analytics can anticipate user behavior on the dark web to discover potential dangers and flaws in the system. For example, machine learning can forecast prime numbers used in the critical generation procedure for RSA encryption.

AI and ML are improving digital forensics by automating the preliminary analysis of digital evidence by recognizing file types, timestamps, and metadata. This accelerates the investigation process, allowing investigators to concentrate on more intricate tasks. AI and ML can also help investigators by automatically organizing and ranking data to uncover significant evidence, simplifying the process of finding crucial information.

AI and ML systems can analyze distinctive malware codes associated with particular malware strains. By recognizing these patterns, investigators can promptly detect malware infections and take steps to eliminate them before they result in substantial harm. Automating data analysis and discovering criminal activity patterns allows detectives to streamline the investigation process and concentrate on more complex tasks. The future of digital forensics appears promising as technology advances, enhancing the effectiveness of combating cybercrime (Sukumar, 2023).

CONCLUSION

Due to its distinctive characteristics and appeal to a wide range of consumers, indications suggest that Bitcoin will progressively integrate into global financial institutions. Consequently, the utilization of cryptocurrency by wrongdoers is increasing due to the uncontrolled and anonymous characteristics of the currency, propelling us towards a future dominated by cybercrime propelled by cryptocurrency. The existing technological capabilities of law enforcement agencies and researchers worldwide may not be adequate, highlighting the need for advancements in digital forensics, specifically with Bitcoin artifacts. Furthermore, it requires the unrestricted dissemination of information concerning cryptocurrency investigations across international agencies, which can then be passed on to local law enforcement organizations.

The studies identified the need to address several areas of digital cryptocurrency forensics, in which gaps can be filled by developing advanced solutions for cryptocurrency forensics. Further investigation is required in digital forensics concerning significant cryptocurrencies like Monero, Ethereum, Verge, Dogecoin, and others. This is necessary because these currencies are becoming increasingly popular among both legitimate users and evil individuals. The survey highlighted another research gap: the limited amount of substantial research on host-based cryptocurrency forensics, particularly in mobile-based cryptocurrency forensics.

Host-based forensics is crucial in identifying initial evidence to guide blockchain forensics investigations in tracking money flows. The majority of research conducted on host-based forensics focuses on outdated operating systems or platforms, highlighting the need for research on more up-to-date versions. When examining forensic methods for cryptocurrencies, it is crucial to consider security and vulnerability assessment studies.

These studies can provide insights into potential exploits or assaults useful for forensic investigations. To summarize, research in Blockchain-based forensics is advancing organically alongside technological advancements. However, there is a need for focused attention on host-based forensics for cryptocurrency.

REFERENCES

Al-Bahouth, A. (2017). Virtual money: Its concept, types, and economic effects. *Scientific Journal of Economics and Trade*. 1;47(1):857-916.

Bahamazava, K., & Nanda, R. (2022). The shift of DarkNet illegal drug trade preferences in cryptocurrency: The question of traceability and deterrence. *Forensic Science International Digital Investigation*, 40, 301377. DOI: 10.1016/j.fsidi.2022.301377

Biddle, P., England, P., Peinado, M., & Willman, B. (2003). The darknet and the future of content protection. In *Digital Rights Management: ACM CCS-9 Workshop, DRM 2002, Washington, DC, USA, November 18, 2002. Revised Papers* (pp. 155-176). Springer Berlin Heidelberg.

Biryukov, A., & Tikhomirov, S. (2019). Deanonymization and Linkability of Cryptocurrency Transactions Based on Network Analysis. *2019 IEEE European Symposium on Security and Privacy (EuroS&P)*, 172-184. DOI: 10.1109/EuroSP.2019.00022

Biryukov, A., & Tikhomirov, S. (2019). Security and privacy of mobile wallet users in Bitcoin, Dash, Monero, and Zcash. *Pervasive and Mobile Computing*, 59, 101030. Advance online publication. DOI: 10.1016/j.pmcj.2019.101030

Bishwas, A., & Advani, J. (2021). Managing Cyber Security with Quantum Techniques. *2021 International Conference on Electrical, Computer and Energy Technologies (ICECET)*, 1-7. DOI: 10.1109/ICECET52533.2021.9698591

Britannica Money. (2024, August 13). https://www.britannica.com/money/what-is-crypto-mining

Brito, J., & Castillo, A. M. (2016). *Bitcoin: a primer for policymakers*. Mercatus Center, George Mason University.

Casino, F., Dasaklis, T. K., & Patsakis, C. (2019). A systematic literature review of blockchain-based applications: Current status, classification and open issues. *Telematics and Informatics*, 36, 55–81. DOI: 10.1016/j.tele.2018.11.006

Chavali, B., Khatri, S., & Hossain, S. (2020). AI and Blockchain Integration. *2020 8th International Conference on Reliability, Infocom Technologies and Optimization (Trends and Future Directions) (ICRITO)*, 548-552. DOI: 10.1109/ICRITO48877.2020.9197847

Chohan, U. (2017). A History of Bitcoin. *PSN: Exchange Rates & Currency (Comparative) (Topic)*. https://doi.org/DOI: 10.2139/SSRN.3047875

Dai, H., Chanphong, S., & Howattanakul, S. (2023). The Effectiveness of Decentralized Autonomous Organization for University in the Web 3.0 Era. *Journal of Roi Kaensarn Academi*, 8(8), 122–140.

Dai, W., & List, C. M. (1998). Bitcoin Whitepaper.

Dhali, M., Hassan, S., Mehar, S., Shahzad, K., & Zaman, F. (2023). Cryptocurrency in the Darknet: Sustainability of the current national legislation. *International Journal of Law and Management*. .DOI: 10.1108/IJLMA-09-2022-0206

Doran, M. D. (2014). *A forensic look at bitcoin cryptocurrency* (Doctoral dissertation, Utica College).

Dudani, S., Baggili, I., Raymond, D., & Marchany, R. (2023). The current state of cryptocurrency forensics. *Forensic Science International Digital Investigation*, 46, 301576. DOI: 10.1016/j.fsidi.2023.301576

Duffield, E., & Hagan, K. (2014). Darkcoin: Peertopeer cryptocurrency with anonymous blockchain transactions and an improved proof of work system. *bitpaper.Info*.

El-kady R, (2021). Combating organized crime via the dark web: an analytical study in Egyptian legislation. *National Criminal Journal*. Nov 1;64(3):44-105.

El-Kady, R. (2023). Handling E-evidence in Egyptian and Comparative Legislation. *Arab Journal of Forensic Sciences & Forensic Medicine*. Dec 26;5(2):191-222.

El-Kady, R. (2024). Artificial Intelligence and Criminal Law. In *Artificial Intelligence Approaches to Sustainable Accounting* (pp. 34–52). IGI Global. DOI: 10.4018/979-8-3693-0847-9.ch003

El-Kady, R. M. (2024). Investigating Forensic Evidence in Metaverse: A Comparative Analytical Study. In *Forecasting Cyber Crimes in the Age of the Metaverse* (pp. 227-258). IGI Global.

FBI, D. (2012). Bitcoin virtual currency: Unique features present distinct challenges for deterring illicit activity. *Intelligence Assessment*.

Gao, Y., Chen, X., Chen, Y., Sun, Y., Niu, X., & Yang, Y. (2018). A Secure Cryptocurrency Scheme Based on Post-Quantum Blockchain. *IEEE Access : Practical Innovations, Open Solutions*, 6, 27205–27213. DOI: 10.1109/ACCESS.2018.2827203

Guccione, D. (2019). *What is the dark web? How to access it and what you'll find, The state of cybersecurity*. CSO Online.

Haminskiy, Y. (2022). ANALYSIS OF INTERNATIONAL CRIMES RELATED TO CRYPTOCURRENCIES. *Advances in Law Studies*. .DOI: 10.29039/2409-5087-2022-10-3-56-60

Harlev, M. A., Sun Yin, H., Langenheldt, K. C., Mukkamala, R., & Vatrapu, R. (2018). Breaking bad: De-anonymising entity types on the bitcoin blockchain using supervised machine learning.

Herskind, L., Katsikouli, P., & Dragoni, N. (2020). Privacy and Cryptocurrencies—A Systematic Literature Review. *IEEE Access : Practical Innovations, Open Solutions*, 8, 54044–54059. DOI: 10.1109/ACCESS.2020.2980950

Hossain, S., Bairagi, M., Aktar, J., Honey, U., & Mithy, S. (2023). The Evolution of Bitcoin: A Historical Analysis and Future Prospects. *iRASD. Journal of Economics*, 5(2), 241–252. Advance online publication. DOI: 10.52131/joe.2023.0502.0124

Huang, S. (2021). Cryptocurrency and crime. *FinTech. Artificial Intelligence and Law*, 125–143. Advance online publication. DOI: 10.4324/9781003020998-11

Hussain, A., & Al-turjman, F. (2021). Artificial intelligence and blockchain: A review. *Transactions on Emerging Telecommunications Technologies*, 32(9), e4268. Advance online publication. DOI: 10.1002/ett.4268

Ilie, D., Karantias, K., & Knottenbelt, W. (2020). Bitcoin Crypto - Bounties for Quantum Capable Adversaries., 9-25. .DOI: 10.1007/978-3-030-53356-4_2

Irwin, A., & Dawson, C. (2019). Following the cyber money trail. *Journal of Money Laundering Control*. .DOI: 10.1108/JMLC-08-2017-0041

Jose, M. (2024, June 6). *The evolution of cryptocurrencies. Part 3: Decentralized Finance (DeFi)*. https://www.linkedin.com/pulse/evolution-cryptocurrencies-part-3-decentralized-finance-jose-manuel-efrkc/

Joshi, C. M. (2023). Cryptocurrency Forensics: The Ultimate Guide to 6 Important Aspects. Indiaforensic. https://indiaforensic.com/cryptocurrency-forensics/

Kadoo, M., & Sodi, M. (2023). An Analysis of Cryptocurrency, Bitcoin and the Future. *International Journal of Advanced Research in Science. Tongxin Jishu*, 287–292. Advance online publication. DOI: 10.48175/IJARSCT-8157

Kethineni, S., & Cao, Y. (2020). The Rise in Popularity of Cryptocurrency and Associated Criminal Activity. *International Criminal Justice Review*, 30(3), 325–344. DOI: 10.1177/1057567719827051

Khan, S., & Mangde, O. (2022). Application of Blockchain in Artificial Intelligence. *International Journal for Research in Applied Science and Engineering Technology*, 10(6), 2066–2070. Advance online publication. DOI: 10.22214/ijraset.2022.44142

Koerhuis, W., Kechadi, M., & Le-Khac, N. (2020). Forensic analysis of privacy-oriented cryptocurrencies. *Forensic Science International Digital Investigation*, 33, 200891. DOI: 10.1016/j.fsidi.2019.200891

Kohut, M. (2023). *The Essence and Place of Cryptocurrency in the Financial System*. Modern Economics., DOI: 10.31521/modecon.V37(2023)-09

Kolachala, K., Simsek, E., Ababneh, M., & Vishwanathan, R. (2021). SoK: Money Laundering in Cryptocurrencies. *Proceedings of the 16th International Conference on Availability, Reliability and Security*. DOI: 10.1145/3465481.3465774

Kreminskyi, O., Kuzmenko, O., Antoniuk, A., & Smahlo, O. (2021). International cooperation in the investigation of economic crimes related to cryptocurrency circulation. *Studies of Applied Economics*. .DOI: 10.25115/eea.v39i6.5247

Kumar, J., Madan, Y., & Mehta, D. (2023). The Evolution of Bitcoin and Other Cryptocurrencies. *International Journal of Advanced Research in Science. Tongxin Jishu*, 13–16. Advance online publication. DOI: 10.48175/IJARSCT-9363

Law, L., Sabett, S., & Solinas, J. (1996). How to make a mint: The cryptography of anonymous electronic cash. *Am. UL Rev.*, 46, 1131.

Lee, J. (2020). The Economics and Politics of Information and its Legal Protection in Cryptocurrencies. *ERN: International Financial Flows (Topic)*. DOI: 10.2139/ssrn.3715632

Li, Y., Susilo, W., Yang, G., Yu, Y., Du, X., Liu, D., & Guizani, N. (2019). Toward Privacy and Regulation in Blockchain-Based Cryptocurrencies. *IEEE Network*, 33(5), 111–117. DOI: 10.1109/MNET.2019.1800271

Majot, A., & Yampolskiy, R. (2015). Global catastrophic risk and security implications of quantum computers. *Futures*, 72, 17–26. DOI: 10.1016/j.futures.2015.02.006

Marian, O. (2014). A Conceptual Framework for the Regulation of Cryptocurrencies. *Criminology eJournal*.

Mark, J., & De Vynck, G. (2022). Crypto winter" has come. And it's looking more like an ice age. *Washington Post*.

Montanez, A. (2014). *Investigation of cryptocurrency wallets on iOS and Android mobile devices for potential forensic artifacts. Department Forensic Science*. Marshall University.

Nakamoto, S., & Bitcoin, A. (2008). A peer-to-peer electronic cash system. *Bitcoin.–URL:*https://bitcoin. org/bitcoin. pdf, *4*(2), 15.

Nath, G. (2020). Cryptocurrency Crimes – Need for a Comprehensive Global Crypto Regulation. *Social Science Research Network*. DOI: 10.2139/ssrn.3683669

Nour, K. (2022). Criminal confrontation of cryptocurrency use in the financing of terrorism. *Jolets*. 16;2(2):79-152. Available from: https://jolets.org/ojs/index.php/jolets/article/view/12

Obeidat, T.. (1996). *Methods and Techniques of Scientific Research*. Dar Sana'a for Publishing. (In Arabic)

Ojha, P., & Niranjan, S. (2023). Potential usage of AI in Blockchain Technology. *2023 International Conference on Intelligent and Innovative Technologies in Computing, Electrical and Electronics (IITCEE)*, 7-8. DOI: 10.1109/IITCEE57236.2023.10091093

Paesano, F., & Siron, D. (2022). Working Paper 38: Cryptocurrencies in Asia and beyond: law, regulation and enforcement. *Basel Institute on Governance Working Papers*. DOI: 10.12685/bigwp.2022.38.1-69

Peck, M. E. (2012). The cryptoanarchists' answer to cash. *IEEE Spectrum*, 49(6), 50–56. DOI: 10.1109/MSPEC.2012.6203968

Pitta, J. (1999). Requiem for a bright idea. *Forbes*, 164(11), 390–392.

Reid, F., & Harrigan, M. (2013). *An analysis of anonymity in the bitcoin system*. Springer New York. DOI: 10.1007/978-1-4614-4139-7_10

Sabry, F. (2021). *Decentralized Finance: The apocalyptic event for the traditional financial institutions* (Vol. 3). One Billion Knowledgeable.

Salah, K., Rehman, M., Nizamuddin, N., & Al-Fuqaha, A. (2019). Blockchain for AI: Review and Open Research Challenges. *IEEE Access : Practical Innovations, Open Solutions*, 7, 10127–10149. DOI: 10.1109/ACCESS.2018.2890507

Salama, R., & Al-turjman, F. (2022). AI in Blockchain Towards Realizing Cyber Security. *2022 International Conference on Artificial Intelligence in Everything (AIE)*, 471-475. DOI: 10.1109/AIE57029.2022.00096

Sereda, I., & Stupina, S. (2021). The Potential of Criminal Legislation in the Field of Counteraction to Crimes Related to Cryptocurrency. *Prologue: Law Journal*. https://doi.org/..DOI: 10.21639/2313-6715.2021.4.10

Sharma, D., Pant, D., & Kumar, A. (2023). Cryptocurrency: An Overview of its History, Technology and Future Prospects. *International Journal of Advanced Research in Science. Tongxin Jishu*, 427–430. Advance online publication. DOI: 10.48175/IJARSCT-9232

Shinde, R., Patil, S., Kotecha, K., & Ruikar, K. (2021). Blockchain for Securing AI Applications and Open Innovations. *Journal of Open Innovation*, 7(3), 189. Advance online publication. DOI: 10.3390/joitmc7030189

Steadman, I. (2013). Wary of Bitcoin? A guide to some other cryptocurrencies. *Ars Technica, 11*.

Sukumar, S. (2023). Digital Forensics in The Dark. https://www.linkedin.com/pulse/digital-forensics-dark-sandhya-sukumar/

Taleby Ahvanooey, M., Zhu, M. X., Mazurczyk, W., Kilger, M., & Choo, K. K. R. (2021, December). Do dark web and cryptocurrencies empower cybercriminals? In *International Conference on Digital Forensics and Cyber Crime* (pp. 277-293). Cham: Springer International Publishing.

Tramèr, F., Boneh, D., & Paterson, K. (2020). Remote Side-Channel Attacks on Anonymous Transactions. *IACR Cryptol. ePrint Arch.*, 2020, 220.

Treasury, H. M. S. (2021). UK regulatory approach to cryptoassets and stablecoins: consultation and call for evidence (2021).

Tsuchiya, Y., & Hiramoto, N. (2021). How cryptocurrency is laundered: Case study of Coincheck hacking incident. *Forensic Science International. Reports*, 4, 100241. DOI: 10.1016/j.fsir.2021.100241

Tziakouris, G. (2018). Cryptocurrencies—A forensic challenge or opportunity for law enforcement? an interpol perspective. *IEEE Security and Privacy*, 16(4), 92–94. DOI: 10.1109/MSP.2018.3111243

Uddin, K. M. N. (2022). On cryptocurrencies: An assessment of bitcoin's prospect as legal medium of exchange. *Advances in Management and Applied Economics*, 12(5), 1–17. DOI: 10.47260/amae/1251

Wang, R., Luo, M., Wen, Y., Wang, L., Choo, K., & He, D. (2021). The Applications of Blockchain in Artificial Intelligence. *Secur. Commun. Networks*, 2021, 6126247:1-6126247:16. .DOI: 10.1155/2021/6126247

Weber, M., Domeniconi, G., Chen, J., Weidele, D. K. I., Bellei, C., Robinson, T., & Leiserson, C. E. (2019). Anti-money laundering in bitcoin: Experimenting with graph convolutional networks for financial forensics. *arXiv preprint arXiv:1908.02591*.

Weber, R. H., & Baisch, R. (2023). Cryptoassets: Taxonomy and Regulatory Approaches. *Banking & Finance Law Review*, 39(3), 467–505.

Xuan, T., & Ness, S. (2023). Integration of Blockchain and AI: Exploring Application in the Digital Business. *Journal of Engineering Research and Reports*. .DOI: 10.9734/jerr/2023/v25i8955

Yousaf, H. (2022). Investigating transactions in cryptocurrencies. *ArXiv*, abs/2203.14684. https://doi.org//arXiv.2203.14684.DOI: 10.48550

Zetzsche, D. A., Arner, D. W., & Buckley, R. P. (2020). Decentralized finance. *Journal of Financial Regulation*, 6(2), 172–203. DOI: 10.1093/jfr/fjaa010

Zhang, T. (2023). Privacy Evaluation of Blockchain-Based Privacy Cryptocurrencies: A Comparative Analysis of Dash, Monero, Verge, Zcash, and Grin. *IEEE Transactions on Sustainable Computing*, 8(4), 574–582. DOI: 10.1109/TSUSC.2023.3303180

Compilation of References

Abduljabbar, R., Dia, H., Liyanage, S., & Bagloee, S. A. (2019). Applications of artificial intelligence in transport: An overview. *Sustainability (Basel)*, 11(1), 189. DOI: 10.3390/su11010189

Ablayev, A. N., Bulychkov, D. A., Sapaev, D. A., Vasiliev, A. V., & Ziatdinov, M. T. (2018). Quantum-Assisted Blockchain. *Lobachevskii Journal of Mathematics*, 39(7), 957–960. Advance online publication. DOI: 10.1134/S1995080218070028

Abulkasim, H., Mashatan, A., & Ghose, S. (2021). Quantum-based privacy-preserving sealed-bid auction on the blockchain. *Optik (Stuttgart)*, 242, 167039. Advance online publication. DOI: 10.1016/j.ijleo.2021.167039

Agoub, A., Filippovska, Y., Schmidt, V., & Kada, M. (2019). Automatic Generation of Photorealistic Image Fillers for Privacy Enabled Urban Basemaps using Generative Adversarial Networks. *Advances in Cartography and GIScience of the ICA*, 1, 1–8. Advance online publication. DOI: 10.5194/ica-adv-1-1-2019

Ahmed, S. A., Dogra, D. P., Kar, S., & Roy, P. P. (2019, July). Trajectory-based surveillance analysis: A survey. *IEEE Transactions on Circuits and Systems for Video Technology*, 29(7), 1985–1997. DOI: 10.1109/TCSVT.2018.2857489

Ahmed, S., Alshater, M. M., El Ammari, A., & Hammami, H. (2022). Artificial intelligence and machine learning in finance: A bibliometric review. *Research in International Business and Finance*, 61, 101646.

Akindele, P. T. (2021). International Conference on Recent Trends in Applied Research (ICoRTAR), *Journal of Physics:Conference Series,* 1734 012013 IOP Publishing DOI: 10.1088/1742-6596/1734/1/012013

Akinode, J. L., & Oloruntoba, S. A. (2017). Design and implementation of a patient appointment and scheduling system. Department of Computer Science, Federal Polytechnic Ilaro Nigeria.

Alahakoon, D., Nawaratne, R., Xu, Y., De Silva, D., Sivarajah, U., & Gupta, B. (2023). Self-building artificial intelligence and machine learning to empower big data analytics in smart cities. *Information Systems Frontiers*, 25(1), 221–240. DOI: 10.1007/s10796-020-10056-x

Al-Bahouth, A. (2017). Virtual money: Its concept, types, and economic effects. *Scientific Journal of Economics and Trade*. 1;47(1):857-916.

Arulmozhiselvan, L., & Uma, E. (2022). QKD in Cloud-Fog Computing for Personal Health Record. *Computer Systems Science and Engineering*, 43(1), 45–57. Advance online publication. DOI: 10.32604/csse.2022.022024

Ateniese, G., Di Pietro, R., Mancini, L. V., & Tsudik, G. (2008). Scalable and efficient provable data possession. In *SecureComm 2008* (pp. 1–10). IEEE., DOI: 10.1109/SecureComm.2008.4761768

Bahamazava, K., & Nanda, R. (2022). The shift of DarkNet illegal drug trade preferences in cryptocurrency: The question of traceability and deterrence. *Forensic Science International Digital Investigation*, 40, 301377. DOI: 10.1016/j.fsidi.2022.301377

Banzi, R., Gujar, D., Liberati, A., Moschetti, I., Tagliabue, L., & Moja, L. (2010). A review of online evidence- based practice point- of- care information summary providers. *Journal of Medical Internet Research*, 12(3), e1288. DOI: 10.2196/jmir.1288 PMID: 20610379

Bathula, A., Merugu, S., & Skandha, S. S. (2022, December). Academic Projects on Certification Management Using Blockchain-A Review. In *2022 International Conference on Recent Trends in Microelectronics, Automation, Computing and Communications Systems (ICMACC)* (pp. 1-6). IEEE.

Bathula, A., Muhuri, S., Gupta, S. K., & Merugu, S. (2023, May). Secure certificate sharing based on Blockchain framework for online education. *Multimedia Tools and Applications*, 82(11), 16479–16500. DOI: 10.1007/s11042-022-14126-x

Bautista, P., & Inventado, P. S. (2021). Protecting Student Privacy with Synthetic Data from Generative Adversarial Networks. *Lecture Notes in Computer Science (Including Subseries Lecture Notes in Artificial Intelligence and Lecture Notes in Bioinformatics)*, 12749 LNAI. https://doi.org/DOI: 10.1007/978-3-030-78270-2_11

Benedetti, M., & Realpe-Gomez, J., Biswas, and Perdomo-Ortiz, A. (2018). Quantum-Assisted Learning of Hardware-Embedded Probabilistic Graphical Models. *IEEE Transactions on Neural Networks and Learning Systems*, 29(12), 5792–5803.

Bernstein, D. J., Buchmann, J., & Dahmen, E. (2019). Quantum-Resistant Cryptography: A Survey. *ACM Computing Surveys*, 51(4), 1–35.

Berry, R. A., Han, Z., Narayanan, K., Poor, H. V., Verikoukis, C., & Yagan, O. (2021). Special issue on communications and networking approaches for combating COVID-19. *Journal of Communications and Networks (Seoul)*, 23(5), 309–313. Advance online publication. DOI: 10.23919/JCN.2021.100030

Bezovski, Z., Singh, R., Davcev, L., & Mitreva, M. (2021). Current adoption state of cryptocurrencies as an electronic payment method. *Management Reseach and Practice*, 13(1), 44–50.

Bhanuteja, T., Kumar, K. V. N., Poornachand, K. S., Ashish, C., & Anudeep, P. (2021). Symptoms Based Multiple Disease Prediction Model using Machine Learning Approach. International Journal of Innovative Technology and Exploring Engineering (IJITEE) ISSN, 2278-3075.

Biamonte, J., Wittek, P. J., & Landsman, N. P.. (2017). Quantum Machine Learning. *Nature*, 549(7671), 195–202. DOI: 10.1038/nature23474 PMID: 28905917

Biddle, P., England, P., Peinado, M., & Willman, B. (2003). The darknet and the future of content protection. In *Digital Rights Management: ACM CCS-9 Workshop, DRM 2002, Washington, DC, USA, November 18, 2002. Revised Papers* (pp. 155-176). Springer Berlin Heidelberg.

Biryukov, A., & Tikhomirov, S. (2019). Deanonymization and Linkability of Cryptocurrency Transactions Based on Network Analysis. *2019 IEEE European Symposium on Security and Privacy (EuroS&P)*, 172-184. DOI: 10.1109/EuroSP.2019.00022

Biryukov, A., & Tikhomirov, S. (2019). Security and privacy of mobile wallet users in Bitcoin, Dash, Monero, and Zcash. *Pervasive and Mobile Computing*, 59, 101030. Advance online publication. DOI: 10.1016/j.pmcj.2019.101030

Bishwas, A., & Advani, J. (2021). Managing Cyber Security with Quantum Techniques. *2021 International Conference on Electrical, Computer and Energy Technologies (ICECET)*, 1-7. DOI: 10.1109/ICECET52533.2021.9698591

Bouzeraib, W., Ghenai, A., & Zeghib, N. (2020). A Blockchain Data Balance Using a Generative Adversarial Network Approach: Application to Smart House IDS. ICAASE 2020 - Proceedings, 4th *International Conference on Advanced Aspects of Software Engineering*. https://doi.org/DOI: 10.1109/ICAASE51408.2020.9380110

Britannica Money. (2024, August 13). https://www.britannica.com/money/what-is-crypto-mining

Brito, J., & Castillo, A. M. (2016). *Bitcoin: a primer for policymakers*. Mercatus Center, George Mason University.

Budiharto, W., Andreas, V., Suroso, J. S., Gunawan, A. A. S., & Irwansyah, E. "Development of Tank-Based Military Robot and Object Tracker," (2019) 4th AsiaPacific Conference on Intelligent Robot Systems (ACIRS), Nagoya, Japan, 2019, pp. 221-224, DOI: 10.1109/ACIRS.2019.8935962

Burger, C., Kuhlmann,A., Richard,P., and Weinmann,J., (2016) "Blockchain in the energy transition. a survey among decision-makers in the german energy industry," Tech. Rep.,.

Cai, Z., Xiong, Z., Xu, H., Wang, P., Li, W., & Pan, Y. (2021). Generative Adversarial Networks: A Survey Toward Private and Secure Applications. *In ACM Computing Surveys* (Vol. 54, Issue 6). https://doi.org/DOI: 10.1145/3459992

Cao, L. (2023). AI in finance: Challenges, techniques, and opportunities. *ACM Computing Surveys*, 55(3), 1–38. DOI: 10.1145/3502289

Cao, X., Sun, G., Yu, H., & Guizani, M. (2023). PerFED-GAN: Personalized Federated Learning via Generative Adversarial Networks. *IEEE Internet of Things Journal*, 10(5), 3749–3762. Advance online publication. DOI: 10.1109/JIOT.2022.3172114

Casino, F., Dasaklis, T. K., & Patsakis, C. (2019). A systematic literature review of blockchain-based applications: Current status, classification and open issues. *Telematics and Informatics*, 36, 55–81. DOI: 10.1016/j.tele.2018.11.006

Chaudhry, B., El-Amine, S., & Shakshuki, E.. (2018). Passenger safety in ride-sharing services. *Procedia Computer Science*, 130, 1044–1050. DOI: 10.1016/j.procs.2018.04.146

Chavali, B., Khatri, S., & Hossain, S. (2020). AI and Blockchain Integration. *2020 8th International Conference on Reliability, Infocom Technologies and Optimization (Trends and Future Directions) (ICRITO)*, 548-552. DOI: 10.1109/ICRITO48877.2020.9197847

Chen, J., Gan, W., Hu, M., & Chen, C. M. (2021). On the construction of a post-quantum blockchain for smart city. *Journal of Information Security and Applications*, 58, 102780. Advance online publication. DOI: 10.1016/j.jisa.2021.102780

Chenna, S. (2022). Application of Generative Adversarial Networks (GANs) for Generating Synthetic Data and in Cybersecurity. SSRN *Electronic Journal.*https://doi.org/DOI: 10.2139/ssrn.4305711

Chen, X., Xu, S., Cao, Y., He, Y., & Xiao, K. (2023). AQRS: Anti-quantum ring signature scheme for secure epidemic control with blockchain. *Computer Networks*, 224, 109595. Advance online publication. DOI: 10.1016/j.comnet.2023.109595 PMID: 36741551

Cheon, J. H., Kim, A., Kim, M., & Song, Y. "Homomorphic encryption for arithmetic of approximate numbers," in *Proc. Int. Conf. Theory Appl. Cryptol. Inf. Secur.*, 2017, pp. 409–437. DOI: 10.1007/978-3-319-70694-8_15

Chi, H., Maduakor, U., Alo, R., & Williams, E. (2021). Integrating Deepfake Detection into Cybersecurity Curriculum. *Advances in Intelligent Systems and Computing*, 1288, 588–598. Advance online publication. DOI: 10.1007/978-3-030-63128-4_45

Chiwande, S. S., Nimje, N., Barbaile, S., Singh, A., Dhote, A., & Pathade, A. (2023) "War Field Spy Robot with Metal Detection and Live Streaming," *7th International Conference on Intelligent Computing and Control Systems (ICICCS)*, Madurai, India, 2023, pp. 1688-1691, DOI: 10.1109/ICICCS56967.2023.10142415

Chohan, U. (2017). A History of Bitcoin. *PSN: Exchange Rates & Currency (Comparative) (Topic)*. https://doi.org/DOI: 10.2139/SSRN.3047875

Chuntang, X. (2020). Quantum Blockchain: A Decentralized, Encrypted and Distributed Database Based on Quantum Mechanics. *Journal of Quantum Computing JQC*, 1(2), 49–63. DOI: 10.32604/jqc.2019.06715

Cici, B., Markopoulou, A., Frias-Martinez, E., & Laoutaris, N. (2016). Assessing the potential of ride-sharing using mobile and social data: D. S'anchez, S. Mart'ınez, and J. Domingo-Ferrer, "Co-utile p2p ridesharing via decentralization and reputation management,". *Transportation Research Part C, Emerging Technologies*, 73, 147–166.

Coeckelbergh, M. (2019). Artificial intelligence: Some ethical issues and regulatory challenges. *Technol. Regulation*, 2019, 31–34.

Coinbase Commerce API documentation https://docs.cloud.coinbase.com/commerce-onchain/docs/welcome

Cottrell,J., and Basden, M., (2017) "How utilities are using blockchain to modernize the grid," PP 257-266.

Dai, W., & List, C. M. (1998). Bitcoin Whitepaper.

Dai, H., Chanphong, S., & Howattanakul, S. (2023). The Effectiveness of Decentralized Autonomous Organization for University in the Web 3.0 Era. *Journal of Roi Kaensarn Academi*, 8(8), 122–140.

Deldjoo, Y., Di Noia, T., & Merra, F. A. (2021). A Survey on Adversarial Recommender Systems: From Attack/Defense Strategies to Generative Adversarial Networks. In *ACM Computing Surveys* (Vol. 54, Issue 2). https://doi.org/DOI: 10.1145/3439729

Deng, R., Yang, Z., Chow, M. Y., & Chen, J. (2015). A survey on demand response in smart grids: Mathematical models and approaches. *IEEE Transactions on Industrial Informatics*, 11(3), 570–582. DOI: 10.1109/TII.2015.2414719

Dhali, M., Hassan, S., Mehar, S., Shahzad, K., & Zaman, F. (2023). Cryptocurrency in the Darknet: Sustainability of the current national legislation. *International Journal of Law and Management*. .DOI: 10.1108/IJLMA-09-2022-0206

Ding, Y., Thakur, N., & Li, B. (2021). Does a GAN leave distinct model-specific fingerprints. In Proceedings of the BMVC. https://www.bmvc2021-virtualconference.com/assets/papers/0197.pdf

Dodis, Y., Vadhan, S., & Wichs, D. (2009). Proofs of retrievability via hardness amplification. *In Theory of Cryptography Conference* (pp. 109-127). Springer. https://doi.org/DOI: 10.1007/978-3-540-69238-9_7

Domingo-Ferrer, J., Farr'as, O., Mart'ınez, S., S'anchez, D., & Soria-Comas, J. (2016). Self-enforcing protocols via co-utile reputation management. *Information Sciences*, 367, 159–175. DOI: 10.1016/j.ins.2016.05.050

Dong, C., Li, Y., & Zhang, M. (2016). Ensuring the integrity of outsourced data with history-based dynamic auditing and trusted computing. *IEEE Transactions on Parallel and Distributed Systems*, 27(5), 1377–1389. DOI: 10.1109/TPDS.2015.2485089

Donghao, C., Bohua, Z., Chaomin, O., & Zhiyu, C. (2021) "Research on Military Internet of Things Technology Application in the Context of National Security," *2nd International Conference on Electronics, Communications and Information Technology (CECIT)*, Sanya, China, 2021, pp. 992-998, DOI: 10.1109/CECIT53797.2021.00177

Doran, M. D. (2014). *A forensic look at bitcoin cryptocurrency* (Doctoral dissertation, Utica College).

D'Orazio, R., Carli, R., & Turchetti, C. (2019). Design and implementation of a wireless charging system for electric vehicles. *Released on July 3, 2019*.

Dudani, S., Baggili, I., Raymond, D., & Marchany, R. (2023). The current state of cryptocurrency forensics. *Forensic Science International Digital Investigation*, 46, 301576. DOI: 10.1016/j.fsidi.2023.301576

Duffield, E., & Hagan, K. (2014). Darkcoin: Peertopeer cryptocurrency with anonymous blockchain transactions and an improved proof of work system. *bitpaper.Info*.

Du, Y., Hsieh, M. H., Liu, T., Tao, D., & Liu, N. (2021). Quantum noise protects quantum classifiers against adversaries. *Physical Review Research*, 3(2), 023153. Advance online publication. DOI: 10.1103/PhysRevResearch.3.023153

El-kady R, (2021). Combating organized crime via the dark web: an analytical study in Egyptian legislation. *National Criminal Journal*. Nov 1;64(3):44-105.

El-Kady, R. (2023). Handling E-evidence in Egyptian and Comparative Legislation. *Arab Journal of Forensic Sciences & Forensic Medicine*. Dec 26;5(2):191-222.

El-Kady, R. M. (2024). Investigating Forensic Evidence in Metaverse: A Comparative Analytical Study. In *Forecasting Cyber Crimes in the Age of the Metaverse* (pp. 227-258). IGI Global.

El-Kady, R. (2024). Artificial Intelligence and Criminal Law. In *Artificial Intelligence Approaches to Sustainable Accounting* (pp. 34–52). IGI Global. DOI: 10.4018/979-8-3693-0847-9.ch003

Erway, C. C., Küpçü, A., Papamanthou, C., & Tamassia, R. (2009). Dynamic provable data possession. *InProceedings of the 16th ACM Conference on Computer and Communications Security (CCS'09)* (pp. 213-222). https://doi.org/DOI: 10.1145/1653662.1653692

Faster Capital. (Apr 3rd 2024). Real estate internet of things: IoT, The Future of Real Estate: Exploring IoT driven Entrepreneurship – FasterCapital, https://fastercapital.com/content/Real-estate-internet-of-things--IoT---The-Future-of-Real-Estate--Exploring-IoT-driven-Entrepreneurship.html, 5/12/24, 10:02 PM Dilmegani (Jan 11th 2024). 4 Use Cases & 2 Challenges of IoT in Real Estate in 2024, https://research.aimultiple.com/iot-real-estate/, 5/12/24, 9:45 PM

FBI, D. (2012). Bitcoin virtual currency: Unique features present distinct challenges for deterring illicit activity. *Intelligence Assessment*.

Fekri, M. N., Ghosh, A. M., & Grolinger, K. (2019). Generating energy data for machine learning with recurrent generative adversarial networks. *Energies*, 13(1), 130. Advance online publication. DOI: 10.3390/en13010130

Fernandes, D. (2018). Financial Literacy, Education, and Behaviour: A Review of the Literature. OECD Working Papers on Finance, Insurance and Private Pensions, No. 44.

Gao, Y., Chen, X., Chen, Y., Sun, Y., Niu, X., & Yang, Y. (2018). A Secure Cryptocurrency Scheme Based on Post-Quantum Blockchain. *IEEE Access : Practical Innovations, Open Solutions*, 6, 27205–27213. DOI: 10.1109/ACCESS.2018.2827203

Gledhill, V. X., & Mathews, J. D. (1972). The clinical synopsis. *Australian and New Zealand Journal of Medicine*, 2(2), 134–141. DOI: 10.1111/j.1445-5994.1972.tb03922.x PMID: 4507090

Gotarane, V., & Raskar, S. (2019) "IoT Practices in Military Applications," *3rd International Conference on Trends in Electronics and Informatics (ICOEI)*, Tirunelveli, India, 2019, pp. 891-894, DOI: 10.1109/ICOEI.2019.8862559

Guccione, D. (2019). *What is the dark web? How to access it and what you'll find, The state of cybersecurity*. CSO Online.

Guggilam, S., DallAnese, E., Chen, Y. C., Dhople, S. V., & Giannakis, G. V. (2016). Scalable optimization methods for distribution networks with high pv integration. *IEEE Transactions on Smart Grid*, 7(4), 2061–2070. DOI: 10.1109/TSG.2016.2543264

Gupta, N., & Kumar, S. (2020). Cyber Threats and Security Measures in FinTech Services: A Comprehensive Review. *Journal of Financial Services Marketing*, 25(2), 89–104.

Gyhm, J.-Y., Šafránek, D., & Rosa, D. (2022). Quantum charging advantage cannot be extensive without global operations. *Physical Review Letters*, 128(14), 140501. DOI: 10.1103/PhysRevLett.128.140501 PMID: 35476489

Hajiesmaili, M. H., Chen, M., Mallada, E., & Chau, C. K. (2017) "Crowdsourced storage-assisted demand response in microgrids," in *Proceedings of the Eighth International Conference on Future Energy Systems*. ACM, pp. 91–100. DOI: 10.1145/3077839.3077841

Haminskiy, Y. (2022). ANALYSIS OF INTERNATIONAL CRIMES RELATED TO CRYPTOCURRENCIES. *Advances in Law Studies*. .DOI: 10.29039/2409-5087-2022-10-3-56-60

Harlev, M. A., Sun Yin, H., Langenheldt, K. C., Mukkamala, R., & Vatrapu, R. (2018). Breaking bad: De-anonymising entity types on the bitcoin blockchain using supervised machine learning.

He, C., Huang, S., Cheng, R., Tan, K. C., & Jin, Y. (2021). Evolutionary Multiobjective Optimization Driven by Generative Adversarial Networks (GANs). *IEEE Transactions on Cybernetics*, 51(6), 3129–3142. Advance online publication. DOI: 10.1109/TCYB.2020.2985081 PMID: 32365041

Herskind, L., Katsikouli, P., & Dragoni, N. (2020). Privacy and Cryptocurrencies—A Systematic Literature Review. *IEEE Access : Practical Innovations, Open Solutions*, 8, 54044–54059. DOI: 10.1109/ACCESS.2020.2980950

Hossain, S., Bairagi, M., Aktar, J., Honey, U., & Mithy, S. (2023). The Evolution of Bitcoin: A Historical Analysis and Future Prospects. *iRASD. Journal of Economics*, 5(2), 241–252. Advance online publication. DOI: 10.52131/joe.2023.0502.0124

Howe, J. (2008). *Crowdsourcing: Why the Power of the Crowd Is Driving the Future of Business* (1st ed.). Crown Publishing Group.

Huang, S. (2021). Cryptocurrency and crime. *FinTech. Artificial Intelligence and Law*, 125–143. Advance online publication. DOI: 10.4324/9781003020998-11

Hussain, A., & Al-turjman, F. (2021). Artificial intelligence and blockchain: A review. *Transactions on Emerging Telecommunications Technologies*, 32(9), e4268. Advance online publication. DOI: 10.1002/ett.4268

Ilie, D., Karantias, K., & Knottenbelt, W. (2020). Bitcoin Crypto - Bounties for Quantum Capable Adversaries., 9-25. .DOI: 10.1007/978-3-030-53356-4_2

Irwin, A., & Dawson, C. (2019). Following the cyber money trail. *Journal of Money Laundering Control*. .DOI: 10.1108/JMLC-08-2017-0041

Ismail, N. S., & Shahreen Kasim, Y. (2017). Yah Jusoh, Rohayanti Hassan, and Ayu Alyani. "Medical appointment application.". *Acta Electronica Malaysia*, 1(2), 5–9. DOI: 10.26480/aem.02.2017.05.09

Iyengar, R. J.. (2020). Fintech for Financial Inclusion: A Review of Existing Literature and Research Gaps. *Pacific Asia Journal of the Association for Information Systems*, 12(2), 1–23.

Jabbar, R., Dhib, E., Said, A. B., Krichen, M., Fetais, N., Zaidan, E., & Barkaoui, K. (2022). Blockchain technology for intelligent transportation systems: A systematic literature review. *IEEE Access : Practical Innovations, Open Solutions*, 10, 20995–21031. DOI: 10.1109/ACCESS.2022.3149958

Janani, K., Gobhinath, S., Santhosh Kumar, K. V., Roshni, S., & Rajesh, A. (2022)"Vision Based Surveillance Robot for Military Applications,"*8th International Conference on Advanced Computing and Communication Systems (ICACCS)*, Coimbatore, India, 2022, pp. 462-466, DOI: 10.1109/ICACCS54159.2022.9785152

Jebaraj, B. S., Sekar, S., & Priyadharshini, S. (2023) "Automated Surveillance and Bomb Diffusing System for Military Applications," *International Conference on Computational Intelligence and Sustainable Engineering Solutions (CISES)*, Greater Noida, India, 2023, pp. 353-357, DOI: 10.1109/CISES58720.2023.10183517

Jemihin, Z. B., Tan, S. F., & Chung, G. C. (2022). Attribute-Based Encryption in Securing Big Data from Post-Quantum Perspective: A Survey. *In Cryptography* (Vol. 6, Issue 3). https://doi.org/DOI: 10.3390/cryptography6030040

Jerald Nirmal Kumar, S., Ravimaran, S., & Sathish, A. (2021). Robust Security with Strong Authentication in Mobile Cloud Computing Based on Trefoil Congruity Framework. *Journal of Organizational and End User Computing*, 33(6), 1–28. Advance online publication. DOI: 10.4018/JOEUC.20211101.oa11

Johnson, M. E., & Lee, J. (2022). Decentralized Finance: The Blockchain Economy. *Journal of Digital Banking*, 6(2), 83–93.

Jose, M. (2024, June 6). *The evolution of cryptocurrencies. Part 3: Decentralized Finance (DeFi).* https://www.linkedin.com/pulse/evolution-cryptocurrencies-part-3-decentralized-finance-jose-manuel-efrkc/

Joshi, C. M. (2023). Cryptocurrency Forensics: The Ultimate Guide to 6 Important Aspects. Indiaforensic. https://indiaforensic.com/cryptocurrency-forensics/

Juels, A., & Kaliski, B. S.Jr. (2007). PORs: Proofs of retrievability for large files. *Proceedings of the 14th ACM Conference on Computer and Communications Security (CCS'07)* (pp. 584-597). https://doi.org/DOI: 10.1145/1315245.1315317

Kabilan, R., R. MallikaPandeeswari, N. Lalitha, E. Kanmanikarthiga,C. Karthica and L. M. H. Sharon, (2022)"Soldier Friendly SmartAnd Intelligent Robot On War Field," Second International Conference on Artificial Intelligence and Smart Energy (ICAIS), Coimbatore, India, 2022, pp. 666-671, doi: DOI: 10.1109/ICAIS53314.2022.9742909.65

Kadoo, M., & Sodi, M. (2023). An Analysis of Cryptocurrency, Bitcoin and the Future. *International Journal of Advanced Research in Science. Tongxin Jishu*, 287–292. Advance online publication. DOI: 10.48175/IJARSCT-8157

Kamara, S., & Lauter, K. (2010). Cryptographic cloud storage. In *Financial Cryptography and Data Security* (pp. 136–149). Springer., DOI: 10.1007/978-3-642-14992-4_13

Kethineni, S., & Cao, Y. (2020). The Rise in Popularity of Cryptocurrency and Associated Criminal Activity. *International Criminal Justice Review*, 30(3), 325–344. DOI: 10.1177/1057567719827051

Khan, S., & Mangde, O. (2022). Application of Blockchain in Artificial Intelligence. *International Journal for Research in Applied Science and Engineering Technology*, 10(6), 2066–2070. Advance online publication. DOI: 10.22214/ijraset.2022.44142

Khoshaman, A., Vinci, W., & Andriyash, W., Amin, and Rieffel, E. (2019). Quantum Variational Autoencoder. *IEEE Transactions on Neural Networks and Learning Systems*, 30(3), 916–927.

Kim, S. K., & Kim, H. J. (2020). Blockchain-Based Peer-to-Peer Energy Trading for Renewable Energy Integration. *IEEE Access : Practical Innovations, Open Solutions*, 8, 222947–222959.

Kitagawa, G., & Tsukada, H. (2020). Securing Bitcoin and Blockchain-Based Systems Against Quantum Attacks. *Journal of Computer Security*, 28(2), 181–196.

Koerhuis, W., Kechadi, M., & Le-Khac, N. (2020). Forensic analysis of privacy-oriented cryptocurrencies. *Forensic Science International Digital Investigation*, 33, 200891. DOI: 10.1016/j.fsidi.2019.200891

Kohut, M. (2023). *The Essence and Place of Cryptocurrency in the Financial System*. Modern Economics., DOI: 10.31521/modecon.V37(2023)-09

Kolachala, K., Simsek, E., Ababneh, M., & Vishwanathan, R. (2021). SoK: Money Laundering in Cryptocurrencies. *Proceedings of the 16th International Conference on Availability, Reliability and Security*. DOI: 10.1145/3465481.3465774

Kreminskyi, O., Kuzmenko, O., Antoniuk, A., & Smahlo, O. (2021). International cooperation in the investigation of economic crimes related to cryptocurrency circulation. *Studies of Applied Economics*. .DOI: 10.25115/eea.v39i6.5247

Kumari, S., Singh, M., Singh, R., & Tewari, H. (2022). Post-quantum cryptography techniques for secure communication in resource-constrained Internet of Things devices: A comprehensive survey. *Software, Practice & Experience*, 52(10), 2047–2076. Advance online publication. DOI: 10.1002/spe.3121

Kumar, J., Madan, Y., & Mehta, D. (2023). The Evolution of Bitcoin and Other Cryptocurrencies. *International Journal of Advanced Research in Science. Tongxin Jishu*, 13–16. Advance online publication. DOI: 10.48175/IJARSCT-9363

Kumar, N., & Ram, S. (2019). Mobile Banking Services in India: Adoption and Future Prospects. *International Journal of Bank Marketing*, 37(6), 1462–1482.

Kumar, P. S., Naveen, I. G., Parameshachari, B. D., & Ramachandra, A. C. (2022, November). Military Robot Design and Implementation For Wireless Communication. In *2022 IEEE North Karnataka Subsection Flagship International Conference (NKCon)* (pp. 1-6). IEEE.

Law, L., Sabett, S., & Solinas, J. (1996). How to make a mint: The cryptography of anonymous electronic cash. *Am. UL Rev.*, 46, 1131.

Lee, J. (2020). The Economics and Politics of Information and its Legal Protection in Cryptocurrencies. *ERN: International Financial Flows (Topic)*. DOI: 10.2139/ssrn.3715632

Li, K., Shi, R., Wu, M., Li, Y., & Zhang, X. (2022). A novel privacy-preserving multi-level aggregate signcryption and query scheme for Smart Grid via mobile fog computing. *Journal of Information Security and Applications*, 67, 103214. Advance online publication. DOI: 10.1016/j.jisa.2022.103214

Liu, A., Zhengy, K., Liz, L., Liu, G., Zhao, L., & Zhou, X. "Efficient secure similarity computation on encrypted trajectory data," in Proc. Data Eng. IEEE 31st Int. Conf., 2015, pp. 66–77. DOI: 10.1109/ICDE.2015.7113273

Liu, F., Chu, M. C., & Ho, D. W. C. (2014). Evaluation of wireless power transfer systems for electric vehicle charging. *Released on September 19, 2014*.

Liu, Z., & Chen, Z. D. (2018). New wireless power transfer systems against misalignments between transmitters and receivers. *2018 18th International Symposium on Antenna Technology and Applied Electromagnetics (ANTEM)*, 1-2. DOI: 10.1109/ANTEM.2018.8572886

Liu, B., Zhang, X., Shi, R., Zhang, M., & Zhang, G. (2022). SEPSI: A Secure and Efficient Privacy-Preserving Set Intersection with Identity Authentication in IoT. *Mathematics*, 10(12), 2120. Advance online publication. DOI: 10.3390/math10122120

Liu, F., Yang, Y., Jiang, D., Ruan, X., & Chen, X. (2017). Modeling and optimization of magnetically coupled resonant wireless power transfer system with varying spatial scales. *IEEE Transactions on Power Electronics*, 32(4), 3240–3250. DOI: 10.1109/TPEL.2016.2581840

Liu, J., Wen, J., Zhang, B., Dong, S., Tang, B., & Yu, Y. (2023). A post quantum secure multi-party collaborative signature with deterability in the Industrial Internet of Things. *Future Generation Computer Systems*, 141, 663–676. Advance online publication. DOI: 10.1016/j.future.2022.11.034

Liu, J., Yu, Y., Wang, H., & Zhang, H. (2022). Lattice-Based Self-Enhancement Authorized Accessible Privacy Authentication for Cyber-Physical Systems. *Security and Communication Networks*, 2022, 1–9. Advance online publication. DOI: 10.1155/2022/8995704

Liu, X., Li, J., & Tan, Z. (2020). Blockchain and Quantum Computing: A Review of Challenges and Solutions. *Journal of Cryptographic Engineering*, 10(1), 23–36.

Liu, Y., He, Y., & Li, Y. (2020). Blockchain-Based Secure and Efficient Energy Trading for Smart Grids. *IEEE Transactions on Smart Grid*, 11(1), 320–329.

Li, Y., Chen, R., Chen, L., & Xu, J. (2015, July/August). Towards social-aware ridesharing group query services. *IEEE Transactions on Services Computing*, 10(4), 646–659. DOI: 10.1109/TSC.2015.2508440

Li, Y., Susilo, W., Yang, G., Yu, Y., Du, X., Liu, D., & Guizani, N. (2019). Toward Privacy and Regulation in Blockchain-Based Cryptocurrencies. *IEEE Network*, 33(5), 111–117. DOI: 10.1109/MNET.2019.1800271

Lloyd, S., Mohseni, M., & Rebentrost, P. (2013). Quantum Algorithms for Fixed Points and Machine Learning. *Physical Review Letters*, 110(19), 190501. PMID: 23705695

Lu, S., & Li, X. (2021). Quantum-Resistant Lightweight Authentication and Key Agreement Protocol for Fog-Based Microgrids. *IEEE Access : Practical Innovations, Open Solutions*, 9, 27588–27600. Advance online publication. DOI: 10.1109/ACCESS.2021.3058180

Madani, S., Roshandel, A., & Safavieh, S. E. (2020). Wireless charging technology for electric vehicles: A comprehensive review. *Released on March 9, 2020*.

Majot, A., & Yampolskiy, R. (2015). Global catastrophic risk and security implications of quantum computers. *Futures*, 72, 17–26. DOI: 10.1016/j.futures.2015.02.006

Malina, L., Dzurenda, P., Ricci, S., Hajny, J., Srivastava, G., Matulevicius, R., Affia, A. A. O., Laurent, M., Sultan, N. H., & Tang, Q. (2021). Post-quantum era privacy protection for intelligent infrastructures. *IEEE Access : Practical Innovations, Open Solutions*, 9, 36038–36077. Advance online publication. DOI: 10.1109/ACCESS.2021.3062201

Management, K., & Mining, D. (2005b). Medical Knowledge Management and Data Mining in. *In Medical Informatics* (Vol. 8). https://doi.org/DOI: 10.1007/b135955

Marian, O. (2014). A Conceptual Framework for the Regulation of Cryptocurrencies. *Criminology eJournal*.

Mark, J., & De Vynck, G. (2022). Crypto winter" has come. And it's looking more like an ice age. *Washington Post*.

Marshall, K., Jacobsen, C. S., Schäfermeier, C., Gehring, T., Weedbrook, C., & Andersen, U. L. (2016). Continuous-variable quantum computing on encrypted data. *Nature Communications*, 7(1), 13795. Advance online publication. DOI: 10.1038/ncomms13795 PMID: 27966528

Mashatan, A., & Heintzman, D. (2021). The Complex Path to Quantum Resistance. *ACM Queue; Tomorrow's Computing Today*, 19(2), 65–92. Advance online publication. DOI: 10.1145/3466132.3466779

Masood, M., Nawaz, M., Javed, A., Nazir, T., Mehmood, A., & Mahum, R. (2021). Classification of Deepfake Videos Using Pre-trained Convolutional Neural Networks. *2021 International Conference on Digital Futures and Transformative Technologies*, ICoDT2 2021. https://doi.org/DOI: 10.1109/ICoDT252288.2021.9441519

Masuda, S., Hirose, T., Akihara, Y., Kuroki, N., Numa, M., & Hashimoto, M. (2017). Impedance matching in magnetic-coupling-resonance wireless power transfer for small implantable devices. *2017 IEEE Wireless Power Transfer Conference (WPTC)*, 1-3. DOI: 10.1109/WPT.2017.7953839

Ma, Y., Kashefi, E., Arapinis, M., Chakraborty, K., & Kaplan, M. (2022). QEnclave - A practical solution for secure quantum cloud computing. *NPJ Quantum Information*, 8(1), 128. Advance online publication. DOI: 10.1038/s41534-022-00612-5

Mendes, J., Pereira, T., Silva, F., Frade, J., Morgado, J., Freitas, C., Negrão, E., de Lima, B. F., da Silva, M. C., Madureira, A. J., Ramos, I., Costa, J. L., Hespanhol, V., Cunha, A., & Oliveira, H. P. (2023). Lung CT image synthesis using GANs. *Expert Systems with Applications*, 215, 119350. Advance online publication. DOI: 10.1016/j.eswa.2022.119350

Mir, A., & Dhage, S. N. (2018). *2018 Fourth International Con- ference on Computing Communication Control and Automation (ICCUBEA)*. IEEE.

Mohan, S., Thirumalai, C., & Srivastava, G. (2019). Effective heart disease prediction using hybrid machine learning tech- niques. *IEEE Access : Practical Innovations, Open Solutions*, 7, 81542–81554. DOI: 10.1109/ACCESS.2019.2923707

Mohanty, D., Anand, D., Aljahdali, H. M., & Villar, S. G. (2022). Blockchain interoperability: Towards a sustainable payment system. *Sustainability (Basel)*, 14(2), 913. DOI: 10.3390/su14020913

Montanez, A. (2014). *Investigation of cryptocurrency wallets on iOS and Android mobile devices for potential forensic artifacts. Department Forensic Science*. Marshall University.

Mosca, M. (2018). Quantum Computing and Cryptography. *IEEE Security and Privacy*, 16(5), 30–37.

Muthu, B. A., Sivaparthipan, C. B., Manogaran, G., Sundarasekar, R., Kadry, S., Shanthini, A., & Dasel, A. (2020). Muthu, BalaAnand, C. B. Sivaparthipan, Gunasekaran Manogaran, Revathi Sundarasekar, Seifedine Kadry, A. Shanthini, and Antony Dasel. "IOT based wearable sensor for diseases prediction and symptom analysis in healthcare sector.". *Peer-to-Peer Networking and Applications*, 13(6), 2123–2134. DOI: 10.1007/s12083-019-00823-2

Nakamoto, S., & Bitcoin, A. (2008). A peer-to-peer electronic cash system. *Bitcoin.–URL:*https://bitcoin. org/bitcoin. pdf, *4*(2), 15.

Nath, G. (2020). Cryptocurrency Crimes – Need for a Comprehensive Global Crypto Regulation. *Social Science Research Network*. DOI: 10.2139/ssrn.3683669

Nour, K. (2022). Criminal confrontation of cryptocurrency use in the financing of terrorism. *Jolets*. 16;2(2):79-152. Available from: https://jolets.org/ojs/index.php/jolets/article/view/12

Nukavarapu, S. K., Ayyat, M., & Nadeem, T. (2022). MirageNet - Towards a GAN-based Framework for Synthetic Network Traffic Generation. *2022 IEEE Global Communications Conference, GLOBECOM 2022 - Proceedings*.https://doi.org/DOI: 10.1109/GLOBECOM48099.2022.10001494

Nukavarapu, S. K., & Nadeem, T. (2021). Securing Edge-based IoT Networks with Semi-Supervised GANs. *2021 IEEE International Conference on Pervasive Computing and Communications Workshops and Other Affiliated Events, PerCom Workshops 2021*.https://doi.org/DOI: 10.1109/PerComWorkshops51409.2021.9431112

Obeidat, T.. (1996). *Methods and Techniques of Scientific Research*. Dar Sana'a for Publishing. (In Arabic)

Ojha, P., & Niranjan, S. (2023). Potential usage of AI in Blockchain Technology. *2023 International Conference on Intelligent and Innovative Technologies in Computing, Electrical and Electronics (IITCEE)*, 7-8. DOI: 10.1109/IITCEE57236.2023.10091093

Paesano, F., & Siron, D. (2022). Working Paper 38: Cryptocurrencies in Asia and beyond: law, regulation and enforcement. *Basel Institute on Governance Working Papers*. DOI: 10.12685/bigwp.2022.38.1-69

Patel, M., Gupta, A., Tanwar, S., & Obaidat, M. S. (2020). Trans-DF: A Transfer Learning-based end-to-end Deepfake Detector. *2020 IEEE 5th International Conference on Computing Communication and Automation,* ICCCA 2020. https://doi.org/DOI: 10.1109/ICCCA49541.2020.9250803

Pathmanathan, M., Nie, S., Yakop, N., & Lehn, P. (2019). Efficiency improvement of a wireless power transfer system using a receiver side voltage doubling rectifier. *2019 21st European Conference on Power Electronics and Applications (EPE '19 ECCE Europe),* P.1-P.8. DOI: 10.23919/EPE.2019.8915022

Peck, M. E. (2012). The cryptoanarchists' answer to cash. *IEEE Spectrum*, 49(6), 50–56. DOI: 10.1109/MSPEC.2012.6203968

Pitta, J. (1999). Requiem for a bright idea. *Forbes*, 164(11), 390–392.

Prasanna, J. L., Ravi Kumar, M., Santhosh, C., Aswin Kumar, S. V., & Kasulu, P. (2022) "IoT based Soldier Health and Position Tracking System," *6th International Conference on Computing Methodologies and Communication (ICCMC)*, Erode, India, 2022, pp. 417-420, DOI: 10.1109/ICCMC53470.2022.9754096

Preskill, J. (2018). Quantum-enhanced Machine Learning. *Proceedings of the Royal Society of London. Series A*, 474(2209), 20170551. PMID: 29434508

Priscila, S. S., Sharma, A., Vanithamani, S., Ahmad, F., Mahaveerakannan, R., Al-rubaie, A. J., Jagota, V., & Singh, B. K. (2022). Risk-Based Access Control Mechanism for Internet of Vehicles Using Artificial Intelligence. *Security and Communication Networks*, 2022, 1–13. Advance online publication. DOI: 10.1155/2022/3379843

Rahimian, F., & Nazemi, E. (2018). Cloud computing security issues and challenges: A survey. *International Journal of Computer Science and Information Security*, 16(6), 164–170. DOI: 10.1007/s10586-017-2202-0

Rahman, M. M.. (2021). A Review on FinTech Security and Privacy: Threats, Challenges, and Research Directions. *Journal of King Saud University. Computer and Information Sciences.*

Rane, M., Jain, M., Kashyap, A., Jajoo, A., Kadam, H., & Kadam, D. (2023) "Mine Detecting Military Bot Using IoT," *International Conference on Emerging Smart Computing and Informatics (ESCI)*, Pune, India, 2023, pp. 1-6, DOI: 10.1109/ESCI56872.2023.10100211

Raveendran, R., & Raj, E. D. (2023). Deep Generative Models Under GAN: Variants, Applications, and Privacy Issues. *Lecture Notes in Networks and Systems*, 494, 93–105. Advance online publication. DOI: 10.1007/978-981-19-4863-3_9

Raya, J. E., Yahya, A. S., & Ahmad, E. K. (2023). Protection from A Quantum Computer Cyber-Attack. Technium. *Technium*, 5, 1–12. Advance online publication. DOI: 10.47577/technium.v5i.8293

Raymaekers, W. (2015). Cryptocurrency Bitcoin: Disruption, challenges and opportunities. *Journal of Payments Strategy & Systems*, 9(1), 30–46. DOI: 10.69554/FBUJ3107

Reid, F., & Harrigan, M. (2013). *An analysis of anonymity in the bitcoin system.* Springer New York. DOI: 10.1007/978-1-4614-4139-7_10

Sabarimuthu, M., Krishna, M. P., Sundari, P. M., Aarthi, L., & Juhair, P. M. and G. GowthamRaj,(2022) "IoT Based Soldier Status Monitoring Using Sensors and SOS Switch, "Second International Conference on Computer Science, Engineering and Applications (ICCSEA), Gunupur, India, 2022, pp. 1-6,DOI: 10.1109/ICCSEA54677.2022.9936125

Sabry, F. (2021). *Decentralized Finance: The apocalyptic event for the traditional financial institutions* (Vol. 3). One Billion Knowledgeable.

Sagar, A., Kashyap, A., Nasab, M. A., Padmanaban, S., Bertoluzzo, M., Kumar, A., & Blaabjerg, F. (2023). A comprehensive review of the recent development of wireless power transfer technologies for electric vehicle charging systems. *IEEE Access : Practical Innovations, Open Solutions*, 11, 83703–83751. DOI: 10.1109/ACCESS.2023.3300475

Salah, K., Rehman, M., Nizamuddin, N., & Al-Fuqaha, A. (2019). Blockchain for AI: Review and Open Research Challenges. *IEEE Access : Practical Innovations, Open Solutions*, 7, 10127–10149. DOI: 10.1109/ACCESS.2018.2890507

Salama, R., & Al-turjman, F. (2022). AI in Blockchain Towards Realizing Cyber Security. *2022 International Conference on Artificial Intelligence in Everything (AIE)*, 471-475. DOI: 10.1109/AIE57029.2022.00096

Sali, S. M., & Joy, K. R. (2023) "Intelligent Rover: An IoT Based Smart Surveillance Robotic Car for Military," *2nd International Conference on Computational Systems and Communication (ICCSC)*, Thiruvananthapuram, India, 2023, pp. 1-6, DOI: 10.1109/ICCSC56913.2023.10143011

Sarkar, S. (2023). Quantum Machine Learning: A Review. *International Journal for Research in Applied Science and Engineering Technology*, 11(3), 352–354. Advance online publication. DOI: 10.22214/ijraset.2023.49421

Schuh, D.. (2023). Understanding DeFi Risks: The Case for Enhanced Financial Education. *Journal of Financial Education*, 49(1), 193–209.

Schuld, M., & Petruccione, F. (2018). *Supervised learning with quantum computers* (Vol. 17). Springer.

Sereda, I., & Stupina, S. (2021). The Potential of Criminal Legislation in the Field of Counteraction to Crimes Related to Cryptocurrency. *Prologue: Law Journal*. https://doi.org/..DOI: 10.21639/2313-6715.2021.4.10

Shacham, H., & Waters, B. (2008). Compact proofs of retrievability. *InProceedings of the 14th International Conference on the Theory and Application of Cryptology and Information Security: Advances in Cryptology (ASIACRYPT'08)* (pp. 90-107). Springer. https://doi.org/DOI: 10.1007/978-3-540-89255-7_6

Shafik, W. (2024a). *An Overview of Computational Modeling and Simulations in Wireless Communication Systems. Computational Modeling and Simulation of Advanced Wireless Communication Systems*. CRC Press., DOI: 10.1201/9781003457428-2

Shafik, W. (2024b). Artificial Intelligence and Machine Learning with Cyber Ethics for the Future World. In *Future Communication Systems Using Artificial Intelligence, Internet of Things and Data Science* (pp. 110–130). CRC Press., DOI: 10.1201/9781032648309-9

Shafik, W. (2024c). Data Privacy and Security Safeguarding Customer Information in ChatGPT Systems. In *Revolutionizing the Service Industry With OpenAI Models* (pp. 52–86). IGI Global., DOI: 10.4018/979-8-3693-1239-1.ch003

Shafik, W. (2024d). *Deep Learning Impacts in the Field of Artificial Intelligence. Deep Learning Concepts in Operations Research*. CRC Press., DOI: 10.1201/9781003433309-2

Shafik, W. (2024e). Ethical Use of Machine Learning Techniques in Smart Cities. In *Ethical Artificial Intelligence in Power Electronics* (pp. 21–47). CRC Press., DOI: 10.1201/9781032648323-3

Shafik, W. (2024f). Shaping the Next Generation Smart City Ecosystem: An Investigation on the Requirements, Applications, Architecture, Security and Privacy, and Open Research Questions. In Majumdar, S., Kandpal, V., & Anthopoulos, L. G. (Eds.), *Smart Cities. S.M.A.R.T. Environments*. Springer., DOI: 10.1007/978-3-031-59846-3_1

Shafik, W. (2024g). Toward a More Ethical Future of Artificial Intelligence and Data Science. In *The Ethical Frontier of AI and Data Analysis* (pp. 362–388). IGI Global., DOI: 10.4018/979-8-3693-2964-1.ch022

Shah, M. A., & Baker, M. (2008). Privacy-preserving audit and extraction of digital contents. *InProceedings of the 2008 ACM Workshop on Cloud Computing Security (CCSW'08)* (pp. 41-52). https://doi.org/DOI: 10.1145/1456458.1456466

Sharma, B., Sharma, L., Lal, C., & Roy, S. (2023). Anomaly based network intrusion detection for IoT attacks using deep learning technique. *Computers & Electrical Engineering*, 107, 108626. Advance online publication. DOI: 10.1016/j.compeleceng.2023.108626

Sharma, D., Pant, D., & Kumar, A. (2023). Cryptocurrency: An Overview of its History, Technology and Future Prospects. *International Journal of Advanced Research in Science. Tongxin Jishu*, 427–430. Advance online publication. DOI: 10.48175/IJARSCT-9232

Shinde, R., Patil, S., Kotecha, K., & Ruikar, K. (2021). Blockchain for Securing AI Applications and Open Innovations. *Journal of Open Innovation*, 7(3), 189. Advance online publication. DOI: 10.3390/joitmc7030189

Singh, S. K., El Azzaoui, A., Salim, M. M., & Park, J. H. (2020). Quantum Communication Technology for Future ICT - Review. *Journal of Information Processing Systems*, 16(6). Advance online publication. DOI: 10.3745/JIPS.03.0154

Singh, S. P. K., Saini, A. K., & Kumar, V. (2019). Blockchain-Based Decentralized Energy Trading Framework for Smart Grids. *IEEE Transactions on Industrial Informatics*, 15(9), 5292–5301.

Smith, A.. (2021). Decentralized Finance: On Blockchain- and Smart Contract-Based Financial Markets. *IEEE Transactions on Services Computing*.

Steadman, I. (2013). Wary of Bitcoin? A guide to some other cryptocurrencies. *Ars Technica, 11*.

Stitt, F. W. (1993). The Problem-Oriented Medical Synopsis: a patient-centered clinical information system. In *Proceedings of the Annual Symposium on Computer Application in Medical Care* (p. 88). American Medical Informatics Association.

Su, H., Liu, S., Zheng, B., Zhou, X., & Zheng, K. (2020). A survey of trajectory distance measures and performance evaluation. *The VLDB Journal*, 29(1), 3–32. DOI: 10.1007/s00778-019-00574-9

Sukumar, S. (2023). Digital Forensics in The Dark. https://www.linkedin.com/pulse/digital-forensics-dark-sandhya-sukumar/

Sun, H., Zhu, T., Zhang, Z., Jin, D., Xiong, P., & Zhou, W. (2023). Adversarial Attacks Against Deep Generative Models on Data: A Survey. *IEEE Transactions on Knowledge and Data Engineering*, 35(4), 3367–3388. Advance online publication. DOI: 10.1109/TKDE.2021.3130903

Taleby Ahvanooey, M., Zhu, M. X., Mazurczyk, W., Kilger, M., & Choo, K. K. R. (2021, December). Do dark web and cryptocurrencies empower cybercriminals? In *International Conference on Digital Forensics and Cyber Crime* (pp. 277-293). Cham: Springer International Publishing.

Tandon, C., Revankar, S., Palivela, H., & Parihar, S. S. (2021). How can we predict the impact of the social media messages on the value of cryptocurrency insights from big data analytics. *International Journal of Information Management Data Insights*, 1(2), 100035. DOI: 10.1016/j.jjimei.2021.100035

Taylor, J. A. (2015). *Convex optimization of power systems*. Cambridge University Press. DOI: 10.1017/CBO9781139924672

Taylor, P. J., Dargahi, T., Dehghantanha, A., Parizi, R. M., & Choo, K.-K. R. (2020). A systematic literature review of blockchain cyber security. *Digital Communications and Networks*, 6(2), 147–156. DOI: 10.1016/j.dcan.2019.01.005

Tinsley, P., Czajka, A., & Flynn, P. J. (2022). Haven't I Seen You Before? Assessing Identity Leakage in Synthetic Irises. *2022 IEEE International Joint Conference on Biometrics,* IJCB 2022. https://doi.org/DOI: 10.1109/IJCB54206.2022.10007948

Tramèr, F., Boneh, D., & Paterson, K. (2020). Remote Side-Channel Attacks on Anonymous Transactions. *IACR Cryptol. ePrint Arch.*, 2020, 220.

Treasury, H. M. S. (2021). UK regulatory approach to cryptoassets and stablecoins: consultation and call for evidence (2021).

Tsolakis, N., Schumacher, R., Dora, M., & Kumar, M. (2023). Artificial intelligence and blockchain implementation in supply chains: A pathway to sustainability and data monetisation. *Annals of Operations Research*, 327(1), 157–210. DOI: 10.1007/s10479-022-04785-2 PMID: 35755830

Tsuchiya, Y., & Hiramoto, N. (2021). How cryptocurrency is laundered: Case study of Coincheck hacking incident. *Forensic Science International. Reports*, 4, 100241. DOI: 10.1016/j.fsir.2021.100241

Tziakouris, G. (2018). Cryptocurrencies—A forensic challenge or opportunity for law enforcement? an interpol perspective. *IEEE Security and Privacy*, 16(4), 92–94. DOI: 10.1109/MSP.2018.3111243

Udaykumar, H., Rathod, S. J., Vinaykumar, R., Pradeep, S., & Savitha, P. B. (2022) "IoT-Based Quadcopter with Automatic Landing System and Object Detection," Fourth International Conference on Emerging Research in Electronics, Computer 64 Technology(ICERECT),Mandya,India,2022,pp.0104, RECT56837. 2022.10059649. DOI: 10.1109/ICERECT56837.2022.10059649

Uddin, K. M. N. (2022). On cryptocurrencies: An assessment of bitcoin's prospect as legal medium of exchange. *Advances in Management and Applied Economics*, 12(5), 1–17. DOI: 10.47260/amae/1251

Vardhini, P. A. H., & Babu, K. M. C. (2022). *"IoT based Autonomous Robot Design Implementation for Military Applications," IEEEDelhi Section Conference*. DELCON., DOI: 10.1109/DELCON54057.2022.9753507

Vijayarani, S., & Dhayanand, S. (2015). Liver disease prediction us- ing svm and na¨ıve bayes algorithms, International Jour- nal of Science [IJSETR]. *Engineering and Technology Research*, 4(4), 816.

Wang, R., Luo, M., Wen, Y., Wang, L., Choo, K., & He, D. (2021). The Applications of Blockchain in Artificial Intelligence. *Secur. Commun. Networks*, 2021, 6126247:1-6126247:16. .DOI: 10.1155/2021/6126247

Wang, C., Kon, W. Y., Ng, H. J., & Lim, C. C. W. (2022). Experimental symmetric private information retrieval with measurement-device-independent quantum network. *Light, Science & Applications*, 11(1), 268. Advance online publication. DOI: 10.1038/s41377-022-00959-6 PMID: 36100587

Wang, C., Wang, Q., Ren, K., Cao, N., & Lou, W. (2012). Privacy-preserving public auditing for secure cloud storage. *IEEE Transactions on Computers*, 62(2), 362–375. DOI: 10.1109/TC.2011.245

Wang, J., Shahidehpour, M., & Li, Z. (2018). Security-constrained unit commitment with volatile wind power generation. *IEEE Transactions on Power Systems*, 23(3), 1319–1327. DOI: 10.1109/TPWRS.2008.926719

Wang, K., Deng, N., & Li, X. (2023). An Efficient Content Popularity Prediction of Privacy Preserving Based on Federated Learning and Wasserstein GAN. *IEEE Internet of Things Journal*, 10(5), 3786–3798. Advance online publication. DOI: 10.1109/JIOT.2022.3176360

Wang, Q., Wang, C., Ren, K., & Lou, W. (2010). Enabling public verifiability and data dynamics for storage security in cloud computing. *InProceedings of the 14th European Conference on Research in Computer Security (ESORICS'09)* (pp. 355-370). Springer. https://doi.org/DOI: 10.1007/978-3-642-15778-2_22

Wang, Z. D., Zhao, J. Z., & Wang, X. G. (2018). Quantum Neural Networks. *Physical Review. A*, 98(3), 032327. DOI: 10.1103/PhysRevA.65.032327

Weber, M., Domeniconi, G., Chen, J., Weidele, D. K. I., Bellei, C., Robinson, T., & Leiserson, C. E. (2019). Anti-money laundering in bitcoin: Experimenting with graph convolutional networks for financial forensics. *arXiv preprint arXiv:1908.02591*.

Weber, R. H., & Baisch, R. (2023). Cryptoassets: Taxonomy and Regulatory Approaches. *Banking & Finance Law Review*, 39(3), 467–505.

Xuan, T., & Ness, S. (2023). Integration of Blockchain and AI: Exploring Application in the Digital Business. *Journal of Engineering Research and Reports*. .DOI: 10.9734/jerr/2023/v25i8955

Xu, Y., Wang, L., Wang, C., & Zhu, H. (2022). Effective Agent Quantum Private Data Query against Malicious Joint Attack with Blind Quantum Computing. *International Journal of Theoretical Physics*, 61(4), 106. Advance online publication. DOI: 10.1007/s10773-022-05104-y

Y. Li, W. Xu, and M. L. Yiu, "Client-side service for recommending rewarding routes to mobile crowdsourcing workers," IEEE Trans. Serv. Comput., early access, Mar. 18, 2019, .DOI: 10.1109/TSC.2019.2905564

Yang, J., Chen, G., Han, T., Zhang, Q., Zhang, Y.-H., Jiang, L., Lyu, B., Li, H., Watanabe, K., Taniguchi, T., Shi, Z., Senthil, T., Zhang, Y., Wang, F., & Ju, L. (2022). Spectroscopy signatures of electron correlations in a trilayer graphene/hBN moiré superlattice. *Science*, 375(6586), 1295–1299. Advance online publication. DOI: 10.1126/science.abg3036 PMID: 35298267

Yang, J., Xiao, S., Li, A., Lan, G., & Wang, H. (2021). Detecting fake images by identifying potential texture difference. *Future Generation Computer Systems*, 125, 127–135. Advance online publication. DOI: 10.1016/j.future.2021.06.043

Yousaf, H. (2022). Investigating transactions in cryptocurrencies. *ArXiv*, abs/2203.14684. https://doi.org//arXiv.2203.14684.DOI: 10.48550

Yu, K.-H., Beam, A. L., & Kohane, I. S. (2018). Artificial intelligence in healthcare. *Nature Biomedical Engineering*, 2(10), 719–731. DOI: 10.1038/s41551-018-0305-z PMID: 31015651

Zetzsche, D. A., Arner, D. W., & Buckley, R. P. (2020). Decentralized finance. *Journal of Financial Regulation*, 6(2), 172–203. DOI: 10.1093/jfr/fjaa010

Zhang, M., Gao, H., & Wu, Z. (2021). Wireless charging for electric vehicles. *Released on March 2, 2021*.

Zhang, Y., Liu, S., & Xu, W. (2020). Wireless charging for electric vehicles: Opportunities and challenges. *Released on November 27, 2020*.

Zhang, T. (2023). Privacy Evaluation of Blockchain-Based Privacy Cryptocurrencies: A Comparative Analysis of Dash, Monero, Verge, Zcash, and Grin. *IEEE Transactions on Sustainable Computing*, 8(4), 574–582. DOI: 10.1109/TSUSC.2023.3303180

Zhang, X., Zhu, X., Wang, J., Bao, W., & Yang, L. T. (2022). DANCE: Distributed Generative Adversarial Networks with Communication Compression. *ACM Transactions on Internet Technology*, 22(2), 1–32. Advance online publication. DOI: 10.1145/3458929

Zhao, A., Jiang, N., Wang, C., Liu, S., & Qiu, K. (2023). Synchronization Optimization of Chaotic Laser Based on Generative Adversarial Network. *Guangxue Xuebao. Acta Optica Sinica*, 43(1). Advance online publication. DOI: 10.3788/AOS220994

Zhou, J., Chen, Y., Shen, C., & Zhang, Y. (2022). Property Inference Attacks Against GANs.

Zhu, S., Cai, Z., Hu, H., Li, Y., & Li, W. (2020). ZkCrowd: A hybrid blockchain-based crowdsourcing platform. *IEEE Transactions on Industrial Informatics*, 16(6), 4196–4205. DOI: 10.1109/TII.2019.2941735

Zhu, X., Li, X., Fang, L., & Chen, P. (2020). An improved proof-of-trust consensus algorithm for credible crowdsourcing blockchain services. *IEEE Access : Practical Innovations, Open Solutions*, 8, 10187–102177. DOI: 10.1109/ACCESS.2020.2998803

Related References

To continue our tradition of advancing information science and technology research, we have compiled a list of recommended IGI Global readings. These references will provide additional information and guidance to further enrich your knowledge and assist you with your own research and future publications.

Aasi, P., Rusu, L., & Vieru, D. (2017). The Role of Culture in IT Governance Five Focus Areas: A Literature Review. *International Journal of IT/Business Alignment and Governance, 8*(2), 42-61. https://doi.org/DOI: 10.4018/IJITBAG.2017070103

Abdrabo, A. A. (2018). Egypt's Knowledge-Based Development: Opportunities, Challenges, and Future Possibilities. In Alraouf, A. (Ed.), *Knowledge-Based Urban Development in the Middle East* (pp. 80–101). Hershey, PA: IGI Global. DOI: 10.4018/978-1-5225-3734-2.ch005

Abu Doush, I., & Alhami, I. (2018). Evaluating the Accessibility of Computer Laboratories, Libraries, and Websites in Jordanian Universities and Colleges. *International Journal of Information Systems and Social Change*, 9(2), 44–60. DOI: 10.4018/IJISSC.2018040104

Adegbore, A. M., Quadri, M. O., & Oyewo, O. R. (2018). A Theoretical Approach to the Adoption of Electronic Resource Management Systems (ERMS) in Nigerian University Libraries. In Tella, A., & Kwanya, T. (Eds.), *Handbook of Research on Managing Intellectual Property in Digital Libraries* (pp. 292–311). Hershey, PA: IGI Global. DOI: 10.4018/978-1-5225-3093-0.ch015

Afolabi, O. A. (2018). Myths and Challenges of Building an Effective Digital Library in Developing Nations: An African Perspective. In Tella, A., & Kwanya, T. (Eds.), *Handbook of Research on Managing Intellectual Property in Digital Libraries* (pp. 51–79). Hershey, PA: IGI Global. DOI: 10.4018/978-1-5225-3093-0.ch004

Agarwal, P., Kurian, R., & Gupta, R. K. (2022). Additive Manufacturing Feature Taxonomy and Placement of Parts in AM Enclosure. In Salunkhe, S., Hussein, H., & Davim, J. (Eds.), *Applications of Artificial Intelligence in Additive Manufacturing* (pp. 138–176). IGI Global. https://doi.org/10.4018/978-1-7998-8516-0.ch007

Al-Alawi, A. I., Al-Hammam, A. H., Al-Alawi, S. S., & AlAlawi, E. I. (2021). The Adoption of E-Wallets: Current Trends and Future Outlook. In Albastaki, Y., Razzaque, A., & Sarea, A. (Eds.), *Innovative Strategies for Implementing FinTech in Banking* (pp. 242–262). IGI Global. https://doi.org/10.4018/978-1-7998-3257-7.ch015

Alsharo, M. (2017). Attitudes Towards Cloud Computing Adoption in Emerging Economies. *International Journal of Cloud Applications and Computing*, 7(3), 44–58. DOI: 10.4018/IJCAC.2017070102

Amer, T. S., & Johnson, T. L. (2017). Information Technology Progress Indicators: Research Employing Psychological Frameworks. In Mesquita, A. (Ed.), *Research Paradigms and Contemporary Perspectives on Human-Technology Interaction* (pp. 168–186). Hershey, PA: IGI Global. DOI: 10.4018/978-1-5225-1868-6.ch008

Andreeva, A., & Yolova, G. (2021). Liability in Labor Legislation: New Challenges Related to the Use of Artificial Intelligence. In Vassileva, B., & Zwilling, M. (Eds.), *Responsible AI and Ethical Issues for Businesses and Governments* (pp. 214–232). IGI Global. https://doi.org/10.4018/978-1-7998-4285-9.ch012

Anohah, E. (2017). Paradigm and Architecture of Computing Augmented Learning Management System for Computer Science Education. *International Journal of Online Pedagogy and Course Design*, 7(2), 60–70. DOI: 10.4018/IJOPCD.2017040105

Anohah, E., & Suhonen, J. (2017). Trends of Mobile Learning in Computing Education from 2006 to 2014: A Systematic Review of Research Publications. *International Journal of Mobile and Blended Learning*, 9(1), 16–33. DOI: 10.4018/IJMBL.2017010102

Arbaiza, C. S., Huerta, H. V., & Rodriguez, C. R. (2021). Contributions to the Technological Adoption Model for the Peruvian Agro-Export Sector. *International Journal of E-Adoption*, 13(1), 1–17. https://doi.org/10.4018/IJEA.2021010101

Bailey, E. K. (2017). Applying Learning Theories to Computer Technology Supported Instruction. In Grassetti, M., & Brookby, S. (Eds.), *Advancing Next-Generation Teacher Education through Digital Tools and Applications* (pp. 61–81). Hershey, PA: IGI Global. DOI: 10.4018/978-1-5225-0965-3.ch004

Baker, J. D. (2021). Introduction to Machine Learning as a New Methodological Framework for Performance Assessment. In Bocarnea, M., Winston, B., & Dean, D. (Eds.), *Handbook of Research on Advancements in Organizational Data Collection and Measurements: Strategies for Addressing Attitudes, Beliefs, and Behaviors* (pp. 326–342). IGI Global. https://doi.org/10.4018/978-1-7998-7665-6.ch021

Banerjee, S., Sing, T. Y., Chowdhury, A. R., & Anwar, H. (2018). Let's Go Green: Towards a Taxonomy of Green Computing Enablers for Business Sustainability. In Khosrow-Pour, M. (Ed.), *Green Computing Strategies for Competitive Advantage and Business Sustainability* (pp. 89–109). Hershey, PA: IGI Global. DOI: 10.4018/978-1-5225-5017-4.ch005

Basham, R. (2018). Information Science and Technology in Crisis Response and Management. In M. Khosrow-Pour, D.B.A. (Ed.), *Encyclopedia of Information Science and Technology, Fourth Edition* (pp. 1407-1418). Hershey, PA: IGI Global. DOI: 10.4018/978-1-5225-2255-3.ch121

Batyashe, T., & Iyamu, T. (2018). Architectural Framework for the Implementation of Information Technology Governance in Organisations. In M. Khosrow-Pour, D.B.A. (Ed.), *Encyclopedia of Information Science and Technology, Fourth Edition* (pp. 810-819). Hershey, PA: IGI Global. DOI: 10.4018/978-1-5225-2255-3.ch070

Bekleyen, N., & Çelik, S. (2017). Attitudes of Adult EFL Learners towards Preparing for a Language Test via CALL. In Tafazoli, D., & Romero, M. (Eds.), *Multiculturalism and Technology-Enhanced Language Learning* (pp. 214–229). Hershey, PA: IGI Global. DOI: 10.4018/978-1-5225-1882-2.ch013

Bergeron, F., Croteau, A., Uwizeyemungu, S., & Raymond, L. (2017). A Framework for Research on Information Technology Governance in SMEs. In De Haes, S., & Van Grembergen, W. (Eds.), *Strategic IT Governance and Alignment in Business Settings* (pp. 53–81). Hershey, PA: IGI Global. DOI: 10.4018/978-1-5225-0861-8.ch003

Bhardwaj, M., Shukla, N., & Sharma, A. (2021). Improvement and Reduction of Clustering Overhead in Mobile Ad Hoc Network With Optimum Stable Bunching Algorithm. In Kumar, S., Trivedi, M., Ranjan, P., & Punhani, A. (Eds.), *Evolution of Software-Defined Networking Foundations for IoT and 5G Mobile Networks* (pp. 139–158). IGI Global. https://doi.org/10.4018/978-1-7998-4685-7.ch008

Bhatt, G. D., Wang, Z., & Rodger, J. A. (2017). Information Systems Capabilities and Their Effects on Competitive Advantages: A Study of Chinese Companies. *Information Resources Management Journal*, 30(3), 41–57. DOI: 10.4018/IRMJ.2017070103

Bhattacharya, A. (2021). Blockchain, Cybersecurity, and Industry 4.0. In Tyagi, A., Rekha, G., & Sreenath, N. (Eds.), *Opportunities and Challenges for Blockchain Technology in Autonomous Vehicles* (pp. 210–244). IGI Global. https://doi.org/10.4018/978-1-7998-3295-9.ch013

Bhyan, P., Shrivastava, B., & Kumar, N. (2022). Requisite Sustainable Development Contemplating Buildings: Economic and Environmental Sustainability. In Hussain, A., Tiwari, K., & Gupta, A. (Eds.), *Addressing Environmental Challenges Through Spatial Planning* (pp. 269–288). IGI Global. https://doi.org/10.4018/978-1-7998-8331-9.ch014

Boido, C., Davico, P., & Spallone, R. (2021). Digital Tools Aimed to Represent Urban Survey. In M. Khosrow-Pour D.B.A. (Ed.), *Encyclopedia of Information Science and Technology, Fifth Edition* (pp. 1181-1195). IGI Global. https://doi.org/10.4018/978-1-7998-3479-3.ch082

Borkar, P. S., Chanana, P. U., Atwal, S. K., Londe, T. G., & Dalal, Y. D. (2021). The Replacement of HMI (Human-Machine Interface) in Industry Using Single Interface Through IoT. In Raut, R., & Mihovska, A. (Eds.), *Examining the Impact of Deep Learning and IoT on Multi-Industry Applications* (pp. 195–208). IGI Global. https://doi.org/10.4018/978-1-7998-7511-6.ch011

Brahmane, A. V., & Krishna, C. B. (2021). Rider Chaotic Biography Optimization-driven Deep Stacked Auto-encoder for Big Data Classification Using Spark Architecture: Rider Chaotic Biography Optimization. *International Journal of Web Services Research*, 18(3), 42–62. https://doi.org/10.4018/ijwsr.2021070103

Burcoff, A., & Shamir, L. (2017). Computer Analysis of Pablo Picasso's Artistic Style. *International Journal of Art, Culture and Design Technologies*, 6(1), 1–18. DOI: 10.4018/IJACDT.2017010101

Byker, E. J. (2017). I Play I Learn: Introducing Technological Play Theory. In Martin, C., & Polly, D. (Eds.), *Handbook of Research on Teacher Education and Professional Development* (pp. 297–306). Hershey, PA: IGI Global. DOI: 10.4018/978-1-5225-1067-3.ch016

Calongne, C. M., Stricker, A. G., Truman, B., & Arenas, F. J. (2017). Cognitive Apprenticeship and Computer Science Education in Cyberspace: Reimagining the Past. In Stricker, A., Calongne, C., Truman, B., & Arenas, F. (Eds.), *Integrating an Awareness of Selfhood and Society into Virtual Learning* (pp. 180–197). Hershey, PA: IGI Global. DOI: 10.4018/978-1-5225-2182-2.ch013

Carneiro, A. D. (2017). Defending Information Networks in Cyberspace: Some Notes on Security Needs. In M. Dawson, D. Kisku, P. Gupta, J. Sing, & W. Li (Eds.), *Developing Next-Generation Countermeasures for Homeland Security Threat Prevention* (pp. 354-375). Hershey, PA: IGI Global. https://doi.org/DOI: 10.4018/978-1-5225-0703-1.ch016

Carvalho, W. F., & Zarate, L. (2021). Causal Feature Selection. In A. Azevedo & M. Santos (Eds.), *Integration Challenges for Analytics, Business Intelligence, and Data Mining* (pp. 145-160). IGI Global. https://doi.org/10.4018/978-1-7998-5781-5.ch007

Chase, J. P., & Yan, Z. (2017). Affect in Statistics Cognition. In *Assessing and Measuring Statistics Cognition in Higher Education Online Environments: Emerging Research and Opportunities* (pp. 144–187). Hershey, PA: IGI Global. DOI: 10.4018/978-1-5225-2420-5.ch005

Chatterjee, A., Roy, S., & Shrivastava, R. (2021). A Machine Learning Approach to Prevent Cancer. In Rani, G., & Tiwari, P. (Eds.), *Handbook of Research on Disease Prediction Through Data Analytics and Machine Learning* (pp. 112–141). IGI Global. https://doi.org/10.4018/978-1-7998-2742-9.ch007

Cifci, M. A. (2021). Optimizing WSNs for CPS Using Machine Learning Techniques. In Luhach, A., & Elçi, A. (Eds.), *Artificial Intelligence Paradigms for Smart Cyber-Physical Systems* (pp. 204–228). IGI Global. https://doi.org/10.4018/978-1-7998-5101-1.ch010

Cimermanova, I. (2017). Computer-Assisted Learning in Slovakia. In Tafazoli, D., & Romero, M. (Eds.), *Multiculturalism and Technology-Enhanced Language Learning* (pp. 252–270). Hershey, PA: IGI Global. DOI: 10.4018/978-1-5225-1882-2.ch015

Cipolla-Ficarra, F. V., & Cipolla-Ficarra, M. (2018). Computer Animation for Ingenious Revival. In Cipolla-Ficarra, F., Ficarra, M., Cipolla-Ficarra, M., Quiroga, A., Alma, J., & Carré, J. (Eds.), *Technology-Enhanced Human Interaction in Modern Society* (pp. 159–181). Hershey, PA: IGI Global. DOI: 10.4018/978-1-5225-3437-2.ch008

Cockrell, S., Damron, T. S., Melton, A. M., & Smith, A. D. (2018). Offshoring IT. In M. Khosrow-Pour, D.B.A. (Ed.), *Encyclopedia of Information Science and Technology, Fourth Edition* (pp. 5476-5489). Hershey, PA: IGI Global. https://doi.org/DOI: 10.4018/978-1-5225-2255-3.ch476

Coffey, J. W. (2018). Logic and Proof in Computer Science: Categories and Limits of Proof Techniques. In Horne, J. (Ed.), *Philosophical Perceptions on Logic and Order* (pp. 218–240). Hershey, PA: IGI Global. DOI: 10.4018/978-1-5225-2443-4.ch007

Dale, M. (2017). Re-Thinking the Challenges of Enterprise Architecture Implementation. In Tavana, M. (Ed.), *Enterprise Information Systems and the Digitalization of Business Functions* (pp. 205–221). Hershey, PA: IGI Global. DOI: 10.4018/978-1-5225-2382-6.ch009

Das, A., & Mohanty, M. N. (2021). An Useful Review on Optical Character Recognition for Smart Era Generation. In Tyagi, A. (Ed.), *Multimedia and Sensory Input for Augmented, Mixed, and Virtual Reality* (pp. 1–41). IGI Global. https://doi.org/10.4018/978-1-7998-4703-8.ch001

Dash, A. K., & Mohapatra, P. (2021). A Survey on Prematurity Detection of Diabetic Retinopathy Based on Fundus Images Using Deep Learning Techniques. In Saxena, S., & Paul, S. (Eds.), *Deep Learning Applications in Medical Imaging* (pp. 140–155). IGI Global. https://doi.org/10.4018/978-1-7998-5071-7.ch006

De Maere, K., De Haes, S., & von Kutzschenbach, M. (2017). CIO Perspectives on Organizational Learning within the Context of IT Governance. *International Journal of IT/Business Alignment and Governance, 8*(1), 32-47. https://doi.org/DOI: 10.4018/IJITBAG.2017010103

Demir, K., Çaka, C., Yaman, N. D., İslamoğlu, H., & Kuzu, A. (2018). Examining the Current Definitions of Computational Thinking. In Ozcinar, H., Wong, G., & Ozturk, H. (Eds.), *Teaching Computational Thinking in Primary Education* (pp. 36–64). Hershey, PA: IGI Global. DOI: 10.4018/978-1-5225-3200-2.ch003

Deng, X., Hung, Y., & Lin, C. D. (2017). Design and Analysis of Computer Experiments. In S. Saha, A. Mandal, A. Narasimhamurthy, S. V, & S. Sangam (Eds.), *Handbook of Research on Applied Cybernetics and Systems Science* (pp. 264-279). Hershey, PA: IGI Global. DOI: 10.4018/978-1-5225-2498-4.ch013

Denner, J., Martinez, J., & Thiry, H. (2017). Strategies for Engaging Hispanic/Latino Youth in the US in Computer Science. In Rankin, Y., & Thomas, J. (Eds.), *Moving Students of Color from Consumers to Producers of Technology* (pp. 24–48). Hershey, PA: IGI Global. DOI: 10.4018/978-1-5225-2005-4.ch002

Devi, A. (2017). Cyber Crime and Cyber Security: A Quick Glance. In Kumar, R., Pattnaik, P., & Pandey, P. (Eds.), *Detecting and Mitigating Robotic Cyber Security Risks* (pp. 160–171). Hershey, PA: IGI Global. DOI: 10.4018/978-1-5225-2154-9.ch011

Dhaya, R., & Kanthavel, R. (2022). Futuristic Research Perspectives of IoT Platforms. In Jeya Mala, D. (Ed.), *Integrating AI in IoT Analytics on the Cloud for Healthcare Applications* (pp. 258–275). IGI Global. DOI: 10.4018/978-1-7998-9132-1.ch015

Doyle, D. J., & Fahy, P. J. (2018). Interactivity in Distance Education and Computer-Aided Learning, With Medical Education Examples. In M. Khosrow-Pour, D.B.A. (Ed.), *Encyclopedia of Information Science and Technology, Fourth Edition* (pp. 5829-5840). Hershey, PA: IGI Global. https://doi.org/DOI: 10.4018/978-1-5225-2255-3.ch507

Eklund, P. (2021). Reinforcement Learning in Social Media Marketing. In Christiansen, B., & Škrinjarić, T. (Eds.), *Handbook of Research on Applied AI for International Business and Marketing Applications* (pp. 30–48). IGI Global. https://doi.org/10.4018/978-1-7998-5077-9.ch003

El Ghandour, N., Benaissa, M., & Lebbah, Y. (2021). An Integer Linear Programming-Based Method for the Extraction of Ontology Alignment. *International Journal of Information Technology and Web Engineering*, 16(2), 25–44. https://doi.org/10.4018/IJITWE.2021040102

Elias, N. I., & Walker, T. W. (2017). Factors that Contribute to Continued Use of E-Training among Healthcare Professionals. In Topor, F. (Ed.), *Handbook of Research on Individualism and Identity in the Globalized Digital Age* (pp. 403–429). Hershey, PA: IGI Global. DOI: 10.4018/978-1-5225-0522-8.ch018

Fisher, R. L. (2018). Computer-Assisted Indian Matrimonial Services. In M. Khosrow-Pour, D.B.A. (Ed.), *Encyclopedia of Information Science and Technology, Fourth Edition* (pp. 4136-4145). Hershey, PA: IGI Global. DOI: 10.4018/978-1-5225-2255-3.ch358

Galiautdinov, R. (2021). Nonlinear Filtering in Artificial Neural Network Applications in Business and Engineering. In Do, Q. (Ed.), *Artificial Neural Network Applications in Business and Engineering* (pp. 1–23). IGI Global. https://doi.org/10.4018/978-1-7998-3238-6.ch001

Gardner-McCune, C., & Jimenez, Y. (2017). Historical App Developers: Integrating CS into K-12 through Cross-Disciplinary Projects. In Rankin, Y., & Thomas, J. (Eds.), *Moving Students of Color from Consumers to Producers of Technology* (pp. 85–112). Hershey, PA: IGI Global. DOI: 10.4018/978-1-5225-2005-4.ch005

Garg, P. K. (2021). The Internet of Things-Based Technologies. In Kumar, S., Trivedi, M., Ranjan, P., & Punhani, A. (Eds.), *Evolution of Software-Defined Networking Foundations for IoT and 5G Mobile Networks* (pp. 37–65). IGI Global. https://doi.org/10.4018/978-1-7998-4685-7.ch003

Garg, T., & Bharti, M. (2021). Congestion Control Protocols for UWSNs. In Goyal, N., Sapra, L., & Sandhu, J. (Eds.), *Energy-Efficient Underwater Wireless Communications and Networking* (pp. 85–100). IGI Global. https://doi.org/10.4018/978-1-7998-3640-7.ch006

Gauttier, S. (2021). A Primer on Q-Method and the Study of Technology. In M. Khosrow-Pour D.B.A. (Eds.), *Encyclopedia of Information Science and Technology, Fifth Edition* (pp. 1746-1756). IGI Global. https://doi.org/10.4018/978-1-7998-3479-3.ch120

Ghafele, R., & Gibert, B. (2018). Open Growth: The Economic Impact of Open Source Software in the USA. In Khosrow-Pour, M. (Ed.), *Optimizing Contemporary Application and Processes in Open Source Software* (pp. 164–197). Hershey, PA: IGI Global. DOI: 10.4018/978-1-5225-5314-4.ch007

Ghobakhloo, M., & Azar, A. (2018). Information Technology Resources, the Organizational Capability of Lean-Agile Manufacturing, and Business Performance. *Information Resources Management Journal*, 31(2), 47–74. DOI: 10.4018/IRMJ.2018040103

Gikandi, J. W. (2017). Computer-Supported Collaborative Learning and Assessment: A Strategy for Developing Online Learning Communities in Continuing Education. In Keengwe, J., & Onchwari, G. (Eds.), *Handbook of Research on Learner-Centered Pedagogy in Teacher Education and Professional Development* (pp. 309–333). Hershey, PA: IGI Global. DOI: 10.4018/978-1-5225-0892-2.ch017

Gokhale, A. A., & Machina, K. F. (2017). Development of a Scale to Measure Attitudes toward Information Technology. In Tomei, L. (Ed.), *Exploring the New Era of Technology-Infused Education* (pp. 49–64). Hershey, PA: IGI Global. DOI: 10.4018/978-1-5225-1709-2.ch004

Goswami, J. K., Jalal, S., Negi, C. S., & Jalal, A. S. (2022). A Texture Features-Based Robust Facial Expression Recognition. *International Journal of Computer Vision and Image Processing*, 12(1), 1–15. https://doi.org/10.4018/IJCVIP.2022010103

Hafeez-Baig, A., Gururajan, R., & Wickramasinghe, N. (2017). Readiness as a Novel Construct of Readiness Acceptance Model (RAM) for the Wireless Handheld Technology. In Wickramasinghe, N. (Ed.), *Handbook of Research on Healthcare Administration and Management* (pp. 578–595). Hershey, PA: IGI Global. DOI: 10.4018/978-1-5225-0920-2.ch035

Hanafizadeh, P., Ghandchi, S., & Asgarimehr, M. (2017). Impact of Information Technology on Lifestyle: A Literature Review and Classification. *International Journal of Virtual Communities and Social Networking*, 9(2), 1–23. DOI: 10.4018/IJVCSN.2017040101

Haseski, H. İ., Ilic, U., & Tuğtekin, U. (2018). Computational Thinking in Educational Digital Games: An Assessment Tool Proposal. In Ozcinar, H., Wong, G., & Ozturk, H. (Eds.), *Teaching Computational Thinking in Primary Education* (pp. 256–287). Hershey, PA: IGI Global. DOI: 10.4018/978-1-5225-3200-2.ch013

Hee, W. J., Jalleh, G., Lai, H., & Lin, C. (2017). E-Commerce and IT Projects: Evaluation and Management Issues in Australian and Taiwanese Hospitals. *International Journal of Public Health Management and Ethics*, 2(1), 69–90. DOI: 10.4018/IJPHME.2017010104

Hernandez, A. A. (2017). Green Information Technology Usage: Awareness and Practices of Philippine IT Professionals. *International Journal of Enterprise Information Systems*, 13(4), 90–103. DOI: 10.4018/IJEIS.2017100106

Hernandez, M. A., Marin, E. C., Garcia-Rodriguez, J., Azorin-Lopez, J., & Cazorla, M. (2017). Automatic Learning Improves Human-Robot Interaction in Productive Environments: A Review. *International Journal of Computer Vision and Image Processing*, 7(3), 65–75. DOI: 10.4018/IJCVIP.2017070106

Hirota, A. (2021). Design of Narrative Creation in Innovation: "Signature Story" and Two Types of Pivots. In Ogata, T., & Ono, J. (Eds.), *Bridging the Gap Between AI, Cognitive Science, and Narratology With Narrative Generation* (pp. 363–376). IGI Global. https://doi.org/10.4018/978-1-7998-4864-6.ch012

Hond, D., Asgari, H., Jeffery, D., & Newman, M. (2021). An Integrated Process for Verifying Deep Learning Classifiers Using Dataset Dissimilarity Measures. *International Journal of Artificial Intelligence and Machine Learning*, 11(2), 1–21. https://doi.org/10.4018/IJAIML.289536

Horne-Popp, L. M., Tessone, E. B., & Welker, J. (2018). If You Build It, They Will Come: Creating a Library Statistics Dashboard for Decision-Making. In Costello, L., & Powers, M. (Eds.), *Developing In-House Digital Tools in Library Spaces* (pp. 177–203). Hershey, PA: IGI Global. DOI: 10.4018/978-1-5225-2676-6.ch009

Hu, H., Hu, P. J., & Al-Gahtani, S. S. (2017). User Acceptance of Computer Technology at Work in Arabian Culture: A Model Comparison Approach. In Khosrow-Pour, M. (Ed.), *Handbook of Research on Technology Adoption, Social Policy, and Global Integration* (pp. 205–228). Hershey, PA: IGI Global. DOI: 10.4018/978-1-5225-2668-1.ch011

Huang, C., Sun, Y., & Fuh, C. (2022). Vehicle License Plate Recognition With Deep Learning. In C. Chen, W. Yang, & L. Chen (Eds.), *Technologies to Advance Automation in Forensic Science and Criminal Investigation* (pp. 161-219). IGI Global. https://doi.org/10.4018/978-1-7998-8386-9.ch009

Ifinedo, P. (2017). Using an Extended Theory of Planned Behavior to Study Nurses' Adoption of Healthcare Information Systems in Nova Scotia. *International Journal of Technology Diffusion*, 8(1), 1–17. DOI: 10.4018/IJTD.2017010101

Ilie, V., & Sneha, S. (2018). A Three Country Study for Understanding Physicians' Engagement With Electronic Information Resources Pre and Post System Implementation. *Journal of Global Information Management*, 26(2), 48–73. DOI: 10.4018/JGIM.2018040103

Ilo, P. I., Nkiko, C., Ugwu, C. I., Ekere, J. N., Izuagbe, R., & Fagbohun, M. O. (2021). Prospects and Challenges of Web 3.0 Technologies Application in the Provision of Library Services. In M. Khosrow-Pour D.B.A. (Ed.), *Encyclopedia of Information Science and Technology, Fifth Edition* (pp. 1767-1781). IGI Global. https://doi.org/10.4018/978-1-7998-3479-3.ch122

Inoue-Smith, Y. (2017). Perceived Ease in Using Technology Predicts Teacher Candidates' Preferences for Online Resources. *International Journal of Online Pedagogy and Course Design*, 7(3), 17–28. DOI: 10.4018/IJOPCD.2017070102

Islam, A. Y. (2017). Technology Satisfaction in an Academic Context: Moderating Effect of Gender. In Mesquita, A. (Ed.), *Research Paradigms and Contemporary Perspectives on Human-Technology Interaction* (pp. 187–211). Hershey, PA: IGI Global. DOI: 10.4018/978-1-5225-1868-6.ch009

Jagdale, S. C., Hable, A. A., & Chabukswar, A. R. (2021). Protocol Development in Clinical Trials for Healthcare Management. In M. Khosrow-Pour D.B.A. (Ed.), *Encyclopedia of Information Science and Technology, Fifth Edition* (pp. 1797-1814). IGI Global. https://doi.org/10.4018/978-1-7998-3479-3.ch124

Jamil, G. L., & Jamil, C. C. (2017). Information and Knowledge Management Perspective Contributions for Fashion Studies: Observing Logistics and Supply Chain Management Processes. In Jamil, G., Soares, A., & Pessoa, C. (Eds.), *Handbook of Research on Information Management for Effective Logistics and Supply Chains* (pp. 199–221). Hershey, PA: IGI Global. DOI: 10.4018/978-1-5225-0973-8.ch011

Jamil, M. I., & Almunawar, M. N. (2021). Importance of Digital Literacy and Hindrance Brought About by Digital Divide. In M. Khosrow-Pour D.B.A. (Ed.), *Encyclopedia of Information Science and Technology, Fifth Edition* (pp. 1683-1698). IGI Global. https://doi.org/10.4018/978-1-7998-3479-3.ch116

Janakova, M. (2018). Big Data and Simulations for the Solution of Controversies in Small Businesses. In M. Khosrow-Pour, D.B.A. (Ed.), *Encyclopedia of Information Science and Technology, Fourth Edition* (pp. 6907-6915). Hershey, PA: IGI Global. DOI: 10.4018/978-1-5225-2255-3.ch598

Jhawar, A., & Garg, S. K. (2018). Logistics Improvement by Investment in Information Technology Using System Dynamics. In Azar, A., & Vaidyanathan, S. (Eds.), *Advances in System Dynamics and Control* (pp. 528–567). Hershey, PA: IGI Global. DOI: 10.4018/978-1-5225-4077-9.ch017

Kalelioğlu, F., Gülbahar, Y., & Doğan, D. (2018). Teaching How to Think Like a Programmer: Emerging Insights. In Ozcinar, H., Wong, G., & Ozturk, H. (Eds.), *Teaching Computational Thinking in Primary Education* (pp. 18–35). Hershey, PA: IGI Global. DOI: 10.4018/978-1-5225-3200-2.ch002

Kamberi, S. (2017). A Girls-Only Online Virtual World Environment and its Implications for Game-Based Learning. In Stricker, A., Calongne, C., Truman, B., & Arenas, F. (Eds.), *Integrating an Awareness of Selfhood and Society into Virtual Learning* (pp. 74–95). Hershey, PA: IGI Global. DOI: 10.4018/978-1-5225-2182-2.ch006

Kamel, S., & Rizk, N. (2017). ICT Strategy Development: From Design to Implementation – Case of Egypt. In Howard, C., & Hargiss, K. (Eds.), *Strategic Information Systems and Technologies in Modern Organizations* (pp. 239–257). Hershey, PA: IGI Global. DOI: 10.4018/978-1-5225-1680-4.ch010

Kamel, S. H. (2018). The Potential Role of the Software Industry in Supporting Economic Development. In M. Khosrow-Pour, D.B.A. (Ed.), *Encyclopedia of Information Science and Technology, Fourth Edition* (pp. 7259-7269). Hershey, PA: IGI Global. DOI: 10.4018/978-1-5225-2255-3.ch631

Kang, H., Kang, Y., & Kim, J. (2022). Improved Fall Detection Model on GRU Using PoseNet. *International Journal of Software Innovation*, 10(2), 1–11. https://doi.org/10.4018/IJSI.289600

Kankam, P. K. (2021). Employing Case Study and Survey Designs in Information Research. *Journal of Information Technology Research*, 14(1), 167–177. https://doi.org/10.4018/JITR.2021010110

Karas, V., & Schuller, B. W. (2021). Deep Learning for Sentiment Analysis: An Overview and Perspectives. In Pinarbasi, F., & Taskiran, M. (Eds.), *Natural Language Processing for Global and Local Business* (pp. 97–132). IGI Global. https://doi.org/10.4018/978-1-7998-4240-8.ch005

Kaufman, L. M. (2022). Reimagining the Magic of the Workshop Model. In Driscoll, T.III, (Ed.), *Designing Effective Distance and Blended Learning Environments in K-12* (pp. 89–109). IGI Global. https://doi.org/10.4018/978-1-7998-6829-3.ch007

Kawata, S. (2018). Computer-Assisted Parallel Program Generation. In M. Khosrow-Pour, D.B.A. (Ed.), *Encyclopedia of Information Science and Technology, Fourth Edition* (pp. 4583-4593). Hershey, PA: IGI Global. DOI: 10.4018/978-1-5225-2255-3.ch398

Kharb, L., & Singh, P. (2021). Role of Machine Learning in Modern Education and Teaching. In S. Verma & P. Tomar (Ed.), *Impact of AI Technologies on Teaching, Learning, and Research in Higher Education* (pp. 99-123). IGI Global. https://doi.org/10.4018/978-1-7998-4763-2.ch006

Khari, M., Shrivastava, G., Gupta, S., & Gupta, R. (2017). Role of Cyber Security in Today's Scenario. In Kumar, R., Pattnaik, P., & Pandey, P. (Eds.), *Detecting and Mitigating Robotic Cyber Security Risks* (pp. 177–191). Hershey, PA: IGI Global. DOI: 10.4018/978-1-5225-2154-9.ch013

Khekare, G., & Sheikh, S. (2021). Autonomous Navigation Using Deep Reinforcement Learning in ROS. *International Journal of Artificial Intelligence and Machine Learning*, 11(2), 63–70. https://doi.org/10.4018/IJAIML.20210701.oa4

Khouja, M., Rodriguez, I. B., Ben Halima, Y., & Moalla, S. (2018). IT Governance in Higher Education Institutions: A Systematic Literature Review. *International Journal of Human Capital and Information Technology Professionals*, 9(2), 52–67. DOI: 10.4018/IJHCITP.2018040104

Kiourt, C., Pavlidis, G., Koutsoudis, A., & Kalles, D. (2017). Realistic Simulation of Cultural Heritage. *International Journal of Computational Methods in Heritage Science*, 1(1), 10–40. DOI: 10.4018/IJCMHS.2017010102

Köse, U. (2017). An Augmented-Reality-Based Intelligent Mobile Application for Open Computer Education. In Kurubacak, G., & Altinpulluk, H. (Eds.), *Mobile Technologies and Augmented Reality in Open Education* (pp. 154–174). Hershey, PA: IGI Global. DOI: 10.4018/978-1-5225-2110-5.ch008

Lahmiri, S. (2018). Information Technology Outsourcing Risk Factors and Provider Selection. In Gupta, M., Sharman, R., Walp, J., & Mulgund, P. (Eds.), *Information Technology Risk Management and Compliance in Modern Organizations* (pp. 214–228). Hershey, PA: IGI Global. DOI: 10.4018/978-1-5225-2604-9.ch008

Lakkad, A. K., Bhadaniya, R. D., Shah, V. N., & Lavanya, K. (2021). Complex Events Processing on Live News Events Using Apache Kafka and Clustering Techniques. *International Journal of Intelligent Information Technologies*, 17(1), 39–52. https://doi.org/10.4018/IJIIT.2021010103

Landriscina, F. (2017). Computer-Supported Imagination: The Interplay Between Computer and Mental Simulation in Understanding Scientific Concepts. In Levin, I., & Tsybulsky, D. (Eds.), *Digital Tools and Solutions for Inquiry-Based STEM Learning* (pp. 33–60). Hershey, PA: IGI Global. DOI: 10.4018/978-1-5225-2525-7.ch002

Lara López, G. (2021). Virtual Reality in Object Location. In Negrón, A., & Muñoz, M. (Eds.), *Latin American Women and Research Contributions to the IT Field* (pp. 307–324). IGI Global. https://doi.org/10.4018/978-1-7998-7552-9.ch014

Lee, W. W. (2018). Ethical Computing Continues From Problem to Solution. In M. Khosrow-Pour, D.B.A. (Ed.), *Encyclopedia of Information Science and Technology, Fourth Edition* (pp. 4884-4897). Hershey, PA: IGI Global. DOI: 10.4018/978-1-5225-2255-3.ch423

Lin, S., Chen, S., & Chuang, S. (2017). Perceived Innovation and Quick Response Codes in an Online-to-Offline E-Commerce Service Model. *International Journal of E-Adoption*, 9(2), 1–16. DOI: 10.4018/IJEA.2017070101

Liu, M., Wang, Y., Xu, W., & Liu, L. (2017). Automated Scoring of Chinese Engineering Students' English Essays. *International Journal of Distance Education Technologies*, 15(1), 52–68. DOI: 10.4018/IJDET.2017010104

Ma, X., Li, X., Zhong, B., Huang, Y., Gu, Y., Wu, M., Liu, Y., & Zhang, M. (2021). A Detector and Evaluation Framework of Abnormal Bidding Behavior Based on Supplier Portrait. *International Journal of Information Technology and Web Engineering*, 16(2), 58–74. https://doi.org/10.4018/IJITWE.2021040104

Mabe, L. K., & Oladele, O. I. (2017). Application of Information Communication Technologies for Agricultural Development through Extension Services: A Review. In Tossy, T. (Ed.), *Information Technology Integration for Socio-Economic Development* (pp. 52–101). Hershey, PA: IGI Global. DOI: 10.4018/978-1-5225-0539-6.ch003

Mahboub, S. A., Sayed Ali Ahmed, E., & Saeed, R. A. (2021). Smart IDS and IPS for Cyber-Physical Systems. In Luhach, A., & Elçi, A. (Eds.), *Artificial Intelligence Paradigms for Smart Cyber-Physical Systems* (pp. 109–136). IGI Global. https://doi.org/10.4018/978-1-7998-5101-1.ch006

Manogaran, G., Thota, C., & Lopez, D. (2018). Human-Computer Interaction With Big Data Analytics. In Lopez, D., & Durai, M. (Eds.), *HCI Challenges and Privacy Preservation in Big Data Security* (pp. 1–22). Hershey, PA: IGI Global. DOI: 10.4018/978-1-5225-2863-0.ch001

Margolis, J., Goode, J., & Flapan, J. (2017). A Critical Crossroads for Computer Science for All: "Identifying Talent" or "Building Talent," and What Difference Does It Make? In Rankin, Y., & Thomas, J. (Eds.), *Moving Students of Color from Consumers to Producers of Technology* (pp. 1–23). Hershey, PA: IGI Global. DOI: 10.4018/978-1-5225-2005-4.ch001

Mazzù, M. F., Benetton, A., Baccelloni, A., & Lavini, L. (2022). A Milk Blockchain-Enabled Supply Chain: Evidence From Leading Italian Farms. In De Giovanni, P. (Ed.), *Blockchain Technology Applications in Businesses and Organizations* (pp. 73–98). IGI Global. https://doi.org/10.4018/978-1-7998-8014-1.ch004

Mbale, J. (2018). Computer Centres Resource Cloud Elasticity-Scalability (CRECES): Copperbelt University Case Study. In Aljawarneh, S., & Malhotra, M. (Eds.), *Critical Research on Scalability and Security Issues in Virtual Cloud Environments* (pp. 48–70). Hershey, PA: IGI Global. DOI: 10.4018/978-1-5225-3029-9.ch003

McKee, J. (2018). The Right Information: The Key to Effective Business Planning. In *Business Architectures for Risk Assessment and Strategic Planning: Emerging Research and Opportunities* (pp. 38–52). Hershey, PA: IGI Global. DOI: 10.4018/978-1-5225-3392-4.ch003

Meddah, I. H., Remil, N. E., & Meddah, H. N. (2021). Novel Approach for Mining Patterns. *International Journal of Applied Evolutionary Computation*, 12(1), 27–42. https://doi.org/10.4018/IJAEC.2021010103

Mensah, I. K., & Mi, J. (2018). Determinants of Intention to Use Local E-Government Services in Ghana: The Perspective of Local Government Workers. *International Journal of Technology Diffusion*, 9(2), 41–60. DOI: 10.4018/IJTD.2018040103

Mohamed, J. H. (2018). Scientograph-Based Visualization of Computer Forensics Research Literature. In Jeyasekar, J., & Saravanan, P. (Eds.), *Innovations in Measuring and Evaluating Scientific Information* (pp. 148–162). Hershey, PA: IGI Global. DOI: 10.4018/978-1-5225-3457-0.ch010

Montañés-Del Río, M. Á., Cornejo, V. R., Rodríguez, M. R., & Ortiz, J. S. (2021). Gamification of University Subjects: A Case Study for Operations Management. *Journal of Information Technology Research*, 14(2), 1–29. https://doi.org/10.4018/JITR.2021040101

Moore, R. L., & Johnson, N. (2017). Earning a Seat at the Table: How IT Departments Can Partner in Organizational Change and Innovation. *International Journal of Knowledge-Based Organizations*, 7(2), 1–12. DOI: 10.4018/IJKBO.2017040101

Mukul, M. K., & Bhattaharyya, S. (2017). Brain-Machine Interface: Human-Computer Interaction. In Noughabi, E., Raahemi, B., Albadvi, A., & Far, B. (Eds.), *Handbook of Research on Data Science for Effective Healthcare Practice and Administration* (pp. 417–443). Hershey, PA: IGI Global. DOI: 10.4018/978-1-5225-2515-8.ch018

Na, L. (2017). Library and Information Science Education and Graduate Programs in Academic Libraries. In Ruan, L., Zhu, Q., & Ye, Y. (Eds.), *Academic Library Development and Administration in China* (pp. 218–229). Hershey, PA: IGI Global. DOI: 10.4018/978-1-5225-0550-1.ch013

Nagpal, G., Bishnoi, G. K., Dhami, H. S., & Vijayvargia, A. (2021). Use of Data Analytics to Increase the Efficiency of Last Mile Logistics for Ecommerce Deliveries. In Patil, B., & Vohra, M. (Eds.), *Handbook of Research on Engineering, Business, and Healthcare Applications of Data Science and Analytics* (pp. 167–180). IGI Global. https://doi.org/10.4018/978-1-7998-3053-5.ch009

Nair, S. M., Ramesh, V., & Tyagi, A. K. (2021). Issues and Challenges (Privacy, Security, and Trust) in Blockchain-Based Applications. In Tyagi, A., Rekha, G., & Sreenath, N. (Eds.), *Opportunities and Challenges for Blockchain Technology in Autonomous Vehicles* (pp. 196–209). IGI Global. https://doi.org/10.4018/978-1-7998-3295-9.ch012

Naomi, J. F. M., K., & V., S. (2021). Machine and Deep Learning Techniques in IoT and Cloud. In S. Velayutham (Ed.), *Challenges and Opportunities for the Convergence of IoT, Big Data, and Cloud Computing* (pp. 225-247). IGI Global. https://doi.org/10.4018/978-1-7998-3111-2.ch013

Nath, R., & Murthy, V. N. (2018). What Accounts for the Differences in Internet Diffusion Rates Around the World? In M. Khosrow-Pour, D.B.A. (Ed.), *Encyclopedia of Information Science and Technology, Fourth Edition* (pp. 8095-8104). Hershey, PA: IGI Global. https://doi.org/DOI: 10.4018/978-1-5225-2255-3.ch705

Nedelko, Z., & Potocan, V. (2018). The Role of Emerging Information Technologies for Supporting Supply Chain Management. In M. Khosrow-Pour, D.B.A. (Ed.), *Encyclopedia of Information Science and Technology, Fourth Edition* (pp. 5559-5569). Hershey, PA: IGI Global. DOI: 10.4018/978-1-5225-2255-3.ch483

Negrini, L., Giang, C., & Bonnet, E. (2022). Designing Tools and Activities for Educational Robotics in Online Learning. In Eteokleous, N., & Nisiforou, E. (Eds.), *Designing, Constructing, and Programming Robots for Learning* (pp. 202–222). IGI Global. https://doi.org/10.4018/978-1-7998-7443-0.ch010

Ngafeeson, M. N. (2018). User Resistance to Health Information Technology. In M. Khosrow-Pour, D.B.A. (Ed.), *Encyclopedia of Information Science and Technology, Fourth Edition* (pp. 3816-3825). Hershey, PA: IGI Global. DOI: 10.4018/978-1-5225-2255-3.ch331

Nguyen, T. T., Giang, N. L., Tran, D. T., Nguyen, T. T., Nguyen, H. Q., Pham, A. V., & Vu, T. D. (2021). A Novel Filter-Wrapper Algorithm on Intuitionistic Fuzzy Set for Attribute Reduction From Decision Tables. *International Journal of Data Warehousing and Mining*, 17(4), 67–100. https://doi.org/10.4018/IJDWM.2021100104

Nigam, A., & Dewani, P. P. (2022). Consumer Engagement Through Conditional Promotions: An Exploratory Study. *Journal of Global Information Management*, 30(5), 1–19. https://doi.org/10.4018/JGIM.290364

Odagiri, K. (2017). Introduction of Individual Technology to Constitute the Current Internet. In *Strategic Policy-Based Network Management in Contemporary Organizations* (pp. 20–96). Hershey, PA: IGI Global. DOI: 10.4018/978-1-68318-003-6.ch003

Odia, J. O., & Akpata, O. T. (2021). Role of Data Science and Data Analytics in Forensic Accounting and Fraud Detection. In Patil, B., & Vohra, M. (Eds.), *Handbook of Research on Engineering, Business, and Healthcare Applications of Data Science and Analytics* (pp. 203–227). IGI Global. https://doi.org/10.4018/978-1-7998-3053-5.ch011

Okike, E. U. (2018). Computer Science and Prison Education. In Biao, I. (Ed.), *Strategic Learning Ideologies in Prison Education Programs* (pp. 246–264). Hershey, PA: IGI Global. DOI: 10.4018/978-1-5225-2909-5.ch012

Olelewe, C. J., & Nwafor, I. P. (2017). Level of Computer Appreciation Skills Acquired for Sustainable Development by Secondary School Students in Nsukka LGA of Enugu State, Nigeria. In Ayo, C., & Mbarika, V. (Eds.), *Sustainable ICT Adoption and Integration for Socio-Economic Development* (pp. 214–233). Hershey, PA: IGI Global. DOI: 10.4018/978-1-5225-2565-3.ch010

Oliveira, M., Maçada, A. C., Curado, C., & Nodari, F. (2017). Infrastructure Profiles and Knowledge Sharing. *International Journal of Technology and Human Interaction*, 13(3), 1–12. DOI: 10.4018/IJTHI.2017070101

Otarkhani, A., Shokouhyar, S., & Pour, S. S. (2017). Analyzing the Impact of Governance of Enterprise IT on Hospital Performance: Tehran's (Iran) Hospitals – A Case Study. *International Journal of Healthcare Information Systems and Informatics*, 12(3), 1–20. DOI: 10.4018/IJHISI.2017070101

Otunla, A. O., & Amuda, C. O. (2018). Nigerian Undergraduate Students' Computer Competencies and Use of Information Technology Tools and Resources for Study Skills and Habits' Enhancement. In M. Khosrow-Pour, D.B.A. (Ed.), *Encyclopedia of Information Science and Technology, Fourth Edition* (pp. 2303-2313). Hershey, PA: IGI Global. https://doi.org/DOI: 10.4018/978-1-5225-2255-3.ch200

Özçınar, H. (2018). A Brief Discussion on Incentives and Barriers to Computational Thinking Education. In Ozcinar, H., Wong, G., & Ozturk, H. (Eds.), *Teaching Computational Thinking in Primary Education* (pp. 1–17). Hershey, PA: IGI Global. DOI: 10.4018/978-1-5225-3200-2.ch001

Pandey, J. M., Garg, S., Mishra, P., & Mishra, B. P. (2017). Computer Based Psychological Interventions: Subject to the Efficacy of Psychological Services. *International Journal of Computers in Clinical Practice*, 2(1), 25–33. DOI: 10.4018/IJCCP.2017010102

Pandkar, S. D., & Paatil, S. D. (2021). Big Data and Knowledge Resource Centre. In Dhamdhere, S. (Ed.), *Big Data Applications for Improving Library Services* (pp. 90–106). IGI Global. https://doi.org/10.4018/978-1-7998-3049-8.ch007

Patro, C. (2017). Impulsion of Information Technology on Human Resource Practices. In Ordóñez de Pablos, P. (Ed.), *Managerial Strategies and Solutions for Business Success in Asia* (pp. 231–254). Hershey, PA: IGI Global. DOI: 10.4018/978-1-5225-1886-0.ch013

Patro, C. S., & Raghunath, K. M. (2017). Information Technology Paraphernalia for Supply Chain Management Decisions. In Tavana, M. (Ed.), *Enterprise Information Systems and the Digitalization of Business Functions* (pp. 294–320). Hershey, PA: IGI Global. DOI: 10.4018/978-1-5225-2382-6.ch014

Paul, P. K. (2018). The Context of IST for Solid Information Retrieval and Infrastructure Building: Study of Developing Country. *International Journal of Information Retrieval Research*, 8(1), 86–100. DOI: 10.4018/IJIRR.2018010106

Paul, P. K., & Chatterjee, D. (2018). iSchools Promoting "Information Science and Technology" (IST) Domain Towards Community, Business, and Society With Contemporary Worldwide Trend and Emerging Potentialities in India. In M. Khosrow-Pour, D.B.A. (Ed.), *Encyclopedia of Information Science and Technology, Fourth Edition* (pp. 4723-4735). Hershey, PA: IGI Global. https://doi.org/DOI: 10.4018/978-1-5225-2255-3.ch410

Pessoa, C. R., & Marques, M. E. (2017). Information Technology and Communication Management in Supply Chain Management. In Jamil, G., Soares, A., & Pessoa, C. (Eds.), *Handbook of Research on Information Management for Effective Logistics and Supply Chains* (pp. 23–33). Hershey, PA: IGI Global. DOI: 10.4018/978-1-5225-0973-8.ch002

Pineda, R. G. (2018). Remediating Interaction: Towards a Philosophy of Human-Computer Relationship. In Khosrow-Pour, M. (Ed.), *Enhancing Art, Culture, and Design With Technological Integration* (pp. 75–98). Hershey, PA: IGI Global. DOI: 10.4018/978-1-5225-5023-5.ch004

Prabha, V. D., & R., R. (2021). Clinical Decision Support Systems: Decision-Making System for Clinical Data. In G. Rani & P. Tiwari (Eds.), *Handbook of Research on Disease Prediction Through Data Analytics and Machine Learning* (pp. 268-280). IGI Global. https://doi.org/10.4018/978-1-7998-2742-9.ch014

Pushpa, R., & Siddappa, M. (2021). An Optimal Way of VM Placement Strategy in Cloud Computing Platform Using ABCS Algorithm. *International Journal of Ambient Computing and Intelligence*, 12(3), 16–38. https://doi.org/10.4018/IJACI.2021070102

Qian, Y. (2017). Computer Simulation in Higher Education: Affordances, Opportunities, and Outcomes. In Vu, P., Fredrickson, S., & Moore, C. (Eds.), *Handbook of Research on Innovative Pedagogies and Technologies for Online Learning in Higher Education* (pp. 236–262). Hershey, PA: IGI Global. DOI: 10.4018/978-1-5225-1851-8.ch011

Rahman, N. (2017). Lessons from a Successful Data Warehousing Project Management. *International Journal of Information Technology Project Management*, 8(4), 30–45. DOI: 10.4018/IJITPM.2017100103

Rahman, N. (2018). Environmental Sustainability in the Computer Industry for Competitive Advantage. In Khosrow-Pour, M. (Ed.), *Green Computing Strategies for Competitive Advantage and Business Sustainability* (pp. 110–130). Hershey, PA: IGI Global. DOI: 10.4018/978-1-5225-5017-4.ch006

Rajh, A., & Pavetic, T. (2017). Computer Generated Description as the Required Digital Competence in Archival Profession. *International Journal of Digital Literacy and Digital Competence*, 8(1), 36–49. DOI: 10.4018/IJDLDC.2017010103

Raman, A., & Goyal, D. P. (2017). Extending IMPLEMENT Framework for Enterprise Information Systems Implementation to Information System Innovation. In Tavana, M. (Ed.), *Enterprise Information Systems and the Digitalization of Business Functions* (pp. 137–177). Hershey, PA: IGI Global. DOI: 10.4018/978-1-5225-2382-6.ch007

Rao, A. P., & Reddy, K. S. (2021). Automated Soil Residue Levels Detecting Device With IoT Interface. In Sathiyamoorthi, V., & Elci, A. (Eds.), *Challenges and Applications of Data Analytics in Social Perspectives* (Vol. S, pp. 123–135). IGI Global. https://doi.org/10.4018/978-1-7998-2566-1.ch007

Rao, Y. S., Rauta, A. K., Saini, H., & Panda, T. C. (2017). Mathematical Model for Cyber Attack in Computer Network. *International Journal of Business Data Communications and Networking*, 13(1), 58–65. DOI: 10.4018/IJBDCN.2017010105

Rapaport, W. J. (2018). Syntactic Semantics and the Proper Treatment of Computationalism. In Danesi, M. (Ed.), *Empirical Research on Semiotics and Visual Rhetoric* (pp. 128–176). Hershey, PA: IGI Global. DOI: 10.4018/978-1-5225-5622-0.ch007

Raut, R., Priyadarshinee, P., & Jha, M. (2017). Understanding the Mediation Effect of Cloud Computing Adoption in Indian Organization: Integrating TAM-TOE- Risk Model. *International Journal of Service Science, Management, Engineering, and Technology*, 8(3), 40–59. DOI: 10.4018/IJSSMET.2017070103

Rezaie, S., Mirabedini, S. J., & Abtahi, A. (2018). Designing a Model for Implementation of Business Intelligence in the Banking Industry. *International Journal of Enterprise Information Systems*, 14(1), 77–103. DOI: 10.4018/IJEIS.2018010105

Rezende, D. A. (2018). Strategic Digital City Projects: Innovative Information and Public Services Offered by Chicago (USA) and Curitiba (Brazil). In Lytras, M., Daniela, L., & Visvizi, A. (Eds.), *Enhancing Knowledge Discovery and Innovation in the Digital Era* (pp. 204–223). Hershey, PA: IGI Global. DOI: 10.4018/978-1-5225-4191-2.ch012

Rodriguez, A., Rico-Diaz, A. J., Rabuñal, J. R., & Gestal, M. (2017). Fish Tracking with Computer Vision Techniques: An Application to Vertical Slot Fishways. In M. S., & V. V. (Eds.), *Multi-Core Computer Vision and Image Processing for Intelligent Applications* (pp. 74-104). Hershey, PA: IGI Global. https://doi.org/DOI: 10.4018/978-1-5225-0889-2.ch003

Romero, J. A. (2018). Sustainable Advantages of Business Value of Information Technology. In M. Khosrow-Pour, D.B.A. (Ed.), *Encyclopedia of Information Science and Technology, Fourth Edition* (pp. 923-929). Hershey, PA: IGI Global. DOI: 10.4018/978-1-5225-2255-3.ch079

Romero, J. A. (2018). The Always-On Business Model and Competitive Advantage. In Bajgoric, N. (Ed.), *Always-On Enterprise Information Systems for Modern Organizations* (pp. 23–40). Hershey, PA: IGI Global. DOI: 10.4018/978-1-5225-3704-5.ch002

Rosen, Y. (2018). Computer Agent Technologies in Collaborative Learning and Assessment. In M. Khosrow-Pour, D.B.A. (Ed.), *Encyclopedia of Information Science and Technology, Fourth Edition* (pp. 2402-2410). Hershey, PA: IGI Global. DOI: 10.4018/978-1-5225-2255-3.ch209

Roy, D. (2018). Success Factors of Adoption of Mobile Applications in Rural India: Effect of Service Characteristics on Conceptual Model. In Khosrow-Pour, M. (Ed.), *Green Computing Strategies for Competitive Advantage and Business Sustainability* (pp. 211–238). Hershey, PA: IGI Global. DOI: 10.4018/978-1-5225-5017-4.ch010

Ruffin, T. R., & Hawkins, D. P. (2018). Trends in Health Care Information Technology and Informatics. In M. Khosrow-Pour, D.B.A. (Ed.), *Encyclopedia of Information Science and Technology, Fourth Edition* (pp. 3805-3815). Hershey, PA: IGI Global. DOI: 10.4018/978-1-5225-2255-3.ch330

Sadasivam, U. M., & Ganesan, N. (2021). Detecting Fake News Using Deep Learning and NLP. In S. Misra, C. Arumugam, S. Jaganathan, & S. S. (Eds.), *Confluence of AI, Machine, and Deep Learning in Cyber Forensics* (pp. 117-133). IGI Global. https://doi.org/10.4018/978-1-7998-4900-1.ch007

Safari, M. R., & Jiang, Q. (2018). The Theory and Practice of IT Governance Maturity and Strategies Alignment: Evidence From Banking Industry. *Journal of Global Information Management*, 26(2), 127–146. DOI: 10.4018/JGIM.2018040106

Sahin, H. B., & Anagun, S. S. (2018). Educational Computer Games in Math Teaching: A Learning Culture. In Toprak, E., & Kumtepe, E. (Eds.), *Supporting Multiculturalism in Open and Distance Learning Spaces* (pp. 249–280). Hershey, PA: IGI Global. DOI: 10.4018/978-1-5225-3076-3.ch013

Sakalle, A., Tomar, P., Bhardwaj, H., & Sharma, U. (2021). Impact and Latest Trends of Intelligent Learning With Artificial Intelligence. In S. Verma & P. Tomar (Eds.), *Impact of AI Technologies on Teaching, Learning, and Research in Higher Education* (pp. 172-189). IGI Global. https://doi.org/10.4018/978-1-7998-4763-2.ch011

Sala, N. (2021). Virtual Reality, Augmented Reality, and Mixed Reality in Education: A Brief Overview. In Choi, D., Dailey-Hebert, A., & Estes, J. (Eds.), *Current and Prospective Applications of Virtual Reality in Higher Education* (pp. 48–73). IGI Global. https://doi.org/10.4018/978-1-7998-4960-5.ch003

Salunkhe, S., Kanagachidambaresan, G., Rajkumar, C., & Jayanthi, K. (2022). Online Detection and Prediction of Fused Deposition Modelled Parts Using Artificial Intelligence. In Salunkhe, S., Hussein, H., & Davim, J. (Eds.), *Applications of Artificial Intelligence in Additive Manufacturing* (pp. 194–209). IGI Global. https://doi.org/10.4018/978-1-7998-8516-0.ch009

Samy, V. S., Pramanick, K., Thenkanidiyoor, V., & Victor, J. (2021). Data Analysis and Visualization in Python for Polar Meteorological Data. *International Journal of Data Analytics*, 2(1), 32–60. https://doi.org/10.4018/IJDA.2021010102

Sanna, A., & Valpreda, F. (2017). An Assessment of the Impact of a Collaborative Didactic Approach and Students' Background in Teaching Computer Animation. *International Journal of Information and Communication Technology Education*, 13(4), 1–16. DOI: 10.4018/IJICTE.2017100101

Sarivougioukas, J., & Vagelatos, A. (2022). Fused Contextual Data With Threading Technology to Accelerate Processing in Home UbiHealth. *International Journal of Software Science and Computational Intelligence*, 14(1), 1–14. https://doi.org/10.4018/IJSSCI.285590

Scott, A., Martin, A., & McAlear, F. (2017). Enhancing Participation in Computer Science among Girls of Color: An Examination of a Preparatory AP Computer Science Intervention. In Rankin, Y., & Thomas, J. (Eds.), *Moving Students of Color from Consumers to Producers of Technology* (pp. 62–84). Hershey, PA: IGI Global. DOI: 10.4018/978-1-5225-2005-4.ch004

Shanmugam, M., Ibrahim, N., Gorment, N. Z., Sugu, R., Dandarawi, T. N., & Ahmad, N. A. (2022). Towards an Integrated Omni-Channel Strategy Framework for Improved Customer Interaction. In Lai, P. (Ed.), *Handbook of Research on Social Impacts of E-Payment and Blockchain Technology* (pp. 409–427). IGI Global. https://doi.org/10.4018/978-1-7998-9035-5.ch022

Sharma, A., & Kumar, S. (2021). Network Slicing and the Role of 5G in IoT Applications. In Kumar, S., Trivedi, M., Ranjan, P., & Punhani, A. (Eds.), *Evolution of Software-Defined Networking Foundations for IoT and 5G Mobile Networks* (pp. 172–190). IGI Global. https://doi.org/10.4018/978-1-7998-4685-7.ch010

Siddoo, V., & Wongsai, N. (2017). Factors Influencing the Adoption of ISO/IEC 29110 in Thai Government Projects: A Case Study. *International Journal of Information Technologies and Systems Approach*, 10(1), 22–44. DOI: 10.4018/IJITSA.2017010102

Silveira, C., Hir, M. E., & Chaves, H. K. (2022). An Approach to Information Management as a Subsidy of Global Health Actions: A Case Study of Big Data in Health for Dengue, Zika, and Chikungunya. In Lima de Magalhães, J., Hartz, Z., Jamil, G., Silveira, H., & Jamil, L. (Eds.), *Handbook of Research on Essential Information Approaches to Aiding Global Health in the One Health Context* (pp. 219–234). IGI Global. https://doi.org/10.4018/978-1-7998-8011-0.ch012

Simões, A. (2017). Using Game Frameworks to Teach Computer Programming. In Alexandre Peixoto de Queirós, R., & Pinto, M. (Eds.), *Gamification-Based E-Learning Strategies for Computer Programming Education* (pp. 221–236). Hershey, PA: IGI Global. DOI: 10.4018/978-1-5225-1034-5.ch010

Simões de Almeida, R., & da Silva, T. (2022). AI Chatbots in Mental Health: Are We There Yet? In Marques, A., & Queirós, R. (Eds.), *Digital Therapies in Psychosocial Rehabilitation and Mental Health* (pp. 226–243). IGI Global. https://doi.org/10.4018/978-1-7998-8634-1.ch011

Singh, L. K., Khanna, M., Thawkar, S., & Gopal, J. (2021). Robustness for Authentication of the Human Using Face, Ear, and Gait Multimodal Biometric System. *International Journal of Information System Modeling and Design*, 12(1), 39–72. https://doi.org/10.4018/IJISMD.2021010103

Sllame, A. M. (2017). Integrating LAB Work With Classes in Computer Network Courses. In Alphin, H.Jr, Chan, R., & Lavine, J. (Eds.), *The Future of Accessibility in International Higher Education* (pp. 253–275). Hershey, PA: IGI Global. DOI: 10.4018/978-1-5225-2560-8.ch015

Smirnov, A., Ponomarev, A., Shilov, N., Kashevnik, A., & Teslya, N. (2018). Ontology-Based Human-Computer Cloud for Decision Support: Architecture and Applications in Tourism. *International Journal of Embedded and Real-Time Communication Systems*, 9(1), 1–19. DOI: 10.4018/IJERTCS.2018010101

Smith-Ditizio, A. A., & Smith, A. D. (2018). Computer Fraud Challenges and Its Legal Implications. In M. Khosrow-Pour, D.B.A. (Ed.), *Encyclopedia of Information Science and Technology, Fourth Edition* (pp. 4837-4848). Hershey, PA: IGI Global. DOI: 10.4018/978-1-5225-2255-3.ch419

Sosnin, P. (2018). Figuratively Semantic Support of Human-Computer Interactions. In *Experience-Based Human-Computer Interactions: Emerging Research and Opportunities* (pp. 244–272). Hershey, PA: IGI Global. DOI: 10.4018/978-1-5225-2987-3.ch008

Srilakshmi, R., & Jaya Bhaskar, M. (2021). An Adaptable Secure Scheme in Mobile Ad hoc Network to Protect the Communication Channel From Malicious Behaviours. *International Journal of Information Technology and Web Engineering*, 16(3), 54–73. https://doi.org/10.4018/IJITWE.2021070104

Sukhwani, N., Kagita, V. R., Kumar, V., & Panda, S. K. (2021). Efficient Computation of Top-K Skyline Objects in Data Set With Uncertain Preferences. *International Journal of Data Warehousing and Mining*, 17(3), 68–80. https://doi.org/10.4018/IJDWM.2021070104

Susanto, H., Yie, L. F., Setiana, D., Asih, Y., Yoganingrum, A., Riyanto, S., & Saputra, F. A. (2021). Digital Ecosystem Security Issues for Organizations and Governments: Digital Ethics and Privacy. In Mahmood, Z. (Ed.), *Web 2.0 and Cloud Technologies for Implementing Connected Government* (pp. 204–228). IGI Global. https://doi.org/10.4018/978-1-7998-4570-6.ch010

Syväjärvi, A., Leinonen, J., Kivivirta, V., & Kesti, M. (2017). The Latitude of Information Management in Local Government: Views of Local Government Managers. *International Journal of Electronic Government Research*, 13(1), 69–85. DOI: 10.4018/IJEGR.2017010105

Tanque, M., & Foxwell, H. J. (2018). Big Data and Cloud Computing: A Review of Supply Chain Capabilities and Challenges. In Prasad, A. (Ed.), *Exploring the Convergence of Big Data and the Internet of Things* (pp. 1–28). Hershey, PA: IGI Global. DOI: 10.4018/978-1-5225-2947-7.ch001

Teixeira, A., Gomes, A., & Orvalho, J. G. (2017). Auditory Feedback in a Computer Game for Blind People. In Issa, T., Kommers, P., Issa, T., Isaías, P., & Issa, T. (Eds.), *Smart Technology Applications in Business Environments* (pp. 134–158). Hershey, PA: IGI Global. DOI: 10.4018/978-1-5225-2492-2.ch007

Tewari, P., Tiwari, P., & Goel, R. (2022). Information Technology in Supply Chain Management. In Garg, V., & Goel, R. (Eds.), *Handbook of Research on Innovative Management Using AI in Industry 5.0* (pp. 165–178). IGI Global. https://doi.org/10.4018/978-1-7998-8497-2.ch011

Thompson, N., McGill, T., & Murray, D. (2018). Affect-Sensitive Computer Systems. In M. Khosrow-Pour, D.B.A. (Ed.), *Encyclopedia of Information Science and Technology, Fourth Edition* (pp. 4124-4135). Hershey, PA: IGI Global. DOI: 10.4018/978-1-5225-2255-3.ch357

Triberti, S., Brivio, E., & Galimberti, C. (2018). On Social Presence: Theories, Methodologies, and Guidelines for the Innovative Contexts of Computer-Mediated Learning. In Marmon, M. (Ed.), *Enhancing Social Presence in Online Learning Environments* (pp. 20–41). Hershey, PA: IGI Global. DOI: 10.4018/978-1-5225-3229-3.ch002

Tripathy, B. K. T. R., S., & Mohanty, R. K. (2018). Memetic Algorithms and Their Applications in Computer Science. In S. Dash, B. Tripathy, & A. Rahman (Eds.), *Handbook of Research on Modeling, Analysis, and Application of Nature-Inspired Metaheuristic Algorithms* (pp. 73-93). Hershey, PA: IGI Global. https://doi.org/DOI: 10.4018/978-1-5225-2857-9.ch004

Turulja, L., & Bajgoric, N. (2017). Human Resource Management IT and Global Economy Perspective: Global Human Resource Information Systems. In Khosrow-Pour, M. (Ed.), *Handbook of Research on Technology Adoption, Social Policy, and Global Integration* (pp. 377–394). Hershey, PA: IGI Global. DOI: 10.4018/978-1-5225-2668-1.ch018

Unwin, D. W., Sanzogni, L., & Sandhu, K. (2017). Developing and Measuring the Business Case for Health Information Technology. In Moahi, K., Bwalya, K., & Sebina, P. (Eds.), *Health Information Systems and the Advancement of Medical Practice in Developing Countries* (pp. 262–290). Hershey, PA: IGI Global. DOI: 10.4018/978-1-5225-2262-1.ch015

Usharani, B. (2022). House Plant Leaf Disease Detection and Classification Using Machine Learning. In M. Mundada, S. Seema, S. K.G., & M. Shilpa (Eds.), *Deep Learning Applications for Cyber-Physical Systems* (pp. 17-26). IGI Global. https://doi.org/10.4018/978-1-7998-8161-2.ch002

Vadhanam, B. R. S., M., Sugumaran, V., V., V., & Ramalingam, V. V. (2017). Computer Vision Based Classification on Commercial Videos. In M. S., & V. V. (Eds.), *Multi-Core Computer Vision and Image Processing for Intelligent Applications* (pp. 105-135). Hershey, PA: IGI Global. https://doi.org/DOI: 10.4018/978-1-5225-0889-2.ch004

Vairinho, S. (2022). Innovation Dynamics Through the Encouragement of Knowledge Spin-Off From Touristic Destinations. In Ramos, C., Quinteiro, S., & Gonçalves, A. (Eds.), *ICT as Innovator Between Tourism and Culture* (pp. 170–190). IGI Global. https://doi.org/10.4018/978-1-7998-8165-0.ch011

Valverde, R., Torres, B., & Motaghi, H. (2018). A Quantum NeuroIS Data Analytics Architecture for the Usability Evaluation of Learning Management Systems. In Bhattacharyya, S. (Ed.), *Quantum-Inspired Intelligent Systems for Multimedia Data Analysis* (pp. 277–299). Hershey, PA: IGI Global. DOI: 10.4018/978-1-5225-5219-2.ch009

Vassilis, E. (2018). Learning and Teaching Methodology: "1:1 Educational Computing. In Koutsopoulos, K., Doukas, K., & Kotsanis, Y. (Eds.), *Handbook of Research on Educational Design and Cloud Computing in Modern Classroom Settings* (pp. 122–155). Hershey, PA: IGI Global. DOI: 10.4018/978-1-5225-3053-4.ch007

Verma, S., & Jain, A. K. (2022). A Survey on Sentiment Analysis Techniques for Twitter. In Gupta, B., Peraković, D., Abd El-Latif, A., & Gupta, D. (Eds.), *Data Mining Approaches for Big Data and Sentiment Analysis in Social Media* (pp. 57–90). IGI Global. https://doi.org/10.4018/978-1-7998-8413-2.ch003

Wang, H., Huang, P., & Chen, X. (2021). Research and Application of a Multidimensional Association Rules Mining Method Based on OLAP. *International Journal of Information Technology and Web Engineering*, 16(1), 75–94. https://doi.org/10.4018/IJITWE.2021010104

Wexler, B. E. (2017). Computer-Presented and Physical Brain-Training Exercises for School Children: Improving Executive Functions and Learning. In Dubbels, B. (Ed.), *Transforming Gaming and Computer Simulation Technologies across Industries* (pp. 206–224). Hershey, PA: IGI Global. DOI: 10.4018/978-1-5225-1817-4.ch012

Wimble, M., Singh, H., & Phillips, B. (2018). Understanding Cross-Level Interactions of Firm-Level Information Technology and Industry Environment: A Multilevel Model of Business Value. *Information Resources Management Journal*, 31(1), 1–20. DOI: 10.4018/IRMJ.2018010101

Wimmer, H., Powell, L., Kilgus, L., & Force, C. (2017). Improving Course Assessment via Web-based Homework. *International Journal of Online Pedagogy and Course Design*, 7(2), 1–19. DOI: 10.4018/IJOPCD.2017040101

Wong, S. (2021). Gendering Information and Communication Technologies in Climate Change. In M. Khosrow-Pour D.B.A. (Eds.), *Encyclopedia of Information Science and Technology, Fifth Edition* (pp. 1408-1422). IGI Global. https://doi.org/10.4018/978-1-7998-3479-3.ch096

Wong, Y. L., & Siu, K. W. (2018). Assessing Computer-Aided Design Skills. In M. Khosrow-Pour, D.B.A. (Ed.), *Encyclopedia of Information Science and Technology, Fourth Edition* (pp. 7382-7391). Hershey, PA: IGI Global. DOI: 10.4018/978-1-5225-2255-3.ch642

Wongsurawat, W., & Shrestha, V. (2018). Information Technology, Globalization, and Local Conditions: Implications for Entrepreneurs in Southeast Asia. In Ordóñez de Pablos, P. (Ed.), *Management Strategies and Technology Fluidity in the Asian Business Sector* (pp. 163–176). Hershey, PA: IGI Global. DOI: 10.4018/978-1-5225-4056-4.ch010

Yamada, H. (2021). Homogenization of Japanese Industrial Technology From the Perspective of R&D Expenses. *International Journal of Systems and Service-Oriented Engineering*, 11(2), 24–51. DOI: 10.4018/IJSSOE.2021070102

Yang, Y., Zhu, X., Jin, C., & Li, J. J. (2018). Reforming Classroom Education Through a QQ Group: A Pilot Experiment at a Primary School in Shanghai. In Spires, H. (Ed.), *Digital Transformation and Innovation in Chinese Education* (pp. 211–231). Hershey, PA: IGI Global. DOI: 10.4018/978-1-5225-2924-8.ch012

Yilmaz, R., Sezgin, A., Kurnaz, S., & Arslan, Y. Z. (2018). Object-Oriented Programming in Computer Science. In M. Khosrow-Pour, D.B.A. (Ed.), *Encyclopedia of Information Science and Technology, Fourth Edition* (pp. 7470-7480). Hershey, PA: IGI Global. DOI: 10.4018/978-1-5225-2255-3.ch650

Yu, L. (2018). From Teaching Software Engineering Locally and Globally to Devising an Internationalized Computer Science Curriculum. In Dikli, S., Etheridge, B., & Rawls, R. (Eds.), *Curriculum Internationalization and the Future of Education* (pp. 293–320). Hershey, PA: IGI Global. DOI: 10.4018/978-1-5225-2791-6.ch016

Yuhua, F. (2018). Computer Information Library Clusters. In M. Khosrow-Pour, D.B.A. (Ed.), *Encyclopedia of Information Science and Technology, Fourth Edition* (pp. 4399-4403). Hershey, PA: IGI Global. DOI: 10.4018/978-1-5225-2255-3.ch382

Zakaria, R. B., Zainuddin, M. N., & Mohamad, A. H. (2022). Distilling Blockchain: Complexity, Barriers, and Opportunities. In Lai, P. (Ed.), *Handbook of Research on Social Impacts of E-Payment and Blockchain Technology* (pp. 89–114). IGI Global. https://doi.org/10.4018/978-1-7998-9035-5.ch007

Zhang, Z., Ma, J., & Cui, X. (2021). Genetic Algorithm With Three-Dimensional Population Dominance Strategy for University Course Timetabling Problem. *International Journal of Grid and High Performance Computing*, 13(2), 56–69. https://doi.org/10.4018/IJGHPC.2021040104

About the Contributors

Christo Ananth got his B.E. Degree in Electronics and Communication Engineering in 2009 and his M.E. Degree in Applied Electronics in 2013. He received his PhD Degree in Engineering in 2017. He completed his Post Doctoral Research work in Co-operative Networks in 2018. Christo Ananth has almost spent a decade in research, instructing, counseling and down to earth application improvement. His exploration skill covers Image Processing, Co-operative Networks, Electromagnetic Fields, Electronic Devices, Wireless Networks and Medical Electronics. He has taken an interest and presented 3 papers in National level Technical Symposiums, 9 Research papers in National Level Conferences, 31 Research Papers in International level Conferences, 80 Research Papers in refereed and indexed International Journals in the field of Embedded Systems, Networking, Digital Image Processing, Network Security and VLSI. He has 3 International Patents and 5 National Patents to his Credit, out of which, 4 had been granted and 4 had been published. He has attended 45 Technical Seminars/Training Courses/Faculty Development Programs. He has contributed 25 Dissertations / Thesis / Technical Reports in International Publication Houses, 28 International Book Chapters in USA and has authored & published 4 National-level Engineering Text books and authored 3 International-level Engineering text books. He has published 10 Monographs in Reputed International Journals. He is a beneficiary of Special note in 6 Engineering Text books associated to Anna University,Chennai. He is the recipient of 15 Honours & Best Faculty Awards including "Best Knowledge Exchange/Transfer Initiative Of The Year- 2017", "Engineering Leadership Award", "Young Scientist Award – 2017", "Sir James Prescott Joule Award", "Outstanding Digital Innovator Award – 2017", "2018 Albert Nelson Marquis Lifetime Achievement Award", "Exemplary Information And Communication Engineer Award" and "Green Peace Award – 2017" for his Excellence in Engineering Education. At present, he is a member of 140 Professional and Social-Welfare Bodies over the globe. He is a Biographical World Record Holder of Marquis' Who's Who in the World (32nd,33rd and 34th

Edition) for his exceptional commitment towards explore group from 2015-2017. He has conveyed Guest Lectures in Reputed Engineering Colleges and Reputed Industries on different themes. He has earned 4 Best Paper Awards from different instruction related social exercises in and outside India. He has organized nearly 23 self-supporting National level Technical Symposiums, Conferences and Workshops in the field of Embedded Systems, Networking, Digital Image Processing, Network Security, VLSI, Biotechnology, Management and Architecture. He is a Technical Advisory Board member of nearly 90 National Level/International Level Technical Conferences over the globe. He is serving as Editorial board member/Reviewer of 381 SCI/ISI/Scopus/Web of Science indexed International Journals and 155 Refereed, Indexed and Reputed International Journals. He has set up about 87 MOUs as Chief with Educational Institutions over the globe. He is chosen as an elected fellow from ISECE (Malaysia) and a Life Member from ISTE (India).

Nitin Mittal is working as Assistant Professor at Shri Vishwakarma Skill University, Palwal, Haryana. He worked as Professor in Department of Electronics and Communication Engineering at Chandigarh University, India. He received his B.Tech and M.Tech degree in Electronics and Communication Engineering from Kurukshetra University, Kurukshetra, India in 2006 and 2009 respectively. He has completed his Ph.D in ECE from Chandigarh University, Mohali, India in 2017. He has 15 years of experience in teaching at graduate and post graduate level. His name is included in the list of Indian Researchers in Stanford University's Top 2% Most Influential Scientists List for the Year 2020, 2021, 2022 and 2023. He has authored/co-authored more than 100 publications including peer-reviewed journals, conferences, Book chapters and Books. He is reviewer of various prestigious journals and he has hosted session chairs in various international conferences. His research interests include Wireless Sensor Networks, Image Segmentation, and Soft Computing.

***

Ramy El-Kady is a full criminal law professor at the Police Academy and holds the position of department chair of criminal law. He was rewarded with the State Encouragement Award in Legal and Economic Sciences, Citizenship and Human Rights Branch, on the topic of "the right of persons cooperating with justice for protection in international conventions and national legislation. He graduated from the Police College in 1999. He obtained a postgraduate diploma in criminal sciences and public law, which is equivalent to a master's degree in criminal law, in 2003. He received a PhD in criminal law from the Faculty of Law, Cairo University, on the topic of (Mediation as an Alternative to a Criminal Case: A Comparative Study. He currently teaches criminal law subjects to college students. He supervised numerous studies submitted for doctoral degrees and higher diplomas and authored a host of research in the criminal law field. He has previously judged multiple research papers in a number of refereed regional scientific journals. He published a host of research in refereed and indexed periodicals and took part in a number of international and local conferences and symposia.

Wasswa Shafik (Member, IEEE) received a Bachelor of Science degree in information technology (BIT) from Ndejje University, Kampala, Uganda, a Master of Engineering degree in information technology engineering (Computer and communication networks) from Yazd University, Iran, and a Ph.D. degree in computer science with the School of Digital Science, Universiti Brunei Darussalam, Brunei Darussalam. He is also the Founder and a Principal Investigator of the Dig Connectivity Research Laboratory (DCRLab) after serving as a Research Associate at Network Interconnectivity Research Laboratory, Yazd University. Prior to this, he worked as a Community Data Analyst at Population Services International (PSI-Uganda), Community Data Officer at Programme for Accessible Health Communication (PACE-Uganda), Research Assistant at the Socio-Economic Data Centre (SEDC-Uganda), Prime Minister's Office, Kampala, Uganda, an Assistant Data Officer at TechnoServe, Kampala, IT Support at Thurayya Islam Media, Uganda, and Asmaah Charity Organization. He has 70+ publications in renowned journals and conferences. His research interests include AI, smart agriculture, health computing and ecological informatics.

Index

A

B

C

D

E

F

G

H

I

M

P

Q

R

S

www.ingramcontent.com/pod-product-compliance
Lightning Source LLC
LaVergne TN
LVHW081334300926
849161LV00008B/1967

* 9 7 9 8 3 3 7 3 1 6 5 7 4 *